PANTHEOLOGIES

PANTHEOLOGIES

GODS, WORLDS, MONSTERS

MARY-JANE RUBENSTEIN

COLUMBIA UNIVERSITY PRESS
New York

Columbia University Press
Publishers Since 1893
New York   Chichester, West Sussex
cup.columbia.edu

Library of Congress Cataloging-in-Publication Data
Names: Rubenstein, Mary-Jane, author.
Title: Pantheologies : gods, worlds, monsters / Mary Jane Rubenstein.
Description: 1 [edition]. | New York : Columbia University Press, 2018. |
Includes bibliographical references.
Identifiers: LCCN 2018019760 | ISBN 9780231189460 (hardback) |
ISBN 9780231548342 (e-book)
Subjects: LCSH: Pantheism. | Religion—Philosophy.
Classification: LCC BL220 .R83 2018 | DDC 211/.2—dc23 LC record
available at https://lccn.loc.gov/2018019760

Columbia University Press books are printed on permanent
and durable acid-free paper.
Printed in the United States of America

Cover image: Photo courtesy of Bodleian Libraries, University of Oxford

For Gabriel, created out of so much.

Turns out I knew less than I'd thought about wonder.

Those who speak of pantheism are wanting in the simplest categories of thought.
—G. W. F. Hegel, *Lectures on the Philosophy of Religion*

CONTENTS

ACKNOWLEDGMENTS

Much like the god-worlds it thematizes, this book is the product of a polyphonic and indeed multispecies cosmogonic effort. Although its shortcomings are the collective responsibility of the riot of organisms currently (de-) composing the author, the work at hand would have remained a set of disincarnate, weird ideas were it not for the companion species, gut bacteria, and quantum intra-actions that have fortuitously concresced into those remarkable humans who have helped bring it into being.

First, last, and in the muddled middle, there has been my research assistant Winfield Goodwin, who discussed the ecofeminist and animist material with me as the project was taking shape, edited the manuscript for submission, and secured permissions for the images. All this with a meticulousness, speed, and wit that have not only improved the project but shaped it, preserving in the meantime the sanity of its signator.

I would also like to thank the students in my experimental Pantheologies seminar, whose insights and enthusiasm enabled me finally to sit down and write. They were Leah Bakely, Anne Dade, Cail Daley, Stephanie Dawson, Amanda Farman, Cheryl Hagan, Noah Hamlisch, Emma Koramshahi, Gretchen LaMotte, Max Luton, Angus Macdonald, Jill Moraski, Daniel Muro,

Emily Pfoutz, Emma Raddatz, Hannah Sokoloff-Rubin, Theodore Sullivan, Sitar Terras-Shah, Claudia von Nostitz, Delaine Winn, and especially Hannah Eisner, who also retrieved untold numbers of volumes from the library for me and conducted some background research on Einstein's pantheism. I was also grateful during these early days for the encouragement of Joanna Brownson, who helped me believe I had something to say.

For the time and space they provided for reflection, collaboration, and writing, I am grateful to the Abbey of Regina Laudis in Bethlehem, Connecticut; the Institute for Cross-Disciplinary Engagement at Dartmouth University, directed by Marcelo Gleiser and administered by Amy Flockton; and the Westar Institute's God Seminar, especially Jeff Robbins, Clayton Crockett, Karen Bray, and Karmen MacKendrick, who looked over a version of chapter 2 with more generosity than it deserved. Justine Quijada's and Laurel Schneider's careful readings of chapters 2 and 3 helped me understand contemporary debates over animist cosmologies. In response to an early incarnation of the introduction, Daniel Miller asked me precisely the questions I was hoping no one would ask, forcing me to get smarter about things like realism and evil.

For his conceptual guidance, I am grateful to Philip Clayton; for his expert assistance with Spinoza, I am indebted to Brian Fay; and for their help with translations, I am thankful for the assistance of Stephen Angle, David Butterfield, Ulrich Plass, and Andy Szegedy-Maszak. Kendall Hobbs helped me chase down a slew of obscure sources and rescued the manuscript more than once from the evil designs of its reference software; Susan Passman and Nara Giannella produced digital images with remarkable speed; Richard King and Ryan Overbey guided me through a thicket of Vedic and Orientalist literature; Joe Rouse provided orientation for the Einstein-Bohr debate; and Courtney Weiss Smith and Wolfram Schmidgen provided historical context for the mechanistic worlds of the seventeenth century.

Lori Gruen spent long afternoons helping me make sense of the relationship between Pan, ecofeminism, and chimpanzees; and saved me more than once from the fear that no one would ever be interested in a book as strange as this one. Also of immeasurable assistance in this regard has been Catherine Keller, who has helped me to clarify the argument, its audience, its contours and stakes; who has read numerous chapters with good humor and care; and whose support has continually strengthened the author as well as the book.

None of this would have been possible without the tireless encouragement of Sheeja Thomas or the constant interlocution of Kenan Rubenstein. I am once again indebted to Wendy Lochner at Columbia University Press for her careful guidance of the project. And finally, for their painstaking reviews of the manuscript, I am grateful to Nancy Frankenberry, who has helped me position the project within the landscape of contemporary critical thought, and to William Robert, who is the most careful and generous reader a multiplicitous riot of hybrid, sympoietic agencies could ask for.

PREFACE

The project at hand grew out of my earlier work on multiverse cosmologies, which concluded on a somewhat frustrated note regarding the so-called public conversation between science and religion. In fact, I came to realize, the ongoing debate over the existence of the multiverse provides a clear picture of the grim state of this conversation. Despite the decades of scholarship illuminating the historical identity, persistent entanglement, and productive crossings of the regimes we now call "science" and "religion," the default assumption among scientists, theists, and their audiences remains that these categories are self-identical and starkly opposed. The "conversation," then, amounts either to replacing a given *thing* called "religion" with another given *thing* called "science"; to rejecting the latter by appealing to a particularly uninteresting form of the former; to supplementing one of them with a strong dose of the other; or, God help us, to "reconciling" them—a task that almost always amounts to orthodox theology's contorting itself around any given scientific discovery so as to hold open an increasingly small space for itself without appearing too backward. As it turns out, we can see all of these strategies at work in the positing, defense, and critique of the *multiverse*—that hypothetical compendium of an infinite number of universes apart from our own.

The question to which the multiverse provides an answer is why the universe seems so finely tuned. Why, physicists ask, do gravity, the cosmological constant, the nuclear forces, and the mass of the electron all happen to have the values they have—especially when it seems that any other values would have prevented the emergence of stars, planets, organic life, and in some cases, the universe itself? What these physicists fear—and with good reason, considering this particular theological strategy's stubborn refusal to die—is the perennial classical theistic answer to this question. The scientist asks: why is the universe so perfect? And the theist predictably responds: because an intelligent, benevolent, anthropomorphic Creator outside the universe set the controls just right, launching the universe on a course "he" knew would produce beings to resemble and worship him.

Strictly speaking, such theological concerns cannot be said to have generated the idea of the multiverse in the first place. Nevertheless, the reason an increasing number of theoretical physicists find it so compelling is that the multiverse provides a metaphysical solution that finally rivals the undead Creator. After all, if there is just one universe, then it is very difficult to explain how the cosmos manages to be so bio-friendly without appealing to some kind of force beyond it. If, however, there are an infinite number of universes, all taking on different parameters throughout infinite time, then once in a while, one of them is bound to turn out right, and we just happen to be in one of those. In short, the infinite multiverse is the only answer big enough to stand up to the infinite God of classical theism, with his omni-attributes and his *ex nihilic* creative powers.

Once again, then, the "conversation" between religion and science amounts to an either/or, metonymically encapsulated in the figures of God and the multiverse, respectively. And once again, popular science books and their recapitulations in social, journalistic, and televised media subject the public to a familiar cadre of (remarkably all male) scientists proclaiming the *final* death of the old father-God. Just to keep things fair and balanced, such media will also trudge out a familiar counter-cadre of (remarkably all-male) religious leaders and theologians decrying the willful ignorance of secular scientists, whom they accuse of being so desperate to avoid God that they will take refuge in the outright absurdity of an infinite number of worlds.

This whole fruitless exchange has led me to believe that the least interesting question one can ask with respect to any given phenomenon (evolution, the big bang, the creation of beetles or mountains, last year's World Series victory) is whether or not God did it. The reason it is so uninteresting to ask this question is that *one can always say God did X*, whatever *X* might be. And if one's opponent makes the counterclaim that, not God, but Y accomplished X, one can always make the counter-counterclaim that God made the Y that went on to do X. These are moves that theists and atheists can always make in antagonistic relation to one another. For the theist, there is always a way to insert a "God of the Gaps" back behind any given physical process, if that is what he is hoping to do. Conversely, the atheist can always find a way to call that God a needless or intellectually dishonest addition to an otherwise elegant, scientific hypothesis. This "debate," I would submit, has always been a dead-end game. It has never gone anywhere and will never go anywhere, in *saecula seculorum*. After all, if it were possible to prove or disprove the existence of a humanoid, extra-cosmic creator, someone would have done it by now.

Apart from being tiresome and unproductive, this deadly back and forth over the existence or nonexistence of an extra-cosmic humanoid misses all the constructive theological work the natural sciences themselves are producing. Those theists and atheists who fret endlessly over their perennial superman tend to miss the new and recycled mythologies pouring out of the scientific sphere. To remain with the example of modern cosmology, they miss the way that some physicists tend to encode dark energy as a malicious demiurge at war with the forces of gravity and light. Or the way that others place mathematics in the position of Plato's Forms, rendering the physical world an imperfect copy of an eternal, unchanging, immaterial realm. Or the way that simulation theorists are trying to ingratiate themselves to the highly advanced scientists whom they believe created humanity out of the more sophisticated equivalent of PlayStations. "How did our simulators make us," they ask, "and why? And how do we get them to love us enough to keep us alive?"

These ruminations amount to speculative and practical theological inquiries in their own right, such that attending to them changes the terms of the science-and-religion game. Rather than asking what sort of God a given scientific discovery still allows room for a theist to believe in, religious studies scholars can turn the critical tables around to ask what sort of gods and monsters such scientific theories are *producing*, and what sorts of ethical values and social formations they reflect and reinforce. And overwhelmingly, the natural and social sciences are currently producing a slew of what I have provisionally called *pantheologies*. Despite their steadily secular self-identification, these sciences are generating rigorous, awestruck, and even reverential accounts of creation, sustenance, and transformation—processes that are wholly immanent to the universe itself.

The plan for this book, then, was to account for the flurry of purportedly secular cosmogonies pouring out of astrophysics, nonlinear biology, chaos and complexity theories, new materialisms, new animisms, post-humanisms, and nonhumanisms as overlapping, nonidentical assemblages of that old philo-theological category of "pantheism." To accomplish this, I thought, I would need first to determine what pantheism is. I would then trace a quick, historical topography of the concept in order to locate the more modern theories of immanence within its multifarious terrain. The moment I set out to do so, however, I discovered that *there is no real conceptual history of pantheism.* What there is instead is a tangle of relentless demonization and name-calling. In short, "pantheism" is primarily a polemical term, used most often to dismiss or even ridicule a position one determines to be distasteful. It is almost never a term of positive identification; rather, it marks a cliff off which a derisive speaker can claim that the position in question threatens to throw thinking— and all existence itself—if it is entertained too seriously. "We cannot possibly affirm *X*," the rhetoric goes, "because *X* would lead to *pantheism*" . . . and such a consequence is thought to suffice as an adequate repudiation of the proposal under consideration.

Having hit this particular wall, the project at hand needed to take a few steps back. Rather than beginning with a genealogy that might be extended to the modern natural sciences, the book begins by examining the perennial disgust with pantheism and asking why it continues to be so repugnant. To be sure, there are plenty of reasons one might decide not to affirm pantheism as one's favorite theoretical framework, or as one's go-to devotional stance. But why, this study asks, does it so rarely get the opportunity to be a stance in the first place? Whence the vitriolic, visceral, automatic, and nearly universal denunciation of pantheism?

As the reader will see momentarily, I have addressed this question by locating in anti-pantheist literature some recurring themes—most notably, those of monstrosity, undifferentiation, (specifically maternal) femininity, dark primitivity, and dreamlike Orientalism. The problem, it seems, is that pantheism not only unsettles, and not only entangles, but *demolishes* the raced and gendered ontic distinctions that Western metaphysics (with some crucial exceptions) insists on drawing between activity and passivity, spirit and matter, and animacy and inanimacy—distinctions that are rooted theologically in the Greco-Roman-Abrahamic distinction between creator and created, or God and world. Insofar as pantheism rejects this fundamental distinction, it threatens all the other privileges that map onto it: male versus female, light versus darkness, good versus evil, and humans over every other organism.

At this point, the broader project shifts from the diagnostic to the prescriptive. If the panic over pantheism has to do with a fear of crossed boundaries, queer mixtures, and miscellaneous miscegenations, and if these monstrosities are said to threaten the carefully erected structures of Western metaphysics, then—at least for those of us who seek a creative destruction of such structures— the question becomes how pantheism, in its most transformative sense, might actually take shape.

The whole book, then, has become a prelude to what I had thought would be its opening question, which is to say, what is pantheism?

PANTHEOLOGIES

INTRODUCTION

THE MATTER WITH PANTHEISM

This is the most monstrous hypothesis that could be imagined, the most absurd, and the most diametrically opposed to the most evident notions of our mind.

— Pierre Bayle, *Historical and Critical Dictionary: Selections*

Monstrosity

On the brink of the eighteenth century, Pierre Bayle published his *Dictionnaire historique et culturelle* (1697, second edition 1702)—an eclectic, rambling compendium whose footnotes comically outweigh its main text and whose essays illuminate the lives and works of biblical figures, monarchs, and an exceedingly strange smattering of philosophers. Known for its thoroughgoing skepticism, its trenchant critique of Roman Catholic authoritarianism, its "lewd anecdotes, moral musings," and defense of religious and political tolerance, the *Dictionnaire* quickly became "the philosophical best seller of the eighteenth century," influencing every classic Enlightenment thinker from Diderot and Voltaire to Berkeley and Hume to Jefferson and Melville.[1]

Bayle's tone throughout the *Dictionnaire* is strident and uncompromising. He seeks to undermine nearly every positive metaphysical position he considers, following them Socratically, and with a heavy dose of crankiness, until they collapse under their own weight. Even for the acclimated reader, however, it can be unsettling, four volumes in, to stumble upon Bayle's unmeasured screed against Baruch Spinoza. Calling Spinoza a "Jew by birth, and afterwards a deserter from Judaism, and lastly an atheist," Bayle does not even take the time to set up the arguments he plainly despises.[2] Such arguments, to Bayle's mind, need no careful treatment, their flaws being "so obvious that no balanced mind could ever be unaware of them."[3] Even the most cursory consideration, he insists, will reveal that Spinoza's teaching "surpasses all the monstrosities and chimerical disorders of the craziest people who were ever put away in lunatic asylums."[4]

What *is* this surpassing monstrosity, this chimerical lunacy? Bayle just says it once, as if dwelling on it any longer might make it contagious. Hiding it in a footnote, in a subordinate clause, he mentions that the insanity at hand is Spinoza's identification of thought and extension.[5] Thought and extension, often colloquialized as mind and body, were for René Descartes two distinct substances, meaning that each of them was self-sufficient, inhering in no greater thing.[6] Reading Descartes against himself, Spinoza insists that thought and extension are merely two attributes of the same substance, which he calls "God, or Nature" (*Deus sive natura*).[7]

Here, then, is our monstrosity: according to Spinoza, God and Nature are equivalent terms. As he phrases it (hastily, as if hoping no one will notice): "the power of Nature is the divine power and virtue, and the divine power is the very essence of God. But I prefer to pass this by for the present."[8] Bayle lets him do no such thing, horrified that if the power of Nature is the divine power and the divine power is the essence of God, then by the transitive principle, "the power of Nature" *is* "the very essence of God." The universe we are in—and which, in turn, is in us—is what we *mean* when we say the word "God"; conversely, "God" is nothing other than the creative work of creation itself. To be sure, the position is unexpected, unorthodox—even heretical. But why does Bayle keep calling it *monstrous*?

In his lectures on abnormality, Michel Foucault explains:

> The monster is essentially a mixture. It is a mixture of two realms, the animal and the human . . . of two species . . . of two individuals . . . of two sexes . . . of life and death. . . . Finally, it is a mixture of forms. . . . the transgression of natural limits, the transgression of classifications, of the table, and of the law as table: this is actually what is involved in monstrosity.[9]

By "the table, and the law as table," Foucault has in mind the whole chart of oppositions that Aristotle ascribes to Pythagoras,[10] and that Western philosophy keeps extending and expanding; namely, the "table" that opposes mind to body, human to animal, male to female, the unchanging to the changing, the rational to the irrational, the spiritual to the material, perfection to imperfection, light to darkness, activity to passivity, etc. As deconstructive thinkers have been pointing out for decades, the first of each of these terms maintains its historical privilege by denigrating and repudiating the second, which turns out to be its condition of possibility. And strikingly, the first set of terms includes all the characteristics that Western metaphysics has traditionally associated with God, while the second set includes the characteristics associated with the world, or creation, or nature. God is said to be anthropomorphic, unchanging, rational, and masculine while the world is coded as animal-vegetal, changeable, irrational, and feminine.

When Spinoza tells us that God *is* the world, then, he is mixing up traits that any sane philosophy would keep separate, transgressing the law of the table. This is what Bayle means when he repeatedly calls Spinoza's philosophy "monstrous"; what kind of divinity could ever be *material*? After all, Bayle reminds us, matter is "the vilest of all beings . . . the theater of all sorts of changes, the battleground of contrary charges, the subject of all corruptions and all generations, in a word, the being whose nature is most incompatible with the immutability of God."[11] By mixing the spiritual and the material, Spinoza therefore produces "the most monstrous hypothesis that could be imagined, the most absurd, and the most diametrically opposed to the most evident notions of our mind."[12]

Again, Bayle tends to be a cantankerous writer. But his essay on Spinoza is a particularly egregious compendium of unsubstantiated name-calling. In addition to the repeated charges of monstrosity, Bayle dubs Spinoza's teachings "absurd," "horrible," and "vile"; his ethics "an execrable abomination," his metaphysics "poppycock," and his *Theological-Political Treatise* a "pernicious and detestable book."[13] Such insults are hardly limited to Bayle; a contemporary detractor wrote that the *Treatise* had been "forged in Hell by a renegade Jew and the Devil."[14] And the source of this abomination, the professed identity of spirit and matter, God and nature, is the position that yet another anti-Spinozist named Jacques de la Faye will derisively name *pantheism*.[15]

Etymologically, "pantheism" names the identification of *pan*, or "all," with *theos*, or "God," but from there, the term shifts wildly depending on how one defines the "all" that God "is." What Benjamin Lazier calls pantheism's "referential promiscuity" is moreover a function of its being initially and more commonly used as a polemical term than as one of positive identification.[16] Simply put, there are more voices saying, "you're a pantheist and that's absurd" than, "my doctrine is pantheist and this is what that means." Casually, the term "pantheism" tends to connote personal or communal reverence for "nature":

that amorphous terrain overseen in Greek mythology by the goat-god Pan. Literarily—and often in the form of Pan himself—pantheism erupts throughout Renaissance, pastoral, Romantic, and Victorian poetry, most notably in the works of Milton, Jonson, Spenser, Goethe, Wordsworth, Shelley, Tennyson, Whitman, and Barrett Browning.[17] Philosophically, however, pantheism is little more than a limit case—the position nearly everyone wants to avoid, regardless of theoretical orientation.[18] For theists, atheists, rationalists, empiricists, and idealists alike, "pantheism" has been from the beginning the school to which one simply does not adhere.

As it turns out, then, Bayle's vilification represents a fairly standard—if uncommonly verbose—instance of what Ninian Smart calls "the horror of pantheism" in Western thought.[19] This horror has been so pervasive that "pantheism" has not developed into a coherent system, or even a clear concept. For the most part, it remains a bad word and a tool of automatic rhetorical dismissal.[20] Indeed, in one of his numerous meditations on Spinoza, Gilles Deleuze reflects on the scores of philosophers who are "constantly threatened by the accusation of immanentism and pantheism, and constantly taking care to avoid, above all else, such an accusation."[21] Such philosophers have included even such "all" thinkers as Hegel, Schelling, and Schleiermacher, and today include the most left-leaning of liberationists; for instance, James Cone carefully distances black theology from any "pantheistic implications," Sallie McFague maintains that her ecotheological "body of God" is "neither idolatry nor pantheism," and Yvonne Gebara insists that ecofeminism's immanent divinity not be read pantheistically.[22] Instead, they affirm along with process theologians the delicately balanced doctrine of pan*en*theism according to which, as Philip Clayton explains, "the world is in God, but God is also more than the world."[23] To be sure, there are numerous reasons one might opt for panentheism rather than pantheism; panentheists might hold an a priori commitment to the ontological distinction between God and the world, or they might worry that pantheism's identity forecloses difference, or both of these at once. As such, panentheists call upon the "en" to ensure the separation between God and world that enables their relation. What is striking, I am trying to suggest, is not the rejection of pantheism *per se*, but rather the haste with which it is rejected. Such haste becomes understandable when one considers that the cost of association with pantheism is often the sort of reckless, incensed invective we find in Bayle's *Dictionnaire*; as Grace Jantzen attests, "if a proposal is seen as pantheistic or leading to pantheistic consequences, that is deemed sufficient reason to repudiate it, often with considerable vitriol."[24]

Of course, Bayle was not the first to repudiate a pantheistic proposal with vitriol. Four decades earlier, Spinoza had been excommunicated from his Jewish community in Amsterdam for his "*monstrous* deeds"; specifically, for the crime of teaching "that God has a body"—namely, the body of the world itself.[25] Having heretically conflated divinity with materiality, Spinoza was expelled bodily from the synagogue with "'the anathema with which Joshua anathematized Jericho,'" to wit:

> Cursed be he by day, and cursed be he by night, cursed be he when he lieth down, and cursed be he when he riseth up; cursed be he when he goeth out and cursed be he when he cometh in; the Lord will not pardon him; the wrath and fury of the Lord will be kindled against this man . . . and the Lord will destroy his name from under the heavens; and, to his undoing, the Lord will cut him off from all the tribes of Israel.[26]

In keeping with this divine genealogical rupture, the elders of Spinoza's Congregation Talmud Torah furthermore imposed a social quarantine: "We ordain that no one may communicate with him verbally or in writing, nor show him any favour . . . nor be within four cubits of him, nor read anything composed or written by him."[27]

Granted, identifying God with a material creation is a highly unorthodox move. As we have already noted, the God of classical theism is said to be eternal, unchanging, simple, infinite, omnipotent, and omniscient: in short, everything the world is *not*. Conversely, the theistic world is thought to be object, not subject; passive, not active; created, not creator—and the pantheistic God-world collapses, or at least entangles, these distinctions. But there are all sorts of heresies, none of which seems to fuel the degree of horror perennially provoked by Spinoza's *Deus sive natura*. One is therefore compelled to ask, *what is so awful about pantheism*? What is it that prompts the council's multidimensional anathema (cursed be he by day, by night; when he's up, down, in, and out); that cuts the pantheist off from all relation, as if to prevent infection; and that constitutes not just an error, but an unforgivable one?[28] Whence stems the *horror religiosus* that not only excommunicates Spinoza, but in the hands of Christian hierarchs condemns John Scotus Eriugena, executes the followers of Almaric of Bena, burns Giordano Bruno at the stake, incinerates Marguerite Porete, suspects even *Jonathan Edwards* of heresy, and would have obliterated Meister Eckhart if he hadn't died first?[29] What is the matter with pantheism?

It might help to address this particular question with its obverse; namely, why does the position in question keep arising, such that it needs to be so repeatedly denounced? The very frequency and tenor of anti-pantheistic proclamations suggests there might be something alluring about this abominable position; in short, there would be no need to reject it so constantly, and so irritably, if it weren't so strangely compelling. In the mid-nineteenth century, for example, a slew of treatises were written to combat the raging pantheism allegedly devouring the American literary landscape—and each of these treatises exhibits a kind of revolted fascination with the heresy in question.[30]

One particularly vilifying treatise is the work of Nathaniel Smith Richardson, an Anglican divine in a transcendental-Spiritualist New England. Over the course of a spirited and even panicked defense of Christian orthodoxy, Richardson calls pantheism a misguided, dangerous, anti-intellectual, and even "appalling movement."[31] The notion that God is not only in, but identical to, the natural world is to Richardson's mind the multiparental offspring of cheap German idealism, an increasingly democratized Puritanism, atheist biblical criticism, and bad poetry, all of which threaten to destroy the moral fabric of the nation. At the same time, even Richardson can see why pantheism has swept up the young and unchurched: "there is a generosity about it," he writes, "and a kindliness, that is captivating."[32] The kindly generosity of pantheism, of course, is its attribution of godliness to all things—its coloring the whole world divine "as if it bore in its hand the wand of an enchanter. . . . It is a gorgeous vision," the anti-pantheist admits, "and no wonder that souls craving for rest and finding none, should gladly yield themselves to its bewitching power."[33]

One might note the sexual metaphorics of this "enchanting," "bewitching," and "gorgeous" power, and indeed, in other works of this time period, pantheism is similarly rendered as temptation, or seduction. Thus the Reverend Morgan Dix of Trinity Church, Manhattan, warns that men lacking in sufficient education "may have been tempted, seduced, tainted, poisoned by [pantheism] . . . unawares"; Alexis De Tocqueville fears that pantheism ranks among those philosophies "most likely to entice the human mind in democratic ages"; and Herman Melville's Ishmael confesses while meditating on the "mysterious, divine Pacific" that, "lifted by these eternal swells, you needs must own the seductive God, bowing your head to Pan."[34] Melville himself evidently struggled with such pantheist seductions; as American literary scholar Richard Hardack has unveiled, his letters reveal both an attraction to "the *all* feeling" and a revulsion from it.[35] Writing to Nathaniel Hawthorne, for example, Melville judges Goethe's injunction to "live in the all" to be "nonsense," and at the same time admits that while "there is an immense deal of flummery in Goethe, [there is also] in proportion to my own contact with him, a *monstrous* deal of it in me."[36] And there is that word again, this time describing the feeling the monster stirs up. The simultaneous attraction and repulsion that pantheism provokes thus becomes its own sort of monstrosity: a chimerical affect prompted by a chimerical subject-object.

SEDUCTION

In her feminist decoding of Plato's Cave, Luce Irigaray reminds us of the raging ambivalence that Western philosophy, like the Freudian subject, sustains toward its feminized origins.[37] Like the Oedipal child, the Western tradition aims to make its way from the dark, maternal womb space to the father's blinding light—from paganism to monotheism, from the cave to the sky, from the dirt to the ideas. The mother, along with the wife who stands in for her, thus becomes a complex site of disgust and desire, of repudiation and nostalgia as the Oedipal man, like the whole phallocentric order, simultaneously commands and rejects everything associated with her. A testimony to the steady reduplication of this violent ambivalence, we find a similar structure at work in orientalist and primitivist discourse. In such renderings, Western scholars and colonial officials both glorify and vilify a simultaneously seductive and repulsive racial other—rendered in consistently dark, primitive, and feminine terms.[38] And indeed, something of the dark, primitive, and feminine fuels the revoltingly attractive power of pantheism.

In his reading of American transcendentalism, Richard Hardack argues that the transcendental movement emerged as a white, romantic appropriation of Native American "animism" on the one hand and African possession traditions on the other. In Emerson and Melville, Hardack shows, the landscape that becomes divine becomes in the same breath primitive, feminine, and racialized—specifically, black.[39] Similarly, Paul Outka demonstrates the persistent haunting of this literature by American Indian genocide on the one hand and West African slavery on the other.[40] For Outka, the transcendental sublime, which shatters the male subject in his overawed encounter with the landscape, is a white enactment of racial trauma from the perspective of privilege and safety.[41] Most likely because it was too close to see, however, this particular heritage tends not to be explicitly avowed in nineteenth-century accounts of the scope and history of pantheism.[42] Rather, the pantheist lineage is routed through another feminized and racialized other: "the Orient."[43]

Reverend Richardson's above-cited anti-pantheist treatise begins by proclaiming, "Pantheism is a child of the mysterious East."[44] As evidence, Richardson imagines the "dim and fragrant grove" of an ancient Indian sage, whose reverie produced the hazy notion that "even dark and earth-born masses are suffused with the divine expression of the one animating spirit."[45] Thanks to its radical egalitarianism, he admits, pantheism is a "captivating philosophy."[46] The problem is that it threatens to keep captivating, advancing its "appalling movement" such that "Pantheism in Europe and the West is destined to become the correlative of Buddhism in the East."[47] Such widespread pantheist seduction, Richardson insists, can only be counteracted by the "plain, distinct, and dogmatic teaching of the Incarnation of the Eternal Word."[48] It must be made known, in other words, that God appeared in the form of a single man; not all of humanity—and much less the whole animal-vegetable-mineral world.

What panics Richardson about the advance of pantheism is not, however, the simple demise of Christendom. Rather, what he seems to fear above all is a collective, racialized unmanning: pantheism, he predicts, will continue to seduce "rosy," Western men into passivity and inertia, until they become like the "earth-born" "Indian sage"—always mentioned in the past tense—who allegedly dreamed his life away in womanly passivity, "in that inactive contemplation which he considered the highest of all states."[49] From this dark, fantastic inertia, Richardson imagines, all things appeared to be engulfed in divinity and all distinctions vanished—most disturbingly, "the distinction between right and wrong, virtue and vice, good and evil."[50] As we saw in Bayle, then, Richardson's own *horror pantheismus* amounts to a revulsion at blurred distinctions and crossed boundaries: of East and West, passivity and activity, femininity and masculinity, darkness and light, immorality and morality. In this vein, Richardson concludes his treatise by lamenting the plan to expand the Parisian Pantheon into a "Pantheistic temple" by expanding its collection to the Eastern world. He shudders to imagine its pristine halls crowded with such horrors as "Brahmin Cow," "Persian Griffin," and "Chaldean Sphynx"—all monstrous mixtures of divinity and animality.[51] By inviting an ungodly swarm of Eastern, chimerical divinities into the anthropomorphic heart of Christian Europe, such a beastly temple would invariably accelerate the "spreading evil" of pantheism, taking the Christian appearance of God in one man and disseminating it indiscriminately out to the whole world.[52]

At the other end of the same orientalist scale, we find British philosopher Constance Plumptre's initially anonymous, two volume *General Sketch of the History of Pantheism* (1878), which celebrates precisely the pantheist consummation of Christianity that Richardson fears. Seeking to ground a fully rational, European religion, Plumptre disavows both polytheistic Greece and Semitic Palestine, looking instead to the more "refined and cultured" East.[53] Relying on

Max Müller's linguistic-religious history, Plumptre argues that the "true ancestors of our race" are the Aryans, whose Vedic texts felicitously exhibit "pantheism . . . in its full growth and maturity."[54] By means of a highly selective reading
of highly selective translations, Plumptre touts the superiority of Vedic oneness
and interiority over Greek multiplicity and externality, which she deems the
products of a "barbarous and savage" race.[55] Ultimately, she hopes the retrieval
of Europe's "true" origins will rectify its misguided present, purifying a hea-
thenized Christianity into the monistic, Aryan pantheism she also attributes to
Jesus of Nazareth.[56]

Although this glowing representation of allegedly Eastern pantheists might
seem a radical departure from Richardson's denunciations, we nevertheless
find in Plumptre's portrayal the same traits, simply transvalued. First, Plumptre
reserves her praise for the light-skinned, monistic Brahmins, ridiculing the
primitive polytheism of the darker castes.[57] Second, just like her anti-pantheist
counterpart, Plumptre attributes a quiet passivity to the "Hindoos" who, she
insists, "may be regarded as a religious, contemplative, and philosophical race,
far more than an active, warlike, or historical race."[58] And although Plumptre
praises these qualities, rather than ridiculing them as effeminate inaction, her
representation underhandedly reaffirms Western dominance over the East.
For as Richard King has argued, these sorts of depoliticized representations of
Indian religion served to justify British colonial rule: the people of India are
not interested in governing, the reasoning goes, so the British might as well
do it for them.[59] Finally, Plumptre assures her reader, as pure and sublime as
the "doctrine of the Vedas" might have been, "the doctrine of Christ"—carefully divested of its Jewish origins—"was far purer and more sublime" than
anything the subcontinent has produced.[60] As in the anti-pantheist literature,
then, Plumptre's fascinated adoption of the "mystical" East eventually reaffirms
the Christian West's spiritual and political superiority over it.

To be sure, it is no surprise to find such fascinations with a feminized "Orient" in the mid- and late-nineteenth century, as the British crown struggled to
gain imperial control over an unruly India (whose inhabitants British scholars
kept wishfully charging with apolitical quietism).[61] But nearly two centuries
earlier, Bayle himself had opened his anti-pantheist tract with what is becoming a familiar Orientalizing move, likening Spinoza's alleged atheism to "the
theology of a Chinese sect."[62] Bayle calls the sect "*Foe Kiao*," a rendition of the
modern Mandarin *fo jiao*, or "the teaching of the Buddha," and attributes to it
a "quietism"—even a "beatific inaction"—in the face of a universal "nothingness."[63] It is at this stage that Bayle grants his lone concession to the loathsome
Spinoza, whose single substance is at least "not . . . so absurd" as that of Bayle's

(bizarrely rendered) Chinese Buddhists.[64] After all, Spinoza's *Deus sive natura* "always acts, always thinks," whereas the "Chinese" generating principle is an allegedly inert, passive vacuum. And there is nothing more inconceivable than an inactive absolute:

> If it is *monstrous* to maintain that plants, animals, men are really the same thing and to base this on the claim that all particular beings are not distinct from their principle, it is still more monstrous to assert that this principle has no thought, no power, no virtue. This is nevertheless what these philosophers say. They make the sovereign perfection of that principle consist in inaction and absolute rest.[65]

Again, at least Spinoza did not go quite this far. But he was close enough that perhaps, thinks Bayle, he *ought* to have been a Chinese philosopher.[66] Respectable Western thought rests, along with allegedly common sense, on the principle of noncontradiction; and in this light, Spinoza's active-passive *Deus sive natura* can only be seen as an untrammeled absurdity . . . or as a foreign invasion. In short, then, the pantheist monstrosity portends the demise of the West itself, collapsing its most central distinctions, seducing it into passive inaction, and perverting its genealogy with decidedly non-Western roots.

PROJECTIONS

For the feminist philosopher of religion Grace Jantzen, pantheism's total unsettling of Western thought was precisely its liberating promise. Beginning in the late 1990s, Jantzen began to attribute all the oppressive dualisms structuring Western philosophy to the binary opposition between a disembodied God and "the physical universe."[67] As she reminds us, the ontological distinction between God and creation does not merely separate the two terms; rather, it establishes the absolute supremacy of the former over the latter. In turn, this logic of mastery secures the rule of everything associated with this God over everything associated with the material world. Again, then, spirit, masculinity, reason, light, and humanity become unconditionally privileged over matter, femininity, passion, darkness, and animal-vegetal-minerality.[68]

Admittedly, this is a well-rehearsed set of hierarchies, which feminist thinkers of both secular and sacred varieties have struggled for decades to dismantle. As far as Jantzen is concerned, however, the only way to collapse this oppressive structure is to go for its root, which is to say the opposition between God and the world. "If pantheism were seriously to be entertained," she ventures, "the whole Western symbolic . . . would be brought into question. Pantheism rejects the split between spirit and matter, light and darkness, and the rest; it thereby also rejects the hierarchies based on these splits."[69] While affirming the spirit of this critique, one might take issue with the absolute priority Jantzen gives to the God/world opposition, which other feminist thinkers have exposed as the product of perennial racisms and shape-shifting patriarchies.[70] It is more likely the fiercely guarded anthropological categories of male and female, light and dark that subtend the theological division between God and world, rather than the other way around. That having been said, once these associations are in place, it is impossible to say which might claim historical or conceptual priority over the others. It might therefore be more helpful to see all these vectors of power as rhizomatically entangled than as arboreally rooted:[71] in such a field, the integrity or destruction of each would depend upon the integrity or destruction of the others. And for Jantzen, the position that promises to unearth the whole thicket of oppressions is pantheism. Therefore, she suggests, feminist philosophy of religion—and feminism tout court—ought to be pantheist.

Understandably, many feminisms—along with queer, critical race, post- and de-colonial theories—want nothing to do with any sort of theism at all, having had more than enough of the patriarchal White Guy in the Sky. From Jantzen's perspective, however, the modern critical circumvention of theology ends up leaving God intact as a *concept*, and the concept of God goes on to reaffirm the very disembodiment, omnipotence, light-supremacy and anthropomorphism such theories seek to dismantle. Insofar as concepts encode and reinforce sociopolitical norms, Jantzen is careful to explain that she is not working from a "realist" stance; rather, she is working at the level of the *symbolic*. When Jantzen affirms pantheism, for example, she is not saying that God *is* the universe or that the universe *is* divine; rather, she is trying to recode "divinity" as a concept. Whether or not an "entity" called God "exists," she is aiming discursively to align God-ness with the vibrant multiplicity of the material world itself.

In this sense, Janzten suggests, pantheism is a far more radical position than atheism, which ends up reinscribing the concept of the God it doesn't believe in. However staunchly they may oppose theism, atheists ironically agree to the terms of the theistic claim—namely that if there were a God, "he" would be anthropomorphic, masculine, all-powerful, and immaterial. These same characteristics constitute the grounds for the theist's affirmation and the atheist's rejection of "him." Whether under the regime of theism or atheism, then, "the *concept* of the divine" remains the same; whether existent or nonexistent, such a God "serves to valorize disembodied power and rationality."[72] And of course, the concept of the divine is the most powerful concept we have, enshrining disembodied power and rationality—which map onto maleness and white European-ness—as our highest values.

For the sake of our threatened planet, in the face of our waning biodiversity, and in solidarity with those living and nonliving beings whom the Father-aligned continue to master, colonize, denigrate, and destroy, Jantzen suggests that feminist philosophers begin deliberately to project a pantheist God—a God who *is* the universe in all its material multiplicity. In her words, "if we took for granted that divinity—that which is most to be respected and valued—*means* mutuality, bodiliness, diversity, and materiality, then whether or not we believed that such a concept of God was instantiated . . . the implications for our thought and lives would be incalculable."[73] Such implications notwithstanding, there has not been a widespread—or even a small-scale—turn toward pantheism among feminist, queer, anti-racist, post- and decolonial, or ecologically oriented philosophers and theologians. Even though Jantzen's work continues to be widely circulated and taught, no one has taken up her call to a pantheist projection.[74] Rather, pantheism continues to serve as a limit-position—marking the boundary of philosophical respectability—for thinkers of nearly every school and political persuasion. And the present work aims to understand why this is the case.

Objections

Godlessness

The stated oppositions to pantheism are numerous, and often perplexingly opposed to one another. "Pantheists" are variously charged with materialism and anti-materialism, irrationality and excessive rationality; fanaticism and coldness, idealism and mechanism—whatever the author's position may be, the pantheist rhetorically incarnates its extreme opposite. The thickest complex of conflicting accusations, however, accumulates around Bayle's first charge against Spinoza, namely, that he is an atheist. At first, this may seem a baffling, even incoherent, claim; as Novalis famously intoned, Spinoza is a "God-intoxicated man" (*ein gottrunkener Mensch*).[75] Everywhere he looks, Spinoza sees the essence and existence of God; thus Goethe reminds us that

"Spinoza does not have to prove the existence of God; existence *is* God."[76] So if Spinoza's God is all things, then how can this same God be *no* thing? How does the *pan-* flip over into an *a-*?

There are two major lines of thinking that produce the conclusion that pantheism is actually atheism, an accusation as old as the term itself.[77] The first is theological, beginning and ending with the insistence that an impersonal, nonanthropic, immanent God would be no God at all. Thus, Reverend Dix laments that with the pantheist onslaught,

> as we comprehend the sacred term, there is left no God. A substance, impersonal, there is; but we cannot imagine that unintelligible, unreasoning, unthinking, unloving state of impotence as our Father, our Creator, our Redeemer, our Sanctifier, our Friend. The God in whom we have believed is gone.[78]

Whether or not it is fair to attribute all of these qualities to the pantheistic deity ("impotence" in particular seems an extension of the orientalist rendering of the passive, feminine, anti-intellectual nonindividual who allegedly dreamed up such visions in the first place), Dix is right to suggest that a God who *is* the world would certainly not be anthropomorphic. As "world," such a God would moreover be material, multiple, malleable, and limited—attributes that cannot possibly apply to the God of classical theism. For the theist, then, to see God everywhere is to see "him" nowhere; this is to say, the word "or" simply cannot conjoin the terms "God" and "Nature."

The second road from pantheism to atheism is more philosophical than theological. With Schopenhauer, it reasons that calling the world "divine" does not add anything to the concept of "world."[79] A universe-as-God is materially and functionally equivalent to a universe-without-God; hence Schopenhauer's declaration that pantheism is merely "a euphemism for atheism."[80] If the world is all there is, then it would be more honest just to call it "world" than to dress it up with divinity; as Nancy Frankenberry concludes, "by assimilating *God* to *Nature* ... [pantheists] raise the suspicion that one of the two of them is semantically superfluous."[81]

Worldlessness

From the foregoing objections, we might think we know which term is superfluous: God. The pantheist world is self-sufficient, auto-creative, and as such, effectively atheistic. Yet a slew of other critiques level precisely the opposite charge: that by swallowing "all things" into God, pantheism eliminates not God, but *the world*. The adjective Hegel uses to describe this Spinozist effect is "acosmic": if all agents are essentially God, then God is the only agent, and the cosmos as such is gone.[82] "There is therefore no such thing as finite reality," he writes; "according to Spinoza what is, is God, and God alone. Therefore the allegations of those who accuse Spinoza of atheism are the direct opposite of the truth; with him there is too much God."[83] Spinoza's alleged "acosmism" deepens the aforementioned attribution of pantheism to the "East"; as Western authors understood it—largely thanks to Hegel[84]—the Vedanta teaches that insofar as "Brahma alone exists," the world itself is "mere illusion."[85] The charge of acosmism also explains the bizarre accusation that even Calvinism amounts to pantheism; as the Unitarian preacher William Ellery Channing argues, the doctrine of predestination, like pantheism, "robs [human] minds of self-determining force, of original activity" and "makes them passive recipients of the Universal force."[86] It is in this sense that Goethe can say that "when others . . . rebuke [Spinoza] with atheism, I prefer to cherish him as *theissimus* [most theistic]."[87] If the world itself is divine, then God is all there is.

For interlocutors less admiring than Goethe, however, Spinoza's acosmic all-God amounts to a denial of human freedom. As Leo Strauss worries, the world-as-God lacks the autonomy to do anything *without* God, or at least without "the threat of divine intervention."[88] Conversely, we find Christian authors worrying that, far from denying human freedom, pantheism grants humanity too much of it, allowing them to do whatever they would like in the absence of a divine overlord and in the presence of an indwelling Spirit.[89] Humans, in effect, drain the freedom out of God and claim it for themselves; as Rudolf Bultmann worries, when God is seen in "nature and natural forces . . . it is only man that is deified."[90] Meanwhile, divine freedom *in itself* is evacuated; after all, if God *is* creation, then God has no freedom not to create—or, for that matter, to act contrary to the laws of nature.[91] Thus Marin Mersenne condemns Giordano Bruno, executed two and a half decades earlier, for the crime "of reducing God to the rank of a natural and necessary agent."[92] In sum, these tortuous and conflicting accusations amount to a remarkably plodding hydraulics: if God is the world, then there is no God; if the world is God, then there is no world; if God acts in humans, then humans can't act; if humans are free, then God is unfree. And once again, we see the anti-pantheist hang on at all costs to the principle of noncontradiction the pantheist so flagrantly violates. It is simply not possible, charges the theist, for these terms to co-inhere.

Clutching his "law of the table," he proclaims any scheme that refuses to line up into two columns "monstrous."

The "Problem of Evil"

Of all the pantheist's conflated binaries, the most commonly cited is the difference between good and evil. Given his wholly good God, the theist is perennially concerned to account for "the problem of evil," which is to say, the presence of suffering in a benevolent creator's creation. The pantheist, says the theist, exacerbates this problem beyond the bounds of reason, because her purportedly God-drenched world is filled with all manner of senseless violence. God becomes in the pantheist register not only responsible for evil, but coextensive with it; if everything is divine, the thinking goes, then war, disease, slavery, and hatred are not only condoned by God—they *are*, in some sense, God. In the face of torture, Schopenhauer argues, at least the theist can defend divine benevolence by appealing to divine inscrutability. The pantheist, on the other hand, has no excuse; the identity of his divinity with a murderous world means that, "the creating God himself is the endlessly tortured [one] who on this small earth alone dies once every second and does so of his own free will, which is absurd."[93] Similarly, Bayle ridicules the notion that within the Spinozist worldview, the sentence "'the Germans have killed ten thousand Turks,'" actually means "'God modified into Germans has killed God modified into ten thousand Turks.'"[94] And C. S. Lewis snipes that in response to the pantheist notion that "a cancer and a slum . . . also is God," the only properly Christian reply is, "'don't talk damned nonsense.'"[95]

As it unfolds, and especially in chapter 4, the present study will address these charges at greater length. For the moment, however, we should note that although a hypothetical pantheist would be just as outraged by the presence of suffering in the world as any theist, she would not view it as a philosophical puzzle, or as grounds for some extended theodicy. Suffering is always a practical problem, calling for a practical response. But "evil" only becomes a *theoretical* problem—something to be explained or explained away—if one holds an a priori commitment to self-evident categories of "good" and "evil" in the first place, to an all-powerful and anthropomorphically "good" creator in the second place, and to an anthropocentric creation—whose felicity is the creator's central concern—in the third. There are numerous cosmologies that do not operate under these premises, and so effectively have no "problem of evil." Evil is not a theoretical problem for Native American or

Black diasporic trickster narratives, for instance, or for Aboriginal Australian stories of the Dreaming; rather, these accounts attribute to the weavers
of the world the same mix of traits that we find *in* the world, offering thereby
a way of finding possibilities in the midst of perennial dangers.[96] As Sylvia
Marcos explains,

> The duality that pervades the Mesoamerican concept of the universe
> included both the positive and negative aspects of nature, the creative as well
> as the destructive, the nurturing and the annihilating forces. . . . There is no
> sentimentality in their perception of the earth. Earth is a great nourishing
> deity and an unpredictable, fearsome monster: in all cases, it is necessary to
> move about the earth with care.[97]

Similarly, evil is a practical but not a theoretical problem for pantheism,
which rejects the anthropomorphic-creator-plus-anthropocentric-creation
that asks, for example, "why does God let bad things happen to good people?"
In the same breath, pantheism rejects the whole table of hierarchical binaries
that would anchor "good" and "evil" as stable referents. Along with her reluctant Nietzschean allies, then, the hypothetical pantheist might ask what it is
that has given rise to our impulse to call certain acts, people, and practices
"good" or "evil" to begin with.[98] And in the absence of a transcendent source
of value, she would have to ask what in any given situation contributes to the
flourishing of creatures, what destroys it, and how best to intervene. But there
would be no assurance ahead of time as to what counts as good or evil, right or
wrong, worthy of care or subject to destruction.

The real difference between theism and pantheism with respect to "evil" is
therefore not that the former rejects it while the latter condones it, or that the
former "takes it seriously" while the latter ignores it in the face of mountains
and rainbows. Rather, the difference is that the pantheist rejects the cosmic
bifurcations that stem from the opposition between God and world and then
regulate theistic ethics from a supposedly transcendent standpoint. And from
this perspective, we see that the turmoil over the problem of evil, like every
other anti-pantheist assertion, boils down to a longing for unchanging, binary
difference. In all its various guises, the anti-pantheist complaint amounts—to
borrow a term from Hermann Cohen and Franz Rosenzweig—to a charge of
Gleichmacherei, or *making everything the same.*[99] In Dix's words, "all boundary
lines are swept away, all differences disappear, all life, all thought, all reason are
struck and heaped and mashed together in one monstrous lump . . . one appalling chaos."[100] And the theist is left calling for order.

The Problem of Difference

One such voice is that of systematic theologian Colin Gunton, who distills all the major objections to pantheism into a common concern for "difference." Reflecting on the manifold ills of pantheism, he writes,

> for there to be freedom, there must be space. In terms of the relation between God and the universe, this entails an ontological otherness between God and the world. . . . Atheism and . . . materialism are in effect identical with pantheism, for all of them swallow up the many into the one, and so turn the many into mere functions of the one.[101]

Succinctly put, the argument is that if there is no difference between God and the world, there can be no difference *at all*. And if there is no difference, then none of the parties involved is sufficiently autonomous to be "free." So, if in our varied political commitments we want to affirm things like freedom, difference, diversity, and multiplicity, Gunton suggests, we'd better hang onto the ontological distinction between God and creation. Otherwise, everything melts, in the words of D. H. Lawrence, into an "awful pudding of One Identity."[102]

At this point, however, one might ask whether the only available options are a two-column hierarchy on the one hand and an awful pudding on the other. One might even go so far as to ask whether the theistic "two" is really so different from the puddingish one in the first place. After all, the metaphysical framework that stems from God-versus-world—opposing in turn form and matter, male and female, eternity and time, colonizer and colonized, good and evil, etc.—does not establish the second as genuinely different from the first, so much as a derivation, deviation, and/or bad copy of it. One might think here of Judith Butler's analysis of lesbianism as a purported imitation of heterosexuality, or of Homi Bhabha's "colonial mimicry," which produces non-Europeans as "almost the same [as their colonizers], *but not quite*."[103] The oppositional logic of classical metaphysics does not, then, give us two; it actually gives us one, and a falling-short of that one.[104] Nor, to part ways with Gunton, does this binary scheme secure the "freedom" of both terms; rather, it secures the freedom of the historically dominant term at the expense of its subjugated other.[105] And so the real concern over pantheism is not the collapse of some abstract notion of "difference"; rather, it is the collapse of one particularly insistent and damaging way of *configuring* difference—one that gathers each instance of "difference" into a static category, forever held in place by an oppositional overlord.

We have already detected an anxiety over racial and gender insubordination woven through nineteenth-century projections of dark, Eastern pantheists. In these texts, a feminized passivity marks the dreamlike Indian sage, who in his erotic reverie attributes divinity even to dark and earthbound things. In more contemporary repudiations, these racialized projections go underground, as authors focus on the (more natural? less contentious?) category of gender. Although Janzten does not explicitly name the persistently racialized nature of this shift, her work turns boldly on the insight that "the fear of pantheism bespeaks a perceived if unconscious threat to the masculinist symbolic of the West."[106] Jantzen detects such panicked masculinity in the surprisingly recurrent language of pantheism's "swallowing," "consuming," and "assimilating" all otherwise "free" beings into some dark abyss—as Hegel ridiculed it, "the night in which all cows are black"[107]—an abyss, moreover, whose racial characteristics Jantzen seems both to notice and not notice. As she puts it,

> from a psychoanalytic perspective, one could speculate about what dread of the (m)other and the maternal womb lurks just below the surface of this fear of pantheism; what exactly is the abyss, this horror of great undifferentiated darkness into which at all costs "we" must not be sucked?[108]

Janzten is thinking primarily of figures like Hegel, Schlegel, and Kierkegaard, but this fear of being pantheistically *swallowed* by a dark, maternal monster can be found even in the lesser-known writings of the nineteenth century.

Reverend Dix, for example, says of pantheism that "the whole system is one vast dream, one shapeless sea of gloom and woe, without light, without life, cold, remorseless, devouring—an abyss in which all honest conviction is engulfed, all *manly* belief buried."[109] By summoning this dark, shapeless, unmanning sea, Dix is calling to mind the waters of Genesis 1, the primordial "deep," or *tehom* that precedes creation.[110] Now in Genesis, a disembodied male voice *speaks* over this darksome deep to bring forth light, and life, and planets and stars. But pantheism eliminates the disembodied creator, leaving us with the abyss that buries manliness alive—the womb that becomes tomb. Revolted, Dix narrates the pantheist cosmogony:

> The mass so indescribable, so incomprehensible, was agitated from within by an equally indescribable and incomprehensible motion. . . . The great belly of blackness and unconscious horror, rumbled as it were, and the abyss, for it seems no better, was in labor and would bring forth.

At the risk of pointing out the obvious, Dix's cosmogonic nightmare is that the *world* might have come into being in the same manner as cats, or donkeys, or humans. For millennia, the cosmological triumph of masculinist monotheism has been its insistence that, while things *in* the world emerge from the bodies of mothers, the world *itself* emerges from a bodiless Father. By rejecting an extra-cosmic deity, then, pantheism delivers us back to—and out of—what Dix characterizes in this passage as a black, maternal, irrational abyss.

This sort of racialized gender-panic is not limited to the Victorian literature; one finds it in more recent rejections of pantheism, as well. For example, evangelical theologian William Lane Craig defends the ontological distinction against pantheism (and its dangerously close cousin, panenetheism) with the following illustration:

> In marriage the antithesis of two persons is *aufgehoben* as husband and wife come together in a deep unity even as their distinctness as persons is preserved. In the same way, the opposition between infinite and finite, God and world, is *aufgehoben* in that God is intimately related to the world in various ways even as the ontological distinctness between God and the world is preserved.[111]

The problem with pantheism, for Craig, is that its demolition of the ontological distinction between God and world is analogous to a demolition of the sexual distinction between man and woman. Unsurprisingly, the first of these terms is aligned with infinity and God, while the second gets finitude and world. Reaffirming this alignment, Craig explains that God "embraces . . . his creatures . . . just as a husband embraces his wife."[112] So we'd better hang onto the ontological distinction—otherwise anyone might embrace anyone else, and who knows what un*aufgehoben*able differences might emerge.

We find a similar fear alarmingly enacted in a critical diatribe that D. H. Lawrence launches against Walt Whitman. Recoiling from Whitman's egotistical, pantheist mass—his ecstatic enfolding of atoms and bicycles and choruses and steam trains, of workers and America and "quadrupeds and birds"[113]—Lawrence lambastes "all that fake exuberance. All those lists of things boiled in one pudding-cloth! No no! I don't want all those things inside me, thank you."[114] Even for the notoriously lascivious Lawrence, Whitman has made himself too porous, too penetrable, too queer: "a pipe open at both ends, so everything runs through."[115] Men, women, Brooklyn, bees—Whitman's pantheism makes him the feminine recipient of all of them—including, Lawrence bristles, "an Esquimo in a kyak . . . little and yellow and greasy."[116]

At the same time as it is universally invaded, Lawrence suggests, Whitman's soul is also infinitely dispersed; the outside-in is turned inside-out. Thus he imagines "Walt" promiscuously scattered into "the dark limbs of negroes . . . the vagina of the prostitute."[117] At this point it seems important to point out that Lawrence's revulsion at Whitman's pantheism is not the product of some commitment to theological orthodoxy. Nor does it stem from an adherence to self-proclaimed philosophical rigor. Rather, such loathing is both prompted and encapsulated by the racial and sexual intermingling it seems necessarily to entail. Whitman is a monster, mixing activity and passivity, creation and reception, and race, sex, gender, species, and class into what Lawrence calls an enormous, snowball-like One,[118] but which frankly looks more like a queer multitude. In fact, the monstrous and the queer perform similar categorical disruptions.[119]

Half a century after Lawrence, Evangelical-turned-Roman Catholic theologian Stephen H. Webb rejects pantheism on more subtly racialized, but similarly gendered ground. In his defense of global capitalism as the economic vehicle for a truly global Christianity, Webb rejects the planetary viability of a pantheist "sacred earth" cosmology. "Judaism, Islam, and Christianity," he cautions, "are unlikely to dismantle their notions of divine transcendence in order to embrace an earth goddess."[120] In this declaration, at the risk of pointing out the obvious, Webb is linking the demise of divine transcendence to the emergence of divine femininity. This femininity is furthermore tied to the earth—the mother *is* matter, and dark matter, at that—and as such, the earth is theistically reduced to "resources" for human (read: male and white) development.[121] Finally, this dark and earthly femininity is tinged with the mild sexuality of an "embrace" that sounds strikingly like Craig's hetero-marital sublation. Meanwhile, at the other end of the theological spectrum, we find even the apocalyptic horseman Richard Dawkins deriding pantheism as a "sexed-up atheism."[122]

Recalling, then, the "temptations" and "seductions" decried in anti-pantheist treatises, it seems that wherever one stands, pantheism is not only "absurd," but also dark, feminized, and dangerously enticing. What each of these authors presents as the "monstrosity" of pantheism—the thing that inspires such panic—amounts to a complicated hybridity of divinity, femininity, darkness, materiality, animality, and sex: undesirable (which is to say, all too desirable) to theists and atheists alike. And this, I would suggest, is the real matter with pantheism: it threatens the Western symbolic not just with a (m)other-womb, but with a wider and more complex range of queer monstrosities: with parts combined that ought to be kept separate and boundaries crossed that ought to be maintained.

Of course, it all depends on what you mean by pantheism.

INDEFINITIONS

1. *The Encyclopedia of Philosophy* defines pantheism as the two-pronged assertion "that everything that exists constitutes a unity and that this all-inclusive unity is divine."[123]
2. The *Routledge Encyclopedia of Philosophy* defines pantheism as "the view that Deity and Cosmos are identical."[124]

Although these definitions can certainly be rendered compatible, the two are hardly equivalent, and in fact tend toward vastly different ontologies. The first hinges the pantheist position on *unity*, attributing a supervening oneness to the things of this world and to the divinity that unifies them. The second anchors pantheism not in oneness but in *immanence*, claiming a this-worldliness for the divinity it cosmicizes. Again, it would be possible to affirm both of these definitions simultaneously; one could say, for example, that "God" is the unified sum of the material universe, and thereby secure unity and immanence at the same time. But one could also affirm the former while rejecting the latter, locating the unity of all things in a spiritual, otherworldly realm and thereby denying the reality or importance of the material universe (as Hegel claims is the case with Spinoza). Conversely, one could affirm the latter definition while rejecting the former, claiming that the material universe is divine but that "it" is not a unity. Ultimately, the difference seems to boil down to an etymological duplicity in this theism's *pan*: does "all" mean "the All," or does it mean "all things"? Is pantheism's cosmic divinity one, or is it many?

These two different meanings of "pan" map onto a distinction William James makes in *A Pluralistic Universe* between "monistic" and "pluralistic" pantheisms.[125] Having dismissed orthodox Christianity as incoherent and childish—even "savage"—and materialism as mechanistic and "cynical," James praises pantheism as providing "the only opinions quite worthy of arresting our attention" (29–30).[126] Yet not all pantheisms are the same; the category, James suggests, "breaks into two subspecies, of which the one is more monistic, the other more pluralistic in form" (31). For the monist, James explains, the world is one "tremendous unity," in which "everything is present to *everything* else in one vast instantaneous co-implicated completeness" (37, 322; emphasis in original). For the pluralist, by contrast, the things of the world are "in some respects connected, [and] in other respects independent, so that they are not members of one all-inclusive individual fact" (55). Monism tell us that everything is connected to everything else, whereas pluralism affirms that connections

come and go—that "a bit of reality when actively engaged in one of these relations is not *by that very fact* engaged in all the other relations simultaneously"
(322–23). Monism is the "philosophy of the absolute," of idealism and "the *all*-
form," whereas pluralism opts for empiricism and "the *each*-form," thinking
that "there may ultimately never be an all-form at all" (34).

Of course, James is a pragmatist, so he knows he cannot say which of these
visions is ultimately "true," or if it even makes sense to speak that way.[127] But
James sides with pluralism for a host of ethical, political, and psychological
reasons: if we affirm a messy plurality rather than a perfect totality, then "evil"
calls for a practical response rather than a speculative explanation; differences of
opinion are signs of health rather than pathology; and our everyday experiences
amount to "intimacy" with the universe itself.[128] This attunement to intimacy
provokes James's most novel critique of the monist tradition: presumably, he
argues, the pantheist locates the divine in and as the world in order to commune
with it. But the monistic "all-form" bears none of the characteristics of the dis-
jointed, imperfect, and changeable world we actually experience. It contains the
so-called *essence* of things, and as such has no imperfections, no traits subject
to development or decay. "It can't be ignorant," James begins. "It can't be patient,
for it has to wait for nothing, having everything at once in its possession. It
can't be surprised; it can't be guilty" (39). In short, the monistic world-as-divine
bears none of the characteristics of the only world we ever experience—with its
desires and mistakes, its passions and pains, its kasha and Kanye—to such an
extent that this type of pantheist places himself even farther from God than the
ordinary theist does, hovering above the world he allegedly divinizes.[129]

Arguably, the most politically expedient problem with monism—a problem
that James allows us to deduce but does not address directly—is that it effaces
the real distinctions among the multifarious constituents of the God-world.
While such indifference might seem at first blush to promise something like
equality, it most often ends up installing an unexamined set of European categories (including "oneness" itself) as its "universal" attributes and then arranging the rest of the world in a stark, racialized hierarchy beneath them. We find
one particularly representative illustration in the work of the nineteenth-century naturalist Ernst Haeckel, a tireless advocate of pantheistic "monism" as the
great reconciler of religion and modern science. Haeckel's "Monistic religion"
or "religion of Nature" will be grounded, he explains, in "the monistic conviction of the unity . . . of mind and body, of force and matter, of God and Universe."[130] Enabled by the novel and seemingly "natural" insights of evolutionary
biology, however, Haeckel's "monistic conviction" is disturbingly reinforced by
an attendant and intensifying scientific racism.[131]

Writing just a few decades after Darwin, Haeckel secures his monism by denying the traditional distinctions between animal, vegetable, mineral, and human life-forms. Nevertheless, in a move not uncommon among his contemporaries, Haeckel goes on to arrange his all-is-one universe into a graduated ontic continuum. As he explains the evolutionary trajectory, the significant beings of the world develop from "birds and mammals" to "the 'ape-man,'" and then to "primitive peoples," the "low civilisation[s]," and finally "the more highly civilised nations."[132] This "progression," he furthermore explains, can be mapped onto a theological journey from pluralism through dualism to monism, "developing" racially from animists and fetishists through pluralists, monotheistic dualists, and ultimately scientific monists.[133] Far from asserting the value of all the beings whose oneness it proclaims, then, monism ironically secures a radical, racialized inequality. Precisely because it denies any *qualitative* differences, it ends up arranging beings *quantitatively*, on a single scale that makes its way from the inanimate to the European.

Less through political or ontological conviction than pragmatic preference, James unsettles this racialized hierarchy by choosing to reject the Germanic monism raging around him in favor of a more modest, pantheistic pluralism. Such manyness makes of the universe what he calls a *multiverse*, by which term he means to designate a loosely coherent, evolving and devolving chain of complex connections that is never quite all-in-all, and so never lumped into a single snowball or arranged into static ranks. Slipping into German to poke fun at the One, James explains that, "The type of [multiversal] union, it is true, is different here from the monistic type of *all-einheit*. It is not a universal co-implication, or integration of all things *durcheinander*. It is what I call the strung-along type, the type of continuity, contiguity, or concatenation" (325).[134]

Inasmuch as James is elucidating monism and pluralism only as "subspecies" of pantheism, and inasmuch as pantheism is the position that James, unlike almost any other self-proclaimed philosopher, *actually professes*, one would expect his vision of divinity to resemble—or indeed, amount to—his vision of cosmology. It is therefore disappointing to find his vision of the former fall so bafflingly short of his vision of the latter. Even as James's "world" amounts to a rich, multiversal plurality of concatenations and stringings-along, his "god" ends up a single, disembodied, anthropomorphic, male agent: a limited force that works alongside other limited forces in the multiverse.[135] Frustratingly, James does not give us the pluralistic pantheism he announces, his diminished, humanoid divinity clashing bizarrely with the complex, entangled vibrancy of the material world—the very world with which James's own pluralist pantheism would ostensibly identify "God."

NAVIGATION

The present study aims to explore the possibility James opens and then closes: to ask what a "pluralist pantheism" might, in fact, be. The task is not a straightforward one; as we have already begun to see, the object of constant denigration is the monistic "all-form" ("The universe," laughs Lawrence, "in short, adds up to ONE. ONE. I. Which is Walt."),[136] and this polemical literature is the venue in which "pantheism" most clearly takes conceptual shape. If it is the case, as Philip Clayton suggests, that "no philosophically adequate form of pantheism has been developed in Western philosophy,"[137] then the absence is even more striking in the case of *pluralist* pantheism—if there even is such a thing. The position will therefore have to come together piecemeal, patchworkily, monstrously arising from the depths of the barely said and unsaid in a wide range of literatures. Far from dreaming up such a position *ex nihilo*, then, this study seeks to show it is already in subtle formation: first, in self-professed pantheisms that present themselves as monistic (at each turn, James writes, "something like a pluralism breaks out");[138] second, in historical philosophies that tend to ignore, sidestep, or actively dismiss the category of "pantheism"; third, in scientific discourses that tend to ignore or actively dismiss "religion" and "theology"—especially general relativity, quantum mechanics, nonlinear biologies, and multiverse cosmologies; and fourth, in the burgeoning, ever-multiplying para-scientific theories these discourses have inspired.

Such para-scientific theories can be loosely assembled under the category of theories of immanence, or of *post-* or *nonhuman studies*, and include such formations as ecofeminisms, "new" materialisms, new animisms, animal studies, vegetal studies, assemblage and actor-network theories, speculative realism, complexity theory, and nonlinear science studies. In their loosely collective, "strung-along" effort to decenter "the human," these modes of immanent analysis open the possibility of something like a pluralist pantheism—or, to mobilize the plurality, "pantheologies." They do so, first, by dislodging agency and creativity from humanity (theism's perennial "image of God") and second, by locating agency and creativity in matter itself. Viewed through the manifold lenses of such studies, the "world" with which the pantheist would identify God is neither inert and passive, as classical theism would have it, nor total and unchanging, as the monist would have it. Rather, "world" names an open, relational, and self-exceeding concatenation of systems that are themselves open, relational, and self-exceeding.

"At any moment," Jane Bennett writes, "what is at work . . . is an animal-vegetable-mineral sonority cluster."[139] Such (monstrous) clustering is at work whether we are speaking about cells, bacteria, the "human" genome, water, air, a cloned sheep, or a "collapsed" wave function: each of them is composed of a mutating band of others. If, with Karen Barad, we add discursivity into the mix,[140] then our multiple-universe becomes an un-totalizable and shape-shifting hybrid of narrative-theoretical-material assemblages that are neither reducible to, nor constitutive of, "oneness." And this multiply unified, multiply divided, constantly evolving multiplicity is what the pantheologies in question would call *divine*. As such, they will look very little like their monistic counterpart, which, to be honest, is easier to find in the philosophical forest. Depending on one's starting point, "pantheism" divinizes either a messy multiplicity or a smoothed-out whole, and this particular expedition is foraging for the mess.

Beginning from immanence rather than unity, the exploration at hand will define "pantheism" minimally as the identification of divinity with the material world. Each of the chapters that follow will focus on one of the four major terms of this definition: *pan* (all), *hyle* (matter), *cosmos* (world), and *theos* (God). Pantheologically speaking, of course, these are all equivalent terms, but they have distinct, if interdetermined, genealogies that this study will examine in turn. For better or worse, the passage from one of these terms to another will be mediated and interrupted by the promiscuous goat-god Pan, who will appear in short, animal-material-vegetal bursts of divinity to keep things monstrous and queer. He will do so even, perhaps especially, in the face of the Christian tradition that tries variously to demonize, romanticize, devour, and assimilate him.

In order to begin its pantheological conjuring, chapter 1 ("Pan") will dive more deeply into the questions of number, identity, and difference. When a hypothetical pantheist affirms that "God is all," what does she mean by "all," and for that matter, what does she mean by "is"? Does "all" denote a seamless unity of existence—whether by virtue of an invisibly shared essence or an enormous sum? Or does it rather refer to "all things" in their shifting plurality—in their different differences from, relations to, and constitutions of one another? What are the stakes of affirming the pantheist one versus its many, and what in either case does it mean to identify God (or anything else) with it?

This chapter will address these questions by evaluating the charges of acosmism and indifference leveled against Spinoza. We will focus in particular on Hegel's accusation that Spinoza's *Deus sive natura* swallows "all that we know as the world" into an "abyss of the one identity" (*Abgrund der einen Identität*)[141]—a conclusion Hegel reached by filtering his reading of the "Oriental" Jew through his limited and romanticized understanding of Hindu cosmology. Revealing the allegedly world-denying monisms of "Spinoza" and "India" to be Orientalizing byproducts of one another, the chapter proceeds to revisit Spinoza's doctrine of substance with an ear toward the concrete, the particular, and the multiple. By reading Spinoza both with and against himself, and alongside his admirer Friedrich Nietzsche, it will argue that, far from transcending or even preceeding the embodied "modes" that express it, Spinoza's substance is in fact constituted by them. As such, *Deus sive natura* is irreducibly many in its oneness, and irresistibly embodied. The "all" that God-or-nature "is" therefore amounts to a dynamic holography: an infinitely perspectival dynamism that unsettles not only the static singularity of substance, but also its eternal determinism, by virtue of the materiality of the modes.

Chapter 2 ("Hyle") will inquire into the meaning of this materiality. Beginning from Bayle's proclamation that matter is "the being whose nature is most incompatible with the immutability of God,"[142] this chapter will ask what matter has historically meant, why Western thought has so obsessively removed divinity from it, and how this anti-materialism has gone on to shape the modern scientific imagination. It will simultaneously locate particularly vibrant exceptions to this materiaphobic trend in the Ionian, Stoic, and Epicurean schools, which produce a generative materiality that arguably finds its culmination in Giordano Bruno (1548–1600). In a body of work that eventually gets him burned at the stake, Bruno deconstructs the Aristotelian privilege of (male) form over (female) matter by configuring the latter as the active, animate, enspirited, and ultimately divine origin of the former.

This particular Brunian maneuver finds a powerful resurgence in the recent post- and nonhumanist transvaluations of materiality that insist on matter's agency, intra-activity, and creativity in the face of mechanistic scientific orthodoxy—transvaluations that have been particularly inspired by microbiologist Lynn Margulis's nonlinear principles of autopoiesis and symbiogenesis. Bruno's heretical materiality also finds unexpected resonances with those "animist" cosmologies derided by colonial anthropologists as primitive, feminine, childish, and incapable of making distinctions. Linking this charge to the perennial anti-pantheist cry of dark, abyssal undifferentiation, this chapter finds in "new animist" accounts of indigenous cosmologies an enlivening of matter that takes Spinoza's and Bruno's insights even further than their authors will go—whether willingly or in spite of themselves. Especially when crossed with nonlinear and new materialist thought, these new animisms produce a pan-animate materiality that amounts to a (largely unintentional) transubstantiation of divinity as multiply, relationally, and irreducibly incarnate—perhaps even pantheological.

Chapter 3 ("Cosmos") will ask what we mean by "world" and what it means to associate God with it. Historically, the pantheist "reduction" of God to world has seemed insulting and absurd; the world, after all, is finite, passive, and given—the theater of just-thereness, whereas God is the source of infinite activity and newness. But what if the world is both more or less than we have thought it to be? What if, far from sitting there self-identically, "world" designates an open, evolving, and interpoietic multiplicity of open, evolving, and interpoietic multiplicities? What would it mean to identify *all of that* as the source and end of all things, which at the end of the day "is what everybody means by 'God'"?[143]

In order to address these questions, this chapter will first track the rise and fall of the deterministic, "clockwork universe" of the seventeenth century, according to which the world is a lifeless set of interlocking machines set in motion by an exclusively agential, extra-cosmic creator. Contemporary reductionist biologies, cosmologies, and neurosciences retain this deterministic mechanism even as they abandon the God who historically secured it, transferring his chief functions to the allegedly timeless and universal laws of nature. Under the global reign of Western capitalism, this vision of a passive, exploitable, and inanimate cosmos has had disastrous racial, gendered, and ecological consequences. It is therefore not only pantheologically instructive but politically expedient to turn to those reanimations of the cosmos both within and beyond the natural sciences, and to track the variously panicked responses they have provoked.

Exemplary in this regard is the ongoing controversy over James Lovelock's and Lynn Margulis's "Gaia hypothesis," which attributes an immanent, non-totalized, and symbiotic creative-destructiveness to the world itself. Amplified by climate change sciences, multiverse cosmologies, speculative realisms, new materialisms, philosophies of science, and the intraspecies creativity of Amerindian cosmogonies, Gaia's "intrusion" allows us to glimpse multiscalar re-worldings amid what Eduardo Vivieros de Castro and Déborah Danowski have called "the ends of the world."[144] Even in the face of genocidal erasure, forced migration, and escalating ecological disaster, interdependent throngs of micro-agencies make and unmake worlds as irreducibly multiple, hybrid, and perspectival, giving us some sense of what a pantheology might mean by "God."

Finally, chapter 4 ("Theos") will take stock of the monster the previous chapters have made of divinity. Summoning this theo-cosmic, materiospiritual many-one, how might pantheological thinking respond to the charges that "pantheism" so often faces of determinism, moral relativism, and atheism? Of all these anti-pantheist accusations, this last one is perhaps the most deeply entrenched: Bayle levels it against Spinoza in the first sentence of his essay; de la Faye builds it into the term "pantheism" the moment he coins it; and over two centuries later, a slew of primarily Christian Americans will revive the charge in collective outrage over Albert Einstein's "cosmic religious feeling."[145] The study at hand will therefore find in this outrage a twentieth-century bookend to the Spinoza crisis, reviving as it does nearly all the familiar charges against pantheism and bringing us toward a more contemporary vision of the monstrosity in question.

Although Einstein will provide a helpful path toward it, however, he will stop well short of the pantheological, retaining as he does an unerring faith in a "rational," deterministic cosmos that maintains absolute distinctions between subjects and objects, causes and effects, and truth and perspective. It was this faith that drove Einstein, over the course of decades, to seek an alternative to quantum mechanics, which asserts the bottomless entanglement of observer and observed, experimental apparatus and measured phenomenon. In the course of recounting the "Great Debate" between Einstein and Bohr, this chapter will mobilize Einstein against himself to dislodge his single, unified, and absolute reality. As we will see, Einstein's metaphysics is at total odds with his physics—especially with the special and general theories of relativity that undermined Newtonian space and time and installed perspective at the heart of any account of the world. Reading this relational perspectivism back into Einstein's theology, we will finally be able to ask what "God" might a look like in a pantheological key. What becomes of divinity as it emerges by means of the ever-growing assemblage of symbiogenesis, animist cosmogonies, Gaia, Amerindian perspectivism, and now relativity and quantum mechanics?

By glimpsing this becoming-divinity in the fictional works of Alice Walker and Octavia Butler, we will ultimately redirect the so-called problem of evil into more productive, practical questions. Rather than asking how an omnipotent and benevolent God could let suffering into "his" creation, we will ask how the ongoing de- and re-worldings of an immanent divinity might condition the possibility of survival, transformation, responsibility, and ethical discernment. Finally, we will ask, if the vibrantly material, complexly emergent, indeterminate, and intra-constituted multiverse can be affirmed pantheologically as the creative source and end of all things, then why not just call this source and end "world(s)"? What difference does it make to call such worldings divine?

Admittedly, it may make no difference at all. To the extent that it is possible to maintain such distinctions, the present work aims for conceptual (re)construction rather than theological apologetics. As such, its hope is not to defend pantheological thinking against this or that rival, much less to win converts, but rather to see what such thinking might look like. To give an ancient-modern heresy a chance to have its say before it gets laughed off the stage—or even to grant it a different reception.

PANIC

panic, n.: "originally and chiefly used allusively with reference to a feeling of sudden terror, which was attributed by the ancient Greeks to the influence of the God Pan."

—Oxford English Dictionary

Half-man, half-goat, the Greek god of shepherds and goatherds originated in Arcadia, "where divine theriomorphism is well attested."[1] Herodotus tells us that the cult of Pan began to spread after the Battle of Marathon (490 BC), when the goat god appeared to the Athenian messenger Phidippides to say that if the Athenians worshipped him, he would terrify the invading barbarians and secure the victory of Athens, which, as legend has it, he did.[2] A cave was quickly built under the Acropolis—Pan is worshipped not in temples but in the womb-like spaces of grottoes—and there his devotees danced and sang, becoming fitfully possessed by their "noise-loving" deity. Pan is said to inspire such fits in friends and strangers alike, springing from nowhere to strike literal "pan-ic" in the hearts of travelers with his riotous "stampeding herds and pipings."[3] Classicist Robin Lane Fox tells us that "in the early fourth century [CE], Iamblichus still referred to 'those seized by Pan' as a distinguishable class among people who had made contact with the gods."[4] The *panic* that pantheism routinely inspires among philosophers and theologians—a mixture of delight and terror, seduction and repulsion—can in this sense be attributed to the influence of the divine chimera himself.

Pan Seated. Roman, 2nd century BCE. Marble, h: 158 cm. MA266. Photo: Hervé
Lewandowski, Musée du Louvre. ©RMN-Grand Palais/Art Resource, NY.

Physiologically and functionally, Pan is a monstrously difficult god to clas-
sify. Having "the horns, ears, and legs of a goat" with the torso and head of a
man,[5] and being moreover a god, he is an irreducible hybridity—a collision of
elements that any sane theology would keep separate. The Stoic philosopher
Cornutus mapped this physiology onto the cosmos itself, explaining that "the
lower part of this god is hairy, and recalls a goat, to designate the roughness
of the earth. The upper part, however, is like a man, for heaven holds sway
over the entire world, because in heaven itself is reason placed."[6] According
to Cornutus, then, Pan's very body recapitulates the Great Chain of Being,
his low parts embodying the lowest ranks of the universe and his upper parts
embodying the highest. In the writings of the "last" Church Father Isidore of
Seville (560–636 CE), however, Pan's animality inadvertently breaks out of its
confinement to his bottom half. Granted, Isidore attests that "his lower part
is filthy, because of trees and wild beasts and herds." But at the very top of his
head, he has "horns in the shape of the sun and the moon."[7] So these elements
of animality vault over Pan's human torso and face to reflect the most rarified
parts of the cosmos.

Upward or down, in his goat-part alone, Pan is already what late-antiquity
religionist Sharon Coggan calls "liminal." A goat, she muses, is "not entirely
tame, yet . . . not entirely wild"[8]—the kind of beast who might bite a kid's palm
at a petting zoo. Part-man, Pan is also represented as a shepherd or goatherd—
even, as we shall see, as the forerunner of the Good Shepherd himself. And
insofar as this odd triunity is human, animal, *and* divine, Pan is also said to be
the guardian of shepherds and goatherds, ensuring their safety as well as that
of their charges. Even bees were said to be under Pan's oversight, in his role as
protector of flocks.[9] Ironically, however, Pan is also known as a hunter—as the
god who ensures a successful kill—and in this vein he is called Pan Lykaios, or
"Wolf-Pan," deadly enemy of flocks.[10] And so the savior is also a destroyer. He
is commonly dressed in the skin of a lynx or a fawn (wolfgoat in deercat cloth-
ing?), and his twin brother is said to be neither a goat nor a sheep nor a bee
nor a wolf, but a *bear*: Arcas, ancestor of the Arcadians.[11] All in all, Pan is what
Donna Haraway might call a "contact zone": a cross-species concatenation of
"world-making entanglements,"[12] within which he is both singular predator
and flockish prey, both protector and pruner of the multitude.

"But when I saw him from behind I was certain he was an animal," attests
G. K. Chesterton's Gabriel Syme after an encounter with Pan, "and when I saw
him in front I knew he was a god."[13]

1

PAN

I am sure that two very different meanings if not more lurk in the word,
One.

—Samuel Taylor Coleridge, *Coleridge's Notebooks: A Selection*

ATTUNEMENT

Having exposed Western philosophy's perennial *horror pantheismus* as a fear of crossed boundaries and perverse categorical mixtures, we now face the task of deliberately summoning this monstrosity from the depths of heretical thinking. The task, to change the metaphor, is one of conceptual rehabilitation—of taking a term that has been indiscriminately applied to a host of misrepresented and incompatible positions, and of determining what it might most compellingly *mean*. As variously denigrated communities have done with terms like "queer," "hag," "Obamacare," and "the big bang," the aim here is to reappropriate and mobilize a ridiculed position to disrupt the very order that finds it so revolting. If something about pantheism threatens the light privilege, misogyny, anthropocentrism, and indeed Western-ness of the energetically guarded "Western tradition," then it seems important at the very least to determine what pantheism *is*. Toward that end, our first challenge is to investigate the *pan*: what is the meaning of the "all" that a pantheology would render divine?

We have already seen William James distinguish "monistic" from "pluralistic" pantheisms: monism presents the universe as "one great all-inclusive fact," whereas pluralism affirms "innumerable little hangings-together, little worlds" that connect, disconnect, and recombine to form more of a multiverse than a universe.[1] The terminology can be a bit confusing, insofar as James also uses the term "monism" to distinguish pantheism—in both its monistic and pluralistic guises—from the dualism of classical theism. If theism proclaims "God" and "world" to be two realities, he suggests, then pantheism insists they are one, and in this sense, pantheism is monistic.[2] As James realized, however, there are at least two ways to configure the single plane of God and world: one might view it as a vast, undifferentiated identity, or one might see it as a proliferation of multiplicities—and thus only an "it" in a semantic sense. The former would therefore amount to something like a monistic monism, whereas the second would amount to a more of a pluralistic monism.

By means of James, then, we can distinguish between two levels of "monism": the first affirms against ontological dualism that the world, or God, is "all there is," whereas the second affirms against ontic pluralism that the world, or God, is "all one." For the sake of clarity, this exploration will use the term "immanence" to refer to the first position and reserve the term "monism" for the second. It is immanence that denies the opposition between God and world; it is monism that declares with Alexander Pope that "All are but parts of one stupendous whole."[3] More wordily, such monism declares with its prophet Ernst Haeckel that "there lives 'one spirit in all things,' and that the whole cognizable world is constituted, and has been developed, in accordance with one common fundamental law."[4] And in this sense, as we will go on to see, pantheological thinking is necessarily immanent, but not necessarily monistic—in fact, a rigorous ontological immanentism tends to stand in the way of ontic monism. The more attuned we become to the vast, material multiplicity of "all things," the less likely we are to declare them to be in any simple sense "one." And yet this is the way "pantheism" is usually construed: as subsuming all particular things into an exceptionless unity—a vast cauldron of indifference. The question is where this reading comes from, and what other possibilities it might be concealing.

Hegel's Snuffbox

Spinozan Retrievals

For more than a century after his death, Baruch Spinoza's name remained just as anathema as the positions he allegedly espoused. As Frederick Beiser reports of the German academy in particular, "until the middle of the eighteenth century it was de rigueur for every professor and cleric to prove his orthodoxy before taking office, and proving one's orthodoxy often demanded denouncing Spinoza as a heretic."[5] The fortunes of this renegade philosopher are said finally to have shifted in the aftermath of the "pantheism controversy" (*Pantheismusstreit*, 1783–1790) catalyzed by Friedrich Jacobi's exposure of the recently deceased Gotthold Lessing as a secret Spinozist.[6] If even Lessing was a Spinozist, Jacobi reasoned, then one could only deduce that all philosophy leads to pantheism—which is also to say to atheism, materialism, and immorality.[7] Although Jacobi had hoped this declaration would inspire German philosophy to throw itself back upon the bedrock of Christian revelation, it in fact produced the opposite effect. Young writers like Goethe, Herder, and Fichte suddenly appealed to Spinozist pantheism as an alternative to what they saw as superstitious theism on the one hand and a cold, mechanical deism on the other. Thus, Beiser proclaims, "the scapegoat of the intellectual establishment became its hero," and "pantheism became, as Heine later put it, 'the unofficial religion of Germany.'"[8]

Although it is certainly the case that German thinkers of the nineteenth century became in numerous ways entranced with "Spinoza" and "pantheism," the depth of this widespread reversal of opinion tends to be overstated. Goethe, for example, does not seem to have studied Spinoza seriously; he almost never wrote about him; and he either dramatically misunderstood or creatively overhauled his doctrine of substance.[9] Furthermore, many of the romantics who ran to Spinoza in their youth—most notably Heine, Schlegel, Schleiermacher, and Coleridge—ended up reverting to anthropomorphic Christian theism in their later writings. The same was the case with Friedrich Schelling, who set forth an organic, dynamic reimagination of Spinoza's pantheism in his early *Naturphilosophie*, but who simultaneously accused Spinoza's own philosophy of neglecting the human and of "lack[ing] life and progression."[10] Ultimately, like so many of his aging colleagues, Schelling eventually abandoned pantheism altogether.[11] And the most extensive, explicit treatment of Spinoza in the wake of the pantheism controversy can be found in the work of G. W. F. Hegel, who indeed "drew heavily" on Spinoza,[12] but who did so in order to move beyond him, characterizing the latter's substance—and pantheism tout court—as excessively monistic and in need of (Christianizing) sublation.[13] It is with Hegel, then, that pantheism becomes most starkly aligned with an undifferentiated, all-consuming monism.

In his *Lectures on the Philosophy of Religion*, Hegel distinguishes between "the all" (*das eine All*) and "all things" (*alles*), stating that only the former definition could serve as the basis of a proper philosophical position. "Pantheism" in the latter or "strict" sense—which would state that all things in their plurality are divine—would simply be absurd, "amount[ing] to the notion that everything taken singularly is God—this [snuff]box or the pinch of snuff."[14] And although many people are *accused* of teaching such absurdities, Hegel insists that no one has actually done so: "it has never occurred to anyone to say that everything, all individual things collectively, in their individuality and contingency, are God—for example, that paper or this table is God. No one has ever held that."[15] With this insistence, Hegel clears Spinoza of the insanity of suggesting that his snuffbox was divine. In the same breath, however, he charges Spinoza with having obliterated the snuffbox altogether: "For Spinoza the absolute is substance," Hegel reminds us, "and no being is ascribed to the finite."[16] Insofar as Spinoza teaches that "what is, is God, and God alone," there is in his philosophy "no such thing as . . . the world" itself—"no such thing as finite reality."[17] As we have seen in the introduction, this is the reason Hegel accuses Spinoza not of atheism but rather of "acosmism": "so strictly is there only God," he maintains, "that there is no world at all."[18] The cost of Spinoza's philosophical propriety is therefore his radical unworldliness: he only avoids the idiocy of calling finite things divine insofar as he also maintains that, thanks to the unity of infinite substance, "the finite has no genuine actuality."[19] Clearly the snuffbox can't be God if it doesn't really exist in the first place.

If it were the case that Spinoza denied the real existence of finite things, then his pantheism would ultimately be of an otherworldly variety. It would locate divinity and existence itself either in some immaterial realm or in a hypothetical mass of undifferentiated matter. Viewed in this light, Spinoza's pantheism would fit the unitive definition of pantheism we have encountered but not the immanent definition; it would proclaim the essential oneness of all that is, but not the divinity of the (constitutively multiple) cosmos itself. Moreover, insofar as genuine materiality—the materiality of experience rather than of abstraction—is necessarily particular, such an acosmic position would amount to what one might call a "spiritual" pantheism as distinct from a "material" pantheism. Far from being divine, the multiple material world along this interpretation of Spinoza's *pan* would be shadowlike and unreal. The question, then, is whether this is a fair reading—whether it is indeed the case, as Hegel claims, that "in the system of Spinoza *all things* are merely cast down into [an] abyss of annihilation" (*Abgrund der Vernichtung*).[20]

Given the patterns we have seen so far, it is perhaps unsurprising to find Hegel likening Spinoza's allegedly pantheistic world-denial to that of "the Orientals."[21] "The profound unity of his philosophy," he explains, "his manifestation of Spirit as the identity of the finite and the infinite in God . . . all this is an echo from Eastern lands."[22] Like the transcendentalists and antitranscendentalists will do overseas,[23] Hegel connects Spinoza's pantheism to India in particular. In fact, he asserts, it was Spinoza who imported the Vedic notion of an undifferentiated, static unity beyond the illusory material realm into Western thinking in the first place.[24] Hegel thus begins to call such unadulterated monism "Oriental pantheism *or* genuine Spinozism."[25] Much as "Krishna, Vishnu, and Brahma" are all the same force that inheres in all finite things,[26] he suggests, Spinoza sinks all distinction and particularity into an undifferentiated, godly oneness. "From this abyss," he insists, "nothing comes out" (*es kommt nichts heraus*); in other words, the "rigid motionlessness" of the Indo-Spinozist substance is incapable of generating a world of actual things.[27]

However "unyielding" and "petrified" this unmitigated oneness might be,[28] it is nevertheless also the starting point of dialectics. As Hegel proclaims in his *History of Philosophy*, "thought must begin by placing itself at the standpoint of Spinozism; to be a follower of Spinoza is the essential commencement of all philosophy."[29] What remains to be thought, he explains, is the generation of concrete particulars out of this initial infinity (negation), and then the historical realization of the infinite in and through the finite itself (double-negation). As is well known, Hegel mapped this dialectical movement geographically, claiming that "religion" properly conceived was evolving from its allegedly unified beginnings in the East, through the Hebrew Bible's divided creator and creation, to a reconciled Christian *cultus*.[30] Hegel furthermore located this progression in the history of modern philosophy, which he claimed was evolving from its "Oriental" Spinozist origins, through its Judaized Enlightenment alienation, to its Christianized Hegelian consummation: if Spinoza denied the reality of the finite and Kant denied our access to the infinite,[31] Hegel would at last reconcile the two to one another, specifically in the form of infinite Spirit working its way through—and as—finite human history.[32] Hegel's former roommate and estranged friend Schelling tells a similarly progressivist story from a slightly different angle, claiming that whereas Descartes "lacerated the world into body and spirit" and Spinoza "unified them into a single, albeit *dead*, substance," he (Schelling) at last would make of unity and duality a "living antithesis."[33] Both Hegel and Schelling, then, are progressivist thinkers of the Absolute as an internally differentiated both/and.

Granted, these two dialectical thinkers have been sufficiently accused of pantheism (charges that Hegel denied vehemently and which Schelling met by redefining pantheism altogether[34]) that one might imagine focusing a pantheological rehabilitation on either or both of their philosophies. Seeking as we are a theory of divine immanence *and* multiplicity, we might imagine appealing to

Hegel's singularly plural Spirit, which generates, inheres in, and reconciles all finite things; or to Schelling's recuperation of "the law of identity," which maintains the irreducible *difference* of its identified terms—in this case, "nature and God."[35] Unfortunately, however, the cost of Hegel's sublation of Spinoza and Schelling's "elevation" of him is a renewed anthropocentrism, a concomitant antimaterialism, and ironically, precisely the antiparticularity with which they both charge their pantheist predecessor.

The problem with Spinoza, Schelling declares, is that he neglects the *human* as the exclusive site of unity between the infinite and the finite.[36] Spinoza misreads nature as inherently divine, forgetting that "it is only *through man* that God accepts nature and ties it to him."[37] In this gesture, Schelling reinstalls the cosmic hierarchy between God and creation, reaffirming its classic mediation by means of the human: "only in [man] did God love the world," Schelling insists, because man alone is "the very image of God."[38] In this bizarrely reimagined "pantheism,"[39] divinity only emerges as living and dynamic because it excludes the nonhuman, material world, which is "dead" and useless on its own. Similarly, Hegel mobilizes Spinoza's allegedly lifeless and inert substance "as spirit" by rendering materiality *itself* lifeless and inert, transferring divinity "from nature to human history," which he considers "a higher and more comprehensive domain of reality."[40] The rest of the cosmos, the entire animal-vegetal-mineral realm that constitutes for Spinoza a dynamic expression of "God or Nature," becomes for Hegel nothing but the inert raw materials for the becoming-divine of human history. As he explains in *The Encyclopedia Logic*, "what human beings strive for in general is cognition of the world; we strive to appropriate it and to conquer it. To this end the reality of the world must be crushed as it were, i.e., it must be made ideal."[41]

From this perspective, the result of this much-touted Romantic reappraisal of Spinoza is ultimately a reconsolidated distinction between God and creation and a reaffirmed privilege of the human over everything else. The only sense in which such configurations might be called "pantheist" is one in which humanity becomes equivalent to the world itself. We see such an elision at work in Heidegger's commentary on Schelling, which perplexingly equates the locution, "God is everything" with the locution, "God is man"—as if the objects of these two sentences were somehow convertible.[42] Whether in the hands of Heidegger's Schelling, Schelling himself, Hegel, Fichte, or even Feuerbach,[43] then, "pantheism" becomes nothing more than what one might call *anthropotheism*—or, more playfully rendered, *mantheism*: God is immanent, not in the material universe, but rather in one (allegedly) exclusively conscious corner of it. Insofar as the pantheology we seek would dismantle the metaphysical privilege of spirit over matter, the one over the many, and the human over everything else, however, such neo-Spinozan mantheism will therefore not be the most productive place to find it. Rather, we will head back to Spinoza's own unanthropic, spiritual-material "God or Nature" in light of its Romantic revisions. We will focus on Hegel's critique in particular, insofar as it both encapsulates and solidifies the received reading of Spinoza as monistic, unparticular, and world-denying, thereby motivating the nineteenth-century re-humanizing of the Absolute.

Vedāntic Projections

To assess the validity of Hegel's undifferentiated and acosmic reading of Spinoza, it is important to interrogate his equally undifferentiated and acosmic reading of Indian philosophy. Hegel was indebted in this regard to J. G. Herder, who declared "the core and basis of Hindu thought" to be "the idea of *one* Being in and behind all that there is, and . . . the unity of all things in the absolute, in God."[44] This interpretation, we should note, is hardly innocent: like the German Romantics more broadly, Herder was seeking in the organic "oneness" of "Hindu thought" a remedy for what he perceived to be the mechanistic rationalism of contemporary Europe. As Wilhelm Halbfass explains,

> Because of Herder's influence . . . the Orient and especially an idealized India . . . became associated with the idea of an original state of harmony and a childlike, unbroken wholeness. Poesy-garbed India, where the people were still "dozing" and dreaming, appeared to be the antithesis of the cold, prosaic Europe of the Age of Enlightenment.[45]

Following Herder's orientalist lead, Friedrich Schlegel learned Sanskrit in order to read the source material behind the "pristine religiousness and . . . wholeness" that Europe had supposedly lost and India had supposedly preserved.[46] Upon studying these sacred texts, however, Schlegel was disappointed to discover, not the cosmic wholeness he had sought, but rather "distortions and misinterpretations of the true pristine teachings."[47] What this accusation demonstrates, of course, is that the "pristine teachings" Schlegel sought were a European projection to begin with. Just as nineteenth-century colonial scholars would go on to proclaim the lived practices of South Asians to be pluralistic and material "debasements" of their monistic, spiritual "source" texts,[48] Schlegel is here proclaiming the texts *themselves* to be debasements of an originally "pure" teaching—a purity that was clearly the invention of a post-Enlightenment longing for unity among disaffected Europeans.

Instead of a "genuine" wholeness, Schlegel found in the Sanskrit sources what he called *pantheism*—a position, he warned, that "is just as pernicious for mortals as *materialism*," which he viewed as its polar opposite.[49] We should note that by opposing these two heresies, Schlegel encodes the pantheist "all" as singular and immaterial, which is to say as completely different from the materialist many. Just as Hegel will go on to do, Schlegel describes the "Oriental" pantheist position as one of pure spirituality and unworldliness, finding such a radical immaterialism at work in both Vedāntic and Buddhist sources. For Schlegel, the broadly Indian *pan* amounts to a "merely abstract and negative concept of infinity . . . [which] ultimately escapes itself and dissipates into nothingness."[50] And from the standpoint of this fatalistic, indeed nihilistic Oneness, he concludes, "all change and all life is mere illusion."[51]

This, then, is the source of Hegel's "Oriental" interpretation of Spinoza: Herder's and Schlegel's Oriental*ist* reading of Indian philosophy. In his own rendition of Vedic substance, Hegel retains the romantic image of an "abstract," "indeterminate," and undifferentiated unity. Nevertheless, he goes on to insist against his predecessors that the indeterminate unity of Indian philosophy could not be nostalgically recovered, but only dialectically sublated.[52] Similarly, he participates in his romantic colleagues' reappropriation of Spinoza in the wake of the pantheism controversy, even as he argues against Goethe and Schelling that Spinoza's thinking is merely the beginning of philosophy.[53] In short, then, it is the romantic longing for holism—which expresses itself in fetishized readings of Indian philosophy on the one hand, and retrievals of the much-maligned Spinoza on the other—that leads Hegel to equate the two positions, declaring them similarly world-denying, similarly undifferentiated, and similarly in need of double-negation.

To be sure, the monistic and acosmic reading of Indian philosophy is not simply a Western invention. The Advaita Vedānta school, attributable to the sage Śaṅkarācārya (c. 700), teaches a radical nonduality between the self (*atman*) and the absolute, or ground of the universe (*brahman*). Along most readings, Advaita also dismisses "the world of diversity," in which things appear to be separate from one another, as "nothing more than an illusory appearance (*māyā*) of a monistic . . . reality."[54] Other Vedāntic schools, however, reject these teachings and insist variously upon the absolute reality of the physical universe, the duality of the *brahman* and *atman*, the duality *and* nonduality of *brahman* and *atman*, or even the fundamental multiplicity of atomic matter.[55] The Western perception that "Oriental" philosophy is acosmic and undifferentiated is therefore built upon a misconception—often encouraged by Indian elites—that Advaita Vedānta, understood to be strictly monistic, constitutes the essence of all Indian thought. As Christopher Isherwood proclaims in his popular collection, *Vedanta for the Western World* (1945), "In India today, as elsewhere, there are hundreds of sects. Vedanta Philosophy is the basis of them all. Indeed, in its simplest form, it may be regarded as a statement of the Philosophia Perennis, the least common denominator of all religious belief."[56]

As Richard King has shown, however, this perception was the complex product of both indigenous and Western interests. Centuries before Europe invaded India, King explains, Indian religions underwent a process of "brahmanization—the process whereby the Sanskritic, 'high' culture of the brahmins absorbed non-brahmanical . . . religious forms" as a way of "maintaining social order and political authority."[57] It was these brahmin elites who eventually presented themselves to Western scholars and colonial officials as the authoritative hierarchs of Indian religion, thereby cocreating along with Orientalist philosophers the notion that India was the home of a primordial unity that Westerners had lost. Ironically, King demonstrates, this vision of a single, ancient "Hinduism" encoded in a monistic Vedānta soon became "a nationalist ideology that could unite Hindus in their struggle against colonial oppression."[58] This nationalist ideology moreover allowed cosmopolitan neo-Vedāntins like Swāmi Vivekenānda (1863–1902) to proclaim spiritual superiority over all other religious traditions—more precisely, to proclaim all other traditions to be derivations of Vedānta, destined to rejoin the nondual fold. "Up, India," Vivekenānda exorted his metaphysically unified continent, "and conquer the world with your spirituality. . . . Ours is a religion of which Buddhism . . . is a rebel child and of which Christianity is a very patchy imitation."[59]

It was Vivekenānda's all-encompassing account of "Hinduism," in fact, that formed the basis of William James's understanding of the monistic "subspecies" of pantheism. Referring to Vivekenānda's address at the 1893 Parliament of World Religions in Chicago, James declared that "the paragon of all monistic systems is the Vedānta philosophy of Hindosan [sic.], and the paragon of Vedāntist missionaries was the late Swami Vivekenānda who visited our land some years ago."[60] The pantheism emerging from German idealism, James suggested, was simply a Westernized and needlessly abstruse version of this more primordial, Indian pantheism. But again, this perception was the result of a complex meshwork of colonial and anticolonial strategies. James came to understand Vedānta as strictly monistic thanks to the missionary efforts of Vivekenānda, whose unified Hinduism was itself the coproduction of indigenous and colonial interests in India.

Whether in the hands of Indian elites or Western scholars, then, the strictly monistic reading of "Oriental" philosophy always serves some political agenda—be it the consolidation of local authority, the establishment of Christian missions, the Romantic appropriation of a colonized people's purportedly timeless spirituality, the consolidation of Hindu nationalism, or indeed the reverse-missionizing of Western religion at the hands of neo-Vedāntins. In each of these cases, an absolute ontological oneness underwrites an aspirational political unity. And in each of these cases, this monistic reading of "Hinduism" deliberately erases the vast plurality of non-Vedāntic philosophies and practices in India, not to mention the interpretive plurality within the Vedāntic lineage itself, and even within Sankara's own philosophy.[61]

As we trace the orientalist lineage of Hegel's reading of Spinoza, one might therefore ask what sorts of ontological and interpretive plurality might be similarly erased by Hegel's strictly monistic reading of Spinoza. Does Spinoza's single substance really do away with particularity and the world of experience as such? If so, then it will clearly be of no help to our search for a pluralist pantheism. But if Hegel is misreading Spinoza—whether strategically or unintentionally—that is, if Spinoza's singularity of substance is somehow also multiple and embodied, then we will need to reconsider the position that Hegel insists no one maintains. Reading the monistic "all" alongside the pluralist "all things," we will ultimately ask in what sense one might affirm that "this complex of everything existing, these infinitely many individual things—that all this is God."[62] In other words, we will need to ask to what extent "that paper," "this table," "or the pinch of snuff" could be said to be divine without tumbling into absurdity.[63] How might a pantheology affirm the concrete manyness of its *pan*?

SPINOZA, REVISITED

In the Image of Man They Created Him

Fourteen years after his singularly irrevocable excommunication, Spinoza published his *Theological-Political Treatise* (*Tractatus Theologico-Politicus*, 1670). Along with his *Principles of Cartesian Philosophy* (1663), the *Tractatus* was one of just two texts that would circulate during his lifetime. Unlike the Cartesian commentary, however, the *Tractatus* did not bear Spinoza's name. Although critics throughout Europe—along with a few "freethinkers" and radicals— would quickly attribute it to the "renegade Jew" anyway, the book initially appeared anonymously, and under the name of a pseudonymous publisher, whose offices claimed to be in Hamburg rather than Amsterdam.[64] Written in Latin, the text is clearly not intended for a general audience. At every major turn, in fact, it sets its teachings against the positions of "the multitude," which Spinoza variously describes as being "wretched," superstitious, deluded, "not guided by reason," emotional, ignorant, obstinate, intellectually "defective," and "unstable and fickle."[65]

Among the many errors of the tragically confused commonfolk, the most fundamental, according to Spinoza, is their anthropocentrism. "They imagine Nature to be so limited," he laments, "that they imagine man to be its chief part."[66] In a critique we can imagine him launching against Hegel, Schelling, and his other Romantic descendants, Spinoza decries the common tendency among human beings to think themselves the most important creatures in existence. From this vantage point, they view the rest of the material world "as means to their own advantage," thereby reducing the entire nonhuman realm to an inert and exploitable "nature."[67] At the same time, they extend their dominion into the heavens, imagining God to be just like them—endowed with intellect, will, passions, and preferences—only perfectly, eternally, and infinitely so. The result is an anthropomorphic creator on the one hand and a subordinate creation on the other: just as humans separate themselves from the material world that they shape and use, so do they separate "God" from the "nature" "he" creates and controls. "Thus they imagine that there are two powers quite distinct from each other," Spinoza explains, "the power of God and the power of Nature, though the latter is determined in a definite way by God, or—as is the prevailing opinion nowadays—created by God."[68] And although Spinoza does not dwell on it at any length, he does acknowledge the gendered alignment of these terms, consistently referring to the anthropomorphic creator as "he" and the instrumentalized creation as "she"—the former being "some royal potentate" and the latter his subordinate, feminized subject.[69]

Even as Spinoza continues for rhetorical purposes to attribute such erroneous notions to "the multitude," he also recognizes that these doctrines have been promulgated by clerical elites toward political ends. The notion of a monarchical God who rules a feminized natural world, for example, "seems to have originated with the early Jews" as they sought to assert cosmological dominance over their (often more powerful) neighbors.[70] Surrounded by "the Gentiles of their time who worshipped visible gods—the Sun, the Moon, the Earth, Water, Sky, and so on," the biblical authors proclaimed the supremacy of their *invisible* God: a God who commanded—who had, in fact, *made*—the very beings their neighbors considered divine.[71] Thus did such incipient monotheism assert its supremacy over rival nations—a theopolitical revolution that arguably was only realized centuries later, in the hands of Western Christendom.[72] In the meantime, especially as they suffered occupation and exile, "the fickle Jewish multitude" could be comforted—sedated, even—by the assurance that God directs all of nature toward the particular ends of the particular humans he prefers over the rest of the universe.[73] "This idea has found such favour with mankind," Spinoza worries, "that they have not ceased to this day to invent miracles with [a] view to convincing people that they are more beloved of God than others, and are the final cause of God's creation and continuous direction of the world."[74] Miracles, after all, are said to be divine violations of the order of nature. What better way to establish the supremacy of our God over all other gods—and of "us" over all other humans, animals, minerals, and plants—than to say that this God stopped the sun in its tracks, divided an ocean, or inhabited a virgin's uterus *for us*?

Against this anthropocentric cosmology and its consequently anthropomorphic theology, Spinoza argues that the notion of a miracle is simply incoherent. God, he insists, is not a monarch who stands outside the creation he commands, establishing his sovereignty over it by occasionally suspending the order of nature. Rather, God works through the order of nature itself. Far from being created, interrupted, or even regulated by episodic divine decrees, Spinoza explains, the "laws of Nature *are* . . . God's decrees."[75] To suggest that God might violate the laws of nature would in this sense be to suggest that God might violate God's own laws—a notion "than which nothing could be more absurd."[76] In short, the laws of nature for Spinoza are nothing other than God's actions in the world—even God's actions *as* the world. If you seek to know God, Spinoza therefore suggests throughout the *Tractatus*, you can do no better than to study natural laws and natural phenomena.[77]

It is at this point that we collide with the fleetingly pantheist passage we first encountered in the introduction. Against the notion that there are two separate powers, an active-masculine God and a passive-feminine Nature, Spinoza insists that "the power of Nature is the divine power and virtue, and the divine power is the very essence of God."[78] Now, if it is the case that all these terms are equivalent, then we can only assume that "the power of Nature" constitutes, for Spinoza, "the very essence of God." As we have seen, however, Spinoza swerves in the very next sentence with a strategic "but I prefer to pass this by for the present."[79] Resuming his refutation of miracles—a project contentious enough in its own right—he leaves us to draw whatever conclusions we might draw about the relationship between the power of nature and the essence of God.

No Substance but Substance

It is only in the posthumously published *Ethics* (1677) that Spinoza explicitly refers to God as *Deus, sive natura* (God, or nature).[80] As he did in the *Tractatus*, Spinoza will attribute scores of metaphysical errors and ethical failures to the anthropomorphic cosmo-theology that imagines God as a king and nature as the exploitable handmaiden for man's flourishing.[81] But whereas the Spinoza of the *Tractatus* can be said at most to *gesture* toward the identity of God and nature, the Spinoza of the *Ethics* derives it philosophically. And his starting point is what one might call a faithful betrayal of René Descartes.

In his *Principles of Philosophy*, Descartes defines "substance" as "a thing which exists in such a way as to depend on no other thing for its existence."[82] Roundness, for example, is not a substance because it always relies on some other entity—a tomato, for example—for its existence. And indeed, for previous philosophers in the wake of Aristotle, a tomato would be an example of a substance, whereas roundness, redness, and sweetness would all be examples of "accidents."[83] For Descartes, however, the tomato cannot be said to be a substance because it depends on a host of other physical processes and things—earth, water, seeds, and sunlight—each of which itself relies on other physical processes and things, all of which ultimately rely on the fact of physicality, or "corporeality," itself. And corporeality relies on nothing other than the God who created it.

Strictly speaking, then, there can only be one substance—only one "thing . . . which can be understood to depend on no other thing whatsoever, namely God."[84] As Descartes goes on to qualify, however, we need not speak so strictly. If we use the term in an analogical rather than a univocal way, then "substance" can indeed refer to things other than God. Specifically, created things can be called substances so long as they depend on nothing *other than God* for their existence. There are two such entities, he reasoned: thinking substance, which gives rise to all mental phenomena; and corporeal substance, which gives rise to all physical phenomena. Each of these two created substances, which Descartes also calls "mind and body," has a "principle attribute"—thought on the one hand and extension on the other[85]—by means of which thinking and corporeal substance are particularized into ideas and emotions, tables and horses. Each of these particularities amounts to what Descartes variously calls an attribute, quality, or mode of either thinking substance or corporeal substance.[86] In this manner, the Cartesian universe is divided into two different categories: mental things on the one hand, and physical things on the other.

Both with and against Descartes, Spinoza argues that there are not two substances, but one. Calling upon his predecessor's own definition of substance, Spinoza reasons that if a substance is that which relies on nothing outside itself, then "there can be, or be conceived, no other substance but God."[87] Rejecting Descartes' analogical compromise, Spinoza insists that thought and extension are in no sense "substances." Rather, insofar as they rely on God for their existence, they must be attributes of God Godself, who alone can be called a substance, according to Descartes' own definition. Moreover, insofar as substance is by definition self-sufficient, there can be nothing outside it to limit or enframe it as such. Substance must therefore be infinite,[88] and this infinite substance, *at once mental and corporeal*, is both what we commonly call "God" and what we mean when we say the word "nature."

Spinoza offers a working definition of God in the sixth and last of the definitions introducing the *Ethics*: "By God," he writes, "I mean *an absolutely infinite being; that is, substance consisting of infinite attributes, each of which expresses eternal and infinite essence.*"[89] In his earlier *Short Treatise on God, Man, and His Well-Being*, Spinoza tells us that "nature" can be similarly defined: "Nature," he explains, "consists of infinite attributes, each of which is perfect in its kind. And this is just equivalent to the definition usually given of God."[90] It is clear, then, that Spinoza means to identify what we call God with what we call nature. But what does this God-or-nature look like? To get a better view of this monstrosity—and to assess the charges of monism, acosmism, and undifferentiation leveled against Spinoza's pantheism—we will work through the *Ethics'* definition of God at some length, seeking ultimately to understand the "all" that its nature-bound *theos* might be.

Infinite Attribution

We begin with the attributes, each of which is said to express "the eternal and infinite essence" of God. If, as we have already seen, thought and extension are not substances (as Descartes would have it) but rather divine attributes, then according to this definition, thought and extension both unfold the eternal and infinite essence of God Godself. As Spinoza explains, "thinking substance and extended substance are one and the same substance, comprehended now under this attribute, now under that."[91] The attributes are in this sense holographic: each of them reflects in its own way the entire essence of God. Moreover, the attributes are, in the quantum sense of the word, *complementary*, which is to say they are parallel and incommensurable.[92] Just as light appears to be particulate under certain experimental conditions and wavelike under others, so does God-or-nature appear to be extended under the attribute of extension and ideational under the attribute of thought. And just as light can be said genuinely to be a set of particles *and* genuinely to be a wave—with no overlap, interaction, or decidability between these perspectives—so is Spinoza's God fully unfolded under the attribute of thought *and* fully unfolded under the attribute of extension. Against Descartes, then, Spinoza is arguing that mind and body are not two different entities, but rather two different ways of expressing the same infinite reality—which is to say God, which is also to say nature.

If God and nature are equivalent by virtue of their both being defined as "consisting of infinite attributes" (*substantiam constantem infinitis attributis*), then we would do well to know what these attributes might be. Thought and extension are two of them, but what are the infinite others? Unfortunately, the text is notoriously inscrutable on this point. God, Spinoza claims, is consists of "infinite attributes," but does this mean there are an infinite number of attributes, or simply that each of the attributes, however many there may be, is infinite? Unsurprisingly, the most conservative reading can be found in Hegel, who writes that, "Spinoza, like Descartes, accepts only two attributes, thought and extension."[93] The attributes, Hegel explains, are infinite in the sense of their being unlimited by anything of their kind. They are not, however, infinite in number.[94] And since Spinoza only speaks of two of them, he must mean there are only two of them.

This interpretation, which makes a residual dualist out of Hegel's purportedly monist Spinoza, seems severely undermined by Proposition 19 of Part I of the *Ethics*, which states that "all the attributes of God (*omnia Dei attributa*) are eternal."[95] If there were only two attributes, then why would Spinoza refer to "all," rather than just both of them? Furthermore, the scholium to Proposition 7 of Part II explains that "whether we conceive Nature under the attribute of Extension or under the attribute of Thought *or under any other attribute*, we find one and the same order."[96] Clearly, then, there are more attributes than just two, but how many more? Some contemporary commentators hedge their bets at this point, suggesting that although there may be more attributes than the two we can discern, there is "no respectable reason for Spinoza to say that Nature has . . . infinitely many attributes."[97] And yet this unrespectable possibility is precisely what Spinoza implies in his *Short Treatise*, which defines God as "a being of whom *all or infinite* attributes are predicated."[98] By rendering "all" equivalent with "infinite," Spinoza does seem to indicate that the attributes are not only qualitatively but also quantitatively infinite—that God, as Gilles Deleuze translates the passage, is "a substance consisting of *an infinity of* attributes (*une infinité d'attributs*), of which each one expresses an eternal and infinite essence."[99]

If it is the case, then, that God-or-nature consists of an infinite number of attributes, the question remains: what are the others, apart from thought and extension? Spinoza's short answer is that he has no idea. Insofar as God is God, God must be infinite. And insofar as God is infinite, God must be expressed in an infinite number of ways. But the human mind only knows two of these ways. The reason for this limitation, Deleuze explains, is that human beings "are constituted by a mode of Extension and a mode of Thought"—namely, body and mind—which are expressions of the (only) two attributes they allow us to understand.[100] Unlike Descartes, however, Spinoza is not suggesting that the human being is made of two components, mind and body, that are mysteriously yet hierarchically connected as the immaterial God is to "his" material creation. Rather, Spinoza explains, a human being is a body with an idea of itself—and that idea *is* the mind. In his words, "the human mind *is* the very idea or knowledge of the human body"; conversely, the body is "the object of the idea constituting the mind."[101] And again, the body and its idea allow us to discern the attributes of which they are particular expressions, namely, extension and thought. We would need to be different sorts of beings in order to perceive (by means of different sorts of minds) the other attributes of which we were finite expressions.[102]

When Spinoza asserts that each of the attributes "expresses eternal and infinite essence," he is saying that each of them unfolds the whole of God-or-nature itself—that God is just as fully expressed in extension as in thought. It is this attribution of corporeality to divinity, of course, that provokes the barrage of revolted denigrations we encountered in the introduction. What is "monstrous" about Spinoza is his heretical conflation of divinity—which is theistically encoded as immaterial, strictly active, anthropomorphic, light-soaked, and male—with matter, understood to be passive, amorphous, dark, and feminine. Indeed, Spinoza summons this divine chimera the moment he suggests in the *Tractatus* that far from being "some royal potentate," God is the material universe itself, and that far from being an inert backdrop to the drama of God and man, the "nature" that unfolds and enfolds all things is what we mean when we say the word "God."[103] To the extent that nature tends to be associated with extension and God with thought, the identification of the two renders Spinoza's one substance an ungainly concatenation, indeed.

The monstrosity grows, moreover, when we consider that there are not merely two attributes of God-or-nature, but an infinite number of them. To be sure, we cannot say what they are, even though we know *that* they are. Much as the cellular constitution of our retinas only allows us to see a tiny fraction of the full electromagnetic spectrum, the corporeal-ideational structure of our being only allows us to know two of the infinite attributes. But again, by virtue of the definition of substance, we know *that* God must be expressed in an infinite number of ways. This means that there are not just two, but an infinite number of holographic channels by means of which minds of all sorts could in principle conceive of God. Our monster is therefore not just a conflation of binaries, but rather an omni-faceted beast appearing under totally different aspects, depending on your point of view.

Such perspectivism might seem to suggest that the attributes are epiphenomenal—that God is one in essence but many "to us." Along this line of thinking, the attributes would be our limited ways of construing substance, but they would not be essential to substance itself, understood as wholly singular. They would be, in a word, illusory—much like the material universe itself according to Western-endorsed strands of Advaita Vedānta. In the contemporary literature, this sort of reading is usually traced back to the historian Harry Wolfson, who "took Spinoza to hold that the attributes are not really distinct from one another even though they are perceived by the intellect as being so."[104] Like most elements of the monistic interpretation of Spinoza, however, this one can also be traced back to Hegel, who declared that the attributes are only real "in the view of the understanding, which falls outside substance," but not real with respect to substance itself.[105]

This illusory or "subjective" interpretation takes its cue from the fourth definition in the first part of the *Ethics*, which defines an "attribute" as "that which the intellect perceives of substance as constituting its essence."[106] Hegel's and Wolfson's assumption, to put it frankly, is that the intellect is not correct— that the intellect *perceives* substance to be constituted by attributes, but that substance is not, in fact, constituted by the attributes. Hence the alignment of Spinoza's supposed acosmism with "Indian philosophy" and its unreal material realm. The chief challenge to this interpretation, however, arises merely two definitions later, when Spinoza calls God "substance *consisting of* infinite attributes" (*hoc est substantiam constantem infinitis attributis*).[107] This phrase is the one element we have not yet discussed in our extended reflection on Spinoza's definition of God, and it seems quite clearly to say that substance is not only expressed in an infinite number of attributes, but is in fact *constituted* by them. The easiest way to reconcile this definition of God with the definition of the attributes would be to say with Valtteri Viljanen that if the intellect perceives the attributes to be the essence of substance, it is "because those attributes really *do* constitute the essence of . . . substance."[108] This would be the realist, or "objectivist" interpretation, and indeed, Spinoza himself goes on to say of substance that "all the attributes it possesses have *always* been in it simultaneously."[109] The attributes are therefore not just temporal access roads to an eternal reality that transcends them—not illusory projections of an undifferentiated Absolute—rather, the attributes really compose God-or-nature itself.

Viewed in this light, our purportedly single substance, Hegel's monistic nightmare that swallows all difference into "the abyss of the one identity,"[110] turns out to be constitutively multiple, and infinitely so. To be sure, Spinoza often resists such a reading, insisting in spite of himself "that God is one; that is, in the universe there is only one substance," and that consequently "the idea of God, from which infinite things follow in infinite ways, must [likewise] be *one, and one only*."[111] But as we have seen, this "oneness" is constitutively multiple by virtue of the reality of the attributes. The oneness of substance is therefore also composite—not in the mereological sense of all the attributes adding up to the wholeness of God—but in the holographic sense of each attribute wholly expressing in its own way God's infinite essence. And this infinitely perspectival many-one is at work even "before" substance expresses itself in any particular thing—any goat, river, toaster, meme, or emotion. Such particularities arise, in fact, by virtue of the multiple singularity of substance itself; in effect, it is the infinite attributes that allow substance eternally to be expressed in the endless run of particular things.

Eternal Modification

At this point, we can finally address the question of the status of the material world in Spinoza. As we have seen, Hegel in particular charges Spinoza with "acosmism" by virtue of the latter's purportedly untrammeled monism. According to Hegel, Spinoza fails to establish the reality of the natural world because his substance is undifferentiated; in effect, Hegel's Spinoza cannot get from the one to the many. If it is the case, however, that Spinoza's one is *already* many—not epiphenomenally, but constitutively—then his singular substance is necessarily multiple, so there is no ontological divide between the one and the many in the first place. The question then becomes: how do the eternal and infinite attributes give rise to the temporal multiplicity of everyday things? To be sure, Spinoza tells us that they *do*, and necessarily so, claiming that "from God's supreme power or infinite nature, an infinity of things in infinite ways— that is, everything—have necessarily flowed or are always following from that same necessity."[112] But as centuries of commentators have complained, it is not clear *how* the attributes as such give rise to particular bodies and ideas[113]—to those ordinary things the *Ethics* designates as "modes."

According to Spinoza, "particular things are nothing but affections of the attributes of God; that is, *modes* wherein the attributes of God find expression in a definite and determinate way."[114] So squirrels and wood planks and humans and socialism and rubber cement—these are all neither objects nor subjects, but rather expressions of God-or-nature by means of its infinite attributes. Bodily things are modifications of God under the attribute of extension; mental things are modifications of God under the attribute of thought; and presumably any given Q_1 is a modification of God under the attribute of Q. The question is, what is it about substance or any of its attributes that *necessarily* modifies itself into such particularities? The first interlocutor to demand such an explanation was the German mathematician and philosopher Ehrenfried Walther von Tschirnhaus, who asked Spinoza in June of 1676, "I should like you to do me the kindness of showing how, from Extension as conceived in your philosophy, the variety of things can be demonstrated *a priori*. . . . I fail to see how from an Attribute considered only by itself, for example, Extension, an infinite variety of bodies can arise."[115] Spinoza responded less than a month later by acknowledging, "as yet I have not yet had the opportunity to arrange in due order anything on this subject," but promises that "perhaps, if I live long enough, I shall some time discuss this with you more clearly."[116] Unfortunately for all of us, he did not, in fact, live long enough—dying in February of 1677.

As Steven Nadler has suggested, the most compelling way to answer *for* Spinoza—to derive on his behalf the necessity of particular things from the singularity of the infinite attributes—is to appeal to the so-called "infinite modes" in Spinoza's system.[117] According to Proposition 21, these "eternal and infinite" modes include "all things which follow from the absolute nature of any of God's attributes."[118] To address Tschirnhaus's example, the infinite modes of the attribute of extension are "motion and rest."[119] That is to say, as Nadler explains it, "what follows from the nature of extension alone, as an attribute of substance, is that motion and rest belong necessarily to an extended universe. . . . *Whatever is extended essentially partakes of motion and rest*."[120] How, then, does Spinoza derive the necessity of multiple, particular, material things—animals, vegetables, minerals, quarks—from the eternal (and single) attribute of extension? He does so, Nadler suggests, by means of motion and rest, which are all that particular, material things *are*. "Bodies for Spinoza," Nadler explains, "are nothing but parcels of extended matter whose parts maintain among themselves a stable ratio of motion and rest."[121] Insofar as extension necessarily entails motion and rest, then, it necessarily expresses itself as the particular bodies that *are* the enactment of motion and rest.

These particular bodies, which is to say everything that is, was, and might yet be is a mode—or expression—of the divine substance. Unlike Neoplatonic "emanation," however, this expression takes place not beyond but rather *within* God Godself; as Spinoza declares early in the *Ethics*, "Whatever is, is *in God*, and nothing can be or be conceived without God."[122] Again, Hegel's interpretation of this passage is that it evacuates the reality of the physical world; if everything is in God, he reasons, then nothing apart from God really *is* at all, and the cosmos is effectively unreal. For Spinoza, however, to say the modes are in God is not by any means to say they are not real. To the contrary, the state of being "in" something else is equivalent to being ontologically dependent upon something else. The relationship between the modes and the substance they are fundamentally *in* is therefore equivalent to the traditional relationship between accidents and substance, taken "up" an ontological notch. Classically, lightness, blueness, and striped-ness are all said to be accidents of the substance "bird." For Spinoza, by contrast, the bird is itself no substance but rather a mode of the substance "nature," or God. The bird—along with the lightness, blueness, and striped-ness that make it the particular bird it is—is a concrete enactment of substance in (and as) a particular node of space and time, and as such the bird, like all of the modes, depends ontologically upon the substance that it modifies. At the same time that they are outward expressions of God, then, particular things can also be said to exist *in* God. The divine unfolding is also a folding in; as Deleuze reminds us, Spinozan *explicare* is also *involvere*.[123]

But none of this is to say that the modes are unreal, that particular things are illusory, or that Spinoza swallows the material world into the womb-tomblike undifferentiation of substance. To the contrary, insofar as the singularity of substance is itself multiple, it is both internally and externally differentiated. And insofar as substance necessarily expresses itself by means of both thinking and extension (among infinite other attributes), it necessarily gives rise both to ideas and to material things. These particular things are "in" God and they express God, but they are not simply the same thing as God, and as such are not "swallowed" into divinity. Neither are they illusory or nonexistent. Rather, each thing for Spinoza has its own essence, which distinguishes it from every other particular thing.

The language of "essence" in Spinoza can be misleading, since the term tends to designate a single and nonrelational core of being. But just as (along our increasingly queer reading of Spinoza) the divine essence is constitutively multiple, the "essences" of particular things are likewise formed in relation to all other particular things. As Yirmyahu Yovel explains it, "the essence of a particular thing is the unique place it occupies in reality; it is, so to speak, the logical or metaphysical 'point' which belongs exclusively to it in the overall map of being."[124] This "map" can be understood from (at least) two perspectives: that of "vertical causality" and "horizontal causality," or better stated, that of eternity and that of temporality. Seen *sub specie aeternitatis*, the modes all exist necessarily in God as a complex whole. One can imagine them mathematically plotted on some infinitely dimensional plane, such that the specific coordinate of any particular thing—its place within the omniplex of things—is what it fundamentally and eternally "is." Seen *sub specie durationis*, however, particular things are not eternal; neither do they form a totality. Rather, they come and go by virtue of their relation to other finite things in a causal progression that has neither beginning nor end. As Spinoza proposes,

> Every individual thing, i.e. anything whatever which is finite and has a determinate existence, cannot exist or be determined to act unless it be determined to exist and to act by another cause which is also finite and has a determinate existence, and this cause again cannot exist or be determined to act unless it be determined to exist and to act by another cause which is also finite and has a determinate existence, and so ad infinitum.[125]

In this sense, the "essence" of any existing thing is nothing more than the point it occupies in space and time by virtue of this endless causality; "in other words, a thing's particular essence is ontologically equivalent to the process of its determination."[126] Far from being "unreal," then, the modes bring one another into being. And far from being self-enclosed, their "essences" are thoroughly relational, existing exclusively in God and coming into the world by means of an endless causal chain of other particularities—an "infinite series of finite modes"[127]—that, likewise, exist exclusively in God, which is to say nature. (Where else would they exist?)

Saving Substance

At this juncture, Spinoza may in fact seem to be veering more toward panentheism than pantheism. One might argue that God is expressed *in* all things and all things are *in* God, but that God is not "all things" as such. The strongest case for such a reading would turn on the ontological distinction Spinoza seems to install between substance and its modes. Whereas substance necessarily exists,

Spinoza maintains, the modes do not necessarily exist; as he phrases it, "the essence of things produced by God does not involve existence."[128] Unlike God, then, particular things can either be or not be; for example, Spinoza explains, "from the order of Nature it is equally possible that a certain man exists or does not exist."[129] With this distinction, then, Spinoza preserves the divine essence from contamination by Snapple® or snuffboxes—or men, for that matter; these things are not necessary to the order of God-or-nature. But even as the contingency of particulars salvages his substance, it also threatens the integrity of his theo-cosmology—most notably, of its infamous determinism.

"Nothing in nature is contingent," Spinoza insists in Proposition 29 of Part 1, "but all things are from the necessity of the divine nature determined to exist and to act in a definite way."[130] Hence the charge of fatalism in Spinoza: like the ancient Greek Stoics, whose cosmos *was* the perfect divinity that suffused it, Spinoza seems to be saying that nothing in the world-that-is-God can be at all different than it is.[131] Unlike the Stoics, however, Spinoza introduces a distinction between God, whose essence entails existence, and particular things, whose essences are eternally in God but whose existence is contingent upon the unfolding or non-unfolding of other particular things. Here, then, is the difficulty: if for Spinoza "a certain man" can either exist or not exist "from the order of Nature," then how can it be the case that everything in existence necessarily exists "from the necessity of the divine nature"? How can particulars be both existentially contingent and thoroughly determined at the same time?

Before resolving this particular dilemma, we will intensify it in an attempt to clarify its stakes. In the *Ethics*, we have just seen Spinoza distinguish between substance and modes by attributing a necessary existence to the former and a contingent existence to the latter. In the *Short Treatise*, Spinoza's character Theophilus translates this distinction, saying that while the modes rely on substance, substance in no way relies on the modes. As he instructs his interlocutor Erasmus, the modes "are not competent to establish an attribute," and as such, "they do not increase the essence of God, however intimately they become united to him."[132] The modes are therefore in substance and substance is in them, but they do not constitute the divine essence as such. Therefore, whereas the necessity of the attributes means that God is essentially thinking and extended, the contingency of the modes means that God is not essentially rabbitlike or mustard-ish. The modes are accidents: like waves in a sea or colors on a chameleon, they appear by virtue of substance, but they do not make substance what it is. Thus Schelling can assure us that, far from identifying the creator with creation, Spinoza provides us with a "complete differentiation" of them; in short, the statement "God is all things" does not mean that the two are equivalent, but that God is the *ground* of all things as *consequents*.[133] God exists independently of the finite modes, whereas the modes exist only by means of God.

But what would happen if we were to reverse the pantheist sentence, asserting that "all things are God"? Would it still be the case, as in line with Schelling's "real meaning of the law of identity," that "subject and predicate" would be related as "antecedent and . . . consequent," so that all things could be called the ground of God? [134] Ontologically, Schelling would need to prohibit such a reversal, insofar as the modes could not possibly contribute constitutively to divinity—itself independent, autonomous, and self-caused. Grammatically and even mathematically, however, there is no reason to prohibit it, and with this realization one starts to wonder whether not only the attributes but also the modes might in some sense make up the substance that God-or-nature is. After all, is it really the case that the sea exists independently of its waves, or the chameleon of its endless colors? What would it even mean to refer to a tomato without its roundness, or a zebra as distinct from its stripes?

As Friedrich Nietzsche will argue throughout his neo-Spinozan[135] corpus, it could very well be that the whole notion of "substance" is a ruse; a product of the "grammatical custom that adds a doer to every deed."[136] Just as we think there is a human "subject" independent of its actions, we also think there is a "substance" independent of its accidents. The philosophical category of substance is therefore an anthropomorphic projection; as Nietzsche explains it, "the belief in substance, accident, attribute, etc., derive their convincing force from our habit of regarding all our deeds as consequences of our will."[137] Just as we think there is a neutral substratum called "I" that chooses to undertake action *X* or *Y*, so do we think there is an entity called "lightning" that undertakes the action of flashing. And yet, as Nietzsche famously reminds us, lightning *is* its flashing. There is no "doer" behind this particular deed; "the deed is everything."[138] Similarly, Nietzsche declares, "there is no such thing as will."[139] In other words, there is no such thing as an "I" independent of the mundane mess of trivialities and events that I seem to undertake and undergo; these "accidents" and "actions" are what—and all—I *am*. And similarly, Nietzsche suggests, "substance" is nothing other than its purported accidents.

Spinoza seems to have half-known this, declaring explicitly that the infinite attributes constitute substance as such. But he goes on to unknow it when he splits this omniattributional substance off from its endless series of modes. Or he half-unknows it. For on the one hand, he says the modes cannot constitute the divine substance. But on the other hand, he says they are eternal, and to say they are eternal is also to say they are eternally bound up with what substance "is." In short, if it is the case that "from the necessity of the divine nature there must follow infinite things in infinite ways (*modis*)," then the modes can be seen as essential to the divine nature, regardless of Spinoza's occasional insistence to the contrary.[140] As Brian Fay has summarized the matter, "for Spinoza, *God/Nature only exists in and through the finite modes that are God/Nature's expression*."[141] After all, Fay suggests, it would be ridiculous to insist that "Nature exists, but no rocks, no cows, no stars, no people . . . Such a view sounds just plain silly: Nature exists in and through the individual entities that express and embody it," and insofar as Spinoza's God *is* nature, the same must be said about God.[142] There is no divine substance apart from its appearance in and as the endless run of worldly things.

According to Nietzsche, the reason the subject-as-substance is such a powerful fiction is that it holds the human above the unending becoming and unbecoming that every "thing" actually "is." We posit the subject "so that the ego, as substance, does not vanish in the multiplicity of change."[143] A similar motivation seems to lie behind Spinoza's protection of substance against its modes: the inessentiality of particular things allows him to preserve the necessity, eternity, and immutability of God-or-nature. As he argues in the *Tractatus*, "Nature . . . always observes laws and rules involving eternal necessity and truth . . . and thus it also observes a fixed, immutable order."[144] In more traditionally theological language, this means that "all things have been predetermined by God,"[145] so that the whole course of natural, human, and more-than-human events is strictly determined from eternity; none of it can happen in any other way. But again, if it is the case that the modes can either be or not be—if there is nothing necessary about their existence or nonexistence—then the modes appear to introduce a contradictory element of contingency in this strictly non-contingent world.

It seems to me that there are two ways to resolve this contradiction. The first would be to preserve the ontological distinction between substance and its modes, and to say with the received interpretation of Spinoza that God bestows upon existent modes the necessity they lack on their own. In this vein, we could argue that although the essence of any particular thing does not necessitate its existence, the essence of *God* does; as Spinoza proclaims, "things could not have been produced by God in any other way or in any other order than is the case."[146] Such determinism would be a function not of God's "free will"—Spinoza insists that neither finite nor infinite will can be "free"[147]—but rather of the eternal necessity of God-as-expressive. In this manner, the independence of substance and the determinism of particular things could hold at the same time.

The (far) less traditional way to address this dilemma would be to reverse the direction. Rather than overriding the contingency of the modes with the necessity of substance, we might allow substance to be undone by the unruly modes. Following Nietzsche's lead—which arguably wanders through an already Spinozan opening—this interpretation would read not only the attributes, but also the modes as constitutive of the divine-natural "substance" itself. Far from conferring necessity upon the complex run of worldly things, this straightforwardly deconstructive reading would confer contingency—and therefore change, imperfection, and redoubled multiplicity—upon the monstrous many-one that God-or-nature "is."

To be sure, the notion that God might be changeable would be utterly anathema to Spinoza, whose God consists of "infinite attributes, each of which expresses eternal and infinite essence."[148] To assert that the divine "essence" is not eternal but rather relational and mutable would be to assert that God—as Spinoza defines the term—does not exist; and as he states in a hasty and unsatisfying echo of the ontological argument, it is not possible to think that God thus construed does not exist.[149] Spinoza therefore believes that he derives divine eternity a priori. But insofar as this argument, much like Descartes' and Anselm's before him, "has satisfied nobody,"[150] it seems rather to be the case that Spinoza derives divine eternity a posteriori. As far as he can see, "Nature is always the same, and its force and power of acting is everywhere one and the same; that is, the laws and rules of Nature according to which all things happen and change from one form to another are everywhere and always the same."[151] And insofar as nature is coextensive with God, God must likewise be everywhere and always the same. At the risk of pointing out the obvious, then, it is the pantheist's experience and understanding of the natural world that gives rise to her understanding of the God-who-is-that-world. As Spinoza explains in the *Tractatus*, "since the laws of Nature . . . are infinite in their scope and are conceived by us as having an eternal quality, and since Nature operates in accordance with them in a fixed and immutable order, the laws themselves give us some indication of the infinity, eternity, and immutability of God."[152] Insofar as nature appears to be eternally unchanging, the pantheist can ascribe the same properties to God.

If it turns out, however, that one conceives of nature differently—if, as far as one can see from a different perspective, the order of nature seems not to be "fixed and immutable" but rather emergent and adaptive—then this post-Spinozan pantheist divinity would similarly shed its eternal necessity and take on the more dynamic, expressive qualities already incipient in Spinoza's own doctrine of God. Incipient: which is to say neither absent nor explicit, but rather both asserted and denied, both opened and foreclosed. For as we have shown against Hegel, Spinoza's substance is neither undifferentiated nor acosmic; rather, it necessarily expresses itself by means of the infinite attributes in the vast proliferation of things and ideas. At the same time, however, it should be admitted that Spinoza does not exactly delight in multiplicity, monstrosity, or even the natural world itself. He repeatedly insists upon the singularity of the substance he nevertheless shows is multiple; he insists upon the logic of noncontradiction; he expresses preference for "fixed and eternal things" over "mutable particular things"; he decries "the hollowness and futility of everything that is ordinarily encountered in everyday life"; and he ridicules the "various confused perceptions of things existing in Nature, as when men are convinced that divinities are present in woods, in images, in animals, and in other things."[153] Spinoza is no awestruck pagan; neither is he a mystic or a naturalist in any common sense of those words. Rather, he soberly entreats us to "understand the works of nature as a scholar, and not just to gape at them like a fool."[154] In short, as F. C. Copleston reminds us, there is "little indication in the pages of Spinoza's writing that he felt any of that emotion in the face of phenomenal Nature which romantic poets have shown."[155]

Nevertheless, it is Spinoza's own philosophy that inspires many of the romantic poets, in large part by giving them the idea that particular things are the concrete expressions of God: "a kind of unfolding of divinity."[156] This is not to say that any particular thing *is* God. The tree is not God; the goat is not God; and no, the snuffbox is not God. But each of them is an expression of God; each of them is *in* God; and God is, by virtue of the constitutive nature of the modes, in each of them. Along this reading, the pantheist declaration that "God is all things" does not mean that God is the compendium of all things—some massively aggregated All. Nor, again, does it mean that God is every or any particular thing. Rather, it means that all things are expressions and modifications of an essentially dynamic, and therefore relationally inessential, divinity; that all things both reflect and compose the God-or-nature that expresses, enfolds, and inhabits all things.

In this sense, the "all" that God-or-nature is, is neither an undifferentiated One nor an unrelated run of things. Nor is it *simply* a unified many or a differentiated unity. Rather, it is both of these, depending on your perspective. From the perspective of "eternity," which is to say if one considers the universe as an abstract whole, it is always possible—even if only discursively—to gather the multiplicity of things under some sort of singular "one." From the perspective of temporality—which is to say, of the world we actually experience—the allness of God-or-nature only ever manifests itself as a complexly connected but *un-totalizable* many. Like the complementarity between particles and waves, or thought and extension, this perspectivism is unresolvable; that is, neither of them is anterior to or derivative of the other. Just as one experimental apparatus will reveal light genuinely to be a bombardment of discrete particles and another will reveal it genuinely to be a smooth undulation of waves, one view of "all things" will reveal "them" to be one, and another will reveal "it" to be many. One might, of course, argue that the very plurality of perspectives here gives a kind of last-minute advantage to the many, and this is the place where I— along with James—prefer *pragmatically* to land.[157] But ontologically, the situation remains genuinely undecidable; after all, someone else might always argue that the compendium of all possible perspectives amounts to some overarching One. (And from here, it would fall upon the pugnacious pluralist to reveal the monist's overarching One as the product of yet another perspective.)

Onward

If the pantheological "all" is irreducibly perspectival, then contrary to Hegel's interpretation and that of his numerous heirs, there is no "problem of the one and the many" in Spinoza[158]—no fundamental incompatibility between the unity of substance and the diversity of the attributes. Rather, as Deleuze has explained, "there is a unity of the diverse in substance, and an actual diversity of the One in the attributes."[159] If it is the case, moreover, that the "diversity of the One" is composed not only of the infinite and holographic attributes, but also of the unending, relational modes that express them concretely, then "substance" is not some eternal mass waiting to be incarnated in particularities. Rather—and this is where thinkers in the wake of Nietzsche would abandon the language of "substance" altogether—God-or-nature is dynamically shaped by the particularities that express it. In short, it *becomes*. This, of course, is the insight with which the Romantics sought to correct Spinoza, whose substance Schelling (like Hegel) called an "eternal, immobile, inactive" monolith, lacking in any dynamism, spirit, or love.[160] As we have seen, however, these thinkers mobilize Spinoza's purportedly inert substance by making it *humanoid*—that is, either by rendering the absolute an anthropomorphic Spirit expressed primarily in, and constituted exclusively by, human history (Hegel); or by appealing to the Fichtean ego as the absolute substance, and to "man" as the "central being" of all creation (Schelling).[161]

The source of this re-centering of humanity is the Romantics' residual conviction that, within the entire visible universe, humanity alone is truly animate, and thus both metaphorically and ontologically the only imaginable locus of genuine creativity. And the effect is that, in spite of all Spinoza's efforts to the contrary, "nature" is relegated once again to the realm of passivity and inertia from which the Romantics are purportedly rescuing "God." As Schelling concludes toward the end of *Freedom,*

> all natural creatures (*Naturwesen*) have a mere being in the depths or in the initial longing which has not yet achieved unity with understanding . . . they are thus mere peripheral entities in relation to God. Only man is in God (*Nur der Mensch est in Gott*). . . . He alone is a central being (*Er allein est ein Centralwesen*) and therefore should also remain in the center. *In him all things are created,* just as it is only through man that God accepts nature and ties it to him.[162]

Insofar as such an ontology installs humanity as the locus of creation and reintroduces absolute, hierarchical distinctions between God and nature on the one hand and humanity and the rest of creation on the other—not to mention the distinction between Schelling's purportedly universal "he" [*er*] and the gender that dare not speak its name—it amounts not to pantheism but rather to what I have called anthropotheism, and what Haeckel dubs "homotheism."[163] As distinct from this materiophobic mantheism, what we seek in the wake of our faithful betrayal of Spinoza is a configuration of matter that finds vibrancy and divinity within it, rather than outside it, and which locates humanity as just one of an infinite number of expressions of material animacy. Toward that end, we now turn to an analysis of the anti-materiality coursing through the Western heritage along with some of its most prominent exceptions, which resonate with indigenous cosmologies to produce contemporary theories of immanence.

PANTERRUPTION

pan, n., adj.: an abbreviation for pansexual.
　　　　　　　　　—Urban Dictionary

In addition to protecting and hunting, Pan is also known to pursue. "Plainly a lusty god," he is usually portrayed with an oversized phallus, looking to seduce anything that moves.[1] He is usually unsuccessful, rebuffed by forest nymphs and shepherd boys alike, and in this context is called by the name "Pan Duserous": "lusty, but 'Unlucky in love.'"[2] In this regard, he can be both mournful and vengeful: when the chaste nymph Syrinx refused him, she ran to a riverbank, calling on her sister nymphs to protect her. They responded by turning Syrinx into reeds along the water's edge, prompting Pan to cry out in agony. Impressed by the beautiful, haunting sound of his own voice across his beloved's newfound "vegetality," Pan cut the reeds to make them (her) into his eponymous flute, the syrinx.

These rejections aside, Pan is said to have had a tryst with Aphrodite, a fairly long-term arrangement with the muse Eupheme, and a fling with "every one of the Maenads," so this queer god's interests range from boys to goddesses to women, and—lest we forget his other half—he is also known as "Mounter of the Goats."[3]

Pan and Daphnis. 1st century BCE. Museo Archeologico Nationale di Napoli.

Topographically, Pan is similarly overdetermined. "Always an outsider to the world of Mount Olympus," Pan inhabits less sacred mountains, the "sure-footed" goat at home in all high, "rugged, rocky places."[4] But he also shows up in the subterranean caves where he is worshipped, and where he sleeps from sunrise to sunset. Pan oversees pastures, of course, but also inhabits forests, where he both strikes terror in the hearts of unsuspecting passers-by and delights his devotees with all-night dance parties set to his nymph flute.[5] So this awesome, awful deity dwells within mountains and caves, fields and woods, vegetation and minerality—and by the way, he was said to have the power to "rescue sailors on a becalmed ship."[6] Indeed, the *Oxford English Dictionary* tells us that, alongside its seemingly endless other meanings, "pan" can refer to an "international radio signal, esp. by ships and aircraft, to alert authorities that the vessel or aircraft requires assistance . . . a step below Mayday."[7] Once again, Pan can thrill and terrify, threaten and save—and from land to sea to sky, there seems to be nowhere he isn't.

Perhaps unsurprisingly, this multilocational misfit—this hypersexual hybrid with multiple personalities—has no clear origin story, there being "no fewer than fourteen different versions of his parentage."[8] As literary scholar Patricia Merivale explains, this "comic-grotesque godling" is a "second-class citizen and non-Homeric latecomer among the Olympians," and as such, he leaves the post-Homeric tradition clamoring to figure out where he might have come from.[9] Pan's father is most often said to be Hermes, messenger of the gods, whose patrilineage establishes Pan—at least for Plato—as the incarnation of "speech."[10] Other accounts name Pan's father as Zeus or Apollo.[11] And although his mother is usually said to be one of any number of nymphs, she is at other times said to be the human Penelope, who in this version of the story did not wait those twenty years for Odysseus to come home; rather, she conceived Pan with one of the gods, or with one of her suitors.[12] In the more vanilla *Homeric Hymns* (wherein this particular god is first mentioned), Pan is said to be the child of Hermes and the nymph Dryope, daughter of Dryops, a mortal whose sheep Hermes had tended. The poet sings, "Dryope bore Hermes a dear son, marvelous to behold: / goat-footed, horned, full of noise and sweet laughter."[13] But as nymphs, shepherd boys, and barbarians will do for centuries, Dryope jumps up in terror and flees at the sight of the goat baby with his "rough, full-bearded face" (line 39). Hermes, by contrast, is delighted with his child and, swaddling him "in the thick fur of mountain hare," flies the strange thing to Olympus to show him off (line 42). The hymn tells us that "All the gods were delighted / in their hearts, but especially Bacchic Dionysos. / 'Pan' they named him, because he delighted them 'all'" (lines 45–47).

2

HYLE

Matter is the vilest of all beings . . . the theater of all sorts of changes, the battleground of contrary charges, the subject of all corruptions and all generations, in a word, the being whose nature is most incompatible with the immutability of God.

—Pierre Bayle,
Historical and Critical Dictionary: Selections

Do not say, "This is a stone and not God." God forbid! Rather, all existence is God, and the stone is a thing pervaded by divinity.

—The Zohar, cited in David Ariel,
Kabbalah: The Mystic Quest in Judaism

Since stones are grammatically animate, I once asked an old man: "Are all stones we see about us here alive?" He reflected a long while and then replied, "No! But some are."

—A. Irving Hallowell,
"Ojibwa Ontology, Behavior, and World View"

Recapitulatio

As we will recall, Pierre Bayle's formidable rancor against Spinoza stems from Spinoza's ascription of *materiality* to the divinity. This was, in fact, the same heresy for which the philosopher had been excommunicated forty years earlier: according to Spinoza, God-or-nature is fully material as well as fully ideational, possessing the attribute of extension as well as that of thought. The hypothesis is "monstrous," Bayle intones, because matter is changeable, corruptible, constantly becoming—and as such diametrically opposed to the immutability, perfection, and eternity of God. Meanwhile, whereas Bayle accuses Spinoza of conflating divinity with the multiple and flawed "generations" of the material world, Hegel levels the opposite charge. Far from collapsing divinity into the corruptible cosmos, he argues, Spinoza swallows the cosmos into an abyss of divinity. This alleged mass of indistinction leaves no room for change, particularity, or contingency—in short, for anything we might associate with the material world.

Navigating between these opposite charges, the previous chapter found that Spinoza's substance is neither atheistic nor acosmic. But it is, in fact, monstrous—in the sense of its holding together seemingly incompatible traits. Spinoza's God-or-nature is constituted not only by the traditionally opposed attributes of thought and extension, but also by an infinite number of others, each of which holographically expresses the whole. These infinite attributes are in turn expressed in the interconnected run of particular, worldly things. Contra Hegel, then, we saw that far from evacuating reality or lacking differentiation, Spinoza's substance unfolds dynamically, relationally, and materially—and does so necessarily rather than accidentally. In other words, there is no such thing as substance without modes; God without creatures; or nature without animals, vegetables, and minerals. That having been said, the very necessity by which substance unfolds all things—and *as* all things—confers an undeniable determinism upon the Spinozan cosmos; in line with the Stoics who preceded him by two millennia, Spinoza tells us that nature's identity with divinity means that "things could not have been produced by God in any other way or in any other order than is the case."[1]

As the last chapter suggested, however, Spinoza's strict determinism begins to tremble if we read, not only the attributes, but also the modes as constitutive of substance itself. Insofar as any given mode is existentially unnecessary—so that this particular siege tower or that particular elephant can either be or not be—the substantially constitutive modes introduce an irreducible contingency into the very heart of "substance." In short, if substance is composed of the modes that express it, then it deconstructs itself *qua* substance, which is to say as self-constituted, self-identical, and independent. The reason Spinoza insisted on the eternal immutability of substance, we therefore concluded, was not that his metaphysics demanded it, but rather that his *physics* seemed to do so. Spinoza understood the natural world to be "everywhere and always the same," and so inferred as much a posteriori of God, "who," he deduced, "now, in the past, and unto all eternity has been, and will remain immutable."[2] Had Spinoza understood "nature" not to be eternal and unchanging but rather emergent and adaptive, however, his divinity as well as his world of particular things would similarly have shed their determinism. The chapter at hand and the one that follows will therefore turn toward such undetermined understandings of nature, hoping to see what sort of pantheologies they might produce. The first will focus on the category of matter (hyle) and the second on that of world (cosmos). What is it we mean, these chapters will ask, when we say that this-or-that "pantheism" reduces God to, or conflates or identifies God with, the material world? With this question in mind, we turn first to what Bayle called the "vilest of all beings": matter itself.

The Matter with Matter

The reason Bayle is so disgusted by Spinoza's ascription of materiality to divinity is that Bayle, like the philosophical tradition that produces and follows him, associates matter with inconstancy, irrationality, and primitivity—in other words, with *chaos*. Matter is the undifferentiated, persistently feminized, often racialized *stuff* that a rational, male principle brings to order to make the natural world. One might think, for example, of the "inharmonious and disorderly" material that the demiurge assembles into a universe in Plato's *Timaeus*.[3] Before the male god came to organize them, Timaeus tells us, these proto-elements "swayed unevenly in every direction," bouncing haphazardly in their pre-cosmic "receptacle" (*khôra*). This space-before-space is variously called "a matrix for everything," "the mother" of the universe, and "the nurse of all becoming"—a feminine non-thing that gives rise to all that is, yet has no properties herself.[4]

Matter is rendered as similarly passive, undifferentiated, and chaotic in the first few verses of Genesis, wherein a silent, primordial "deep" (*tehom*) awaits the divine breath that calls creation forth from it—or her.[5] In her theopoetic study of *tehom*, Catherine Keller has unveiled the dark, feminized metaphorics of this pre-cosmic sea in the work of modern theologians and the church fathers alike, playfully encoding their reliable denigrations of maternal materiality as *tehomophobia*.[6] Indeed, over the course of the second and third centuries, *tehom* herself will be hidden from theological view as the church fathers begin to insist that God creates, not out of these pre-cosmic depths (*ex profundis*), but out of nothing at all (*ex nihilo*). Retrieving the cosmogonic principle hiding in plain sight at the biblical beginning, Keller reminds us that the Hebrew *tehom* is etymologically connected to the Babylonian Tiamat, a goddess-turned-chaos-monster whose great-grandson kills and dismantles her to establish the cosmos in the *Enuma Elish*.[7] In this story, as in Genesis and the *Timaeus*, matter is destructive at worst and lifeless at best, contributing the raw materials for creation but lacking any ability to create on its own. In all three accounts, writes Rosemary Radford Ruether, "the metaphor for cosmogenesis is taken from the work of the [male] artisan, who shapes things from dead stuff, not from the reproductive process of begetting and gestating.'"[8]

In Aristotle's demythologized cosmogony, we similarly find matter lying in wait for another principle to discipline, order, and shape it; as he explains, it is matter's "own nature to desire and yearn for [form]."[9] Form, for Aristotle, provides the unity, order, and animacy that makes anything what it is, transforming matter's pure potentiality into actuality.[10] This means that matter itself has no qualities apart from "privation"; as he explains in the *Metaphysics*, matter "is of itself neither a particular thing nor of a particular quantity nor otherwise positively characterized; nor yet negatively, for negations also will belong to it only by accident."[11] And lest we think the persistent gendering of these terms is merely implicit or accidental, the *Physics* clearly states that "what desires the form is matter, as the female desires the male and the ugly the beautiful."[12]

At first glance, then, Aristotle seems simply to offer a secular translation of Plato's creation narrative, with his unqualified femininity awaiting an external male creator. Yet it was precisely the externality of the Platonic Forms—their supposed transcendence of the material universe—that prompted Aristotle's most pronounced departure from Plato in the first place. Far from existing in some perfect, extra-cosmic realm, form for Aristotle is "not independent of matter."[13] Rather, as one commentator glosses a famous illustration from the *Metaphysics*, "all natural forms are like something which is 'snub,' where something is snub only if it is concavity-realized-in-a-nose."[14] Unlike the Platonic Forms, then, Aristotelian form is totally bound up with matter; in fact, matter allows form to come into being in the first place. Matter is, in Aristotle's words, the "ultimate substratum"—that which precedes, underlies, and follows each evanescent configuration of matter-and-form.[15] So when a tree becomes logs or wood chips, the forms change dramatically, but the material of the wood persists throughout the transformations. And when a log becomes fire, the proximate material of the wood disappears, but *matter itself* persists as fire, smoke, and ash.

Matter is, in sum, the condition of possibility of all substance—a primordium of which nothing can be properly predicated because it enables predication itself. Those who have ears to hear might pick up traces in such primordial, ineffable materiality of some apophatic divinity—and a feminized one at that. Indeed, the medieval philosopher David of Dinant (1160–1217) took Aristotle's "ultimate substratum" to mean that the divine intelligence was identical to primal matter—or in a Christian register, to the "deep" or *tehom* of Genesis 1:2.[16] Such divine materiality led him furthermore to proclaim the equivalence of creator and creation. If, as David reasoned, "the matter of the world is God himself, and the form that comes to animate matter is nothing other than God making himself sensible," then "the world is therefore God himself (*mundus est ipse Deus*)."[17] For this crime, which *The Catholic Ency-clopedia* continues to brand "the most thoroughgoing pantheism,"[18] David's books were burned, his followers executed, and his ideas given a particularly uncharitable treatment by Albertus Magnus and his pupil Thomas Aquinas.[19]

David's theo-materialist interpretation of Aristotle did not, therefore, become the received reading of Aristotle. This is not to say that David was the only person to identify the divine intelligence with prime matter; to the contrary, a similar position has been ascribed to the Islamic philosopher Ibn Rushd (Averroes), who asserted the eternity of matter against the doctrine of *creatio ex nihilo*. It has also been ascribed to the Jewish Neoplatonist Ibn Gabi-rol (Avicebron), whom early modern Christians often mistook for a Muslim Aristotelian hylo-theologian.[20] The extent to which these philosophers actually divinized matter is a question of ongoing debate,[21] but they certainly held it in higher esteem than Aristotle did—his own critique of Plato notwithstanding. For despite matter's interiority and anteriority to form, and despite its resis-tance to all conceptualization, Aristotle hardly divinizes it. Rather, he ascribes divinity to a (sometimes singular, sometimes plural) "Prime Mover" positioned sufficiently beyond the fixed stars to give them a cosmogonic push.[22] This god is pure actuality, which is to say form uncontaminated by matter. Matter, in the meantime, continues throughout the authorship to embody pure passivity, privation, and longing. In relation to form, it is unquestionably the inferior term—the ugly, womanly, shapeless gunk that needs something manly to bring it to order and life.

This, then, is the source of the conception of matter that becomes the inheritance of modern Europe, whose techno-capitalist operations depend upon "the idea of matter as passive stuff, as raw, brute, or inert."[23] Hence the rise in the seventeenth century of the "mechanistic" view of nature, which envisioned the universe as a massive clock composed of lifeless matter.[24] The only exception to such "brute" mechanism was specifically human con-sciousness; as Descartes infamously insisted, even nonhuman animals were soulless "automata," unable to think and guided by strictly "physiological laws . . . derivable from mathematical principles."[25] As moral philosopher Mary Midgley has pointed out, one might expect that such a "disillusioned view" would have parleyed matter into something devoid of personal charac-teristics, which is to say something genderless. As it turned out, however, the "mechanistic campaigners [of the early modern era] . . . went on for a long time enthusiastically treating [nature] as female and suggesting new ways of attacking her, searching out her inmost secrets, piercing her armor and gen-erally bringing her into submission."[26] Like Marduk, who used the dead body of Tiamat to shape the cosmos, the new science used the purportedly dead body of matter herself to make the modern world.

Such science furthermore operated in concert with the theology of the Protestant Reformation—whose iconoclasm and denial of transubstantiation drained spirit out of the material world—and, of course, with early capitalism. As Karl Marx insists, it is only when matter is understood to be lifeless that it can be used unconditionally, and without permission, to create profit or property.[27] It is only because we assume that rivers, soils, mountains, and rocks are not animate—let alone divine—that we can even imagine rerouting, poisoning, removing, or fracking them. These sorts of ecological concerns form a good deal of the motivation behind Jane Bennett's retrieval of materiality as agential, or "vibrant": "Why advocate the vitality of matter?" she asks. "Because my hunch is that the image of dead or thoroughly instrumentalized matter feeds human hubris and our earth-destroying fantasies of conquest and consumption."[28]

This is not to say that a living, active matter is necessarily benevolent or eco-friendly; it is simply to say that such matter *does things* that call into question the ontic dominance of "conscious" animals. Omega-3 actively alters the moods of the earth's purported hierarchs; trash actively generates gases and reconfigures landscapes; and the multifarious "assemblage" of gunpowder, gun, human volition, and bodily mechanics enables a bullet to hit whatever it hits and kill whomever it kills.[29] Agents marked as natural, cultural, material, immaterial, animal, vegetable, and mineral constantly function in such intermingled assemblages to get everything done that is done; "the electrical grid," for example, is for Bennett "a volatile mix of coal, sweat, electromagnetic fields, computer programs, electron streams, profit motives, heat, lifestyles, nuclear fuel, plastic, fantasies of mastery, static, legislation, water, economic theory, wire, and wood—to name just some of the actants."[30] Mel Chen similarly animates the allegedly inanimate in their analyses of environmental toxins, which enter animal and vegetable bodies in a constant "merging of forms of 'life' and 'nonlife.'"[31] Such toxins, they argue, undertake cultural work, as one can detect in the case of lead's producing a racist panic among white, heterosexist, American parents when it appears in toys manufactured in China.[32] In the work of Bennett, Chen, and other "new materialist" authors,[33] we find a refusal to divide the world into spirit and matter, life and nonlife, or activity and passivity—refusals that find resonance with the "new animist" movement in anthropology, which we will encounter later in this chapter. First, however, we turn to some *older* animacies that are agonistically entangled with their anti-material counterparts.

ANTIQUE MATERIALISMS

Matter Beyond Mechanism

The term "materialism" has been deployed in so many contradictory senses that it is tempting to abandon it altogether. It has been associated with untrammeled consumerism as well as its Marxist critique, with mechanistic determinism as well as its vital-organic alternative. For the sake of consistency with some of its contemporary interlocutors, however, this study will use the term chiefly in this last sense. The philosophies we will call "materialist" are those that locate creative agency—whether it be called life, spirit, animacy, or emergence—within matter itself. Understood in this particular way, materialist philosophies contest the mechanistic reductionism that often goes by the same name: a reductionism that ascended with the new science and still thrives in certain areas of particle physics, neo-Darwinism, and neuroscience. These "materialisms" purport to reject the dualisms of modernity, but insofar as they reduce any given phenomenon to the thoughtless collisions of particles, programs of genes, or firing of neurons, they are actually the product of these very bifurcations. Far from integrating the traditional functions of, say, "spirit" with those of "matter," or of "mind" with "body," such philosophies simply choose the latter terms over the former, all the while preserving the ontological humiliation those categories suffered under the reign of anti-materialist metaphysics. Matter is still irrational, lifeless, and chaotic—it's just that now such "matter" is all there is. Ecofeminist philosopher Val Plumwood summarizes the situation thus:

> Materialist positions, which have become popular and self-consciously modern positions, attempt to reduce the mental side of the dualism to the bodily, as in physicalism which reduces mind to brain . . . to bodily behavior . . . or to complex organisational machine states. . . . *But the original dualism remains in the wings* in such a conception to the extent that an impoverished and polarized conception of the material or bodily sphere deriving from the original dualism is affirmed as the ground of reduction.[34]

To be sure, the easiest way to elude the persistent grasp of this "original dualism" and to locate creativity, animacy, or divinity *within* a materiality undistinguished from spirit, intelligence, or form would be to appeal to traditions that lie outside the Greco-Roman-Hebraic lineage we incoherently call "the Western canon." For example, the Cheyenne nation (which, geographically speaking, is far more Western than Athens or Jerusalem), tells a creation story in which "water people," or people of the sea, participate with a limited god in the creation of land, who becomes known as Grandmother and in turn helps create trees and plants that bear fruits, flowers, and seeds.[35] Commenting on this story, Paula Gunn Allen explains that unlike Genesis, which clearly distinguishes between an active creator and a passive creation, "American Indian thought makes no such dualistic division, nor does it draw a hard and fast line between what is material and what is spiritual, for it regards the two as different expressions of the same reality."[36] Likewise, in Aboriginal Australian cosmogony, the earth itself produces "the great creative beings" that travel the continent, making and "singing up" everything that emerges. In this case, as Deborah Bird Rose explains, the creative agent is neither a disembodied spirit nor a superhuman power, but rather "country"—the relational network of minerals, elements, animals, and plants that brings forth and sustains all beings in interdependent "creature communities."[37]

In this chapter and the next, we will find many such indigenous cosmogonies inspiring the work of contemporary theorists of immanence. Plumwood and Rose both appeal to what they call a "philosophical animism," according to which the world is "buzzing with multitudes of sentient beings," whose relational creativity establishes nature itself as "self-inventive and self-elaborative."[38] Similarly, in the work of "new animist" anthropologist Tim Ingold, matter and organisms form one another in (and as) an "ever-evolving" meshwork of existence, within which "beings grow or 'issue forth' along the lines of their relationships."[39] Plumwood, Rose, and Ingold offer these accounts as indigenous corrections to the toxic dualisms of Western modernity. As we have already seen, however, one of the chief architects of "modern Western thought" also contested the very distinctions between creator/creation, mind/body, and spirit/matter upon which the tradition relies; indeed, Spinoza, the "renegade Jew," could happily affirm the Cheyenne teaching that such seemingly opposed terms are merely "different *expressions* of the same reality." As we wend our way toward contemporary reanimations of matter against the stubborn striations of the "modern West," it might therefore be useful to trace a quick path through some of the pre-Spinozan counterontologies internal to the tradition such reanimations seek to critique.

Ionian Immanence

In the Greek-speaking world, the first materialists on record are the Ionian philosophers. The Ionians were *hylozoists* (etymologically, "matter life-ists"), meaning that, contrary to the post-Socratic philosophers to come, they taught that "matter as such has the property of life and growth."[40] As such, the Ionians attributed the creation of the whole world to the internal stirrings of one or more material elements: for Thales of Miletus, the generative substance was water; for Anaximenes of Miletus and Diogenes of Apollonia, it was air; for Heraclitus of Ephesus, it was fire; and for Empedocles of Acragas, it was all four elements in alternating cycles of "love" and "strife."[41] Xenophanes of Colophon seems to have been alone in ascribing the origin of the universe to the element of earth, which mixes itself with water to bring all things into being.[42] Epitomizing what Victorian intellectual historian Constance Plumptre calls an "earnest and consistent pantheist," Xenophanes also taught two millennia before Spinoza that God and Nature were equivalent, and that mind and matter were similarly identical.[43] For this reason, he insisted against Homer, Hesiod, and their devotees that divinity was nothing like humanity. The anthropomorphic gods of Olympus were no more than anthropocentric projections, with their strong arms and marital strife and unruly tempers. As one fragment proposes, "if cattle or lions had hands . . . they would paint their gods and give them bodies in form like their own—horses like horses, cattle like cattle."[44] The true god, for Xenophanes, is much closer to that of Spinoza: a mental and extended substance unlike anything in the world and yet expressed in each part of it.[45]

Stoic Cyclicism

We find a similarly pantheist concatenation of God, nature, spirit, and matter two hundred years later in the Stoic school (founded 300 BCE), which taught that "the whole world is a living being [zoon], endowed with soul and reason [empsychon kai logikon]."[46] Far from ordering matter from without, from being mystically joined to matter, or even from inhabiting matter to animate it, the Stoic world-soul *was* material. Specifically, it was a rational type of matter that some teachers called breath (*pneuma*), some called ether (*aither*), and others called fire (*pyr*).[47] This cosmic breath or fire was said to be the active, dry, rational principle, which worked on a passive, wet, mindless, and "formless material" (*apoios hyle*) to generate the universe.[48] Out of these two opposing *archai* (principles) was everything made that was made.

At first, this bifurcation might sound strikingly Aristotelian, with its elevation of spirit as the sole animating principle and its relegation of materiality to passivity and privation. The association intensifies when we learn that the Stoic founder Zeno of Citium often likened the inert *hyle* to "female secretion" and the active *pneuma* to the sperm that allegedly brings it to life.[49] In fact, the school's third leader, Chrysippus of Soli, likened *hyle* to Hera and *pneuma* to the sperm of Zeus, in one fragment going so far as to illustrate the creation of the world with a then-familiar image of Zeus penetrating Hera's mouth.[50] To be sure, such associations make it difficult to appeal directly to the ancient Stoics for anything like a feminist cosmology. At the same time, it is important to note that, beneath this unsavory allegory, the Stoics' gendered hierarchy is not quite the same as Aristotle's—first, because the Stoic universe does not oppose spirit to matter (again, spirit *is* matter); second, because these two *archai* can be seen as different incarnations of the same primordial fire[51] (and therefore somewhat akin to Spinoza's attributes, expressing the same omni-attributional substance); third, because for teachers other than Chrysippus, the god of the Stoic universe inhabits a range of genders, being called not only "Zeus," but also by the names of all the other gods and goddesses (Dia, Athena, Hera, Hephaestus, Poseidon, and Demeter);[52] and finally, because the Stoic universe does not oppose divinity to the material world. Rather, the Stoic god is utterly internal to the world—sometimes characterized as the breath or life within all that is, but more often rendered as both reason (*nous*) and nature, which is to say as the world in its entirety.[53] Indeed, for Diogenes Laertius, the most straightforward reading of the Stoic cosmos is that it *is* the god who creates, sustains, destroys, and remakes it.[54] This process takes place in an ongoing cycle of birth, destruction, and rebirth called *ekpyrosis* (out of fire)—an endless cosmogony by which the god-world periodically consumes itself in flames, burns everything in existence, and then starts all over again with a remnant of *pneuma* and a remnant of *hyle*.[55] And since the Stoic universe is divine—and therefore perfectly ordered, totally unified, and wholly rational—this new world would be effectively identical to the one that came before it, with another Stoic school, another Spinoza, and another rancorous Bayle; another Brexit and another threatened wall between the United States and Mexico; another series of empires rising and falling only to rise and fall the same way the next time around.

Indeed, it was political expedience above all that prompted the later, Roman Stoics to abandon this cyclical theo-cosmology; if the whole world was destined to end and start again, they feared, then the imperial order would be seen as impermanent. These Roman Stoics therefore abandoned their predecessors' immanentism in favor of a singular, governing deity outside the (unique) universe.[56] As is well known, this later form of Stoicism would prove both politically and theologically compelling for an emerging Christian orthodoxy,[57] especially as the latter sought in the first few centuries of the common era to establish the singularity of the church, the transcendence of its singular, monarchical God, and the exclusive authority of his representatives on earth. The early Stoics, by contrast, would have been far less useful to such a cause, being "thoroughgoing pantheists,"[58] and occasionally pluralist ones at that. After all, they affirmed a single principle expressed as two *archai*; a single god-nature expressed as all the gods and goddesses; and an infinite series of *kosmoi* born, destroyed, and remade both by *and as* the god(s) throughout infinite time. In sum, they affirmed a materiality that not only contained but *was* the singularly plural creative power of creation—a considerable departure from Aristotle's purely passive matter and Plato's formless, god-dependent chaos alike.

Atomist Animations

The Stoics' chief rivals in the ancient world were the Epicureans, whose "Garden" was established in the last years of the fourth century BCE, and whose version of vibrant materialism led them to a pantheism that looks remarkably like atheism—or vice versa. Their central physical doctrine was that of atomism, first taught two hundred years earlier by Leucippus and Democritus. In line with the Ionians, these early atomists taught that the world was the product of an internally animate materiality. Against the Ionians, however, the atomists taught that the elements were not primary; rather, earth, air, fire, and water were all composed of invisible, indivisible particles of matter called atoms (from *atomos*, the Greek word for "uncuttable"). These atoms moved eternally in a void (*kenon*), either moving uniformly "downward" or jostling and colliding until one atom happened to swerve in such a way as to draw the others into a vortex (*dine*). Within the furious rotation of this vortex, light and heavy atoms joined together, gradually assembling each of the elements and the cosmos they came to compose.[59]

The fullest extant elaboration of Epicurean cosmology can be found in *De rerum natura*, a lengthy didactic poem written by the Roman author Lucretius (99–55 BCE). Theologically speaking, the text's most consistent argument is that "Religion [*superstitio*] breeds wickedness"—namely, irrationality, fear, and violence—and as such must be replaced by the true knowledge of "Nature and her laws."[60] Humanity's chief error in this regard is its (remarkably perennial) conviction that the harmonious order of the universe—its tides and crops and seasons—are evidence of one or more all-powerful deities who made the world "for *our* sake," and who did so in excess of all existing physical principles, which is to say "out of nothing" (2.172, 1.150; translation altered slightly). Insofar as people perceive the world to be an unmatchable gift, they feel perpetually indebted to the gods who gave it. And insofar as they perceive the divine function to be supernatural (bringing forth everything out of nothing), they believe the gods to lie beyond the bounds of earthly power, reason, or morality. In an effort to repay these inscrutable gods, or to win their favor, people thus deceived will enact endless rituals, no matter how pointless, demeaning, or even murderous. Lucretius is particularly troubled by Agamemnon's willingness to sacrifice his daughter, Iphigenia, so that the gods might grant his fleet favorable winds to sail into battle: "so potent [is] Religion in persuading to do wrong."[61]

The surest way to end this madness, Lucretius suggests, would be to realize that the world is not nearly as well ordered as we have been led to believe. Rather than marveling at the regularity of its sunrises and sunsets, or of its evaporation and rain, we might reflect instead upon its arid land, hostile plants, "savage beasts," or "rocky crags and desolate fens"—not to mention death, disease, and misery. "My point," Lucretius summarizes, is that "the universe was not created for our sake / By powers divine, since as it stands it is so deeply flawed" (5.198–226).

Having uprooted the chief argument for the existence of a benevolent, omnipotent creator (a line of thinking that later centuries will variously christen the teleological argument, the argument from design, and the principle of intelligent design), Lucretius offers Epicurean cosmology as an alternative. Far from having been wrought by eternal providence, he explains, the world was born in a series of random collisions that just happened to give rise to things as they are: "by trying every motion and combination, they at last / Fell into the present form in which this universe appears" (1.1026–27). Such collisions have not only produced our world, but they also continue to produce others—in fact, an infinite number of them—far beyond the bounds of what appear to be our "fixed stars." Everywhere in the infinite universe, atoms are smashing themselves together to make, sustain, and unravel worlds (2.1052–75). Along this line of thinking, then, matter is hardly lifeless or inert, nor does it lie in wait for some masculine principle to bring it to order. Rather, it gets things done. "Nature"—which Lucretius consistently feminizes—is restless, active, and constantly bringing new forms out of the recombined remains of the old. As such, Lucretius calls her "Nature the Creator" (1.628), insisting that there is no principle of generation apart from the internal stirrings of matter itself.

At this juncture, one might be tempted to align Lucretius's *natura* with Spinoza's *Deus sive natura*, even to declare the latter an early modern revival of the former. And indeed, it is certainly the case that each of them affirms the cosmic immanence of creation, as well as the identity of the creator with the world itself. That having been said, the creative agent for Lucretius is utterly lacking in a quality that is central to Spinoza's theo-cosmology (and to that of the Stoics, for that matter): namely, *reason*. Whereas Spinozan thought, like the Stoic *nous*, is inherent to the material order, it is simply absent for the Epicureans; "for certainly the elements of things do not collect / And order their formation by their cunning *intellect*," reasons Lucretius, "Nor are their motions something they agree on or propose" (1.1021–23). There is no plan, no goal, no *mind* in matter—just particulate bumblings that occasionally form remarkable things by the sheer power of accident, enacted through infinite time.

Therefore, although one *could* designate Epicurean matter as the divine principle of a materialist pantheism, one could also call it the unconscious conduit of a "strict," "sheer," or "mere" materialism—the kind that gives rise to the reductionist mechanisms still haunting modern science.[62] Just as its critics fear, then, we have collided with a genuine confluence of pantheism and atheism, and in this case I will refuse to come down on one side or the other. Rather, it seems to me that atomism can amount to all-god or no-god, depending on your point of view. Clearly, it is not self-evidently pantheism, thanks to its steady denunciation of "religion" and its unintelligent, ateleological creative principle. But neither is it self-evidently atheism, because as it turns out, the atomists do not simply abandon the gods. Rather, they *transvalue* them.

Flouting the terms of contemporary theism and atheism, Epicurean philosophy is not suggesting that the gods "don't exist." Rather, it is suggesting that we have misunderstood what it means to be a god. In Lucretius's words, we have configured the gods as "proud masters" (*dominis superbis*) who rule over a creation they keep in fear and ignorance (2.1091; translation altered). As we have seen, a true understanding of the nature of things will allow us to recognize such gods as the illusory projections of a misguided physics. But even as it rids us from the dominion of these cosmic overlords, such knowledge does not allow us to abolish the gods altogether. Rather, it makes us akin to the *true* gods, whom Lucretius portrays as enlightened sages, living in quiet contemplation in the space between worlds.[63] In short, the Epicurean gods are self-consciously modeled on Epicurean philosophers, whose ultimate goal was to attain, through contemplation of the universe, an unperturbed state of well-being called *ataraxia*. For this reason, although the impassivity of the gods is a reason not to fear or propitiate them (why would they care about human affairs?),[64] it is not a reason not to "believe" in them. To the contrary, the gods' implacable calm is a reason to *imitate* them, however deliberately projected such gods might be. And again, the clearest path toward such godliness is the knowledge of the godless unfolding of the cosmos, a knowledge perfectly attained by Epicurus himself, whom Lucretius goes so far as to call, with ironic reverence, "a god—a god indeed" (5.8).

We might rest here, with the gods relieved of all cosmic function and relegated (or elevated) to blissed-out irrelevance, were it not for the poem's opening lines. True to generic form, Lucretius begins with an invocation: "Life-stirring Venus," he calls, "Mother of Aeneas and of Rome. . . . I invite / You, Goddess, stand beside me, be my partner as I write" (1.1, 1.23–24). To be sure, there would be nothing remarkable about such an invocation if the reader had no familiarity with Epicurean theology, which maintains the deities' total removal from all human affairs, a category that presumably includes the composition of didactic poems. And perplexingly, Lucretius summarizes this impassive theology immediately after the very Hymn to Venus that asks her to stand beside him, aid him, and grant the nation peace.[65] Not only does this hymn ask a constitutively uninvolvable goddess to involve herself in his fleeting, mortal concerns, but it also ascribes to her the very cosmogonic functions Lucretius will go on to remove from the deities. "Pleasure of men and gods," he writes, "*you make all things* beneath the dome . . . every species comes to birth / Conceived through you" (1.2–5). Such conception is, moreover, a delightful one, with Venus's "delicious yearning" inspiring the earth to make flowers, the oceans to laugh, all species to procreate "lustily," and the beasts to romp and "pant after you . . . caught in the chains of love" (1.7–20). If, as the remaining thousands of lines explain in detail, "all things" come about through the mindless concourse of imperceptible particles, then how can a pleasure-ridden goddess of love have anything—let alone everything—to do with the process?

Commentators have investigated this dilemma for centuries, and there is still no consensus on the matter. Some say Lucretius is merely following poetic convention; others say he is following Roman convention; others that he is honoring Memmius (the poem's addressee) by invoking the patron goddess of the nobleman's family; others that he is modeling cultic practice within the bounds of reason; and still others that he is trying to make the "bitter pill" of Epicurean philosophy as generally palatable as possible.[66] As Lucretius writes toward the end of the poem's first book,

> Consider a physician with a child who will not sip
> A disgusting dose of wormwood: first, he coats the goblet's lip
> All round with honey's sweet blond stickiness, that way to lure
> Gullible youth to taste it, and to drain the bitter cure. . . .
> That's what I do. Since those who've never tasted of it think
> This philosophy's a bitter pill to swallow, and the throng
> Recoils, I wished to coat this physic in mellifluous song.[67]

It is likely that many of these factors are at work in the Hymn to Venus, but I follow Elizabeth Asmis in believing all of them to be secondary to the invocation's broadly allegorical function. Venus, she suggests, is a mythic representation of nature or the universe itself, and as such serves as "an allegorical rival" to the Stoic divinity.[68] If, she argues, the Stoic god orders the universe by imposing divine reason upon it (and we should recall here that the Stoic divinity grows more monarchical and transcendent during the Roman period), then by contrast, the Epicurean goddess "stands for pleasure and a world ordered by its own spontaneous impulses," a world free to pursue its pleasures without the oversight of the *dominis superbis* (459).

At this point, two divergent interpretations become possible. The first, which Asmis offers, and which is in line with nearly every received reading of Lucretius, is that Venus thus understood becomes the ironic savior of the cosmos from gods of any sort. "Venus stands for the liberation of nature," Asmis argues, "whether this is [from the] Stoic Zeus or the platonic demiurge or Aristotle's first mover or, above all, the gods of the priests" (468). In other words, the Hymn does away with its own addressee, praising a godless nature as the autopoietic life in all things. The second possibility is that Lucretius's Venus announces an alternative pantheology—one in which nature unfolds an infinity of creatures in unanticipated, divergent, and non-totalized ways; whose materiality contains within itself everything it needs to create, unravel, and remake an endless number of worlds; and whose *hyle*, while persistently feminized, is recoded as active, creative, and exuberant. Such nature is, we should recall, unintelligent. But insofar as intelligence performs no cosmic function for Lucretius, his refusal to ascribe it to matter is not a denigration of materiality. Rather, it is an effort to dislodge the anthropocentrism that deludes centuries upon centuries of people into believing our world to be the contrivance of a humanoid divinity, possessed above all of the rational faculty that purportedly distinguishes humans from the rest of creation. When Lucretius denies reason to "Nature the Creator," he is refusing to anthropomorphize it; indeed, even when he does resort to humanoid descriptions of "Venus," her traits are stubbornly un-gubernatorial, anti-monarchical, even anarchic—bearing far more resemblance to the acentric proliferation of vegetality than to the linear teleology of gods and men.[69]

Two possibilities, then: atheism and pantheism; divinity either retired from useful service or reconfigured as the anarchic abundance of matter. Asmis implicitly acknowledges the second when she admits that "Venus . . . is identical, just like Zeus, with the material cosmos."[70] Nevertheless, she edges

Lucretius into atheism by maintaining that while "the Stoics . . . exalt the physical to the divine[,] Lucretius . . . uses the identity to eliminate divinity altogether."[71] This is certainly the case if we understand divinity to mean mastery, imposed order, and universal teleology—whether transcendent or immanent. But if divinity is sufficiently categorically flexible to designate an immanent, ateleological, delightful abundance, then Lucretius is not eliminating divinity; he is reimagining it. Granted, "the gods" remain calm observers of this constant unfolding, rather than its agents. But along this pantheological interpretation, the most vibrant site of divinity would not be the gods but rather nature itself, which continually brings all things out of—and back into—all things. And the best humans can do is to understand, love, and even celebrate this endless cosmic dance—to abandon their own projects of mastery and domination and get, like the gods, out of the way.

RECOMBINATIO: ON GIORDANO BRUNO

Although some early Renaissance authors seem to have had access to it, Lucretius's work was largely lost to the European world until Poggio Bracciolini infamously rediscovered De rerum natura in a monastic library in 1417.[72] Among the text's numerous latter-day adherents was Giordano Bruno (1548–1600), an Italian polymath from Nola who is best known for his execution by the Inquisition at the dawn of the seventeenth century. The reasons for his condemnation are manifold,[73] but theologically speaking, most of them can be encapsulated in his veritable equation of God with the universe—a universe that he configured in atomist fashion as infinite in expanse and filled with innumerable worlds.[74] We will learn more about Bruno's cosmology in the next chapter, focusing in the meantime on its physical foundations—namely, Bruno's reconfiguration of Aristotelian form and matter in light of the work of his "living teacher," Lucretius.[75]

In a dialogue-within-a-dialogue titled De la causa, principio e uno (1584–1585), Bruno's mouthpiece Teofilo ("reliable reporter of the Nolan philosophy") proclaims his admiration for "Democritus and the Epicureans."[76] Nevertheless, he disagrees with their insistence that "matter alone is the substance of things, and that it is also the divine nature, as the Arab named Avicebron has said."[77] Unlike the Epicureans, then, Bruno will argue that matter is not the sole principle in (or of) the universe. Strikingly, however, unlike nearly every other ancient or modern reader of the Epicureans, Bruno's Teofilo does not call their materialism "atheism." Rather, he refers to it as a fully material (pan)theology—one in which "matter alone is the substance of things, and . . . also the divine nature." As is probably clear from his racialized aside about Avicebron (Ibn Gabirol), however, Teofilo will nevertheless proceed in this dialogue to distance himself from both prongs of this position, at least initially. He will not straightforwardly assert the divinity of matter—ultimately doing so only by (unsubtle) implication. Nor will he straightforwardly reduce all substance to matter—leading us instead on a long dialectical journey that may or may not lead us to draw that conclusion for ourselves. Rather, Teofilo's clearest and earliest-stated position is that true philosophy must make an absolute distinction between form and matter, which is to say between "active potency" and "passive potency," and between "the power to make" and "the power to be made" (55). In short, true philosophy must distinguish creator from creation.

As we will no doubt notice, perhaps with a bit of consternation considering the iconoclasm we might be expecting from Teofilo, these are strictly Aristotelian categories, traditionally mapped in implicitly gendered opposition and held together under the distinction between God and the world. The likeliest explanation for Teofilo's beginning with these standard dualisms is that he is meeting his audience at their own level. Insofar as the universities of Bruno's time were filled with neo-Thomist Christians (scholars whom he had ridiculed in an earlier, more audacious dialogue as "Peripatetics who get angry and heated for Aristotle"),[78] Teofilo is staking his eventual implosion of these terms on an analogical premise his interlocutors will find unshakeable: *form* is different from *matter* as *activity* is from *passivity*, as *maker* is from *made*.

Even though these categories traditionally line up under the headings of "God" and "creation" respectively, Teofilo makes it clear from the beginning that his investigation into the "cause and principle" of the universe will have nothing to do with God. He is only a natural philosopher, he explains, and as such he is dealing with only natural causes (34). In any event, Teofilo continues, sounding remarkably like an early iteration of David Hume's Philo,[79] it is impossible to reason analogically from dependent things to the "first principle" on which they depend, insofar as we have no experience of that which precedes and exceeds the whole universe (34–35). Moreover, he adds, we see the universe only in parts. Without knowledge of the whole, we have no hope of discerning its cause (35). At this point, Teofilo's friend Discono jumps in, and like Hume's Demea cites a slew of apophatic theologians, from "the Talmudists" to Paul, who claim we can never see God directly and must therefore refrain from impiously ascribing to the Creator attributes derived from earthly forms. For all these reasons, Teofilo concludes, "we shall do well to abstain from discussing such a lofty subject" as God (35). Bracketing the question of the *first* principle and cause, he will therefore "look into the principle and cause insofar as . . . either it is nature itself or it shines in the elements and the bosom of nature" (36)—that is, the source of all things insofar as it either is or animates the material world itself.

In line with tradition, Teofilo (along with his doppelgänger Filoteo, who presides over the framing dialogue) begins with the "form" of the universe, which he calls "the world soul" (*l'anima de l'universo/l'anima del mundo*): "a vital, vegetative, and sensitive principle in all things which live, vegetate, and feel" (6).[80] The chief faculty of the world soul is what Bruno calls "the universal intellect" ("*l'intelletto universale*") which he moreover designates as "the universal physical efficient cause ("*l'efficiente phisico universale*") (37, 39). The world soul is therefore the *principle* of the universe, meaning it precedes, contains, and fills everything that exists; whereas the intellect is the *cause*, meaning it brings all that is into being.[81] Matter, by contrast, is the stuff on which the world soul works through the power of intellect. Strictly speaking, it "has no natural form by itself, but may take on all forms through the operation of the active agent which is the principle of nature," that is, the world soul (56). But precisely because matter is, in this sense, the "receptacle of forms" (61),[82] matter is indispensable to the emergence of anything that is. After all, Discono asks, "how can the world soul . . . act as shaper, without the substratum of dimensions or quantities, which is matter?" (55). Insofar as form cannot exist independently of matter, it must therefore be wholly internal to it, "forming [matter] from inside like a seed or root shooting forth and unfolding the trunk" (38).

At this point in the dialogue, we have come as far as Aristotle will go, with matter figured as the surprisingly formidable "universal substratum"—the stuff that remains even as accidental forms arise in it and fall away. As we have seen, however, Aristotle nevertheless persists in denigrating matter as sheer passivity, as possessing neither powers nor qualities, and as "yearning" for form to come make it into something. The contradiction is enough to make one want to ask with Discono, "Why do you claim, O prince of the Peripatetics, that matter is nothing, from the fact of its having no act, rather than saying that it is all, from the fact that it possesses all acts?" (82). In other words, why have you failed to adhere to your own central insight? If form does not exist without matter, but is rather preceded, followed, and even generated by it, then matter is not empty of all qualities but rather full of them, containing *in potentia* all the forms it actualizes over time. This, says Filoteo, is what David of Dinant knew (7), and what Averroes almost knew ("he would have understood still more," says the voice of the Nolan, "had he not been so devoted to his idol, Aristotle" [80]):[83] *matter does not lack form* and so cannot desire it. Rather, matter can only be said to be "deprived of forms and without them" in the same way that "a pregnant woman lacks the offspring which she produces and expels forth from herself" (81).

According to all the characters whom the dialogue presents as respectable (chiefly Filoteo, Teofilo, Discono, and Gervasio), the reason so few people have reached the insight that matter contains and gives rise to all things is that, crudely stated, Aristotelians hate women. As we have seen, the *Physics* explicitly aligns matter with femininity (and ugliness), which lies in wait for masculine form to bring it to order and beauty. This position finds a comical, exuberant spokesman in *Cause, Principle, and Unity* through the character Poliinnio, "one of those stern censors of philosophers . . . reputed to be a follower of Socratic love, an eternal enemy of the female sex" (29). The fourth dialogue opens on Poliinnio alone, who in the absence of his quick-witted interlocutors is free to deliver his thoughts on the manifold ills of matter in an uninterrupted, verbose, and increasingly ridiculous rant.

"And the womb never says 'enough,'" Poliinnio begins, likening the operations of matter to the hysterical longings of a sex-crazed woman (70). According to Poliinnio, matter displays "the insatiable craving of an impassioned female" (10) inasmuch as "she" is "never sated with receiving forms" (70). For this reason, he explains, matter is

called by the prince of the Peripatetics . . . *chaos*, or *hyle*, or *sylva* [abundant material], or . . . cause of sin . . . disposed to evil . . . not existing in itself . . . a blank tablet . . . unmarked . . . litter . . . field . . . or *prope nihil* (almost nothing). . . . finally, after having taken aim with several comparisons between various disparate terms . . . *it is called "woman"* (70).

Citing Helen of Troy, Delilah, and Eve, Poliinnio goes on to charge women with causing the downfall of all great men and nations. Similarly, he reasons, matter is the ruin of all form, which on its own "does not sin, and no form is the source of error unless it is joined to matter" (71). It is therefore no accident, Poliinnio concludes, that the *Physics* compares matter to femininity. For it cannot be denied that matter shares all the qualities of

the female sex—that sex, I mean, which is intractable, frail, capricious, cowardly, feeble, vile, ignoble, base, despicable, slovenly, unworthy, deceitful, harmful, abusive, cold, misshapen, barren, vain, confused, senseless, treacherous, lazy, fetid, foul, ungrateful, truncated, mutilated, imperfect, unfinished, deficient, insolent, amputated, diminished, stale, vermin, tares, plague, sickness, death (72).

This lengthy and progressively absurd monologue ends up serving three purposes in this text. First, it exposes the traditional philosophical denigration of matter as a product of sheer sexism. Second, it exposes such sexism as baseless and anti-intellectual, coming as it does from the mouth of a character whom Gervasio calls "the biggest, most bumbling beast that exists in human form" (34). And third, it provides Teofilo with the metaphorical basis of his transvaluation of matter. Turning the Peripatetics' own associations against them, Teofilo provokes them to demonstrate, in spite of themselves, the preeminence of *hyle*, which "sends all forms forth from its womb" and is, as such, the origin of all that is (82). In effect, Teofilo's strategy is to retain the traditional gendering of matter while shifting our focus from the heteronormative sex act to the act of giving birth. From this vantage point, he is able to assert that far from lacking, desiring, or indeed receiving anything, matter already "possesses" within itself everything it eventually brings forth (82). Therefore, as his dialogic twin Filoteo suggests in his summary of the proceedings, matter is "not a *prope nihil*, an almost nothing, a pure and naked potency, since all forms are contained in it, produced by it, and brought forth by virtue of the efficient cause (which . . . can even be indistinguishable from matter)" (9).

And with this cryptic, parenthetical remark, Filoteo foreshadows the dialogue's most radical maneuver. Having initially insisted upon the distinctions between form and matter, act and potency, activity and passivity, and maker and made, he proceeds in the light of matter's revivification to establish the collision of all these terms by means of a mechanism he inherits from Nicholas of Cusa: the coincidence of opposites.[84] The key to this deconstructive project lies in the category of "intelligible matter," which Teofilo introduces immediately before and after Poliinnio's misogynist rant against materiality (69, 75–76). Intelligible matter is a Neoplatonic category, designating the substratum of intelligible things just as "prime" or "natural" matter designates the substratum of sensible things. The difference between intelligible and sensible matter, Teofilo explains, is that "one is freed from dimensions and the other is contracted to them," so that the former possesses all forms at once, whereas the latter "becomes everything successively" (80–81).

Devoted Spinozists might hear in this distinction a prelude to the difference between "vertical" and "horizontal" causation, which is to say between the perspective of eternity and the perspective of duration.[85] And indeed, just as these perspectives (like thought and extension themselves) are not separate realities for Spinoza but rather differing points of view, so are Bruno's intelligible and sensible matter merely differing attributes of the same substance. "There is a single matter," Teofilo announces, "by which everything that exists does so in act . . . this applies equally to both corporeal and incorporeal substances" (77). Although he is using the term "substance" in the Aristotelian sense, Teofilo's message here is proto-Spinozan: there is just one "matter" that produces both sensible and intelligible things.[86]

It is at this point that Teofilo is able to unify all the distinctions he has taken such pains to separate. Insofar as it is the condition of possibility of all things, this one matter is the principle of creation, which is to say the world soul itself. And insofar as matter brings all things forth, it is also the efficient cause of creation, which is to say the universal intellect. Hence the coincidence of corporeality and intellect, body and soul, principle and cause, activity and passivity, and—most centrally for our purposes—matter and form (8, 66). Crucially for Bruno, however, this cascade of coincidence does not erase the distinctions it holds together. Rather, as Filoteo explains, the assertion that "all is one" means "there is unity in the multiplicity and multiplicity in the unity . . . being is multi-modal and multi-unitary" and, as Teofilo puts it, "multiform and multifigured" (10, 90).[87]

The pressing question then becomes whether this many-oneness of form and matter, act and potency, intellect and material, and every other cosmic principle also amounts to a differential coincidence of *God* and *world*. Filoteo tempts us with this possibility when he suggests that "what is supreme and divine is all that it can be" and that likewise, "the universe is all it can be" (8). Perhaps this means that the universe itself is "supreme and divine"? Teofilo, however, is understandably reluctant to assert this particular identity, and so he qualifies it with another Cusan move: the distinction between "contracted" and "uncontracted" infinities.[88] "The universe is all that it can be, in an unfolded, dispersed, and distinct manner," he explains, "while its first principle is all it can be in a unified and undifferentiated way" (66). Therefore, he implies, the two do not coincide. If, however, the divine first principle relies upon the universe that incarnates it as form relies upon matter, then creator and creation would coincide after all. Discono tries numerous times to get Teofilo to extend his dialectics in this manner, but Teofilo keeps reminding him that their conversation has deliberately excluded "the supreme and most excellent principle" (81), restricting itself to physical causation. None of this, he repeatedly insists, has anything to do with God.

Rhetorically and strategically speaking, Teofilo's restraint here is understandable. Logically speaking, however, there is no reason to limit the coincidence of opposites to physical causes—especially insofar as the physical and the metaphysical presumably coincide in the unity of sensible and intelligible matter. By leading us to this possibility without quite entertaining it, Bruno therefore allows his reader to entertain the notion of God's identity with the universe, should she be so inclined—while himself stopping a hairbreadth short of heresy. Even so, Bruno does allow Teofilo to conclude that if matter indeed contains all forms, then it "must, therefore, be called a divine and excellent parent, generator and mother of natural things—indeed nature entire in substance" (83–84). And at this point, one starts to wonder just what use the perennially bracketed "supreme first principle" might ultimately be. If nature is itself divine, if it generates all sensible and intelligible things from itself and is, as such, an omni-gendered parent (both "generator" and "mother"), then what on earth would we need from a God above or beyond or before this spiritual-material divinity? One might suggest such a God is perhaps required to give the universe a first push at the beginning of time, but this would limit rather severely the function and continuing relevance of God. Besides that, there *is* no "beginning of time" for Bruno; the universe is eternal and so needs no first push.

Theologically speaking, then, what this "strictly physical" dialogue has done is to call each of the divine faculties down into nature itself—all the while pretending not to speak of God. It is precisely by bracketing the "supreme first principle" that Bruno goes on to render such a principle irrelevant, leaving us with an omni-formed, ensouled matter as the creator and end of all things. Insofar as this created creator is both intellectual and extended, Bruno's "cause and principle" of the universe looks less like the riot of Epicurean atoms than the "multi-unitary" Spinozan substance it goes on to influence—whether directly or indirectly.[89] And indeed, just as Spinoza will proceed to do, Bruno argues that each of the particular things of the world is a mode of this cause and principle; in his words, "the uniform substance is one . . . which manifests itself through innumerable particularities and individuals, showing itself in countless, concrete, individual substances" (9). Again, Bruno is not as careful as Spinoza will be (in the wake of Descartes) with respect to his use of the term "substance." Nevertheless, the conviction is the same: the manifold animals, vegetables, and minerals around us are all physical and ideational expressions of the same substance, which does not exist independently of its expressions and for that reason is many in its oneness—or in Filoteo's words, "multi-modal."

Furthermore, just as this thinking will lead Spinoza to deduce the divinity of all things, it leads Bruno to proclaim the vitality of all things. Insofar as everything in existence is an expression of the world soul, Bruno reasons, *everything has a soul*—and is therefore animated. The logic seems to him so sound that he asserts in a prefatory summary of the dialogue, "It is . . . unworthy of a rational subject to believe that the universe and its principle bodies are inanimate" (6). And although this statement seems to limit the scope of animacy to the world as a whole and the sun, moon, and stars (or, for more contemporary readers, to the principle forces of gravity and the cosmological constant), Teofilo proceeds over the course of his instruction to extend animacy to all inner-worldly beings. The teaching, his interlocutors object, is a strange one: "common sense tells us that not everything is alive," cautions Discono, only to be immediately countered by Teofilo's reply: "the most common sense is not the truest sense" (42).

This exchange stirs the ire of Poliinnio who, much like Hegel with his snuff-box, attempts to force the argument into absurdity. "So my clogs," Poliinnio asks, "my slippers, my boots, my spurs, as well as my ring and my gauntlets are supposedly animated? My robe and my palladium are animated?" (43). Teofilo's answer to his overdressed underling sounds remarkably like what Spinoza might have responded to Hegel, had he had the chance to explain the sense in which this snuffbox, that table, this academic regalia, or those all-weather boots were divine: "the table is not animated as table," says Teofilo, "nor are the clothes as clothes, nor is leather as leather . . . but . . . they have within them matter and form. All things, no matter how small and minuscule, have in them part of that spiritual substance which, if it finds a suitable object, disposes itself to be plant, or to be animal" (44). The omni-creativity of this multi-unitary spiritual substance—which, we will recall, is also a material substance—means that all things, "even if they are not living creatures, are animate" (44). Nothing is inert, dead, mere (or for that matter, exploitable) matter.

For Teofilo, this universal animacy means, finally, that the pre-Socratic philosopher Anaxagoras was right, in a sense, when he said that "all things are in all things."[90] After all, the same spiritual-material world soul that animates the cactus also animates the polar bear, so the whole universe appears in contracted form in each of them; as Teofilo puts it, "each thing in the universe possesses all being" (89). Far more recently than Anaxagoras, Nicholas of Cusa had taught this same precept as a theological principle: God is present everywhere throughout the boundless universe, he argued, and as such God is as fully present in a mustard seed as in a man.[91] This radical indwelling is, in fact, what it means for Cusa to call God "creator" in the first place: "creating," he ventures, "seems to be not other than God's being all things."[92] And to the extent that God is the being of all things and all things dwell reciprocally in God, it can in fact be said that "all are in all and each are in each."[93]

Although the logic is nearly indistinguishable from Cusa's, Teofilo does perform two major but subtle departures from his more orthodox predecessor. First, as we will continue to see, he effectively eliminates the Cusan difference between God and the universe, entreating us by virtue of this entangled animacy not to "look for the divinity outside of the infinite world and the infinity of things, but inside that world and those things" (82). Second, he qualifies the Cusan-Anaxagoran proclamation of "all things in all things" with a pre-Spinozan principle of particularity: "Everything is in everything," Teofilo affirms, "but not totally or under all modes in each thing" (90). So, this piece of toast has carbon, wheat, yeast, salt, fire, human labor, mechanical production, time, space, and, most likely, traces of polycarbonate or polyvinyl chloride in it—indeed, it has the *substance* of the whole universe within it—but it does not, for all that, contain a teabag. To be sure, the toast contains and reflects the same "being" (and earth and vegetality and water and air and probably trace plasticity) that also finds itself expressed as a teabag, but the teabag as teabag is not in the toast as toast. Hence the universal interrelation *and* the irreducible particularity of all things—a differential holography enacted through the divine generativity of matter itself. In his bold sort of qualified stutter, Teofilo is therefore led once again to conclude that matter is what we have meant by the origin, end, and life of all things: matter, he suggests, is indeed "so perfect that, if well pondered, [it] is understood to be a divine being in things, as perhaps David of Dinant meant, who was so poorly understood by those who reported his opinion" (86). This, at least, is the position of Teofilo, proponent of "what the Nolan holds," reaching from one heretic to another, backward and forward through the centuries.

AFTERLIFE

Against the chaotic or inert matter of Platonism, Aristotelianism, dualism, and mechanism alike, Bruno gives us a matter unopposed to form, spirit, or intelligence. Matter, both sensible and intelligible, *is* the world soul itself, and as such it contains, brings into being, and inheres in all that is. Far from "yearning" for the order and properties it lacks, matter is nothing short of everything: a "divine being" that bestows animacy upon everything it generates and constitutes. Animacy is therefore a shared property of all that is. At the same time, it is that which makes anything the particular thing that it is. For this reason, all things are substantially interrelated with all other things even as they are modally distinct from one another; each thing is both relationally constituted and irreducibly itself. And yet even this "itself-ness" is constituted (as it is in Spinoza) by the infinite chain of components, interactions, and causes that makes any particular animal, mineral, or vegetable both what and more-than-what it "is": both itself and a slew of others, both finite and divine.

Inasmuch as his animate and indeed godly materiality amounted to a closure of the abyss between creator and creation, Bruno was burned alive on an
Ash Wednesday in 1600 at the Campo de' Fiori in Rome. His books suffered
a similar fate in St. Peter's Square, and were placed on the Inquisition's Index
of Forbidden Books.[94] Perhaps needless to say, then, Bruno's theo-cosmology
was never adopted into orthodox theology. What is more perplexing is that it
has never been seriously entertained even by the most heterodox post-Christian theologies, concerned as they perplexingly remain to keep themselves at
a safe distance from anything that looks too much like pantheism. Precisely
because he is so dramatically repudiated by "the church" in all its guises, however, Bruno becomes in the centuries after his death a secular hero, heralded by
historians of science as having broken the stranglehold in which "religion" had
held critical thinking—either since the collapse of the Roman Empire or since
the dawn of time, depending on the narrator.[95] This sort of secular hagiography
was arguably consolidated in 1889 with the installation of Ettore Ferrari's stone
monument to Bruno at the site of his execution: a stern, cowled figure holding
an oversized book, directly facing the Vatican. The celebration reportedly gathered an "immense crowd," who witnessed the unveiling to the sound of trum-
pets and who cried out, "*Viva Bruno! Viva il martire del libero pensiero!* (Long
live Bruno! Long live the martyr of free thought!)."[96] An inscription at the base
of the statue reads, "*A Bruno—il secolo da lui divinato—qui dove il rogo—arse*
(To Bruno—from the age he predicted—here where the fire burned)."[97]

At the time, one popular science writer celebrated Bruno as having taken
"unbridled license" against "the complete self-prostration of intellect dogmati-
cally demanded by the Church of Rome," setting a course for Galileo, Newton,
Voltaire, and the eventual liberation of secular thought.[98] Well over a century
later, Neil deGrasse Tyson delivers the same story in the first episode of his
televised *Cosmos* series, a reimagination of the Carl Sagan classic that ran in the
1980s. Tyson's segment on Bruno, which lasts a full ten minutes, is composed
of footage of the modern astrophysicist strolling through modern Rome, inter-
spersed with a full animation of Bruno's trial and execution. As the flames are
finally kindled at his feet, we see Bruno turn his head away from the crucifix the
executioner places in front of his eyes. The camera pans upward from his defiant face to the infinite, starry sky above him, at which point this final animation
dissolves to a live-action shot of Tyson, standing in front of a similar starry sky
to advance the narrative of this condemned renegade into the modern, secular-
scientific world. "Ten years after Bruno's martyrdom," Tyson reports (ironically
enshrining the religious language from which Bruno allegedly freed us), "Galileo first looked through a telescope."[99]

Considering Bruno's august place in this scientific lineage, it is perplexing that so few of his teachings have been incorporated into the purportedly secular domain of inquiry to which he purportedly gave birth. Although he can perhaps be credited with circulating Copernican cosmology and contributing to its eventual victory over geocentrism, almost none of Bruno's own ideas was adopted by his alleged successors. Neither Galileo nor Bacon nor Newton nor Einstein believed the universe to be infinite, much less filled with infinite, inhabited worlds.[100] None of them embraced his turn to theurgy and necromancy to describe the interactions of bodies.[101] And absolutely none of them proclaimed the divine animacy of all things by virtue of the spiritual-material world soul. Rather, modern science "freed" the material world from its ecclesiastical imprisonment only to intensify matter's traditional degradation. This intensification is well encapsulated in the words of the late eighteenth-century physiologist Richard Saumarez, who called the material component of an organism "as imbecile and inert as the shoe without the foot."[102] This total denial of agency to materiality culminated in the determinism of Newtonian mechanics and the mechanical compulsion of neo-Darwinist evolution.[103] In short, the modern-scientific matter allegedly catalyzed by Bruno was programmed, inanimate, and just as devoid of divinity as it had been under the Socratic-Christian regime.

Thus it happened that when colonial anthropologists set out to study the residents of the lands that Europe had conquered and seized, they were genuinely confounded by what they learned there. Informed by people from the Americas to Africa to Australia that rivers, rocks, and trees were alive; that humans could communicate with foxes, pigs, and salmon; or that turtles and snakes helped create the universe, these European scholars acted as though they had never heard such ideas before—at least not from grown men in full possession of their rational faculties. And as William Pietz has argued, this bafflement stemmed from their fiercely guarded distinction between animacy and inertness:

> The special fascination that Egyptian zoolatry and African fetishism exerted
> on eighteenth-century intellectuals derived not just from the moral scandal
> of humans kneeling in abject worship before animals lower down on the
> "great chain of being" but from the inconceivable mystery (within Enlight-
> ement categories) of . . . animateness in material beings.[104]

The inconceivability persisted throughout the long nineteenth century; indeed, even as England prepared to send hundreds of delegates to celebrate the unveiling of the monument to Bruno,[105] it managed simultaneously to forget his having taught that matter was divine, or that slippers were in some sense alive. This is certainly not to say that Bruno somehow anticipates what we hastily call "indigenous cosmologies"—much less that his post-Christian account of creation even approaches the texture, complexity, and staggering range of non-European philosophies. It is simply to say that, had Bruno's deconstruction of Aristotelian metaphysics wielded nearly the influence it is reported to have wielded over the secular sciences, then anthropologists of the nineteenth century would have been far less unsettled than they were by the seemingly global-indigenous phenomenon they came to call "animism."

ANIMIST PROJECTIONS

Although theories of the phenomena grouped under the category of animism can be found in the writings of scholars as wide-ranging as David Hume, Max Müller, Emile Durkheim, James Frazer, and Mircea Eliade,[106] the most thorough elaboration of the term can be found in the work of the man who coined it: Edward Burnett Tylor (1832–1917). According to Tylor, *animism* can be defined simply as "the belief in spiritual beings," and as such it constitutes the conceptual and historical root of all religion.[107] By virtue of its central "belief" in spirits, animism is starkly opposed for Tylor to the "materialistic philosophy" of his day, which teaches that matter is insensate and inert.[108] (Here we should note for clarity's sake that the vital "materialisms" we have been exploring in this chapter are therefore closer to what Tylor calls "spiritualism" than they are to what he calls materialism.)

Unlike contemporary, adult Europeans, Tylor explains, "primitive" animists affirm the existence of spirits—in particular, spirits that dwell mysteriously within animal, vegetal, and mineral formations. Tylor accounts for this phenomenon as the narcissistic projection of the human spirit onto everything else in the world. Thus, he describes the cognitive emergence of animism: "savages" first deduce the existence of human souls from the difference between a dead body and a living one, and from the appearance of their ancestors in dreams (12). Rather than understanding such appearances to be the product of their own minds, such uninformed people believe that dreams amount to apparitions of an actual being, a spirit that used to animate a now-lifeless body. Having thus created a basic concept of the human soul (*anima*), the animist philosopher goes on to attribute this sort of soul to everything he sees—first to animals, then to plants, and finally to the so-called environment itself, so that "what we call inanimate objects—rivers, stones, trees, weapons, and so forth, are treated as living intelligent beings" (61). These beings can be propitiated, angered, mollified, and bargained with as though they were not only persons but gods; hence animism is, in essence, the "religion of the savages" (5).

Although this alleged progression in thinking works downward through the perennial "great chain of being"—ascribing ensoulment to humans, then animals, then vegetables, and finally to minerals and elements—the alleged *historical* progression of religion works in reverse. This reversal allows Tylor and his colleagues to offer a racial hierarchy of humanity mapped along temporal lines, with the "earliest" and "lowest" races worshipping material objects and the earth (which, he notes, is almost always female); slightly later and higher races worshipping animals; and subsequent, even higher races worshipping national, humanoid deities; until finally, religion and humanity both culminate in the worship of a *super*human God: male, singular, imperial, and utterly immaterial (356–59).[109] Tylor does not offer evidence or justification for this hierarchy, simply assuming it will be intuitive to his Euro-American readers: "to the modern educated world," he writes, "few phenomena of the lower civilizations seem more pitiable than the spectacle of a man worshiping a beast" (315). After all, "Natural History" has taught the inhabitants of this "modern educated world" a lesson it has denied to, say, the "Red Indians": that "it is our place not to adore [animals] but to understand and use [them]" (315).

Tylor's instrumentalizing disdain intensifies as he moves farther "down" the ontological ladder to consider the worship of trees ("preposterous and absurd") or the reverence of amulets, bones, or "stocks and stones" (those "monstrous and most potent fetishes" of the "Gold Coast negro") (387, 231). We will address the monstrosity in a moment, pointing out in the meantime that such practices inspire in Tylor a sudden burst of unprecedented theological judgment: "Fetishism," he explains, is "the doctrine of spirits embodied in, or attached to, or conveying influences through, certain material objects, and thence it passes by an imperceptible gradation into idolatry" (230). Despite this momentary appeal to Mosaic law, however, it is clear that Tylor's primary allegiance is not to monotheism, but rather to modern science. Although it has not yet reached the "primitive cultures" of his study, he imagines that science will eventually conquer the animist cosmos, having already occupied and civilized Europe's own primordial cultures with its multilateral army: "Physics, Chemistry, Biology," Tylor boasts, "have seized whole provinces of the ancient Animism, [exchanging] force for life and law for will" (268). Unlike even Aristotle[110]—and certainly unlike his unruly commentator Bruno—these modern sciences teach us that plants are not moved by spirits, but by gravity, and that animals are not driven by souls, but by instinct. The implication is that, in the process of draining vitality and personhood from the things of the world, these disciplines have in turn given Europe animals it can *use*, plants without souls it might need to appease, matter that is just raw material, and "primitive" humans who are not quite human. Being insensate, inanimate, irrational, or all of these at once, every non-European category of creature is now available for untrammeled "human" consumption. In short, the natural sciences have allowed "educated modern" citizens to draw rigid ontological distinctions between themselves and everything else on earth, so that the whole world—including darker-skinned non-Europeans—can be exploited unconditionally for the sake of "human" "development."

For Tylor, this rigid binarism marks the central difference between Western and non-Western ontologies. In fact, he charges, indigenous people are unable to make distinctions at all, and this failure becomes the source of their pitiable theologies. As Tylor explains it, the people of the "lower races" simply do not make the "absolute psychical distinction between man and beast, so prevalent in the civilized world"; nor do they seem capable of dividing animals from plants or living things from inert objects (53). According to Tylor, these categorical errors are the product of an even more fundamental indistinction, namely, that between self and other, interiority and exteriority. "The savage," writes Tylor, "is a man who scarcely distinguishes his subjectivity from objectivity, hardly knows his inside from his outside."[111] This inability to distinguish is the reason the "savage" thinks his dreams are external apparitions rather than internal projections, the reason he can identify totemically with animals and plants, and the reason he is able to project his own sort of subjective being onto objects (rocks, rivers, bones) to make them seem alive—even conscious. And the result is a riot of animacies—the "metaphysical cacophony" depicted throughout eighteenth- and nineteenth-century European sources as a "swarming horde" of fetishists and their idols that renders the animist universe a "socially undifferentiated mob."[112]

As we might recall from the introduction, a similar charge of indistinction is continually leveled against people accused of pantheism: their denial of the ontological difference between God and creation is said to amount to a collapse of spirit and matter, agent and patient, good and evil, and by association, male and female. Rather than a reassuringly binary system, pantheists are said to produce something like the "awful pudding" that D. H. Lawrence attributed to Walt Whitman, or indeed the "Irish porridge" that Pope Honorius III attributed to John Scotus Eriugena (and it is a testament to the homogeneity of antipantheist revulsion that the scandalous Lawrence would choose a metaphor so close to that of a thirteenth-century pope).[113] We furthermore heard Hegel level a similar charge against Spinoza, whose substance also allegedly swallowed all difference into an "abyss of annihilation."[114]

In these anti-pantheist sources of the eighteenth through the twentieth centuries in particular, we have seen such accusations regularly filtered through orientalist lenses: pantheist indistinction is continually said to be an infiltration of mystical, Eastern monism into the soberly dualist West. With Lawrence in particular, we also saw glimpses of primitivism behind this anti-pantheist panic, and the contours of such primitivism become clearer when we consider the colonial anthropology of the nineteenth and early twentieth centuries. Just like Eastern "pantheists," indigenous polytheists allegedly fail to make distinctions. Tylor himself likens these two errors at one point by comparing indigenous animism to South Asian reincarnation, which likewise presumes that all beings have souls, and that such souls could just as well inhabit a reptile or a bird as a human being.[115] There is an uncanny resemblance, then, between the monstrous indistinction of the one (monistic pantheism) and the monstrous indistinction of the many (multitudinous, horde-like animism): both of them unsettle the tidy charts and tables structuring Western metaphysics. Indeed, between "Eastern" pantheists and "primitive" animists, colonial Europe had surrounded itself with cosmologies that threatened the fundaments of its private individual and steady either/ors.

As we have already witnessed in Spinoza, however, the charge of indistinction is often a false one. It may hold for a self-professedly monistic pantheist like Ernst Haeckel, who proclaims that "we cannot draw a sharp line of distinction between [the inorganic and organic], any more than we can recognize an absolute distinction between the animal and the vegetable kingdom, or between the lower animals and man . . . [or] the natural and the spiritual. . . . *both are one.*"[116] But such oneness is multiplied and undermined in Spinoza's cosmos, for example, which is teeming with particularity and difference—just not with the sort that consent to line up beneath "God" on one side and "nature" on the other, or mind over here and body over there. Similarly, contemporary anthropologists have argued that indigenous philosophers make plenty of distinctions—just not the kind Victorians were looking for.

REANIMATIONS

The ongoing effort to "reframe and reclaim" the traditionally insulting and ironically indistinct category of animism—an effort often encoded as "new animism"—can be traced back to Irving Hallowell's renowned study of the Ojibwa (Ojibwe/Anishinaabeg) nation of the Great Lakes and Central Canada.[117] According to Hallowell, the "worldview" of the Ojibwa breaks open and relativizes the central category of *anthro*-pology because its structuring concept of personhood, unlike that of Euro-American anthropologists, is not confined to humanity.[118] A *person* for the Ojibwa is a being who can act, speak, move, and change—and as such, the sun is not a thing or an object, but rather a person "of the other-than-human class."[119] Likewise, flint (the mineral), mythological characters, "entities 'seen' in dreams," thunderbirds, bears, and thunder and lightning are also said to be persons.[120] Other beings are said to be "animate," a category that sometimes overlaps with that of personhood and sometimes does not, and which sometimes obtains and sometimes does not, so that "*some, but not all* [beings]—trees, sun-moon, thunder, stones, and objects of material culture like kettle and pipe—are classified as animate."[121] By "some, but not all," Hallowell means that while some beings under particular circumstances are treated as animate and/or personal, others are not; it all depends on the circumstance. A "string of wooden beads" can come to life in the hands of powerful men, but this does not mean that all wooden beads everywhere are living beings.[122] Hallowell's oft-cited lesson in this regard comes from an elder, whom Hallowell approached after he had become conversant in the Ojibwa language. "Since stones are grammatically animate," Hallowell explains, "I once asked an old man: Are *all* stones we see about us here alive? He reflected a long while and then replied, 'No! But *some* are.'"[123]

In the course of his analysis, Hallowell implicitly contests nearly every element of Tylor's classic definition of animism as "the belief in spiritual beings." First, bear-persons and animate rocks do not "contain" anthropomorphic spirits; rather, they themselves are living beings.[124] As such, their animacy is not a matter of belief but rather of relation; to affirm that this tree, that river, or the-bear-looking-at-me is a person is to affirm its capacity to interact with me—and mine with it. As Tim Ingold phrases the matter, "we are dealing here not with a way of believing *about* the world, but with a condition of living in it."[125] When animacy is thus understood, it turns out not to be a projection of human selfhood onto other beings, as Tylor had imagined. Rather, according to Deborah Bird Rose, human selfhood in the animist cosmos is a derivation of a wider category of selfhood; humans are just a small subclass of the wide range of persons with whom humans are in relations of care, predation, and exchange.[126] Hence Graham Harvey's redefinition of "animists" as "people who recognise that the world is full of persons, only some of whom are human, and that life is always lived in relationship with others."[127] Finally, as Hallowell's living stones illustrate, to affirm the animacy, or indeed the personhood, of this desk, those mountains, or that snake is not to affirm the animacy or personhood of everything everywhere—much less is it to say that all things are the same. To the contrary, it is to affirm that things are differently different from one another, depending on their circumstances.

From Hallowell's account, it is clear that the Ojibwa do not make a priori distinctions between animals, humans, living things, nonliving things, internality (dreams, psychic states), and externality ("reality"). But this does not mean the Ojibwa cannot make distinctions at all; to the contrary, the bear who becomes a person in relation to a threatened human is ontologically different from all other bears. The beads that come alive in certain men's hands become inert on a table or in the display case of a European museum, whereas medicine objects might become even more dangerous when deprived of their social relations in such exhibitions.[128] Far from abolishing or preventing distinctions, then, this sort of animacy produces differences *locally* and *interactively*. Beings become the kind of beings they are in relation to the other beings who interact with them in a particular time and place. In short, beings do not carry properties around with them; rather, like quantum particles, they obtain those properties by means of the relational apparatus that produces them.[129] Categories like "living," "nonliving," "personal," and "animate" are not static; they are emergent and adaptive. They take shape, as anthropologist Eduardo Viveiros de Castro explains with philosopher Déborah Danowksi, "according to the practical context of interaction with them."[130]

Rose's work on Aboriginal kinship structures is particularly instructive in this regard. In her two years among the Yarralin community in Australia's northern territory, Rose endeavored to understand the complex kinship structure that binds human and nonhuman animals.[131] As her instructor Daly taught her, each Yarralin is related to the more-than-human world along multiple lines of descent; Daly, for example, is catfish on his mother's side and dingo on his father's. Other members of his patrilineal group, by contrast, are not catfish but brogla (an Australian crane), flying fox, or snake. This means, first, that each Yarralin is related to *some, but not all* local animals. As such, they have different and overlapping obligations from one another. Daly cannot eat the catfish with whom he "shares flesh" but his non-catfish wife can eat them, so long as she buries the bones respectfully afterward.[132] Moreover, these differential obligations shift according to circumstance, so that, for instance, "when an emu person dies, nobody eats emus until the emu people tell them they can, and the first emu to be killed is treated with special ritual."[133] Particular creatures become forbidden and protected under particular circumstances, just as particular creatures become kin to *some but not all* other creatures. The result of this dynamic, relational structure is not uniformity, all-is-oneness, or a "pudding of one identity," but rather what Rose calls "a web of interdependencies."[134] Each creature is directly responsible for the well-being of many beings at many times, but not for all beings at all times, and these "overlap[ping] connections" sustain a community united not by its identity to itself, but by its complex, mobile, and interrelated differentiations.

What, then, do these animist ethico-ontologies have to do with our pan-theological investigation?

For early colonial anthropologists, the "totemic" kin structure of indigenous Australia amounted to a straightforwardly theriomorphic theology: the dingo is an ancestor, a taboo and therefore sacred being; and as such, the dingo is *the god* of that kinship group.[135] Emile Durkheim sought to correct this notion— and to counteract the ridicule it tended to prompt among European scholars (think of Tylor's "pitiable spectacle" of "a man worshipping a beast")—with the Melanesian term *mana*, which he conflated with the Sioux *wakan* and the Iriquois *orenda* to form a general theory of totemism.[136] According to Durkheim, *mana* is an impersonal force that courses through all totemic life and is more highly concentrated in some beings than in others. It is not, then, the dingo, snake, or cow as such that is sacred; rather, these animals are thought to possess a high level of *mana*, the life force itself, which "animates" all things on earth.[137] "In other words," he explains,

> totemism is not the religion of certain animals, certain men, or certain images; it is the religion of a kind of anonymous and impersonal force that is identifiable in each of these beings but identifiable to none of them. . . . Taking the word "god" in a very broad sense, one could say that it is the god that each totemic cult worships. But it is an impersonal god, without name, without history, immanent in the world, diffused in a numberless multitude of things.[138]

What Durkheim has effectively done with his theory of *mana* is to transpose totemic animism into full-fledged, spiritual-monistic pantheism: everything on earth contains the same disembodied, sacred force that precedes and gives life to all that is.

Unfortunately for would-be monists, however, this notion of a sacred, universal life force among indigenous nations has been contested by scores of anthropologists, from Durkheim's contemporary Paul Radin through Hallowell to Harvey, who insists that *wakan*, for instance, "does not refer to an impersonal power but ... defines all kinds of persons"—animal-, earth-, human-, and plant-persons—"as relationally, socially powerful."[139] As these authors all explain, the power in question is neither singular nor transcendent. "It" is not a unified, disembodied force that incarnates itself in various creatures. Rather, creatures *produce* this life force by means of their differential relations with one another. It is Rose's earthly, embodied, and utterly material "web of interdependencies" that gives rise to, sustains, and eventually reclaims all creatures in the Yarralin landscape—and each creature contributes to and in some small way alters the very web that brings it forth.

In his metatheoretical work on animism, Ingold offers a similarly reconfigured animist ontology as an antidote to "the canons of Western thought."[140] Such canons operate, he argues, by means of a "logic of inversion," whereby embodied practices are said to be "the outward expression of an inner design."[141] This inside-out metaphysics gives us the "doers behind the deed" we have seen Nietzsche attempt to dismantle: those purported individuals who are said to *be* before they *act* in accordance with that being. The same inversion gives us a being-itself (or a divinity, or the Forms, or Substance) that primarily exists in some disincarnate, extra-cosmic realm and only secondarily decides to manifest itself in the bodies and minds of particular beings. In the works of Spinoza and Bruno, we have found theories of nature that strain against this Western inversion, with Spinoza's single substance (arguably) constituted by the multiple particularities that "express" it, and with Bruno's utterly material "world soul" generating the very forms that order and shape it. Even in these authors, however, we find a commitment to the ultimacy of oneness—however manifold—and to the universe as the necessary unfolding of some inner design—however much their own thinking might work against itself in this regard.

In Ingold's "new animism," then, one could say that metaphysics finally collapses into the embodied multiplicity and total immanence on whose brink Spinoza and Bruno keep it balanced. Animacy, Ingold maintains, is not a spiritual force that resides in the material world—nor is it some internal life force that gets expressed in outward ways. "Rather," he suggests, "it is the dynamic, transformative potential of the entire field of relations within which beings of all kinds ... continually and reciprocally bring one another into existence."[142] Unlike spirits, Spirit, God, or Substance, animacy thus configured does not inhere in beings, create beings, or even express itself in beings. More radically, it is *produced* by beings, whose movement, growth, interweavings, and ruptures *constitute being itself*. Being is thus in irreducibly embodied and perpetually relational becoming. "To elaborate," writes Ingold, "life in the animic ontology is not an emanation but a generation of being, in a world that is not preordained but incipient." Rather than unfolding what is already there, the "domain of entanglement" in which we live, move, and have our being produces new and unanticipated movements—movements that reconfigure the field of growth and becoming itself.

From an anthropological perspective, the chief danger of the "new animism" seems to be its familiar, universalizing tendencies. There is as much a risk that one might seek to apply Rose's web or Ingold's entanglement to every "indigenous cosmology" as there was with Durkheim's *mana*, or indeed Tylor's *anima*. By tracking the contours of this immanent animacy, I am not, therefore, commending it as a way to describe the conceptual structure of any given culture—such work could only be evaluated in relation to the ethnographic records of particular field sites, each of which would undoubtedly demand unique articulations of how it is that beings come to be. In other words, I am not reading these new animacies primarily as accounts of "indigeneity itself," or even of some carefully pluralized "indigeneities." Rather, I am appealing to them as philosophies born out of encounters between Euro-American and native conceptual regimes. Rose has argued that in contemporary animist philosophies, "at least one strand of Western philosophy now seeks to meet indigenous philosophy on its own ground," and I would suggest that this description is helpful so long as one emphasizes the *meeting* (rather than the ownness) that produces such a strand.[143] New animist philosophies are not unmediated reflections of *any* of the cultures that coproduce them; rather, they are hybrid philosophies. Moreover, these hybrid philosophies look remarkably like what William James has called *pluralist pantheisms*. After all, they locate creativity wholly within the material world—a world whose complex but differential and non-totalized connections and disconnections resist any effort to gather "it" into a tidy singularity. It is therefore not surprising to find philosopher Scott Pratt demonstrating that American pragmatism is *itself* the product of the interaction between European and Native American thinkers.[144] If indigenous communities produce ontologies that resemble James's pragmatist-pluralist pantheism, it is arguably because they helped form the notions of pragmatism, pluralism, and pantheism in the first place.

Granted, the resonance with theism of any sort would make most of the new animists uncomfortable. Considering the history of European fascination and revulsion with variously monstrous "savage" displays of animal, vegetable, and fetish worship, such contemporary thinkers understandably hesitate to call indigenous philosophies "theologies" or even "religions" at all. This hesitation usually comes in the form of sheer absence—one rarely encounters explicitly devotional or godlike categories in the new animist literature—but it occasionally finds more direct elaboration. One representative in this regard is Matthew Hall's study of the "animist plant ontologies" that stem from numerous Aboriginal and Native American cultures. Against Tylor and Frazer in particular, Hall maintains that "animist relationships with plants" absolutely do not amount to deification of them.[145] Drawing on Rose's work, Hall argues that plants are not gods, but kin. And "as kin and as proper persons," he explains, "plants are recipients not of worship, but of respect and moral consideration. . . . [For instance,] the reticence of the Ojibwe in chopping down trees is an ethical act rather than an act of worship."[146] This ethical act sustains earthly relationships, Hall insists; it has nothing to do with metaphysical reverence or aspirations toward salvation. As one might note, however, these distinctions (between the physical and the metaphysical, the this-worldly and the other-worldly, or the religious and the ethical) are rooted in the oppositions between spirit and matter, creator and created, that "animism" purportedly rejects.[147]

For some reason, the irony is lost on many of the new animists, who go to great lengths to demonstrate the extent to which such practices are not at all "religious." Hall, for example, takes pains to connect animist ontologies to contemporary *scientific* studies, which variously establish the sentience, intentionality, cognition, memory, social behavior, decision-making, and symbiotic or anti-symbiotic properties of plants.[148] The implication is that the indigenous attribution of agency and even personhood to vegetal life is not irrational, infantile, narcissistic, or delusional (which is to say, religious); to the contrary, these insights are so sophisticated that "plant science" has *confirmed* them. What Hall does not acknowledge is that the particular plant studies in question are largely indebted to the theories of autopoiesis and symbiogenesis championed in the late twentieth century by the microbiologist Lynn Margulis, whose work on bacterial agency, symbiosis, and even cognition provoked raging controversy precisely because it looked too much like religion—in particular, like "that 'Earth Mother' crap" most commonly associated with pantheism.[149]

Symbiology

The term "autopoiesis" was coined by the Chilean biologists Humberto Maturana and Francisco Varela in 1972, but the concept was advanced and popularized in the following few decades by Margulis and her frequent co-author (and son) Dorion Sagan.[150] In essence, autopoiesis is a principle of immanence, asserting life's "continual production of itself" rather than its derivation from some external principle.[151] To say that life is autopoietic is to say that it generates, regulates, and even regenerates itself, so that far from being created—or for that matter, animated—by some force outside themselves, autopoietic organisms produce the very processes they need to emerge and flourish. "Consider, for example, the case of a cell," writes Sagan: "it is a network of chemical reactions which produce molecules such that . . . through their interactions [they] generate and participate recursively in the same network of reactions which produced them."[152] Insofar as it is reciprocally constituted and changed by the very beings it produces, such a "network" sounds remarkably like Ingold's animic "domain of entanglement," itself an unconscious, fully dynamic, and pluralized rendition of Bruno's "matter."

Indeed, the resonance intensifies when we consider the Margulisian theory of "symbiogenesis," according to which new traits, organs, organisms, and species are produced through the symbiotic interaction of existing organisms.[153] Margulis's most significant breakthrough in this regard was her "serial endosymbiotic theory" (SET) of *eukaryosis*, which explains the emergence of complex cells as the product of primordial bacterial mergers.[154] Against the neo-Darwinist insistence that the primary engines of evolution are random mutations and competition, Margulis demonstrates that organisms evolve by means of interspecies exchange, cooperations, and co-optations.[155] "The major source of evolutionary novelty is the acquisition of symbionts," Margulis explains; "it is never just the accumulation of mutations."[156] Producing new and unanticipated structures out of recombinations of the old, symbiosis takes place in reciprocal relationship with the "environment," to such an extent that it makes no sense to set the two apart from one another. As Bruno Latour argues, Margulis erases "the inside/outside boundary . . . by bringing inside the organism those other aliens who used to be part of its 'environment.'"[157] In this manner, Margulis replaces the endless antagonism of the classic origin of species with what Myra Hird has called "an ontology of primordial entanglement": organisms are not individuals struggling against other individuals to survive, but rather, interdependent crowds of creatures working adaptively together.[158]

According to Margulis, any complex organism[159] is a collective, or *symbiont*, "itself" produced by and composed of an infinite series of symbionts reminiscent of Spinoza's infinite horizontal causation. The result, says Margulis, is that "we are walking communities"; a sentiment Sagan echoes by explaining that "all macroscopic beings are, evolutionarily and currently, microbial colonial composites."[160] In this light, as the two of them argue in their appropriately co-authored *What is Life?*, "independence is a political, not a scientific term."[161] Following this lead, biologists Scott Gilbert, Jan Sapp, and Alfred Tauber have proposed that the basic units of biology ought not to be individuals but rather "holobionts"—multispecies assemblages that are both more and less than one. "All organisms," they suggest, are effectively "chimeric."[162] Similarly, and strikingly for those who might be listening out for categorical transgression, Sagan goes so far as to celebrate this irreducible chimerism as "monstrous": a "breach of Platonic etiquette in favor of polymorphous perversity."[163] And it is this very monstrosity that prompts Donna Haraway to argue that the "autopoiesis" by which life produces, sustains, and transforms itself would more appropriately be called "sympoiesis."[164] The "auto" is misleading, Haraway suggests, "because nothing self-organizes—it's relationality all the way down."[165]

This perverse and wholly immanent relation, we might note, is far from undifferentiated, abyssal, or pudding-like; to the contrary, it relentlessly produces different kinds of difference precisely by virtue of its steady refusal to gather beings under the traditional categories of activity and passivity, creator and created, animate and inanimate, or spirit and matter. In this chapter's crossing of animist, nonlinear, and new and old materialist thought, what we have therefore found is a vibrant, this-worldly materiality that produces, sustains, and remakes all things—a multiple and multiplying "substance" or "cause and principle" that is itself transformed by the beings that compose it. Perhaps appropriately, this dynamic, adaptive, and generative vision of what heretics of numerous traditions have dared to call not only matter, but God, is a coproduction of indigenous, Western, philosophical, biological, and social-scientific thinkers: a methodological mash-up that refuses to be assembled under any particular discipline and which threatens in turn the very symbionts that give rise to it, considering its proximity to "religion."

Such proximity became apparent for Margulis, at least, when she expanded her theory to the level of planetarity. Having finally gained the reluctant and near-universal admiration of evolutionary biologists for her symbiogenetic account of eukaryosis,[166] Margulis began to argue in the early 1970s that earth itself is an autopoietic set of symbionts.[167] Adopting and advancing physical chemist James Lovelock's "Gaia hypothesis," Margulis spent the rest of her career accumulating evidence for the reciprocal interactions between the atmosphere and the biosphere, which exerts "active control" over earthly conditions in service of the proliferation and evolution of life.[168] Organisms, she argued alongside Lovelock, create the very conditions they need to live, interact, and evolve; in their words, "the earth's atmosphere is actively maintained and regulated by life on the surface, that is, by the biosphere."[169] We will explore the details of this sympoietic Earth momentarily, concluding this exploration of materiality with a glimpse of some of the familiar ridicule the Gaia hypothesis has provoked.

In their rejection of her 1992 grant proposal, a panel at NASA lauded Margulis's reputation as a "distinguished scientist" whose endosymbiotic theory had "alter[ed] the way we think of life on Earth."[170] In recent years, however, the panel judged that she had "gone perhaps too far. This is primarily due," they explained, "to her defense of the Gaia hypothesis."[171] According to James Strick, the chief stumbling block to broad scientific acceptance of this theory was and remains Margulis's and Lovelock's ascription of *agency* to what mainline researchers still hold to be mechanistic biological processes. Insofar as this agency amounts to the creation of life itself, critics accuse the Gaia hypothesis of "secretly slipping a supernatural Creator . . . in through the back door."[172] But far from being supernatural, such a Gaian creator would be—as it is for the Stoics, Lucretius, Bruno, and Spinoza—nothing other than nature itself. It is not therefore theistic, but rather pantheistic, and as such would more appropriately be denounced as "an unscientific attempt to deify the biosphere"[173] than an unscientific attempt to sneak in an extra-cosmic God. For the sober-minded, however, this pantheological correction is no improvement; in fact, the insult to "science" only increases with the unsubtle gendering of Gaia, that "ancient Greek Earth goddess" whose maternal materiality connotes what one author calls "vague New Age mysticism," what another dubs "new-age goddess worship," what Lovelock dismisses as "Pagan goddesses and things," what Margulis herself calls "Earth Mother crap," and what Sagan admits are "scientifically unwelcome teleological, feminist, and animist connotations."[174]

What we have witnessed, then, is a complete reversal of the charges with which this chapter opened—a reversal that nevertheless retains the logical structure of the initial position: the heretics of the medieval and early modern periods ascribed materiality to divinity, whereas the heretics of the contemporary world ascribe divinity to materiality. Either way, the sexed and raced categories of "feminism and animism" are unwelcome within the dominant discourse in question. And now as then, these ungodly and pseudoscientific philosophies continue to generate the pantheological possibility that what we call "God" is nothing other than the material multiplicities of the sympoietic world itself. It is to this world that we now turn.

PANFUSION

"'Pan' they named him, because he delighted them 'all.'"
—Homeric Hymns

It is the *Homeric Hymns* (7–6 BCE) that inaugurated the rich and strange tradition of associating Pan (*Pán*) with "the all" (*tò pân*), which is the closest term the Greeks have to "universe." As Patricia Merivale explains, the "correct derivation" would stem, not from *tò pân*, but rather "from *pa-on* (grazer)."[1] And yet once the association was made, it stuck: the pastoral collided with the metaphysical and stayed there. Some of the bawdier sources perform this elision in a pluralistic fashion, saying that Penelope was unfaithful to Odysseus not just with one god or suitor, but with them *all*, "and that from this intercourse was born Pan."[2] Others render Pan monistically, in line with the Orphic Hymn of late antiquity. It is this text that attributes to the "Goat-footed, horned, Bacchanalian Pan" a fully cosmogonic function, calling him "the substance of the whole" and that "fanatic pow'r, from whom the world began."[3] Thus Pan is at once a riot of manyness and a principle of unity—an anti-Oedipal monster-god who is also the "universal god, or god of Nature," "the pantheistic divinity," "the All."[4]

Porphyry (ca. 234–305 CE) encapsulates Pan's many-oneness by attesting that his devotees "made Pan the symbol of the universe and gave him horns as symbol of the sun and moon and the fawn skin as emblem of the stars in heaven, or of the *variety of the universe*."[5] This "variety" drops away in the work of most other neo-Platonist and Scholastic authors, who follow Plato and Aristotle in rejecting the manyness of *tò pân* (along with the Stoic and Epicurean thinkers who had asserted it) and insisting upon a universal *oneness*.[6] The later poets tend to be split on the matter, with the Romantics rendering Pan a cosmic whole and the Victorians keeping him particular and categorically paradoxical.[7] Either way, in the persistent universalizing of the goat-god, we see a "Pan" of manifold hybridities, transgressed boundaries, and material multiplicities collide head-on with a "pan" which, depending on how you configure your universe, either means the "variety" of all things or all-things-as-one.

Christian apologetic sources go on to conflate and toggle between these monistic and pluralistic *pan*s, using whichever strategy serves them best in any given situation. Most notably, Eusebius of Caesaria (ca. 260–340 ce) devotes two sections of his *Preparatio Evangelica* to a strange story in Plutarch that announces "the death of Pan." Opening on a boat piloted by an Egyptian man named Thamus, the story recalls the passengers' hearing a voice from the shore of Paxi calling, "Thamus, Thamus, Thamus; the Great Pan is dead!" Astonished that the voice somehow knows his name, the captain agrees to pass the news onto the next island they reach—news whose delivery elicits "a loud lamentation, not of one but of many, mingled with amazement."[8] Once the ship returns to Rome, the captain files a report with Emperor Tiberius, who commissions an investigation that concludes that the deceased in question was, in fact, "Pan the son of Hermes and Penelope."[9]

For a century now, many classicists have argued that the whole story was based on a misunderstanding that went over Plutarch's head.[10] Eusebius, however, interprets the tale as a historical report of the death of Pan, who stands metonymically for "all" the pagan gods. Noting that the account takes place during the reign of Tiberius, Eusebius reminds his reader that these were the days of Christ's "sojourn among men," during which he "ri[d] human life from demons of every kind."[11] For Eusebius then, the death of Pan is coincident with the life of Christ, who rids the world of "'All' the Greek gods, that is . . . all the evil demons."[12] And so the Lamb of God overcomes the goat-god, who goes on to become not just one evil spirit among many in the Christian imagination, but the demon of demons himself. Singling him out for his unbridled sexuality, Christian mythology parleys the "horns, hooves, shaggy fur, and outsized phallus" of Pan into the paradigmatic "image of Satan."[13]

Thus the simultaneous revulsion from and attraction to this mythic creature-creator intensifies. In the American literary tradition in particular, the powerful ambivalence of the Pan symbol often amounts to his being represented as black, Native American, or both. "[Nathaniel] Hawthorne, for example, reifies a long-standing transcendental association in imagining a group of runaway slaves, in their 'primeval simplicity,' as 'not altogether human . . . and akin to the fawns and rustic deities of olden times.'"[14] Hawthorne's *Marble Faun* moreover presents the character Donatello as what Richard Hardack calls an "aboriginal Pan in a kind of blackface," an African-descended slave who, like Pan, occupies the "liminal" spaces of American society.[15] In Hawthorne's words, the black faun constitutes, like the Native American, "a natural and delightful link between human and *brute* life, with something of the divine character intermingled."[16] Hardack finds similar strings of associations in Emerson, Stowe, and Melville, all of whom racialize, demonize, romanticize, and then appropriate Pan, who, for the transcendentalists in particular, becomes a means of escaping white male subjectivity and merging with a dark, feminized, and animal universe.

One finds a slightly more circumspect longing for a lost, racialized pagan unity in D. H. Lawrence's "Pan in America," which declares that, "still . . . among the Indians, the oldest Pan is alive. But here, also, dying fast."[17] And at any rate, he shrugs, "we cannot return to the primitive life, to live in tepees and hunt with bows and arrows."[18] Yet Lawrence longs intensely for the very life he denigrates—for "the living universe of Pan" as distinct from "the mechanical conquered universe of modern humanity."[19] And although he stops short of recognizing it, one might point out that "modern humanity" (white humanity) has mechanized and conquered the universe precisely by mechanizing and conquering those black and native others whom it animalizes, naturalizes, denigrates, and elevates.

"Pan!" exclaims Lawrence, "All! That which is everything has a goat's feet and tail! With a black face! This really is curious."[20]

3

COSMOS

Earth's crammed with heaven,
And every common bush on fire with God.
　　　　—Elizabeth Barrett Browning, *Aurora Leigh*

This world: a monster of energy, without beginning, without end... as a play
of forces and waves of forces, at the same time one and many... eternally
changing... the eternally self-creating, the eternally self-destroying....
do you want a name for this world?
　　　　—Friedrich Nietzsche, *The Will to Power*

DEUS SIVE MUNDUS

Stated most simply, pantheism is the hypothesis that identifies God with the
world. As we saw in the introduction, however, there is another definition—
often conflated with this one—which states that pantheism assimilates all
things into a single, divine unity.[1] In the course of the reconstructive part of this
analysis, we have opted for the first, "immanent" definition over the second,
"unitive" definition because the latter tends to locate its oneness either in a
disembodied realm of otherworldly "essence" or in a this-worldly monism that
forces all beings into a static ontic hierarchy of race and species. Insofar as the
position in question might genuinely disrupt the violent categories of Western
metaphysics, it is not unity but immanence, in all its constitutive multiplicity,
that forms the pantheological premise (and promise): what we mean by God
(*theos*) is nothing other than the world (*cosmos*) itself.

It is this foundational claim that theists and atheists alike find objectionable; to atheists, the term "God" does not seem to add anything to the category
of "world," and to theists—including panentheists—it seems "incoherent to
assert that God *just is* the world."[2] We glimpsed some of the indeterminacy

between atheism and pantheism in our encounters with Spinoza and Lucretius and will revisit this problem in the next chapter. For the moment, however, we will focus on the purported incoherence of God's "just" being the world. Philip Clayton worries that such a straightforward identification lodges both terms in eternal necessity, robbing God of "conscious agency" and leaving the world a deterministic machine, incapable of being otherwise.[3] With Clayton, I worry about the ethical stagnancy (not to mention scientific outdatedness) of theo-cosmic determinism, and indeed have already set forth a reading of Spinoza that undermines this classically Spinozan ideal. Against Clayton, however, I am reluctant to predicate divine agency on "consciousness," modeled as this trait so often is on specifically human cognition. And either way, it seems to me that although people of various persuasions might find the pantheist identification of God and world objectionable, offensive, or even redundant, it can only be said to be "incoherent" if the claimant or the addressee is working with an impoverished notion of the concept "world."

To be sure, if the term "world" designates a finite, inert, mechanistic back-ground for creaturely existence—an entity that is simply *given*, whether by bare fact or by an anthropomorphic deity—then it clearly makes very little sense to identify that static entity with the forces of creation, transformation, destruc-tion, and vitality inherent to divinity. If, however, whatever we mean by "world" is open, emergent, and sympoietic—if a world is, in Nietzsche's words, "a mon-ster of energy . . . at the same time one and many . . . eternally self-creating . . . eternally self-destroying"—then the pantheological premise sheds its incoher-ence. Facing such an energetic monstrosity, those who maintain the anthro-pomorphism, immutability, immateriality, strict singularity, or strict triunity of God may very well reject pantheological thinking—not as incoherent, but as incompatible with what they hold to be necessary attributes of God. For those who hold no such commitments, however, the identity of such an open, emergent, and sympoietic world with "God" might transvalue the latter term, reconfiguring the creativity, infinity, and moreness of divinity as immanent, processual, embodied, and multiple. Before approaching the category of divin-ity as such, we will therefore endeavor to determine what a hypothetical pan-theologian might mean by "world."

WORLD, WORLDING, WORLDS

Granted, it is difficult to determine what *anyone* might mean by "world." The Greek word *kosmos* (pl. *kosmoi*) originally meant "order," as in the order of soldiers preparing for battle or the order of a well-functioning state.[4] Gradually, the word came to designate the arrangement of the planetary bodies, and by Plato's time (429–347 BCE), it signified the "ordered whole" of the physical universe itself.[5] Plato and Aristotle used the words *kosmos* and *tò pân* (the all) interchangeably, each of them insisting that there was only one world in the universe. According to the Academy's major rivals, however, there were many *kosmoi* within *tò pân*—even an infinite number of them. As we saw in the previous chapter, Epicurean worlds arose, lived, and decayed in spatial distribution throughout an infinite universe, whereas the Stoic world was a temporal unity, born, ignited, and reborn in nearly identical form throughout infinite time.[6]

In Latin, the spatial sense of *kosmos* is rendered *mundus*, whereas the temporal sense becomes *saeculum*, or "age," referring in particular to the era of creation as distinct from the eternity of God. The English word "world" maintains both of these valences, stemming etymologically from the Germanic *were* (man) and *old* (age), and coming to mean both "the age of man," which is to say the time of human existence, and the space in which humans dwell.[7]

Cosmologically, this dwelling-spacetime we call "world" has often designated the planet Earth, but during the seventeenth century in particular, it came to designate other planets and stars on which humanlike creatures were thought to live.[8] Nicholas of Cusa used the term *mundus* in the fifteenth century to mean the region of spacetime visible in all directions from the vantage point of any given cosmic body—a perspectival expanse that contemporary cosmologists now call the (or an) "observable universe." Cusa's more radical and less ecclesiastically tolerated descendant Giordano Bruno made his sixteenth-century *mundi* less perspectival but equally innumerable under the dual influence of Copernicus and the newly rediscovered Lucretius, equating a world with a solar system, and announcing that there were necessarily an infinite number of them. In contemporary astrophysics, the term "world" is used loosely, referring variously to any visible region of spacetime (or "observable universe"), to the product of the big bang taken as a whole, to a universal bubble within the hypothetical compendium of universes called the "multiverse," to everything within the event horizon of a black hole, or indeed to the cosmic era between the big bang and whatever is coming at the end of time—whether it be a crunch, a rip, or a "whimper."[9]

In a geological register, the term "world" tends to refer to the Earth and its atmosphere. Biologically, it can mean the earthly biosphere as a whole or it can designate an ecosystem within it, as in "the oceanic world" or "the world of the rainforest." "World" can also refer to the natural-cultural milieu of a particular kingdom or species—hence "the microbial world," "the floral world," or "the world of bears." Indeed, insofar as any given organism is what Lynn Margulis calls a "symbiont"—the ongoing, multisystemic product of countless consonant and dissonant agencies—an organism can itself be called a world.

Historically, the term is chiefly temporal, as in "the medieval world" or "the modern world"; whereas politically, it is spatial, cultural, racial, religious, or all of these at once ("the Muslim world," "the Western world," "the two-thirds world"). Anthropologically, "world" encapsulates the cultural-linguistic norms of a national, racial, sexual, or indeed scientific community. Sociologically, it can refer to any number of loosely defined groups or associations, such that one might simultaneously inhabit the otherwise nonoverlapping "worlds" of Reconstructionist Judaism, CrossFit, autism awareness, and experimental jazz. Psychologically, "world" denotes the affective-relational structure of the psyche, composed as it might variously be of ancestors, parents, ex-lovers, old novels, and bad pop songs. And theologically, "world" traditionally refers to creation as distinct from the creator—Augustine's "kingdom of man" as distinct from the "kingdom of God"—the fallible, changeable order that anticipates some "other world" with which it falls tragically short. In this same register, "world" can designate more narrowly that part of creation that lies outside the physical or spiritual bounds of the community, monastery, or temple—"the secular" insofar as it is carefully demarcated from "the sacred."

*Pan*theologically, of course, these last two terms would be folded into one another, "the world" itself being the site of the sacred, of creation, destruction, and salvation—however those terms might be immanently understood. As such, there is nothing fixed or inert about such a world; nor, as we have already begun to see, can such a world be simply called singular or whole. Even in their broadest, most cosmic sense, worlds tumble into multiplicity and excess—and yet the sense persists both conceptually and linguistically that ultimately, there is "a world": a singular, gridlike structure across which more or less animate beings move, and which is in some sense different from the force that creates it—hence the charge of pantheistic incoherence. The first question to address, then, is where the idea of this singular, gridlike, derivative "world" came from.

A CLOCKWORK COSMOS

Living Alternatives

The notion that the world is a mechanical backdrop to organic life—which itself is a mechanical backdrop to human consciousness—has a fairly recent and culturally specific history. It cannot be found in Aboriginal cosmologies, whose "country" is composed of an entangled network of cocreative plants, animals, rivers, creeks, rocks, and mountains—all of which are "not primarily markers in the ground but interlocutors in the world."[10] Nor can such an insentient cosmic stage be derived from any number of indigenous American cosmologies, which often tell of primordial people who have morphed "into the biological species, geographical features, meteorological phenomena, and celestial bodies that compose the present cosmos."[11] By virtue of this originary and persistent personhood, Shawnee philosopher Thomas M. Norton-Smith explains, the multispecies assemblage that American Indians call "world" is "animate, creative . . . and constantly unfolding . . . interconnected and interdependent."[12] One striking illustration of such ongoing relational animacy can be found in Robin Wall Kimmerer's retelling of the Iroquois narrative, according to which the world of Turtle Island ("our home") is an intra-active concatenation of animals, labor, mud, gratitude, and dance.[13]

Likewise, for all its perennial dualisms, the "West" has, for the most part, animated its cosmoi. As we will recall from the previous chapter, the pre-Socratic Ionian philosophers explained the world as the autopoietic product of one or two elements; the Stoics configured it as a living divinity; the atomists imagined worlds as living and dying in an ongoing vortical dance; and Giordano Bruno proclaimed them temporary arrangements of animate, enspirited matter—alive and infinite in number. Even the alleged source of Western dualisms "himself," through the voice of his astronomer Timaeus, presents the cosmos as a "visible living being" that "contains within itself all living beings."[14] The planets and stars in this Platonic cosmology are all said to be "divine and eternal," and the earth is said to be "our foster-mother . . . the first and oldest of the gods born within the heaven."[15] To be sure, as the product of a male manufacturer-god, or demiurge, this *foster*-mother has lost the absolute priority and creative agency that previous centuries had attributed to the earth. A testament to such divine anteriority survives, however, in the Homeric Hymns (700–600 BCE) that present Gaia, or earth, as "the strong foundation, the oldest one," derived from no previous source. As "mother of all," the "Hymn to Gaia" intones, the earth "feeds everything in the world[,] / Whoever walks upon her sacred ground / or moves through the sea / or flies in the air." More fundamentally, Gaia is the one who "give[s] life to mortals and who take[s] life away."[16]

The Hymn to Gaia thus presents us with a straightforward pantheological utterance—a God-world alignment that could not possibly be accused of incoherence. To the contrary, insofar as she serves as creator, sustainer, and destroyer of all that is, the Homeric Gaia fulfills all the major functions of the deity of classical theism (who manages perennially to set the terms of philosophical coherence). The only major differences between these divinities are Gaia's immanence, materiality, and, of course, her femininity. Affirming such a world as the most fundamental of gods might therefore be aesthetically unappealing, politically undesirable, metaphysically unsatisfying, or technologically inexpedient, but it is hardly irrational. This particular god-world might not shore up the phallic preferences of mind over body, male over female, light over darkness, and a phantasmic other world over the one we are in. She might even assemble such terms into monstrous concatenations and dangerous hybridities, as does the protective-scheming, nurturing-violent Gaia of Hesiod's *Theogony*.[17] But the divinity of such a creative-destructive cosmos would not, for all that, be "absurd."

In fact, the pantheist identity between God and world becomes unthinkable only when divinity, creativity, life, and agency are fully drained from the latter—a process that culminates in the "clockwork cosmos" theory that ushered in the "new science" of the early Enlightenment. As Jessica Riskin has shown, this omnipresent metaphor configured the world "as a machine—a great clock, in seventeenth- and eighteenth-century imagery—whose parts [were] made of inert matter, moving only when set in motion by some external force, such as a clockmaker winding a spring."[18] Thus, she argues, the scientific revolution functioned theologically in its very effort to overcome theology. For on the one hand, the "brute mechanism" in this imagery sought to avoid the "mysticism" of an animate universe by insisting that the world and its constituents were mindless, insentient, and passive; but on the other hand, this same brute mechanism needed *some* sort of power to set and sustain it in motion—and if no such power could be found within the suddenly inanimate universe, then one would have to be postulated beyond it. Ironically, Riskin concludes, "a material world lacking agency assumed, indeed required, a supernatural god"—one who in fact came into being with the modern world that allegedly destroyed him.[19]

Boyle's "Admirable Automaton"

This clockwork cosmos and its sovereign engineer find exemplary pairing in Robert Boyle's *Free Enquiry into the Vulgarly Received Notion of Nature* (1686), which is concerned above all with contradicting the allegedly rampant seventeenth-century understanding that the world was animate—even divine, and maternally so. Boyle attributes varieties of this view to the pre-Socratics, the Orphic Hymns, the Stoics, and a host of Roman authors including Cicero, Pliny the Elder, and Seneca ("'There is no nature without God or God without nature: the two are identical'");[20] also Origen of Alexandria, Moses Maimonides, Menasseh Ben Israel, and an unnamed, contemporary "sect of men" who were allegedly proclaiming the identity of God and world.[21] In an alchemical text called *Atalanta Fugiens* (1617), with which Boyle was most likely familiar,[22] Michael Maier presents an image of just such an animate Mother Earth, accompanied by the epigram:

> Romulus is said to have been nursed at the coarse udders of a wolf
> But Jupiter to have been nursed by a goat, and these facts are said to be believed:
> Should we then wonder if we assert
> That the earth suckles the tender Child of the Philosophers with its milk?[23]

His Nurse Is the Earth. Michael Maier, *Atalanta Fugiens* (1617). Public domain.

Images such as Maier's have conflated cosmology and theology in order to produce what Boyle calls the contemporary "vulgar notion of nature" (9). According to this notion, the "merely material world" (106) is misconstrued as a "true and positive being" (9)—variously figured as a parent (9), "a goddess and semi-deity" (23), and most perniciously, an "intelligent and powerful being" whom God appointed at the beginning of time as "vicegerent" to manage his cosmic affairs (13). And in all of these cases, the uneducated come to mistake "nature," "the world," or "the universe" (Boyle notes the equivalence of the three terms [23]), for an active, creative, sustaining force.

As far as Boyle can see, this erroneous depiction of nature has two disastrous and interrelated consequences: it impedes the investigation of the natural world (9–10) and it "undermin[es] the foundation of religion" (62). After all, unless the world is understood as a machine rather than an animated being, natural philosophers will not be prompted to discover how its vast machinery works. And unless the world is so de-animated, God himself will be humiliated: his glory and praise usurped by the inferior power of "nature" or "world," which, Boyle insists, is so "dark and odd a thing" as not even to be a power at all (60). This divine usurpation forms the central concern of the *Free Enquiry*.

Despite his repeated insistence that he is undertaking a physiological and philosophical study rather than a theological one (4, 38), Boyle is primarily concerned in this text with defending the sovereignty of God. His chief objection to proclaiming the divinity or even the animacy of the world is that it amounts to piracy: such nature worship "defrauds the true God of divers acts of veneration and gratitude that are due to him from men . . . and diverts them to that imaginary being they call nature" (62). Rather than looking beyond the visible world to its invisible source, the adherents of this "idolatrous" metaphysic stop with the world itself, attributing to some dark-and-odd "her" the light-filled wonders that "he" has wrought. Once again, then, we hear a familiarly racialized gender panic suffusing this anti-pantheology: "instead of the true God," Boyle fumes, "they have substituted for us a kind of a goddess with the title of 'nature,'" and have given to *her* the "praise and glory" due to *him* (62). And although Boyle assures us once again that the present *Enquiry* is no work of theology, he is also eager to point out that the very first lines of Scripture contradict the "idolatrous" notions of the vulgar (30): "'In the beginning God made the heavens and the earth,'" Boyle recalls, "and in the whole account that Moses gives of the progress of it, there is not a word of the agency of nature" (38).[24] Therefore, he announces, "I hope I shall be excused, if with Moses, Job and David, I call the creatures I admire in the visible world 'the works of God' (not of nature), and praise *him rather than her* for the wisdom and goodness displayed in them" (30; emphasis added).

Ultimately, the primary mechanism of this *him*-directed praise will be mechanism itself. In the place of a living, sentient, personal, or divine cosmos, Boyle offers us a "great" or "admirable automaton" of a world composed of "subordinate" animal, vegetable, and mineral "engines," all of which have been designed, built, and set in motion by a disembodied and reassuringly male God (39, 160). Once this God establishes the overall "cosmical mechanism," Boyle explains, its numerous "particular mechanisms" merely enact the movements their maker has foreseen, executing God's eternal program according to the inexorable laws of nature (37). Referring to a famed Alsatian assemblage of mechanical animals, biblical automata, and rotating planets, Boyle therefore explains that the world

> is like a rare clock, such as may be that at Strasbourg, where all things are so skillfully contrived that the engine being once set a-moving, all things proceed according to the artificer's first design, and the motions of the little statues that at such hours perform these or those things do not require . . . the peculiar interposing of the artificer or any intelligent agent employed by him, but perform their functions upon particular occasions by virtue of the general and primitive contrivance of the whole engine.[25]

Far from requiring nature to administer his will, and even farther from being nature "herself," Boyle's clockmaker God is a supremely powerful, entirely incorporeal, and exquisitely mathematical engineer. Conversely, far from creating or animating anything at all, Boyle's world is a procession of "little statues": a predetermined, mechanical enactment of divine providence. The world is a "mere contrivance of brute matter, managed by certain laws of local motion" (11), and therefore as different as possible from its exclusively animate creator. In sum, by severing "world" completely from "God," Boyle's clockwork cosmos secures the New Science *and* a particularly totalitarian theology; more precisely, it secures the former by means of the latter. The inanimate world guarantees the regularity and calculability of the universe insofar as it augments the untrammeled power of its creator.

Newton's Demonic Determinism

We find a similarly deterministic, mechanical cosmos secured by a similarly transcendent engineer in Newtonian physics. According to Newton's

Astronomical Clock in the Cathedral in Strasbourg. Tobias Stimmer (1574).
Woodcut printed from two blocks on two sheets with letterpress text, sheet: 22. 7/16 ×
14 15/16 in. (57 × 38 cm). Anonymous Gift, 2009 (2009.157). Image copyright ©
The Metropolitan Museum of Art. Image source: Art Resource, NY.

Principia (1687), published just a year after Boyle's *Free Enquiry*, space and time are "absolute," which is to say wholly independent of the things and events that take place within them. Space is universally extended, "always similar and unmovable," and time flows inexorably from the past to the future "without regard for anything external."[26] Together, Newtonian space and time form an inert, graphic background of a world through which bodies move according to the fixed and eternal laws of physics. Infamously, however, although Newton could explain with astonishing precision the ways in which bodies moved, he could not say what it was that did the moving (in other words, he had no idea what gravity was); nor did he know how bodies came to be in the first place.[27] Indeed, Newton located numerous gaps in his law of universal gravitation, each of which he eventually concluded could only be filled by a transcendent God.[28] Moreover, and much to the consternation of his rival Gottfried Leibniz, Newton began to suggest not only that God must have created and organized the universe, but also that he must regularly intervene to keep it in equilibrium and correct irregularities.[29]

Newton uncovered most of these godly gaps in his 1692–1693 correspondence with the theologian Richard Bentley, who at the time was in the process of delivering an eight-part lecture series at Cambridge University, endowed by none other than the recently deceased Robert Boyle, for the purpose of combatting atheism. Bentley had resolved to base his lectures on Newtonian mechanics, convinced that this discipline provided incontrovertible proof of the existence of God ("Nothing," Newton wrote to Bentley, "can rejoice me more than to find it useful for that purpose").[30] And much like Boyle's, Bentley's proof lies precisely in the inanimate, mechanical workings of the world itself. Calling his lecture series "Matter and Motion Cannot Think," Bentley insists that the lifelessness of material bodies is clearly demonstrated by the unerring mathematical precision according to which they move—along with the testimony of "common" sense. After all, Bentley asks, if "sensation and perception" were "inherent in matter as such . . . [then] what monstrous absurdities would follow? Every stock and stone would be a percipient and rational creature."[31] (Once again, the animist monster rears its head.) Insofar as such universal animacy is clearly absurd, matter must be lifeless; and insofar as it is lifeless, its determinate motion through space and time must be the work of an "eternal, immaterial, intelligent Creator" who brought such machines "out of nothing," wound them up, and let them go.[32]

In the centuries that followed, Newtonian mechanics did not so much abandon its omnipotent God as it did perfect him and then take his place. In his 1814 *Philosophical Essay on Probabilities*, Pierre-Simon Laplace infamously imagined "an intelligence which could comprehend all the forces by which nature is animated and the respective situation of the beings who compose it— an intelligence sufficiently vast to submit these data to analysis."[33] If such an intelligence (whom later generations would come to call "Laplace's demon") could but know the positions, velocities, and surrounding forces of every particle in existence, Laplace promised that it would be able to predict the entirety of natural and human history: "nothing would be uncertain and the future, as the past, would be present to its eyes."[34]

According to scientific lore, when Laplace presented his fully deterministic mechanics to Napoleon, the latter asked why he had not mentioned God, and was surprised to hear Laplace respond, "I had no need of that hypothesis."[35] As numerous scholars have shown, however, Laplace was not in this gesture denying the existence of a creator; rather, he was denying the ongoing "tinkering" that Newton had imagined God must perform upon the cosmos.[36] Indeed, Laplace says clearly in his *Exposition du système du monde* (1796) that if Newton had fully understood the behavior of physical bodies, he would have realized that the "conditions of the arrangement of the planets and satellites are precisely those that ensure its stability."[37] In this case, far from needing the hypothesis of a divine tinkerer, Newton would have affirmed God as the creator of a flawless cosmic clock (much like Boyle's)—a perpetual motion machine that needs no further intervention.

Inanimacy and Dominion

Lest we think modern science has overcome its theological origins, this mechanistic divinity persists in the strict determinism proclaimed by—to name a few—classical physicists, "many-worlds" quantum theorists, mathematical realists, neo-Darwinian biologists, and those bio-cognitivists who privilege material reduction over emergence or plasticity. "Within this [classical mechanical] view of nature," Lee Smolin explains, "nothing happens except the rearrangement of particles according to timeless laws, so . . . the future is already completely determined by the present, as the present was by the past."[38] Seen in this light, the "timeless laws" of the contemporary natural sciences retain the function of the New Scientists' God: they establish and maintain the being and movement of everything that is and moves, transcending the world of materiality and change that they impassively govern.

As we have therefore begun to see, the allegedly immanent sciences born in the wake of Bruno's execution produce a surprisingly transcendent theology:

as in the early-modern period, the mechanistic regularity of the contemporary scientific world attests to the existence of a creator beyond it, whether this be a personal divinity or impersonal, eternal law. Far from beginning with the scientific revolution, however, this denigration of the world—and its concomitant elevation of one or another extramundane god—can be said to take initial hold during the long Christian battle with, and eventual victory over, all that it branded as "paganism." Historian Lynn White has famously tracked the ecological consequences of this effort, which removed all traces of vitality from the earth and its constituents in order to augment the power of its extra-cosmic Father. In turn, this Father shored up the privilege of those humans said to be made in his image—those beings to whom God granted dominion over the rest of the cosmos.[39] And although White does not mention this particular doctrine, it seems important to emphasize that from the third century onward, this Father was also said to create the universe, not out of a preexisting primordial material, but rather out of nothing at all (*ex nihilo*).[40] Far from having creative capacities of its own, materiality under orthodox construction does not even *exist* independently of God.

This "materiaphobic" theology, which took root in late antiquity and found its apotheosis in the clockwork cosmos of the seventeenth century, had the embodied effect and indeed the motivation of subjecting "nature" and its "resources" to private and colonial possession. Such ownership increased, in turn, the techno-scientific *use* of such "resources." In other words, the recoding of animal, mineral, vegetable, and nonwhite human lives as *machinery* conditioned their unrestrained exploitation—an exploitation that would have been impossible without the rigorously anti-pantheological operations of imperial Christianity. As White explains,

> In Antiquity every tree, every spring, every stream, every hill had its own *genius loci*, its guardian spirit. These spirits were accessible to men, but were very unlike men; centaurs, fauns, and mermaids show their ambivalence. Before one cut a tree, mined a mountain, or dammed a brook, it was important to placate the spirit in charge of that particular situation, and to keep it placated. By destroying pagan animism, Christianity made it possible to exploit nature in a mood of indifference to the feelings of natural objects.[41]

Of course, the chimera that White names (centaurs, fauns, mermaids) are all specific to Greek antiquity. But the drive to de-animate the landscape has persisted throughout the spatiotemporal adventure of Christian imperialism in its tentacular entanglement with industrial capitalism and techno-science.

In nearly every continent on earth, over the course of centuries, the steady denial of life to the earth and its constituents has secured cheap (even "free") materials for Western overdevelopment, overriding countervailing indigenous and endogenous cosmologies by converting, enslaving, disciplining, and destroying their adherents ("the smell of the burned witches still hangs in our nostrils," writes the ecofeminist Neopagan Starhawk.[42]) In short, the pantheological *divinity of the world* is only unthinkable under the historically specific regime of a theo-techno-politics whose ascendance has had disastrous racial, gendered, and ecological consequences. What, then, would it mean to think the world—or a world, or many worlds—otherwise?

THE UNGODLY, UNGAINLY REBIRTH OF GAIA

Revelation

In the late twentieth and early twenty-first centuries, the lifeless world and its inagential inhabitants have undergone a particularly dramatic process of reanimation at the hands of the ever-contentious Gaia hypothesis. The idea first occurred to the chemist and inventor James Lovelock, who realized while developing instruments for NASA's extraterrestrial pursuits in the mid-1960s that the chemical composition of other planets was strikingly different from that of Earth. Carbon dioxide makes up 95 percent of the atmospheres of Venus and Mars, but only .03 percent of the atmosphere of Earth.[43] Venus and Mars maintain a chemically stable balance of gases, whereas the Earth's atmosphere is "far from chemical equilibrium," containing far too much oxygen relative to its levels of methane, hydrogen, and nitrogen.[44] Of course, most living things need oxygen, so it is fortuitous that Earth has so much of it. The question is, *why*? Why does the Earth, unlike any other planet around us, have such bio-friendly tendencies?

Positioned as it is between Venus and Mars, one would expect Earth to resemble them with respect not only to oxygen levels, but also "to acidity, [gas] composition, redox potential, and temperature history"—and yet Earth differs dramatically from its neighbors in each of these respects, enabling the emergence and proliferation of life as we know it.[45] What, then, has produced this "anomalous atmosphere"?[46] The theistic temptation, of course, is to attribute our finely tuned earth-world to an intelligent designer, who set the planet's conditions just right for "us." The scientific convention, by contrast, is to chalk it up to accident. Unlike every other planet around us, the thinking goes, Earth just happens to be well-suited to the existence of slime molds and grasses and donkeys—and if any variable were different, "life would have been annihilated."[47] Caught between the two equally unsatisfying possibilities of God and chance, Lovelock (in what he tends to recount as a road to Damascus experience) was hit in a flash by a third: "it suddenly dawned on me that somehow life was regulating climate," Lovelock testifies; "suddenly the image of the Earth as a living organism able to regulate its temperature and chemistry at a comfortable steady state emerged in my mind."[48]

This, then, is the origin story of Lovelock's suggestion that "the temperature and composition of the Earth's atmosphere are actively regulated by the sum of life on the planet—the biota."[49] Living things, Lovelock declared, produce the very conditions they need to live. Along this interpretation, then, the "environment" is no inert background to organic life; neither can organisms be reduced to mechanical "engines" set in preordained motion. Rather, the Earth and its inhabitants form an emergent, cocreative, "complex entity involving the Earth's biosphere, atmosphere, oceans and soil; the totality constituting a feedback or cybernetic system which seeks an optimal physical and chemical environment for life on this planet."[50] Immediately upon conceiving this idea, Lovelock sensed that it needed a less ponderous name than "self-regulating, homeostatic, cybernetic system." He appealed to his classically trained friend, the novelist William Golding (author of *Lord of the Flies*), who "without hesitation . . . recommended that this creature be called Gaia, after the Greek Earth goddess."[51]

Perhaps unsurprisingly, however, the idea was instantaneously and nearly unanimously ridiculed: "The biologists hated [Gaia] right from the beginning," Lovelock reports in an interview; "they loathed it."[52] Indeed, members of the neo-Darwinist establishment rejected the idea on numerous grounds: the Earth, they quibbled, does not reproduce or take part in natural selection and so cannot be called an "organism;"[53] life-forms are strictly self-interested and therefore could not behave "altruistically" for the good of other species;[54] plants, bacteria, and the Earth itself cannot be said to act with anything like "intention";[55] Gaia makes the earth seem too harmonious and kind;[56] and, of course, an earth goddess has no business occupying the center of a respectable biological theory.[57] "Gaia is just an evil religion," wrote one biologist; Lovelock is a "holy fool," cautioned another.[58] But perhaps none was as colorfully dismissive of Lovelock's "pseudoscientific mythmaking" as the English microbiologist John Postgate. In a *New Scientist* article dismissively titled, "Gaia Gets Too Big for Her Boots," Postgate scoffs, "Gaia—the Great Earth Mother! The planetary organism! Am I the only biologist to suffer a nasty twitch, a feeling of unreality, when the media invite me again to take it seriously?"[59]

What makes Postgate particularly twitchy is the gendered, theological personification of this Great Earth Mother—who began as an "amusing, fanciful" figure, but who has become surprisingly popular in the public eye, rapidly "metamorphos[ing] . . . first into a hypothesis, later into a theory, then into something terribly like a cult."[60] Faced with such terrifying irrationality, Postgate can hardly bear to imagine what might happen next: "Will tomorrow bring hordes of militant Gaiaist activists enticing some pseudoscientific idiocy on the community crying, 'There is no God but Gaia and Lovelock is her prophet?'"[61] Although he is doubtless unaware of the generic resonance, Postgate's vitriolic tone and visceral disgust in the face of an animate earth are strikingly reminiscent of the anti-pantheist literature of the seventeenth through nineteenth centuries. And true to convention, Postgate's fear is encoded as multitudinous (hordelike), feminine ("the Great Earth Mother!"), irrational ("pseudoscientific idiocy"), and orientalist ("there is no God but Gaia"—a mockery of the Muslim *Shahada*). The only real distinction is that, far from being construed as passive—as they were construed under colonial rule—the racialized hordes in the "post"-colonial 1980s are now rendered "militant." The threat of an Eastern takeover is still palpable, but the dark pantheists at

Gaia Gets Too Big for Her Boots. Peter Schrank (1975). Permission granted by the artist.

the gates have morphed from drowsy ladies in waiting into hysterical mothers threatening revolt. "Lovelock's Earth goddess," the subheading reads, "has ideas above her station."

Co-Implications

Perhaps in part because she had been subject to similarly gender-based denigrations,[62] Lynn Margulis became an early ally of Lovelock's, advancing the hypothesis significantly by identifying the specific microbial sources of the Earth's thermochemical anomalies.[63] Her earlier work on symbiosis and symbiogenesis made her particularly well-suited to this effort, insofar as Gaia, in the words of one critic, can be seen as "symbiosis . . . of global dimensions."[64] This work also led Margulis to perform a significant conceptual departure from Lovelock: whereas he was happy to call Gaia "a single organism"—at least for the sake of getting a point across[65]—Margulis was insistent that the Earth is not by any means a single organism.[66] Just as interdependent cells and bacteria, or fungi and trees, amount not to individuals but to "symbionts," the chimerical multitudes of Gaia compose not a monistic whole but interdetermined multiplicities. "Much more appropriate is the claim that Gaia is an interacting system," Margulis writes with microbiologist Oona West, "the components of which are organisms."[67] And of course, any given organism is itself a microbial multitude, or in Darwin's own words, "a microcosm—a little universe, formed of a host of self-propagating organisms, inconceivably minute and numerous as the stars in heaven."[68] So "it is symbionts all the way down,"[69] and it is multiplicity all the way up: Margulis's Gaia can be neither reduced to individuals nor gathered into a whole.

Even as Margulis resists the micro- and macrocosmic structures of singularity, however, she affirms and augments the *agency* that Lovelock attributes to this mutliplicitous monster of energy. According to the Gaia hypothesis, the atmosphere is not simply given—not just accidentally the way it is—rather, it is affected and even "actively controlled" by the biosphere. This work takes place primarily through the tireless activity of microorganisms, whose metabolic processes create the gases that organisms need to live.[70] For example, prokaryotic microbes generate and release the molecular oxygen that is toxic to many of them but crucial to all larger life-forms. In fact, Margulis and Lovelock venture, it was most likely these prokaryotes that transformed the earth from an anaerobic to an aerobic environment two billion years ago, setting the stage for larger and more complex (but arguably less industrious) organisms to evolve.

Algae and green plants, of course, increase this oxygen production by process-ing photosynthetically the carbon dioxide released by aerobic respiration and combustion. Soil bacteria convert dissolved nitrates into the stable nitrogen gas needed to form proteins and nucleic acids. The list goes on and becomes recur-sive, with waste turning into fuel and byproducts turning into building blocks.

Taken all together, then, the system amounts to a negative feedback mecha-nism—like a thermostat—wherein thermochemical disturbances are absorbed and redistributed to maintain relative homeostasis throughout the system.[71] The oceans' alkalinity holds steady at about 3.5 percent; oxygen levels remain high enough to keep breathing things breathing but low enough not to set the planet on fire; and the temperature of the Earth—at least until recently—has remained within a bio-friendly band of about 10 degrees Celsius, even though the sun's luminosity has increased somewhere between 40 and 300 percent over the course of its lifetime.[72] In short, Gaia is autopoietic (or, to accept Haraway's lexical correction, sympoietic):[73] in their various symbioses, compostings, recombinations, and parasitisms, living things produce and sustain the condi-tions that produce and sustain them.

It is in this sense that Gaia can be said to be alive: "her" innumerable, inter-locking, and non-totalized systems do the active work of regulating the climate. For Lovelock, however, speaking this way is a matter not of metaphysics but of expedience. He came upon the idea that the Earth, far from being accidentally suitable for life, was itself creating the conditions that made it so suitable, and "at such moments," he quips, "there is no time or place for such niceties as the qualification, 'of course it is not alive—it merely behaves as if it were.'"[74] And it is precisely at this point that indigenous philosophies might congratu-late earth-systems science for having finally caught up to what it has known all along; as Vine Deloria attests, "traditional Indians," who have always asserted the animacy of the universe, "are quite amused to see this revival of the debate over whether the planet is alive."[75] But it is here that Lovelock draws the line, on those occasions when he is interested in drawing lines. In a popular book from 1991 titled *Healing Gaia: Practical Medicine for the Planet* (note Gaia's metaphoric demotion from agent to patient, from creator to victim), Lovelock concedes that, technically speaking, the Earth is not alive. "When I talk of a living planet," he explains, "*I am not thinking in an animistic way*, of a planet with sentience, or of rocks that can move by their own volition and purpose. I think of anything the Earth may do, such as regulating the climate, as auto-matic, not through an act of will, and all of it within the strict bounds of sci-ence."[76] Even for this notorious renegade, then, "the line" still lies between a persistently mechanistic science and a perennially denigrated animism. Even for Lovelock the "holy fool," rocks are not persons, and Earth neither feels nor wills nor intends. Rather, the system, which his syntax almost always renders in the singular, operates automatically and unconsciously to maintain planetary homeostasis.

Margulis, by contrast, is far less concerned than Lovelock to protect "science" from animism, the automatic from the intentional, the one from the many, or homeostasis from change. In fact, Margulis explicitly appeals to "Native American perception" as one way of countering the neo-Darwinist mechanism to which Lovelock is arguably still in partial thrall.[77] Citing the Squamish leader Chief Seattle, Margulis insists that "humanity belongs to the Earth"—not, as the anthropocentric biological establishment would have it, the other way around. From the perspective of Chief Seattle's and Margulis's "autopoietic and nonmechanical" belonging-to-the-Earth, it becomes clear that humans are not by any measure the most important or evolved beings on earth. Rather, the "truly productive organisms," the ones who truly matter and act and (therefore) *are*, are the earth-others who condition the possibility of everything we tend to consider superior to them.[78] Specifically, for Margulis, the most significant life-forms are the protists and bacteria that build, shape, and constitute Gaia.

Margulis thus turns the Great Chain of Being on its head, attributing agency primarily to those previously "subordinate engines" relegated to the lowest ranks of the Neoplatonic-turned-neo-Darwinist hierarchy. Against the dominant lineage of Western metaphysics—including Descartes, his latter-day disciples who obsess over the "hard problem of consciousness," and even Lovelock with his "engineeristic and physiological automatisms"—Margulis insists that there are "cognitive symbiogenetic processes operating at [the level of] elementary matter."[79] Chemostatic bacteria can "smell" their surroundings so as to "swim toward sugar and away from acid."[80] Protists refuse to interact with the particular mold spores that they know they can't ingest.[81] Bacteria of all "species" choose to congregate rather than live separately; they perform "hypersex" (horizontal gene transfer rather than direct filiation); they know how to clone; they manipulate their chemical surroundings; and they generate new technologies and life-forms by incorporating external bodies into their chimerical "own."[82] As Margulis and Sagan therefore conclude with microbiologist Ricardo Guerrero, the idea "that bacteria are simply machines, with no sensation or consciousness, seems no more likely than Descartes' claim that dogs suffer no pain."[83]

It should be noted that Descartes himself did not go nearly so far as to suggest that nonhuman animals do not suffer—even though the position was immediately ascribed to him and even though some of his philosophical descendants did, indeed, adopt it.[84] What Descartes *did* deny was that nonhuman animals could *think*, a denial Margulis flatly rejects by attributing cognition not only to dogs and plants but also to the microbes that compose dirt and rocks themselves. "When I describe the origin of the eukaryotic cell merger," she insists, "I emphasize that the components that fused in symbiogenesis are already 'conscious' entities."[85] They are conscious, again, in the sense that they are able to interpret their surroundings and weigh and make decisions—both for their own benefit and for that of the larger organic symbionts whose existence they make possible. In Margulis's inverted cosmology, then, bacteria become the intelligent designers. Indeed, she goes so far as to confess in a burst of upside-down Neoplatonism that "we animals . . . *emanate* from the microcosm."[86]

Protestations

Even as she rigorously reanimates the tiny lives that compose and decompose the cosmos, however, Margulis is careful to stop short of explicit deification. Indeed, she is far more reluctant than Lovelock even to personify the animate Earth. Her concern in this regard seems to be threefold: first, she is trying to avoid the singularity such personification seems to consolidate; second, she is hoping to forestall the gendered associations of love and care that "Mother Earth" tends to import into existentially neutral systems theories; and third, and most energetically, she is seeking to guard biology against the intrusion of those enthusiasts she at one point derides as "anti-intellectual and hysterically toned New Age . . . crystal swingers."[87] Margulis speaks to all of these concerns at once when she insists, "I cannot stress strongly enough that Gaia is not a single organism. My Gaia is no vague, quaint notion of a mother Earth who nurtures us. The Gaia hypothesis is *science*."[88]

Considering the venomous accusations leveled against Lovelock and Margulis, alleged priests of some dark cult of Gaia, and considering the ongoing refusal of the politically influential American Christian Right to acknowledge or fund research in evolution and climate change, it is certainly understandable that both of these scientists seek to distinguish their hypothesis at all costs from "religion." At the same time, they are in some sense aware that they have spent their adult lives summoning and reconfiguring an ur-goddess, and they are in some sense aware that a metaphor can never quite *just* be a metaphor. Thus, we hear the stammering in Lovelock's otherwise rigorous repudiation: "[Gaia] *sort of* precludes religion *almost*. It is the atheist's dream *in a way*."[89] This is absolutely not religion, he insists . . . sort of, almost, in a way.

What Lovelock's charming string of unsayings allows us to specify is that the sympoietic Gaia "precludes," not so much "religion," as it does a particular way of conceiving divinity. An Earth whose interlocking systems assemble and maintain themselves has no need for an extra-cosmic, anthropomorphic deity to get or keep it going; as Lovelock insists, Gaia has from the beginning been "running itself. It doesn't need God interfering."[90] Similarly, Margulis and Sagan maintain that "there is nothing mystical in the process at all . . . no unknown conscious forces need be invoked."[91] But the God they are all denying is a God who would be *different* from the self-creative, self-destructive world. What they do not consider explicitly—even as they lay nearly all its groundwork and even call it by name—is that the pan-agential set of sympoietic assemblages we deceptively singularize as "world" might themselves be divine. There are, however, microscopic openings to such a possibility, peeking here and there through the exuberant denials. Lovelock concedes at one point that Gaian science "begins to veer into that area previously occupied by religion," but admits that such geobiology is poorly equipped to come to terms with "the ethical significance" of an animate earth.[92] And Margulis and Sagan go so far as to admit that "the 'feminization' of a patriarchal god into an Earth mother, from a sky-based deity to an atmospherically veiled yet a measurable entity: these are in need of rigorous mythological analysis."[93] That said, they leave it to others to undertake such analysis.

How to Avoid Godding

The seeming divinity of Lovelock's and Margulis's Gaia continues to prompt spirited objections to it—most recently in the form of earth system scientist Toby Tyrrell's 2013 *On Gaia*. The aim of this compendium of oceanography, geology, biology, and ecology is to discredit the Gaia hypothesis by enumerating the climatic imbalances endemic to, and escalating throughout, the biosphere. Contrary to the position Tyrrell attributes to Lovelock (he mentions Margulis only once, as the [derivative] advocate of endosymbiosis who became Lovelock's negligible "co-author"), Tyrrell maintains that "life" clearly does not "promote stability and keep conditions favorable to life."[94] There is, in other words, no such thing as "Gaia"—no benevolent mother-god who keeps the earth in balance and who, in the face of an increasingly toxic atmosphere, deforestation, mass extinctions, refugee crises, and a rising and acidifying sea,

might step in to save us from ourselves.[95] In terms of its argumentative framing, at least, the book therefore amounts to an anti-teleological argument, or
an argument for un-design: whereas natural theologians marshal evidence of
cosmic beauty and function to prove the existence of an intelligent creator,
Tyrrell marshalls evidence of cosmic inharmony and chaos to undermine "the
existence of Gaia."[96]

Tyrrell's book becomes the critical point of departure for a lecture that
Bruno Latour called, "How to Make Sure Gaia is Not God?" As far as Latour
is concerned, Tyrrell's argument is a questionable endeavor to begin with:
"attempting to prove the [non] existence of God," he writes, "seems to me
a strange exercise for a grown up."[97] Its puerility aside, Latour argues that
Tyrrell's anti-demonstration is moreover based on a dramatic misconstrual of
Gaia. Lovelock's and Margulis's Gaia, Latour counters, is neither providential
nor kind—especially not with respect to human concerns. Nor, crucially, can
Gaia be said to be a single being guiding the earth. Rather, "she" stands in the
way of individuals and totalities alike by naming the persistent interdetermi-
nation of beings and world. The point, Latour reminds us, is precisely not that
there is a being called "Evolution capital E, or Life capital L, or Gaia capital
G" that molds or regulates bio-atmospheric processes "from the outside."[98]
Rather, what we are facing—what we are in the inescapable midst of—is an
"extended pluralism" wherein the alleged whole exists on the same plane as
the parts. More precisely, the "parts" are not parts and as such do not form
a whole; rather, what "Gaia" means is that "you cannot distinguish between
organisms and their environments any longer."[99] The boundary between
"inside" and "outside"—the very one that nineteenth-century anthropologists
accused animist "primitives" of being unable to abide—has disappeared. And
so "there is no whole"—no force or being back behind or up above the constant interplay of forces or beings.[100]

It is for this reason, Latour points out, that Lovelock keeps changing the way
he talks about Gaia: as far as Latour can see, Lovelock is trying at every turn "to
make sure Gaia is not a God." Citing one short passage in which Lovelock refers
to Gaia in rapid succession as a "control system," "a self-regulating system,"
a "thermostat," an "evolving system," and an "emergent domain," Latour suggests that Lovelock is using names strategically, provisionally, fleetingly—aware
that none of them is quite right: "it is difficult to describe," sighs Lovelock at
the end of his onomastic outpouring.[101] Filled with admiration, Latour asks,
"See how he struggles? How he makes sure each metaphor is seen as such
and counterpoise[es] it, immediately, with another linguistic precaution?"[102]
This, Latour suggests, is the only way (not) to speak of Gaia, the only way to

make sure she does not become a whole, or a "level 2" unity beyond the biotic fray—in other words, a god. The interdeterminate non-totality of Gaia must be named by many names so as not to be encompassed by any of them. In fact, the point is the over-saying itself, which according to Latour prevents the "godding" of Gaia.

True to form (and content), Latour himself performs this overnaming in the course of the lecture, calling out some of the countless ways that Gaia has already been invoked. To be sure, these names are not equal. Latour is clearly suggesting that "Nanny-Gaia," " Gaia-Nurturing Mother," "Gaia-Kaiser," and "Gaia-Air Conditioning System" are not nearly as heuristically, critically, or ecologically promising as "Gaia the Party Spoiler," "Gaia the Gate-Crasher," "Gaia-Sympoietic," or "Gaia the Uncommon-Commons."[103] Again, Latour enacts this multiplicitous outpouring to "make sure Gaia is not God." And yet in all of these over- and unsayings, Latour recapitulates a classic theological strategy—namely, the "negative" or "apophatic" effort to call God by every name, thereby acknowledging and preserving God's transcendence of all of them.

It is not clear to what extent Latour is aware that he is in such deceptively theological waters. The most straightforward sign of such awareness is his parenthetical admission that his numerous Gaian epithets sound like their Marian analogues ("'Queen of Heaven,' 'God-Bearer,' 'Star of the Sea,' 'Mater Misericordiae,' 'Rose of the Garden,' and so on") and that such an enumeration constitutes "a nice ritual indeed worth extending to Gaia's cult!"[104] Another clue can be found in the very title of the lecture ("How to Make Sure Gaia is Not a God"), which sounds uncannily like Jacques Derrida's "How to Avoid Speaking: Denials," in which the latter demonstrates in relation to Pseudo-Dionysius and Meister Eckhart the tragicomic impossibility of asserting that a negative-critical strategy—in this case, deconstruction—is *not* negative theology.[105] Finally, Latour comes closest to admitting the theological resonances of his anti-theological effort in the last line of his lecture. "Let us ask this Gaia," he implores his audience, "to save us from taking her as a God."[106] At first, the utterance seems playful: Latour is couching an impassioned denial of Gaia's godhood in a prayer to the one it denies, thereby lampooning the divinity in question. At the same time, however, this playfulness mirrors the utter seriousness of the apophatic quest, famously encapsulated in Eckhart's own proto-Latourian "therefore I pray to God to make me free of God."[107]

What Eckhart meant with this prayer was that, as the soul seeks to divest itself of every conceptual idol that might stand between itself and God, it eventually needs to give up not only itself, but "God," as well, which is to say the God who stands as an object of and for the appropriative subject. It is only when the

soul knows and has and is nothing—"not God or created things or himself"—
that the nothingness of God can take place within the nothingness of the soul,
making it fully divine.[108] (Perhaps unsurprisingly, Eckhart's theology was condemned as heretical because of teachings that would later be called "pantheist.")[109] If it is the case that Latour is indeed channeling this line of (un)thought,
then his prayer to Gaia to free him of "Gaia" can be understood as an effort to
abandon all conceptual abstractions—all "level 2" holisms—and to bring Gaia
down to the mundane sphere she both constitutes and interrupts. In Latour as
in Eckhart, the extreme edge of apophatic transcendence would thus give way
to cataphatic immanence, *the no-God tumbling into the all-God*—as long, once
again, as "all" is understood as irreducibly many and motley: both more and
less than "one." And indeed, in the revised version of this lecture, Latour has
changed the title to "How to Make Sure Gaia is not a God *of Totality*," leaving
open the possibility of other ways of configuring divinity.[110] But we are getting
ahead of ourselves. Back to the "world" that Gaia both composes and decom-
poses, both interrupts and is.

Unworlded World

Anthropocenities

Latour delivered this lecture on ungodding Gaia as part of a 2014 international
conference organized by philosopher Déborah Danowski and anthropologist
Eduardo Viveiros de Castro in Rio de Janeiro, titled, "The Thousand Names of
Gaia: from the Anthropocene to the Age of the Earth." The conference sought
to deploy both indigenous and Western perspectives on the concept of "world"
in order to unsettle the increasingly omnipresent language of "the Anthropocene."[111] As is well known, climate change scientists proposed use of this term at
the start of the millennium and adopted it in 2016 to mark the epoch in which
humans began to exert climatic and geological influence over the planet, changing the composition of the air, rocks, waters, and soils that create and sustain
terrestrial life.[112] Although theorists debate the precise timing of this epoch,[113]
the events that most directly catalyzed the Anthropocene escalated "in the latter part of the eighteenth century, when analyses of air trapped in polar ice
showed the beginning of growing global concentrations of carbon dioxide and
methane. This date also happens to coincide with James Watt's design of the
steam engine in 1784."[114] Object-oriented philosopher Timothy Morton therefore credits Watt's invention with having brought about "the end of the world,"

which is to say the end of any romantic, harmonious holism that might quell our anxieties and dull our thinking. For Morton, the advent of the Anthropocene marks the impossibility of gathering the unassimilable mess of things into "some abstract entity such as Nature or environment or *world*."[115] Caught as we are within the toxic, inexorable, massively distributed "hyperobject" of anthropogenic climate change, there is, Morton insists, no "world" left to speak of. But just as there may be ways of thinking about divinity without capitulating to the "level 2" holism of "God," there may well be worlds beneath the unworlded World of the Anthropocene. In fact, this very terminology might be preventing us from imagining worlds otherwise.

Insofar as the term "Anthropocene" might help to alert policy-makers about the gravity of our self-imposed terrestrial condition, it might well prove strategically useful for this or that climate summit, recycling initiative, or set of emissions regulations. One problem with the apocalyptic "Anthropocene," however, is that it tends to inspire a disturbing level of "cynicism," "defeatism," or indeed "passive nihilism" by granting the disaster the seemingly inexorable status of a geological epoch: there is, it might seem, nothing to be done—no way to live otherwise.[116] A twin danger is that the Anthropocene risks elevating and even celebrating the untrammeled power of the agents of global disaster, "ascrib[ing] to *Homo sapiens* a 'destinal' (even if only destructive) power over the planet's history."[117] Moreover, the Anthropocene falsely universalizes these destructive agents as "the *anthropos*," when the blame lies not with "humanity" as such but with its particularly eco-cidal, white Euro-American, industrial-capitalist subspecies. This backdoor deification of those who regulate the boundaries of "humanity" can be detected above all in the escalating suggestions that any number of geoengineering techniques might patch up the ozone layer, scrub the atmosphere, and refreeze the glaciers.[118] We should beware, Donna Haraway cautions, of capitulating to the alluring "cosmofaith in technofixes."[119] After all, such technologies—which reliably promise to deliver profit as well as a habitably hacked planet—are the product of the colonially and genocidally fueled white-industrial capitalism that created the disaster they now endeavor to fix. As James Cone asks, "Do we really think that the culture most responsible for the ecological crisis will also provide the moral and intellectual resources for the earth's liberation?"[120]

Less impending than already underway, the late-capitalist end of the world has prompted a growing number of anthropological, political, new-materialist, and science-studies theorists to try to come to different terms with the cataclysm that "the Anthropocene" only seems to escalate. Summoning variously minoritarian and multispecies assemblages, they seek to imagine and build worlds otherwise, right here at the end of the world. And strikingly, many of them turn in these endeavors to the figure of Gaia. Gaia, for these authors, names the nearly impossible injunction "to exit the Anthropocene both intellectually and 'phenomenologically'"—to re-world in the midst of a planetary unworlding.[121]

Living in Question

A common touchstone for these re-worlders is Isabelle Stengers' annunciation of Gaia's "intrusion."[122] Far from guaranteeing a stable climate, a breathable atmosphere, or well-behaved oceans—and even farther from remaining an unchanging, inanimate stage for human "progress"—Stengers tells us that Gaia has intruded into a smug human history to upend all of it. Neither inert background nor loving mother, Gaia is the "event" that "calls us into question"—we self-appointed masters of creation who thought we were somehow in charge.[123] Stengers calls this event "transcendent" in the sense that it exceeds and unsettles the order and aims of "Man."[124] But of course, Gaia is a wholly immanent transcendence: a worldly disruption that is none other than the world itself, an uncanniness that is not only in our midst, but which *is* our midst. An interruption of that which we thought was a background—whether lifeless, maternal, or both—and whose unassimilable animacy ought, frankly, to terrify us. (Here we may recall that the goat-god of nature, much like Stengers' Gaia, strikes panic in the hearts of those he interrupts.)

Although this disruptive event may seem a departure from Lovelock's homeostasis and Margulis's sympoiesis, Stengers' Gaia is in a sense fully consistent with "the Gaia hypothesis," even in its earliest incarnations. Convinced of this consistency, Latour summarizes Lovelock's discovery as a perfect inversion of Galileo's: if the latter discovered that the Earth was just another planet, the former discovered that the Earth was, in fact, special: unlike every other planet in our solar system, it is way out of equilibrium, which is to say, alive.[125] But as Danowski and Viveiros de Castro remind us, disequilibrium is by definition an unreliable state. "What led Lovelock to Gaia," they write, "was precisely the incongruity and fragility of this niche of negentropy that is [the] living Earth—which can of course cease to exist at any moment."[126] Life on a Gaian earth is therefore neither a providential nor an evolutionary necessity, but rather a "cosmological hapax," subject to dramatic change in the hands of the very organisms that compose it.[127] Gaia, in this light, *is* the intrusion that calls (especially human) order into question.

Lovelock's and Margulis's central insight, we will recall, was that living things change the "environment" to such an extent that it is incoherent to speak of an environment at all; Gaia is the open, interlocking biotic systems that determine her condition. Stengers admits that "Lovelock perhaps went a bit too far in affirming that this processual coupling ensured a stability."[128] In recent years, however, Lovelock has clearly announced the end of anything like planetary homeostasis—an end he attributes primarily to "overpopulation." "It's not simply too much carbon dioxide in the air or the loss of biodiversity as forests are cleared," he insists; "the root cause is too many people, their pets, and their livestock—more than the Earth can carry."[129] As feminist and de-colonial interlocutors are quick to point out, however, the problem is not "people" as such; it is the wealthy inhabitants of overdeveloped nations who have built their industrial and now informatic worlds on the desecration of the worlds of others. It would take five earthlike planets to sustain the energy "needs" of the average American, Stengers reminds us; hence the growing theoretical preference for the term "Capitalocene" over "Anthropocene."[130] The *anthropos*, if there is such a thing, isn't the problem.

Perhaps the cruelest irony of this Gaianic interruption is that the first beings to suffer from our violently changing climate have been and will continue to be those nonhumans and humans who have had little or no hand in provoking it: the poor, the unincorporated, the unrepresented, the forcibly invisible, and the allegedly inaudible. Eventually, however, the planet will become uninhabitable for even the whitest and wealthiest bipeds—a fate that Margulis, never a prophet of homeostasis, judges to be in the planet's best interests. "Gaia, a tough bitch, is not at all threatened by humans," she assures us. In fact, she suggests, Gaia will be far better off once she is rid of the "upright mammalian weeds" to which *homo sapiens* amount.[131] After the Anthropocene, the real agents of life will do the work they have always done of creating *ex mortuis*: as Margulis reminds us, "bacterial life is resilient. It has fed on disaster and destruction from the beginning."[132] Indeed, it has made whole worlds out of it.

Unbecomings

To touch base with our reading of Spinoza, then, it turns out that "nature" is not the eternal, unchanging source of all things that allowed the "renegade Jew" to equate "her" with a fairly traditional—if impersonal—God. Far from unfolding a determinate order, "nature" changes—becoming, unbecoming, and becoming-otherwise. And as it turns out, the agents of this (un)becoming are precisely those "expressions" of *Deus sive natura* that Spinoza calls "modes": namely, concrete, particular organisms. With the intrusion of Gaia, we are therefore confronted with the full collapse of the distinction we anticipated in Spinoza between a purportedly singular substance and "its" multiplicitous modes. What we have come to call "the environment" is none other than those living things that, far from being secondary to nature "itself," compose and decompose it in an ongoing process of un- and re-worlding.

Gaianically speaking, then, there is no independent, Newtonian grid across which beings move. To the contrary, insofar as organisms make and unmake Gaia, they condition the possibility of space and time themselves, which is to say "the world," "the beginning," and "the end." As Danowski and Viveiros de Castro therefore proclaim, "our world has ceased to be Kantian."[133] Far from being a priori categories, it seems that space and time, those allegedly transcendental conditions of experience, are themselves experientially conditioned: The situation is indeed remarkable. As Latour muses, even the most stalwart "social constructivists" of the pre-Skokal era would never have dared to suggest that the air and rocks around us, much less *space* and *time*, were culturally conditioned.[134] And yet this is precisely what the sturdily scientific Anthropocene announces: the "natural world" in which we live, move, and have our being is shaped and unraveled by the cultural patterns of the livers, movers, and beings who form its entangled multitude.

As such, "the world" cannot be said to be *one* except as what James calls a "subject of discourse."[135] It will always make grammatical sense to refer to "the world" in the singular; nevertheless, "it" cannot at this point be distinguished from its constitutive "they" and as such tumbles inexorably into multiplicity—into the "little hangings-together, little worlds" of James's pluralistic pantheism.[136] In this case, what we mean by "world" consists of innumerable, interconstituted agencies that work in astonishing resonance and excruciating dissonance both with and against one another (well, many-another), amounting not to a *uni*verse but to a *multi*verse in the Jamesian sense: an open set of coherences and incoherences that refuse to be assembled into oneness—except, again, as a subject of discourse. We can always refer for strategic purposes to "the world," but as Latour reminds us, the Stengerian "intrusion of Gaia" means that "*cosmos* has become, to put it bluntly, a mess, certainly a cacophony, or to use another blunt Greek term, a *cacosmos*."[137]

Insofar as "world" tends to connote an ordered whole, unaffected by the carryings-on of its inhabitants, the intrusion of Gaia does indeed mean the end of the world. And the end of the world means the end of worlds of all sorts: not only conceptually, but experientially, we are undergoing the loss of island nations, ecosystems, and of course innumerable animal and vegetable organisms, each of which amounts to a biosocial *world* composed of countless trans-species symbionts. Danowski and Viveiros de Castro have noted that ever since the geophysical sciences reached a consensus in the 1990s regarding greenhouse gases and anthropogenic climate change, there has been an intensified outpouring in popular and scholarly productions of apocalyptic narratives: a "disphoric [sic.] efflorescence" of "grim catastrophism"[138] that continually confronts us with any number of thermo-military-oceanic-nuclear-biotoxic-zombie-alien generalized death-scapes. There is, it seems, a justifiably widespread *panic* over the escalating loss of *tò pân*.

Although Danowski and Viveiros de Castro concede that some messy, globalized "we" is facing "'the end of the world' in the most empirical sense possible," they nevertheless remind "us" that this is hardly the first time the world has come to an end.[139] To the contrary, indigenous peoples across the planet have undergone apocalyptic destruction at the hands of invading Europeans for the sake of the birth of the Capitalocene. For the Euro-descended agents of global climate change, then, the end of the world may well be on its way. But "for the native people of the Americas," to take just one example, "*the end of the world already happened*—five centuries ago. To be exact, it happened on October 12, 1492,"[140] when Columbus made landfall in the Lucayan lands that would become the Bahamas. Over the next century and a half, the "combined action" of "viruses . . . iron, gunpowder, and paper" would proceed to massacre 95 percent of indigenous Americans and untold numbers of animal, vegetable, and mineral life-forms.[141] Danowski and Viveiros de Castro therefore suggest that, having already undergone the worst imaginable cataclysms, "indigenous people have something to teach us when it comes to apocalypses, losses of world, demographic catastrophes, and ends of History."[142] What "they" have to teach "us," in short, is that the end of the world need neither be suicidally hastened nor nihilistically endured. Rather, just as the Yanomami and the Maya have lived "diminished yet defiant" after the end of the world, it must be possible to live out the Anthropocene "in a mode of resistance."[143] It must be possible, in other words, to find ways of world-making in an unworlded world.

Re-Worldings

If it is the case that worlds are not given but made, and if they are made by means of innumerable, interrelated micro-agencies whose personhood has been denied, erased, and assaulted, then the question becomes how such agencies might be assembled or convoked into practices of re-worlding. In this vein, Latour imagines in his penultimate Gifford lecture a singular "people of Gaia" who, unlike their falsely universalized enemy "Man," would belong to a clearly "delineated" "territory."[144] United under the secular deity of Gaia, these "Earthbound" people must fight against the earth-ravaging "Humans" in what Latour imagines as an ultimate "War of the Worlds"—a war *for* the world itself.[145] Now, considering the lengths to which Latour has gone in these lectures to deny any sort of singularity or wholeness to Gaia, it is puzzling that he would suddenly insist on total unity among "its" people (Latour singularizes and de-genders Gaia the moment he imagines "it" might assemble this army). And considering his decades-long effort to unsettle the logic of war (nature vs. culture, science vs. religion, realism vs. constructivism), it is even more perplexing to find him drawing his lines around the Earthbound and declaring war to the end of the world against "Humans." After all, it was territory, opposition, and war that got us into this mess in the first place.

Stengers voices some of this discomfort with war and its forced unities when she insists that "struggling against Gaia makes no sense—it is a matter of learning to compose with her."[146] To be sure, Latour would respond that his Earthbound army is not struggling against Gaia, but *for* "it"—in the name of it and by virtue of it. Unlike Latour's, however, Stengers' Gaia is a force of divine *interruption* rather than a (secular-) divine unifier. Unlike Latour's "it," Stengers' "she" does not call diverse people into a unified *demos*; rather, she provokes the collaborative response of disunified communities whose distance and disagreement might actually condition "*relations* worthy of that name."[147] Meanwhile, navigating between Latourian unity and Stengerian difference, William Connolly calls for resistance to the Anthropocene in the form of "an active, cross-regional pluralist assemblage composed of multiple minorities in different parts of the world."[148] Both unified and multiple, this world-affirming, world-making assemblage takes shape in Connolly's earlier work as a "counter-resonance machine" and in his more recent work as "entangled humanism."[149]

Each of these theorists seeks a way to make livable worlds at the end of the world—to create *with* Gaia in response to her intrusion. Even as they declare the entanglement, interruption, or necessary demise of "the human," however, Connolly, Stengers, and Latour all manage to reaffirm a certain humanity (however minoritarian, pluralistic, or post-) as the primary or even exclusive agent of re-worlding. Considering Gaia's teeming throngs of nonanthropic animacies, these reconstructed humanisms are perplexingly un-Gaian, even Anthropocene-tric. Given "humanity's" stubborn capacity always to find itself back in the center of a newly inert cosmic stage, it would therefore seem that any

effort to live otherwise would have to be the work of multispecies multitudes—
the very sort of intra-active assemblages that constitute worlds in the first place.

The most consistent vision of such symbiogenetic re-worldings can be
found in the work of Donna Haraway, who continually seeks ways to imagine
"worlds we might yet live in" amid the techno-convulsions of late capitalism.[150]
Steadily refusing the twin temptations of pure beginning and total apocalypse
("the world has always been in the middle of things"), Haraway's worlders
are always already hybrid and contaminated: natural-cultural concatenations
who affirm that "there *can* be an elsewhere, not as utopian fantasy or relativist
escape, but an elsewhere born out of the hard (and sometimes joyful) work
of getting on together in a kin group."[151] Constantly breaking the traditionally anthropic and reproductive bounds of "kinship," Haraway's world-makers
include "cyborgs and goddesses," "femalemen," "companion species" in symbiotic partnerships, the "bacteria, fungi, protists, and such" who compose fully
90 percent of the human genome, "inappropriate/d others," sacrificial trans-
genic mice, and "chimeras of humans and nonhumans"—in short, *monsters* of
all imaginable sorts.[152]

In her most recent work, Haraway proposes the term "Chthulucene" as an
immanent elsewhere to the Anthropocene and Capitalocene, each of which
manages to reaffirm the untrammeled power of the particularly white, overdeveloped human agents at their centers, and to make them once again in
the image of God. Reminding us that "the Greek *chthonios* means 'of, in, or
under the earth or seas,'" Haraway configures the Chthulucene as the ongoing
project of the irreducibly terrestrial.[153] "The Chthonic ones are precisely not
sky gods," she insists, "not a foundation for the Olympiad . . . and definitely
not finished."[154] They are, rather, earthly creators, working from the messy
middle of things to make the multispecies kinship structures that amount to
worlds. In this work, Haraway's "chthonic ones" are led not by Man, but by
those fungal, bacterial, vegetable, and animal earth-others who know best
how to become-with one another in order to compose and decompose cosmoi. Margulis, we will recall, has taught us that microbes are the primary
creative force on (and of) earth, making worlds even out of the most thoroughgoing destruction. Led and instructed by these symbiotic demiurges,
Haraway imagines that "the unifinished Chthulucene must collect up the
trash of the Anthropocene, the exterminism of the Capitalocene, and chip-
ping and shredding like a mad gardener, make a much hotter compost pile for
still possible pasts, presents, and futures."[155]

Although she sets this relationally earthy work in stark opposition to that
of any autonomous, transcendent designer, Haraway does occasionally mark

her re-worlding as a pseudo-theological project. Much like Latour's omni-epithetic Gaia, Haraway's Chthulucene "resists figuration . . . and demands myriad names," among them "Naga, Gaia, Tangoroa, Terra, Haniyasu-hine, Spider Woman, Pachamama, Oya, Gorgo, Raven, A'akuluujjusi, and many, many more."[156] Alongside Latour, then, Haraway stages a collision of the apophatic and the cataphatic in the Chthulucene: its resistance to temporal, spatial, or conceptual encapsulation means that it must be called by as many names as possible. So the unsayable gives way to unending over-saying. Indeed, Haraway most clearly (un)affirms her chthonic ones as apophatic rivals to the sky-gods when she channels Exodus to intone that *they are who are.* No wonder the world's great monotheisms have tried again and again to exterminate the chthonic ones."[157] In their ongoing cosmogonic labors, the chthonic ones therefore allow us to begin to form a fully immanent, nonanthropic vision of divinity: what we mean by god(s) in a Harawayan register would be nothing more or less than the sympoietic world(s) in ongoing (de)composition.

COSMOLOGY AND PERSPECTIVE

Insofar as Haraway's chthonic re-worldings ascribe creative agency to precisely those life-forms that the Aristotelian-Christian-Boylean cosmos relegates to passivity, Danowski and Viveiros de Castro have noted that her multispe-cies cosmogonies—like Elizabeth Povinelli's Aboriginally inflected "geontolo-gies"[158]—begin to "converge with the world 'made of people' of Amerindian cosmologies."[159] In this sense, Haraway and Povinelli have learned from these "veritable end-of-the-world experts" something about how to live after the apocalypse, which is to say, how to respond to Gaia's intrusion—and this response has something to do with affirming a "world made of people."[160] With this phrase, Danowski and Viveiros de Castro are referring to indigenous cre-ation narratives that begin with a throng of primordial humans, who morph over the course of the stories into the rocks, rivers, stars, plants, and animals that compose the cosmos. In these accounts, as in Haraway's Chthulucene and Povinelli's geongologies, "what we call 'environment' is . . . a society of societ-ies . . . a *cosmopoliteia*":[161] a living world of intra-active persons.

Just as it is for Haraway, Stengers, Margulis, and Latour, however, it is mis-leading to refer to this indigenous "living world" in the singular. Such a ref-erence is misleading in part because, as we have already learned from these Western theorists, the agents who constitute "the world" are fundamentally symbiotic, multiple, and non-totalizable. More radically, however, "the world" cannot be said to be singular because, as Viveiros de Castro shows in a series of reflections on numerous ethnographies, Amerindian cosmology is thoroughly *perspectival*.[162]

Throughout his authorship, Viveiros de Castro gives numerous examples of what he and Tânia Stolze Lima have named "Amerindian perspectivism." Perhaps the most commonly cited of these examples is the category of "humanity" itself: as Viveiros de Castro explains, any being that can call itself a subject "sees itself as a member of the human species" and sees others as nonhuman predators or prey.[163] So, according to the Jurana (Tupi) people of central Brazil, when a jaguar looks at a jaguar, she sees a human being. When that same jaguar looks at a Tupi man, however, she sees a monkey, or perhaps a peccary: "Every existing being in the cosmos thus sees itself as human, but does not see other species in the same way."[164] Humanity and animality, then, are not static or essential categories; rather, a being is only human or nonhuman from a particular perspective.

As it turns out, every other ontic grouping, no matter how mundane, works the same way. From a vulture's perspective, what the Ashanika (Campa) people call maggots are actually grilled fish; from a jaguar's perspective, blood is beer; from a tapir's perspective, mud is a hammock.[165] "What seems to be happening in Amerindian perspectivism," explains Viveiros de Castro, "is that substances named by substantives like *fish . . . hammock*, or *beer* are somehow used as if they were relational pointers."[166] In other words, there are no "substances" at all—no self-constituted entities that precede the relations that locally determine them. Rather, every term is akin to the designation "mother-in-law": any *thing* is only what it is from the perspective of the one *for whom* it is that thing. So, as Lima points out, a Jurana person will not say that it rained yesterday, but that "to me, it rained."[167] After all, in this multiperspectival social system, where "peccaries" see flutes in the things that "humans" judge to be coconuts,[168] it would be hard to say whether it rained from anyone's perspective other than "mine."

Cosmologically, then, Amerindian perspectivism opens onto an irreducible multiplicity. Unlike relativism, which would affirm differing representations of the same world, such perspectivism amounts for Viveiros de Castro to *the same representations of different worlds*. As he explains, the "categories and values" remain the same from jaguar to peccary to tapir: "their worlds, like ours, revolve around hunting and fishing, cooking and fermented drinks, cross-cousins and war, initiation rituals, shamans, chiefs, spirits, and so forth. Being people in their own sphere, nonhumans see things just *as* people do. But the *things* that they see are different."[169] The signs are the same, but the referents are different; culture is the same, but natures are different; representations are the same, but the worlds themselves are different. Specifically, worlds in Amerindian cosmologies are constituted by virtue of any given perspective. The perceiving subject, or "human" (whether jaguar, Jurana, or snake) stands at the center of the world and organizes everything else relationally around her. And this perspectival worlding *is* what the world is—what worlds are. As Viveiros de Castro puts it, "there is no distinction in Amerindian metaphysics between 'the world-in-itself' and the indeterminate series of existing beings understood as centers of perspectives."[170]

Viewed in this light, Viveiros de Castro's and Lima's "Amerindian metaphysics" looks remarkably like the perspectivism of Giordano Bruno's cosmological predecessor, the Roman Catholic cardinal and early Renaissance philosopher Nicholas of Cusa (1401–1464). As we saw briefly in the previous chapter, it was Cusa who demolished Ptolemy's bounded, geocentric cosmos and proclaimed a (contractedly) infinite universe: as the unmediated outpouring of the (uncontracted) Creator, the Cusan universe is spatiotemporally boundless. Insofar as there is no periphery to the universe, Cusa reasoned, there is no center, either; more precisely, there is no absolute center. Rather, everything in the universe occupies the center of the universe *from its own perspective*.[171] Even those stars that earthlings see at the outer edge of the cosmos occupy the center of creation from their own vantage point. Against the Platonic-Aristotelian insistence on the singularity of the cosmos, then, Cusa proclaimed an unending number of worlds, each of them centered on any given cosmic body. Like the worlds of the Jurana and Ashanika, Cusan worlds overlap with one another: just as the jaguar's peccary is what we would call a human, Star Q's outermost light is what we would call the sun. Cusan worlds therefore *compose* one another: our earth occupies at once the "center" of its own world, the midranges of other planets' worlds, and the peripheries of far-off planets' worlds.

From the perspective of creation, therefore, "the world" amounts to an endless number of interconstituted worlds, none of which can claim to be any more real than the others. So far, so Amerindian. A considerable difference opens in our cross-cultural comparison, however, when we shift with Cusa to the perspective of *God*, from whose vantage point creation is "a single universal world."[172] Holding on as the cardinal of Cusa understandably does to the absolute distinction between creator and creation—a distinction that paradoxically secures the immanence of God in every creature—Cusa stops well short of affirming the divinity of the omnicentric universe. Bruno, as we have witnessed, will plow us right into such an affirmation, all but denying any distinction between God and a rigorously understood creation. In the hands of Bruno, however, the innumerable worlds lose their Cusan perspective. Claiming to consummate the revolution Copernicus initiated, Bruno configures worlds as solar systems, each of them revolving around their own central star.[173] Unlike Cusa's, then, Bruno's worlds do not compose one another, nor do they shift according to one's position in the universe. Rather (given infinite time), one could in principle map out Bruno's infinite worlds spatially, affirming from a single perspective the objective and separate existence of an endless number of worlds.

From the perspective of quasi- and fully-heretical European cosmology, then, what Viveiros de Castro's perspectivism amounts to is a Cusan omni-centrism refracted through Brunian immanence. The makers of the endless worlds are none other than the intra-active elements of those worlds themselves, each of which assembles itself in a relationally ongoing cosmogony, even in the midst of—even after—the end of the world.

Multicosmic Coda

In recent years, the generalized panic over the end of the world has extended itself even into the ordinarily serene realm of theoretical astrophysics. The crisis hit in 1998, when two independent teams of American researchers set out to measure the universal "deceleration parameter," which is to say the rate at which cosmic expansion is slowing down now, 13.82 billion years after the big bang sent space and time hurtling out of whatever had been there before. Using Type 1a supernovae to measure the distance of far-off galaxies, however, both teams discovered to their bewilderment that there *is* no deceleration parameter—that, far from slowing down, the expansion of the universe is speeding up.[174] Everything that *is* is racing away from everything else, the universe flinging itself outward with increasing velocity as time goes on. And the cause of this cosmic freneticism is a negative pressure that suffuses the universe: a repulsive gravitational force that physicists call "the cosmological constant," or more colloquially, "dark energy."[175]

If dark energy remains at a steady density throughout the life of the universe, then its unyielding repulsion will gradually cause distant galaxies to fly off beyond our cosmic horizon. In the meantime, gravity will create a temporary supercluster of the Milky Way, Andromeda, and a few dwarf galaxies. At that point, this supercluster will seem to a hypothetical earthling to constitute the entire universe, since every other galaxy will have disappeared from view. Eventually, however, the outward push will win out over the inward tug and even this local supercluster will be ripped apart. Dead planets and burned out stars will be drawn into black holes, and the universe will consist of nothing more than a "thin gruel of particles," a sea-like quantum vacuum still madly racing out into nothing at all.[176] Channeling T. S. Eliot, physicists therefore predict that the universe that began with a big bang is destined to end in a "big whimper."[177]

Enter panic. Not only did physicists not see this subtly racialized "dark energy" coming, but they also hate what they now see, capitulating to uncharacteristic—and unexceptionally visceral—affective outpourings. Thus we find cosmologist Marcelo Gleiser calling dark energy "ugly and unexpected" and theoretical physicist Brian Greene imagining its end-time usurpation as "vast, empty, and lonely."[178] Robert Kirshner, a member of one of the two teams that uncovered (or summoned) this ugly monstrosity, similarly envisions the final scene it will bring about as "lonely, dull, cold, and dark," and his team-leader Brian Schmidt calls the dark-energetic unraveling "the coldest, most horrible end to the universe I can think of. I don't know," he stammers; "it's creepy."[179] This creepy, lonely, horrible apocalypse finds a particularly agonized roundup in the astronomer Seth Shostak, who thus summarizes his colleagues' widespread revulsion at their own discovery:

> This, then, is the story of the universe. A Big Bang, a hundred billion years of light, life, and late-night television, and then an infinitude of nothingness. Am I getting through to you? Not a long time—not a really long time—but an *infinitude*. A flash of activity, followed by a never-ending darkness. Our universe is destined to spend eternity in hell, without the fire.[180]

Facing the prospect of this hellish eternity, a surprising number of physicists began around the turn of the millennium to look for some sort of way out. The result has been the exuberant proliferation over the past two decades of "multiverse" cosmologies, which suggest that our universe is just one of a staggering number of others.

To be sure, it was not existential panic alone that motivated the turn to the multiverse. Nor did such panic produce the idea in the first place; rather, during the second half of the twentieth century, numerous multiple-universe scenarios had emerged from the fields of quantum mechanics, inflationary cosmology, loop quantum gravity, and string theory.[181] As many of these early multiversalists have argued, however, their theories tended to be derided and ignored until the apocalyptic revelation at the end of the millennium. In the face of dark energy, the multiverse became suddenly thinkable—even almost respectable—partly because it "appeared to offer hope" of viable universes else-where, and partly because it seemed to be the only solution to the so-called fine-tuning problem.[182] Briefly stated, the "fine-tuning problem" asks how the fundamental constants of nature came to assume the values they did, when nearly any other value would have made life in the universe impossible.[183] Dark energy raises the stakes of this conundrum significantly, insofar as nearly any other value for the cosmological constant would have made the universe *itself* impossible—either blowing it outward to shreds or pulling it inward to an infer-nal "big crunch." How, then, did the cosmological constant come to have the bafflingly small, quantum-field-theory-violating value that it seems to have?

As we will recall, planetary scientists were faced with a similar conundrum when it came to the atmospheric composition of Earth. How is it, they asked, that (in this solar system, at least) our planet alone is suitable to the emergence of life? The Gaian answer, of course, is that "life" has made the planet suitable to life; metabolic processes have produced the very conditions they need to proliferate and evolve. The multiverse provides a very different solution. Rather than suggesting that the universe itself is an animate assemblage of sympoietic agents, the multiverse renders the universe a mechanically inevitable accident. There are, the dominant models suggest, an infinite number of universes tak-ing on all imaginable cosmic parameters throughout infinite time. Under these conditions, the vast majority of worlds will fail—blowing up thanks to too much dark energy or caving in under too much gravity—but now and then, a universe will just happen to have the "right" combination of physical forces, and that sort of universe is the only kind that will produce planets and stars and beings like us.[184]

In its magisterial efforts to explain not only this but all possible universes—indeed, the actuality of all possible universes[185]—the multiverse is certainly *aiming* to become a theory of everything. In the terms more familiar to the study at hand, one could even call it an aspirationally monistic pantheism. For whether in the hands of inflationary, quantum, loop quantum, or string theorists, multiverse scenarios seek a single, immanent, generative-destruc-tive principle (be it an energy, an equation, an evolutionary mechanism, or a landscape of vacua solutions) that might unify every imaginable world into a single, hypothetical mega-world. In practice, however, multiverse cosmologies are hardly narrowing down or approaching consensus. Rather, they are pro-liferating with each passing year, their differences amplifying into a Latourian cacophony. One might be inclined to explain this cacophony as a function of the relative youth of these sciences, imagining that the theories are bound at some point to converge in a single account of cosmic multiplicity. But as Latour has argued, this is simply not the way the natural sciences work. Despite their promises of impending "unification" or "reductionism," the experimental and theoretical sciences are far from approaching "one tiny equation from which everything else would be deduced." Rather, "every discipline, every specialty, every laboratory, every expedition, *multiplies* the surprising agents with which their world is made," branching out into dizzying manyness rather than zeroing in onto oneness.[186]

The problem of disciplinary consensus is intensified when it comes to cosmology, which unlike every other natural science, cannot even pretend to get outside its subject matter and see it as an object. We are irremediably inside the universe that cosmology tries to see as a whole, so all our accounts of it are inexorably situated. To be sure, this inexorable *situation* is the case with every discipline; it is simply more transparent when it comes to cosmology, which now endeavors not only to see our universe as a whole, but others, as well. And insofar as the contemporary meaning of the term "universe" is the (earth-centered) region of spacetime we can see in any given direction, "other universes" lie by definition beyond the bounds of what we are able, even in principle, to measure or observe.

Given, then, that it will never be possible to see such "other" cosmic realms, one can safely assume that their nature, number, and sheer existence will remain a matter of (highly sophisticated) conjecture. Granted, it may indeed be that a particular set of thermal *in*homogeneities on our cosmic microwave background constitutes evidence of our universe's "birth" from a primordial, multiversal sea.[187] But the same inhomogeneities might attest instead to the collision of our universe with any number of its neighbors.[188] Or they might demonstrate the existence of a partner world across an unbridgeable fourth dimension.[189] Or they might be the signature of a race of superscientists who have simulated our universe to *appear* as though it is bound up with others.[190] Or perhaps the markings are just random abnormalities, and our universe is all there is to isness.

As I have suggested elsewhere, then, it seems highly unlikely that we will ever get a single account of cosmic multiplicity—if it even makes sense to speak this way.[191] Rather, the manyness of "all things" seems only to proliferate with each investigation. Just as light appears to be a wave under certain experimental conditions and a set of particles under others; just as God/Nature appears as thought under one attribute and extension as another; and just as substance X is beer to a jaguar (who is human to herself) and blood to a human (who is a peccary to a jaguar)—so will the cosmos appear to be singular or multiple, connected or disconnected, or this multiverse or that, depending on the theoretical-material apparatus any given team uses to investigate-construct it. And just as there is no objectivity back behind the perspectivism of particles and waves—no answer to the question of what light (or God/Nature, or jag-uarness/humanness) *really is*—so is there no "world" back behind our end-less, situated acts of worlding. As in Amerindian perspectivism, one might say that in contemporary cosmology "there is no distinction . . . between 'the world-in-itself' and the indeterminate series of . . . perspectives."[192] And these "monsters of energy"—these sympoietic, self-exceeding assemblages of per-spectival assemblages—are what our hypothetical pantheologian might mean by "worlds."

PANCARNATION

Pan, n.: allusively. A person with responsibility for shepherds and flocks; a chief shepherd (occas. applied to Jesus Christ).
—Oxford English Dictionary

As a queer and racialized "all," Pan tends to be the object of longing and loathing, animality and divinity, denigration and exaltation. And strikingly, the author who is most noted for his Pan-based portrait of Satan ("horns, hooves, shaggy fur, and outsized phallus"[1]) *also* wrangles Pan into a forerunner of Christ. Calling us back to those pastures outside Bethlehem, where angels would announce the arrival of a human-divine protector of flocks, John Milton imagines,

> The shepherds on the lawn
> Or ere the point of dawn
> Sat simply chatting in a rustic row
> Full little thought they then
> That the mighty Pan
> Was kindly come to live with them below.[2]

As the incarnation of speech (*logos*), the conflation of opposites, and the Good Shepherd of "all," Christ becomes for Milton the *true* Pan. Milton was not quite the first author to notice the parallels between these chimeric divinities; in fact, François Rabelais had given voice to it a century earlier through his "absurd" character Pantagruel, who interprets Plutarch's "death of Pan" as an account of the crucifixion.[3] So named by his father, who imagined him "thirsting after *the all*,"[4] Pantagruel defends his bizarre conflation with extraordinary rhetorical flourish. The death of Pan can be interpreted as the death of Christ, he explains, "for in Greek [Christ] can rightly be called *Pan*, seeing that he is our All, all that we are, all that we live, all that we have, all that we hope, is in him, of him, by him."[5] The hapless scholar goes on to remind us that both Pan and Christ are shepherds, and that at the moment of the crucifixion, "plaints, sighs, tumultuous cries and lamentations throughout the entire machine of the Universe: Heaven, earth, sea, and Hell."[6] This, then, was the source of the cries off those Grecian shores that "the great Pan [was] dead." Reversing the Eusebian interpretation, Pantagruel presents the "death of Pan" *not* as the death of the pagan gods exorcised by Christ, but as the death of the exorcist himself: "for that Most-good, Most-great Pan, our Only Servator, died in Jerusalem during the reign in Rome of Tiberius Caesar."[7]

As classicist Wilfred Schoff illustrates, and to his great consternation, this exegetical absurdity becomes "noble verse" when Milton misses the joke and imports the whole set of associations into his Nativity Ode.[8] From there, the conflation of Christ, Pan, and allness becomes commonplace: Edmund Spenser reminds us that "The great Pan is Christ, the very God of all shepherds," whose death coincides with "the death of Pan";[9] Ben Jonson writes that "PAN is our All, by him we breathe, we live, / We move, we are";[10] and Elizabeth Barrett Browning tunes into that moment "When One in Sion / Hung for love's sake on the cross" to hear forests, fields, mountains, and seas cry out in agonized uniformity that "Pan, Pan, is dead."[11]

This co-optation of Pan is just one of countless Christian theological efforts to limit the scope of divinity in the world and gather it all into the person of Christ—an effort whose constancy bespeaks a perilous fragility. Indeed, if the most revolted charges and dismissals of "pantheism" have come from Christian authors, it is because, Christianly speaking, the idea is so seductive. The central Christian profession is the doctrine of the incarnation, which is to say the identity of eternity and time, spirit and flesh, and even God and world—but precisely because it threatens these distinctions, the scope of this incarnation must be swiftly and continuously limited to the person of Jesus of Nazareth. As Søren Kierkegaard's most devout pseudonym Anti-Climacus suggests, "No teaching on earth has ever really brought God and man so close together as Christianity"—the risk being that, especially in the hands of second-rate preachers, "the qualitative difference between God and man is pantheistically abolished."[12] This is the reason, Anti-Climacus argues, that Christianity properly conceived has "protected itself so painstakingly against [this] most dreadful of all blasphemies . . . by means of the offense."[13] By "the offense," he means the absolute, unassimilable singularity of God's appearance in the world. And indeed, we might recall the Reverend Dix prescribing just this doctrinal cure: the spreading disease of pantheism can only be counteracted, he insists, by preaching "the Incarnation of the Eternal Word."[14]

In a notoriously inflammatory address at Harvard Divinity School, Ralph Waldo Emerson called this sort of Christian self-protection a "perversion" of its prophet's own teachings. As far as Emerson was concerned, Christians ought to be following (Emerson's) Jesus, proclaiming like him the presence of God in all human beings. Instead, they end up producing a "noxious exaggeration about the person of Jesus," proclaiming not that God's radical indwelling unites all people, but that "this was Jehovah come down from heaven. I will kill you, if you say he was a man."[15] And indeed, there has been no shortage of people who have been killed for saying—or even implying—that Jesus was no more divine than anyone else, from Arians to Unitarians to Muslims to Jews, and including, of course, the heretic from Nola who seemed to assert the incarnation of God in and as *the world itself.*

As the ongoing fascination with Bruno reveals, however, and as Laurel Schneider has argued, the reason the Christian tradition has needed so energetically to protect its theological and ecclesiastical boundaries is that incarnation cannot be so tidily contained within a single man living for thirty years in occupied Palestine. "The coming to flesh completely disrupts the smooth otherness of the divine," Schneider writes; "its separateness from the changeable stuff of earth, its abhorrence of rot, its innocence of death, and its ignorance of life or desire."[16] Moving even beyond Emerson's anthropotheism, Schneider breaks divinity into the tangled spheres of the non- and more-than-human by virtue of the inherent porosity of *flesh*. Flesh, she argues, is inherently "promiscuous," exhibiting an "indiscriminate . . . interconnection with everything."[17] For this reason, the word-become-flesh refuses to stay still, tumbling promiscuously into the multiple "bodies," queer "mixtures," and intraspecies worlds from which orthodoxy tries so fiercely to guard it.[18] In other words, the incarnation already performs the monstrous conflations of which the Christian accuses the pantheist, introducing a dark, feminized, sexualized, and changeable materiality into the very substance of God.

And although orthodoxy tries to keep such concatenations contained, Donna Haraway reminds us that the container himself is a monstrous, anti-Oedipal half-breed: "a mother's son, without a father, yet the Son of Man

claiming *the* Father," who shows up amid sheep and goats; is kin to the colonized; violates the principle of noncontradiction; and keeps company with
sex workers, the poor, and disabled.[19] A leaky container indeed, the figure of
Jesus "threatens to spoil the story, despite or because of his odd sonship and
odder kingship, because of his disguises and form-changing habits."[20] For
this reason, "the story has constantly to be preserved from heresy, to be kept
forcibly in the patriarchal tradition of Christian civilization."[21] But as this constant effort attests, incarnation keeps slipping through every effort to wall it
in—perhaps most strikingly in the work of the not-executed Cardinal of Cusa.
As Catherine Keller has shown, Cusa breaks the *imago dei* out of its Christic
and even human confines, opening it out to the universe itself so that "every
creature is, as it were, a finite infinity or created God."[22] The result, then, is
not the incarnation of God in a single body at a single point in spacetime, but
rather "a pan-carnation of God equally distributed."[23] For Cusa, God shows up
just as fully in a mustard seed as in a man as in anything we might call a world.

4

THEOS

All things are full of gods.
—Thales of Miletus

Dear God. Dear Stars, dear trees, dear sky, dear peoples.
Dear everything. Dear God.
—Alice Walker, *The Color Purple*

FINALLY

In the face of pantheism's perennial philo-theological denigration, the study at hand has undertaken both a diagnosis of this widespread panic and a conceptual reconstruction of the offending term. Attributing the vitriolic name-calling that so often attends "pantheism" to a fear of crossed boundaries and queer mixtures, we have sought to cobble together the sort of position that might actually perform the thoroughgoing disruptions that anti-pantheists fear. Responding in particular to the charges of pantheist indistinction, passivity, and givenness, the last three chapters have unearthed a ceaselessly multiple, destructive-creative, animate materiality that both produces and emerges from "all things" in their various worldings and re-worldings. The remaining question, then, is what it might mean to call such monstrous operations theological. What does it do to the categories of divinity, the gods, or even "God" to identify them with such polycosmic sympoiesis? And reciprocally, what does it add to the polycosmically sympoietic to call it divine?[1] Addressing these questions will force us to revisit the problem of determinism we first glimpsed in Spinoza and then, finally, to confront the remaining challenges to pantheism as it is usually construed: namely, its alleged moral relativism (or sanctioning of "evil"), and its equivalence to atheism. If "God" is nothing other than "the world," then why would anyone bother to act responsibly, to make worlds otherwise, or in fact to appeal to divinity at all?

At this point, one might be tempted to take refuge in either of the admittedly more straightforward positions of theism and atheism, appealing either to the transformational covenant of an extra-cosmic deity or to the awesome and awful unfoldings of "strictly" biological processes. Conceptually, ethically, and for the sake of minimizing cognitive dissonance, one would certainly be justified in taking one or the other of these stances. It has been the wager of this particular exploration, however, that it is precisely pantheism's unthinkability that calls for thinking. Less dramatically stated, pantheism's promise lies in its discomfiting refusal of those traditional Western metaphysical divisions of theism and atheism, God and world, spirit and matter, and indeed science and religion—divisions that manage, *regardless of the camp one chooses*, consistently to privilege light over darkness, male over female, and a carefully circumscribed "humanity" over everything else.

Of course, not all pantheisms will unsettle such privileges. As we have seen, monistic schemes tend to consolidate the dualistic inequalities they purportedly reject by gathering the whole world into one side or another of the binary in question. By proclaiming absolute unity, they moreover assemble "all things" under "progressive" categories of race and species, often marshaling evolutionary theory to produce a strikingly familiar Great Chain of Being. In this way, monistic pantheisms deny all qualitative difference only to solidify quantitative difference, reaffirming European-descended male humans as the pinnacle of creation. What we have therefore sought instead are Jamesian "pluralist" pantheisms—those provisionally named "pantheologies"—that attribute divinity not to some "force" within the universe, "essence" behind it, or totality around it, but rather to the multiform, "theotic" worldings of consonant and dissonant symbionts: those created creators to which "all things" amount.[2]

Having opened with the centuries-long outcry against Spinoza's "monstrous" *Deus, sive natura*, this study now concludes with the resurgence of anti-pantheist sentiment in the midst of yet another resurrection of "the renegade Jew." The conjurer at hand is none other than Albert Einstein, whose professed fidelity to "Spinoza's God" provoked a familiar yet updated onslaught of condemnations at the hands of American Christian clergy in the early- to mid-twentieth century. As we shall see, Einstein's Spinozism both approaches and recoils from the pantheological. But this very ambivalence—along with the decidedly unambivalent accusations of his critics—allows us to address the

questions that previous chapters have glimpsed and left open: namely, those of
ethics and atheism. What, we now ask, is the place of newness and responsibility in pantheological worldings, and what difference could it possibly make to
calls such worldings divine?

THE EINSTEIN CRISIS

The public outcry over "Einstein's God" or "Einstein's religion" flared up and
for the most part died down in the second quarter of the twentieth century.
Far from being a strictly ecclesiastical affair (if such a thing even exists), this
"Einstein crisis" was the hybrid product of inter-resonant theological, political,
scientific, economic, and epistemological operations, including the devastation
of the First World War, the overturning of Newtonian physics by general and
special relativity, the rupture between science and religion staged in the 1925
Scopes Trial, the rise of fascism in Europe, the crash of the U.S. stock market,
and Einstein's decade-long debate with Niels Bohr over quantum mechanics
and the nature of reality. Arising from all of these factors in complex relation,
the Einstein crisis can be organized into three major waves.

The first wave hit in April of 1929, one week before a lavish gala at the
Metropolitan Opera House in honor of Einstein's fiftieth birthday, which drew
3,500 people in support of the Jewish National Fund and the Zionist Organization of America.[3] As American Jews prepared to celebrate their most famous
kinsman—whose works the Nazi regime would burn six years later as incarnating an unacceptable "Asiatic spirit in science"[4]—Cardinal William Henry
O'Connell of Boston delivered an address to the New England Province of
Catholic Clubs of America, urging their members to pay no attention to this
modern-day renegade Jew. Having previously denounced Hollywood and
radio technology for proliferating a monstrous cadre of "masculine women"
and "effeminate men," the cardinal now charged Einstein's theory of relativity with endorsing the categorical indistinction of the topsy-turvy era.[5] The
theory, he insisted, was nothing more than "befogged speculation producing
universal doubt about God and his creation [and] cloaking the ghastly appa-
rition of atheism."[6] O'Connell did not quite explain the connection between
relativity and atheism, except to say that the theory was too confusing to be
true and that it made no mention of God.[7] But one can surmise from the
controversies that followed that the mere name of "relativity" connoted moral
laxity—the sort that had allegedly devoured law, economics, politics, and
gender in the post-war era, and which church leaders believed could only be

held in check by an unchanging, immovable, extra-cosmic lawgiver.[8] In short, relativity's denial of any absolute reference point for space and time seemed a denial of the Absolute altogether.

Seeking to defend his assailed hero against the incensed cardinal, Rabbi Herbert S. Goldstein of the Institutional Synagogue in New York sent a cable to Einstein in Berlin, asking, "Do you believe in God? Stop. Prepaid reply 50 words."[9] As it turned out, Einstein only needed half as many words, responding, "I believe in Spinoza's God who reveals himself in the orderly harmony of all things, not in a God who concerns himself with the fates and actions of human beings."[10] In an interview with the German-American author and eventual Nazi sympathizer George Sylvester Viereck (whom Einstein insisted on misreading as Jewish, Viereck's protestations notwithstanding), Einstein would go on to clarify that his reply to Rabbi Goldstein "was not intended for publication." Laughing with Viereck, he added, "No one except an American could think of sending a man a telegram asking him: 'Do you believe in God?'"[11] Nevertheless, the earnest American rabbi took Einstein's cabled profession as proof that the physicist was not, in fact, an atheist, and went on to publish it in *The New York Times* as a rejoinder to Cardinal O'Connell. Einstein was by no means a ghastly atheist, Goldstein announced; after all, he had invoked Spinoza. And "Spinoza, who is called 'the God-intoxicated man' and who saw God manifest in all of nature, certainly could not be called an atheist."[12] In fact, Goldstein went on to insist, Spinoza's unflagging faith in the rational unity of nature made him—along with Einstein—an unmitigated monotheist, which was certainly more than anyone could say of the trinitarian O'Connell.[13] Of course, Goldstein's defense of Einstein's orthodoxy was hardly watertight; as we have seen, Spinoza most certainly *can* and has been called an atheist, as well as a pantheist, as well as an atheist disguised as a pantheist. And in an uncanny recapitulation of these accusations, the modern Osservatore Romano went on to proclaim on behalf of Pope Pius XI that Cardinal O'Connell was correct: Einstein's theory of relativity amounted to "authentic atheism even if camouflaged as cosmic pantheism."[14]

The second wave of controversy hit just seven months later, when Einstein published a piece in the *New York Times Magazine* titled, "Religion and Science."[15] Subtly informed not only by Spinoza but also by Kant, Nietzsche, Schleiermacher, Schopenhauer, and the colonial anthropology of the late nineteenth and early twentieth centuries, Einstein suggests in this short essay that "religion" develops in three historical stages. First comes the "religion of fear," in which "primitive peoples" install anthropomorphic beings behind the terrifying forces of nature—beings whom they try to appease by means of ritual and sacrifice, and whose whims are communicated by means of a power-hungry "priestly caste." Eventually, this allegedly primordial expression "develops" into a "moral religion," whose people are united under the eternally binding command of a single lawgiver. Although this moral stage dominates "the religions of all the civilized peoples," Einstein explains that it tends nevertheless to be intermingled with the earlier stage of fear. And regardless of the preponderance of morality or fear in any given tradition, divinity is understood in each of them to be wholly "anthropomorphic," with an anthropocentric set of preoccupations.

We will recall that Spinoza accused contemporary religious doctrines of being similarly modeled and centered on human pursuits. And indeed, fueled by his oft-professed love for Spinoza,[16] Einstein rejects not all divinity, but rather the God who looks like humanity and who concerns himself primarily with human flourishing, human punishment, and human commerce. The highest stage of religion, he therefore concludes, manages to break free of this anthropomorphic deity and his anthropocentric carryings-on, revolving instead around what Einstein calls a "cosmic religious sense." This awestruck, humbling feeling reveals "the vanity of human desires and aims" in comparison to "the nobility and marvelous order which are revealed in nature." And it is this "cosmic religious sense," Einstein concludes, that not only suffuses "the religious geniuses of all times," but that animates scientific geniuses as well, inspiring the likes of Kepler and Newton to persist in their solitary labors for the sake of "understand[ing] even a small glimpse of the reason revealed in the world."[17]

Einstein's brief theory of religion and its relationship to science hit the New York newsstands early on a Sunday morning. Hours later, it was decried in mainline Christian pulpits throughout the city, with Methodists, Presbyterians, Episcopalians, and Roman Catholics alike denouncing Einstein's "cosmic religious sense" as amoral, overly intellectual, impersonal, and anticlerical.[18] Einstein's lone defender—at least according to the next day's *Times*—was Rabbi Solomon B. Freehof of Chicago, who maintained at Carnegie Hall to the Free Synagogue congregation that Einstein was in no sense an atheist. Whereas, half a year earlier, Rabbi Goldstein had defended Einstein's theism based on his comprehension of cosmic reason, Rabbi Freehof now defended it based on Einstein's humble sense of its *mystery*: "the anti-religious view of the universe looks upon the world as a clearly understood machine in which every 'riddle' is either solved or on the way to solution," Freehof explained. For Einstein, by contrast, "the universe is essentially mysterious. He confronts it with awe and reverence."[19] As we will continue to see, this tension between the rational and the incomprehensible comes to constitute the auto-deconstructive core of

Einstein's philosophy of religion: for Einstein, the persistence of the mysterious renders the rationality of the universe a constant matter of faith.

The final wave of "the Einstein crisis" crashed a full ten years after the publication of "Religion and Science," in response to Einstein's academic address titled "Science and Religion" (Einstein's nearly unfathomable creativity seems to have bottomed out when it came to titles). Einstein offered the lecture as part of a symposium at Jewish Theological Seminary in New York that gathered scholars from a wide range of disciplines to confront the ongoing political "disintegration" of "Western civilization," a destruction the conference organizers attributed to "our failure to harmonize science, philosophy and religion in their true relation to the democratic way of life."[20] It was their hope that Einstein might assist "the reconciliation of science and religion separated 80 years ago by the conflict between six-day Creation and the theory of evolution."[21] And Einstein certainly thought he was offering a means toward such reconciliation, arguing as he did that religion and science occupy separate but supplementary "spheres." Science, he ventured, is concerned with "what *is*," whereas religion tells us "what *should be*"; science uncovers "facts," whereas religion prescribes "human thoughts and actions."[22] As such, neither is sufficient on its own; in Einstein's now-iconic words, "science without religion is lame, religion without science is blind" (46).

Whence, then, comes the perceived opposition between these mutually beneficial regimes? "The main source of the present-day conflict between the spheres of religion and science," Einstein ventures, "lies in [the] concept of a personal God" (47). Channeling Spinoza's denial of miracles,[23] Einstein declares the scientific inadmissibility of an anthropomorphic power that might violate the eternal order of nature in response to human need, petition, or sacrifice. Moreover, he criticizes the ethical uselessness of such a God, whose purported omnipotence relieves human beings of responsibility for their own actions. After all, Einstein reasons, if God is all-powerful, then "every occurrence, including every human action, every human thought, and every human feeling and aspiration is also His work," rather than the work of human actors (46). "How is it possible," Einstein asks, "to think of holding men responsible for their deeds and thoughts before such an almighty Being?" (46).

To be sure, Einstein admits, the sciences can never disprove the existence of a personal God. But they have increasingly displaced this God as an explanatory power, forcing his adherents to cram their outdated deity into "those domains in which scientific knowledge has not yet been able to set foot" (48). Like Dietrich Bonhoeffer's "God of the gaps," this anti-scientific superman can only continue to lose ground, influence, and relevance as the sciences push him into the ever-smaller spaces of the inexplicable (the bacterial flagellum, a single still-perplexing ocular synapse, or the 10^{-34} of a second just after the big bang).[24] For scientific, ethical, and theological reasons alike, Einstein therefore insists that "*teachers of religion must have the stature to give up the doctrine of a personal God*" (48; emphasis added). Once people are free from this divine overlord, Einstein promises, they will likewise be delivered "from the bondage of egocentric cravings," breaking through the "shackles of personal hopes and desires" to attain that comportment his earlier essay called the cosmic religious sense (48–49). Infused at last with "that humble attitude of mind toward the grandeur of reason incarnate in existence," the religious person becomes affectively identical to the scientist, both of them singularly focused on that which, "in its profoundest depth, is inaccessible to man" (49).

Again, Einstein had thought that this lecture might help his colleagues in the natural and theological sciences repair the rift between their disciplines. As far as most of his audience was concerned, however, Einstein's attempted reconciliation with religion amounted to a full-scale attack. As *The Chicago Daily Tribune*, *The New York Times*, the front page of *The Washington Post*, a flurry of local newspapers, and a feature article in *Time* magazine all declared, Einstein's call "to give up the doctrine of a personal God" amounted to a denial of God altogether.[25] "There is no other God but a personal God," an anonymous Roman Catholic priest wrote in the *Hudson Dispatch*; "Einstein does not know what he is talking about."[26] We may recall that the same conviction coursed through the American anti-pantheist treatises of the mid-nineteenth century, which similarly denied the coherence of affirming any "God" other than "our Father, our Creator, our Redeemer, our Sanctifier, our Friend."[27] Having perhaps overestimated the overseas effect of Germany's own late-modern retrieval of Spinoza, Einstein accomplished precisely the opposite of what he had set out to do in this lecture, proclaiming the grandeur of a God his audience considered to be incoherent, and thereby intensifying the divisions among the disciplines the conference had set out to unify. Thus the *New York Times* reported that, as far as the philosophers and theologians were concerned, "the famous unifier of time and space expounded his own atheism" in this allegedly pantheist lecture—an atheism, in fact, "which has been . . . never before so emphatically stated."[28] As the physicist and philosopher Max Jammer has discovered in Einstein's personal letters, Einstein was baffled by this vitriolic response, and by the multidenominational excoriations that arrived by mail for months after the address was sensationally summarized in the press.[29]

For the most part, the charges were predictable—many of them familiar from the sermonic kerfuffle ten years earlier, or indeed from the centuries-long critique of Spinoza. Einstein was an atheist; he was a pantheist; he was an atheist dressed as a pantheist; he had insulted God by denying "His" personalism; he had insulted "man" by denying his resemblance to God; his cosmic religion was "absurd," "the sheerest kind of stupidity and nonsense," and "full of jellybeans"; he was unfit as a scientist to weigh in on matters of theology; and he had undermined the very possibility of ethics by "remov[ing] the Supreme Being so remotely from the sphere of human comprehension as to make His influence on the individual's conduct negligible."[30] Although nearly all of these critics were Christian, there were a few orthodox and conservative Jewish voices among them, including Rabbi Hyman Cohen of Hudson County, who concluded that "Einstein is unquestionably a great scientist, but his religious views are diametrically opposed to Judaism."[31] Even his defenders ascribed these "religious views" to some foreign source; thus we find Rabbi Jacob Singer of Chicago lauding Einstein's ethics while dismissing his theology as non-Abrahamic pantheism, and Reverend Burriss Jenkins of Kansas City explicitly likening Einstein's vision to that of "the Hindu religion."[32]

One unprecedented set of claims, however, and one leveled exclusively by self-professed Christians, asserted that Einstein's orientalizing (a)theology offered aid to the Nazi extermination of his own people. For example, extending the typically theistic logic of "the problem of evil" to Einstein's deliberately impersonal pantheism, Monsignor Fulton John Sheen of Catholic University objected that a cosmic divinity could hold no one responsible for his actions. Einstein's "rational knowledge," so reliable in scientific matters, had failed him theologically, for "if God is only impersonal Space-Time, there is no moral order; then Hitler is not responsible for driving Professor Einstein out of Germany. It was only a bad collocation of space-time configurations that made him act this way."[33] Of course, Einstein had made just the opposite claim in "Science and Religion," arguing that if God were personal, then *God* would be responsible for the violent convulsions of human behavior—including, presumably, Hitler's expulsion of the Jews. Yet Monsignor Sheen does not consider this position, taking it as given that only an anthropomorphic lawgiver can secure moral conduct on earth (the obvious objection being that he hadn't).

Other incensed Christians pushed Einstein's alleged excusing of Hitler's behavior into a full-fledged justification of it. As one Roman Catholic attorney and self-described interfaith activist dared to assert, Einstein's denial of a personal God made a case for the "exp[ulsion of] the Jews from Germany," making it seem as though the Jews actually deserved such treatment by virtue of their inadmissible theology.[34] Thus we find an endorsement of anti-Jewish violence masquerading as a defense of Judaism, a phenomenon most clearly displayed in the letter of a Christian Zionist from Oklahoma who fulminates,

> I have done everything in my power to be a blessing to Israel, and then you come along and with one statement from your blasphemous tongue do more to hurt the case of your people than all of the efforts of the Christians who love Israel can do to stamp out anti-Semitism in our Land. Professor Einstein, every Christian in America will immediately reply to you, "Take back your crazy, fallacious theory of evolution and go back to Germany where you came from, or stop trying to break down the faith of a people who gave you a welcome when you were forced to flee your native land."[35]

Perhaps needless to say, Einstein's major contributions to science had very little to do with any "theory of evolution." By associating Einstein with a teaching that self-identified "fundamentalists" of the early twentieth century had determined to be anti-Christian, however, the author charges Einstein not only with aiding the destruction of Einstein's own people, but also with a refusal to assimilate himself into mainstream Christian culture—a refusal that amounted in the author's eyes to an act of aggression against this culture. In the course of this letter, then, this critic's stated effort to "stamp out anti-Semitism" ends up duplicating its logic. For centuries, European Christians had accused European Jews of aggressively flouting the conventions of their host cultures. Such stubborn anti-assimilationists included, of course, those members of Spinoza's family expelled from Spain in 1492 for their imperfect Christian conversions.[36]

FAITH IN REASON

Viscera and vitriol aside, however, what did Einstein mean when he professed adherence to "Spinoza's God?" On the most elementary level, he meant that he was most certainly not an atheist.[37] Depending on the day and context, he also meant either that he was a pantheist or that he was perhaps not a pantheist.[38] Whether or not he accepted this label, however, Einstein certainly used the word "God" interchangeably with "Nature." This theo-cosmic identity becomes clear in a conversation with a colleague who asked Einstein to explain what he had meant when he said, "subtle is the Lord, but malicious He is not." Einstein replied, "Nature hides her secret because of her essential loftiness, but not by means of ruse."[39] God and Nature are equivalent and nondeceptive, which is to say rational: this is the essence of Einstein's theology. Indeed, what the heretical physicist means above all when he says, "I believe in Spinoza's God" is that the world is rationally structured, and that this cosmic reason is divine. Unlike Spinoza, however, who thought he could demonstrate such a precept geometrically, Einstein admits that his unflagging faith in "the rationality or intelligibility of the world" is, precisely, a matter of faith.[40] "The basis of all scientific work is the conviction that the world is an ordered and comprehensive entity," he writes, "which is a religious sentiment."[41]

Insofar as the universe is fully rational, Einstein goes on to reason with Spinoza and Newton alike that it must also be fully determined. Again anchoring his rationalism in a para-rational source, Einstein explains that "the scientist is *possessed* by the *sense* of universal causation. The future, to him, is every whit as necessary and determined as the past."[42] Possessed by this overwhelming feeling that everything is ordained, Einstein joins the more sober Spinoza in denying anything like free will. "Man acts in accordance with an inner and outer necessity," Einstein maintains in 1930, "as little responsible as an inanimate object for the movements which it makes."[43] Ten years later, he will complicate this position in light of the Nazi atrocities, suggesting as we have seen that the doctrine of a personal God impedes human responsibility more than determinism does.[44] As he later clarifies, each of these opposed worldviews threatens to evacuate human freedom at a theoretical level, but personal theism evacuates it on a practical level as well, assuring us that there is an extra-cosmic ur-agent outside the cosmos who will step in to save the day. It is only when we give up this idea that we might finally take responsibility for our actions, determined or not. As Einstein explains to Viereck, then, even if "I" do not actually have free will, "practically, I am nevertheless, compelled to act—as if freedom of the will existed. If I wish to live in a civilized community, I must act on the assumption that man is a responsible being."[45]

In his earlier work, however, Einstein is less concerned than he is in this later essay to attribute blame to human agents for their actions. In fact, he explains, the understanding that we are not actually free "is a perpetual breeder of tolerance, for it does not allow us to take ourselves or others too seriously; it makes rather for a sense of humor."[46] In addition to securing an ethic of radical tolerance, Einstein's denial of human freedom in this early work helps him to deny the doctrine of a personal God: it would make no sense, he reasons, for God to punish or reward humans for their actions, because humans cannot do otherwise. Nor would it make sense for God to interrupt the course of history or the order of nature with some inexplicable miracle, because God is the explicable order itself. In response to a query from 11-year-old Phyllis Wright of the Riverside Church in New York, Einstein therefore asserts that scientists do not, in fact, pray. The universe operates according to deterministic laws, he explains, so we cannot hope to have our particular wishes granted by a supernatural being. That having been said, Einstein also admits once again that this universal rationality is itself an undemonstrable premise. As he summarizes the matter to his adolescent interlocutor, "our actual knowledge of these laws is only an incomplete piece of work, so that ultimately the belief in the existence of fundamental all-embracing laws also rests on a sort of faith."[47]

Grounded in this sort of faith, it is the aim of Einstein's scientist to rise above anthropocentric concerns and anthropomorphic imaginings in order to attune himself (Einstein was unimpressed by the rational capacities of most women)[48] to the rational order of the universe. The same is true, Einstein insists, of the "religiously enlightened" person, which is to say, the "one who has, to the best of his ability, liberated himself from the fetters of his selfish desires and is preoccupied with thoughts, feelings, and aspirations to which he clings because of their superpersonal value."[49] As we have already seen, such "thoughts, feelings, and aspirations" constitute what Einstein calls the "cosmic religious sense" shared by scientists and "religious geniuses" alike.[50] Much like Friedrich Schleiermacher's longing "to intuit the universe," or indeed Spinoza's *amor dei intellectualis*, Einstein's cosmic religious sense seeks to perceive the unity of all things at once—to see everything holographically reflected in each thing.[51]

More like Spinoza than Schleiermacher, Einstein describes this quest as a rational pursuit rather than a strictly emotional one. More like Schleiermacher than Spinoza, he also acknowledges reason's insufficiency with respect to this pursuit. In short, Einstein's cosmic religious sense amounts to reason at its limits: the more ardently it attempts to grasp the order of the universe, the more it understands how feebly it grasps it. And yet this constant falling-short only inspires the devout scientist to intensify his effort to comprehend as much as he can. Einstein's universe is thus fully rational *and* persistently mysterious; as he famously encapsulates the matter, "the eternal mystery of the world is its comprehensibility. . . . The fact that it is comprehensible is itself a miracle."[52] Again, however, this commonly cited aphorism does not mean that the universe is *fully* comprehensible—at least not to the hopelessly insufficient human mind. Rather, it means that the universe is rationally structured and that the human mind participates to a limited extent in that universal reason. To be sure, Einstein believes that the scientific effort is in some sense progressive, revealing increasingly more of the universal order as the individual scientist ages and the collective centuries unfold.[53] At the same time, he suggests that the more the scientist uncovers, the more mysteries he also reveals.[54] It is this dance between the comprehensible and the incomprehensible that constitutes for Einstein the essence of religion and science alike, practices that aim to grasp in some way the rationally mysterious order of things he calls "God."

In one light, one might therefore see Einstein's theo-cosmology as a fairly straightforward apophaticism (whether Cusan, Eckhartian, Maimonidean, or indeed Socratic): knowledge here is both compelled and held in check by the unknowable. In another light, however, one might perceive this same theo-cosmology to be in perplexing conflict with itself. After all, if Einstein himself maintains that the rational order of things always lies beyond our grasp, then how can he be so sure it is rational in the first place? If the impersonal God lifts us out of all anthropomorphism, then to what extent can God be said to possess, or indeed to *be*, that intellect whose structure is inescapably human? Granted, Einstein concedes nearly every time he mentions it that his premise is undemonstrable, and that as such, "the intelligibility of the universe [remains] a matter of faith."[55] But what does it mean for faith to assert the ultimacy of rea-son? To what extent can the indeterminate secure a strict determinism? These questions were not particularly pressing in our exploration of Spinoza, who admitted no such faith beneath his reason and whose study of nature revealed it to be as eternal, unchanging, and absolute as he understood God to be. But they become particularly expedient in relation to Einstein, who simultaneously asserts and denies the sufficiency of reason, and who inadvertently calls into question the rational determinism of the universe the moment he professes *faith* in it. Above all, Einstein's fidelity to a natural-divine Absolute stands in baffling tension with his insight that the spacetime it amounts to is relative.

EINSTEIN VS. EINSTEIN

Relativity

As we saw in the previous chapter, it was Isaac Newton who asserted and in turn solidified the "absolute" nature of space and time.[56] To say that space and time are absolute is to say that they are independent of any particular perspec-tive on them. Measurements therefore hold for all observers: regardless of the different vantage points of person A and person B, each of them will measure a mile as a mile and ten minutes as ten minutes. Moreover, as Newton argued against his opponent Gottfried Leibniz, to say that space and time are absolute is to say they are independent of the objects within them, forming an inert grid across which beings move. Even if the universe were totally empty, space according to Newton would still be extended, and time would still pass from the past through the present to the future.

With his early twentieth-century papers on the theories of special and general relativity, however, Einstein demonstrated against Newton that space and time are not by any means independent of perspective, their inhabitants, or one another.[57] Rather, space is curved from one perspective and straight from another;[58] time passes differently depending on the velocity of the observer;[59] and space and time form a four-dimensional fabric that bends and warps according to the matter and energy "within" it. This bending and warping of spacetime is nothing other than the "gravity" that Newton declined to define: the mass of the sun, for example, creates paths within which planets travel, while the mass of planets determines the path of the moons and comets that in turn exert their own gravitational force, all of them composing the dynamic shape of the solar system. Bound up as it is with space, time likewise does not progress uniformly throughout the cosmos; rather, it passes more slowly for bodies near massive, gravitationally powerful objects than it does for bodies far from them.

As Einstein therefore summarizes the matter, vindicating Leibniz posthumously, "spacetime is not . . . something to which one can ascribe a separate existence, independently of the actual objects of physical reality. Physical objects are not *in space*, but these objects are *spatially extended*. In this way the concept 'empty space' loses its meaning."[60] There is no such thing as extension without modes, a universe without inhabitants, space without time, or "the world" without perspective. As Niels Bohr therefore remarks, Einstein's theory of relativity shatters the Newtonian clockwork, calling into question "our most elementary concepts, like space and time, and cause and effect"; anything that happens, happens from a particular standpoint. If it is the case that two bolts of lightning can hit a train one after another from the perspective of the train, but simultaneously from the perspective of the embankment that runs alongside it, then there is an "element of subjectivity" built into everything we might try to say about the universe.[61] Much like the animist cosmoi sketched by Lima, Viveiros de Castro, Ingold, and Rose, Einsteinian spacetime therefore not only appears different, but *is* different from one constituent-observer to the next. Worlds take place differently depending on your perspective.[62]

For Newton, absolute time and space reflected and reaffirmed their absolute Creator, incarnating "God's infinite extension and eternal duration" in and as the material universe.[63] One would therefore be justified in expecting nothing short of a theological revolution to attend Einstein's cosmo-physical revolution. Especially if Einstein's God *is* the order of the cosmos itself, one might hope that this divinity would be at least as manifold as trains and embankments—at least as relative as matter and spacetime. Erwin Schrödinger gestures toward such a theological revolution when he marvels that physicists can now manipulate "before and after" just by changing the velocity or gravitational field of their frame of reference. In this light, he suggests, relativity accomplishes nothing less than "the dethronement of time as a rigid tyrant imposed on us from outside." And insofar as this rigid, extra-cosmic tyrant mirrors the God of classical theism, Schrödinger concludes that the very thought of his dethronement "is a religious thought, nay, I should call it *the* religious thought."[64]

Surely, then, the physicist's ability "to play about with such a master's program" ought to change our vision of the master—as well as "his" program.[65] And yet, Schrödinger stops short of thinking through this supremely "religious thought," seeking to avoid any conflict with science by "turning against religion" altogether.[66] Such a turn is, of course, his prerogative. Far more perplexing is Einstein's own refusal to reevaluate divinity in light of his dethronement of time, considering that unlike Schrödinger, he couldn't stop talking about God. For as we have already seen, Einstein does not come close to constructing a theology of relativity. Rather, he reconsolidates a straightforward theology of the absolute—of a single, unified, deterministic, cosmic divinity in which effect always follows cause, subject is separate from object, and God retains the sturdy invariance (not to mention the anthropomorphic intelligence) "he" had enjoyed under the regime of classical and scholastic physics alike.[67] In short, Einstein's theology looks almost nothing like the cosmology his "pantheism" would presumably recapitulate.

Constant Cosmos

Granted, Einstein's neoclassical theology is not the only instance of his recoiling from his own insights. In fact, as soon as he completed his theory of relativity, he seems to have realized it posed a challenge to his faith in the absolute. We will recall that general relativity states that spacetime takes shape in relation to the matter and energy that do not so much inhabit as constitute it. For this reason, Einstein realized, it is possible that the entire universe might either be expanding or contracting—that the whole of spacetime might be either running away from or collapsing in on itself. But of course, he reasoned, a mutable universe would be absurd. Thanks, perhaps, to his thoroughgoing Spinozism, or to his enduring Newtonianism, Einstein was simply certain that the universe must be eternally unchanging. Therefore, even though it ran contrary to his own discovery of the dynamism of spacetime, Einstein introduced a term he called the "cosmological constant" (represented by the Greek letter lambda [Λ]), whose repulsive force he set in perfect counterbalance to gravity's attraction.[68] Together, gravity and lambda worked to keep the cosmos in eternal stasis.

Just a few years later, however, Edwin Hubble discovered that the distant "nebulae" he had recently determined to be galaxies were not staying in place, as they would do in a static cosmos.[69] Rather, they were all racing away from one another. More precisely, the spacetime around them was stretching out, pushing galaxies apart like polka dots on an inflating balloon. Upon hearing that the universe was not only changing but in fact careening outward into nothing at all—a realization that lent credibility to the emerging big bang hypothesis—Einstein rescinded his cosmological constant.[70] Surely it was not the error alone, but rather the degree to which Einstein had overridden his own insights, that prompted him (as astrophysical legend has it) to refer to this attempted calibration as his "biggest blunder."[71] That having been said, his hasty acceptance of an expanding universe did not make Einstein any more comfortable with the possibility that it might be indeterminate, perspectival, or less than fully "rational."

Quantum Disturbances

The conflict between Einstein's science and his metaphysics comes into clearest relief in his protracted debate with Niels Bohr over the nature of quantum mechanics. As was the case with the expanding universe and its concomitant big bang hypothesis, the quantum put Einstein in the position of being unable to tolerate the implications of his own discoveries. Indeed, although Einstein does not tend colloquially to be associated with quantum mechanics, he did play a significant role in its early stages by quantizing light in his special-relativity paper. And just four years later, he ascribed probability coefficients to these light quanta, putting an end to the centuries of toggling back and forth between particle and wave theories by suggesting that light was, in fact, both.[72]

Beginning with our study of Spinoza, the theory of particle-wave duality has provided a helpful illustration of perspectivism. Just as God-or-nature can be fully described under the attribute of thought or the attribute of extension, which are parallel and incommensurable perspectives; and just as a particular liquid is blood to a human and beer to a jaguar; so can light be fully described as particulate or wavelike, depending on the experimental arrangement one uses to observe it. If a beam of light is sent through two slits, it will produce a wavelike pattern on the screen behind them. If one slit is closed, the same beam will produce a particle pattern. If photons are fired one at a time through two slits, they will land in a wave. But if a "which-path" detector is added to determine how this is possible, the photons will behave as particles.[73] Niels Bohr's name for such mutually incompatible outcomes is *complementarity*: differing experimental arrangements produce different phenomena. And just as special relativity proclaims it equally correct to say that the embankment is moving as that the train is moving, just as a creature is a tapir under some circumstances and a human under others, so does quantum mechanics proclaim it equally correct to say that light is a particle as that light is a wave. The two phenomena are complementary: they arise under equally precise yet incompatible conditions, such that there can be no un-perspectival adjudication between them— or, for that matter, any combination or reconciliation of them. Complementary phenomena are irreducibly parallel and perspectival.

Einstein first heard Bohr present his theory of complementarity in 1927 at the Fifth Solvay Conference in Brussels. Bohr's focus was not so much particle-wave duality as properties of individual particles that could not be determined simultaneously. We may recall from our brief tour of Newtonian physics that Pierre-Simon Laplace wagered he could predict the future of the whole universe if he could at just one point in time determine the position and momentum of every body in existence.[74] Quantum particles unsettle any such cosmic determinism not just in practice but in principle because, as Bohr explained, it is not possible simultaneously to discover the position and momentum of *any* quantum particle, let alone all of them. The reason for this impossibility is that determining each of these values requires mutually exclusive experimental arrangements: position can only be calculated according to a fixed apparatus (which introduces a significant degree of uncertainty into the measurement of momentum) and momentum can only be calculated according to a moving apparatus (which introduces a significant degree of uncertainty into the measurement of position). Position and momentum—along with other values like energy and time, or the measurement of spin around different axes—are complementary: they cannot be determined simultaneously.

This quantum recalcitrance is most commonly explained as a function of Heisenberg's "uncertainty principle." Briefly stated, the problem as far as Heisenberg could see was one of instrumental interference: the moment an experimenter goes to measure a particle's position, she disturbs its momentum, and vice versa. The implication here is that, left to its own devices, a particle *has* both position and momentum, but the minute the particle is measured, one or the other of these properties necessarily changes. As Karen Barad explains, however, Heisenberg's principle is "fundamentally different" from Bohr's theory of complementarity, which amounts not to uncertainty but to *indeterminacy*.[75] According to Bohr, it is not the case that a particle possesses properties that our measurements then disturb; rather, the "intra-actions" between the particle and the act of measurement produce these properties in the first place. In short, if the problem for Heisenberg is epistemological, then the problem for Bohr is ontological: it is not the case that certain values remain unknown to us as we go to measure others, but that certain values do not exist at all as others become determinate. As molecular biologist and philosopher of science Gunther Stent summarizes the matter, "there is no such thing in the world as an electron with definite position and momentum."[76]

Rather than definite properties, what the electron, photon, or other sub-atomic particle "has" is a "wave function" (described by the Schrödinger equation) that encodes all its possible states. Any given electron will be most likely to be found in those places where the probability wave is high, least likely to be found where it is low, and unable to be found where it does not exist. In short, rather than properties, particles have probabilities. Gone, then, is the Laplacian dream of a determinate universe, as well as the sturdy logic of cause and effect that anchored it. At the quantum level, at least, identical causes produce differing and unanticipatable effects. To be sure, the sum of these possible effects can be mapped along the particle's probability wave. But any single effect remains unknown—and unknowable—in advance.

Again, there is a sense in which Einstein anticipated quantum indeterminacy. In addition to formulating particle-wave duality and introducing perspectivism with his trains and embankments, Einstein called into question the logic of cause and effect by undermining the absolute temporality on which they rely. The "effect" observed by one witness might, according to another observer, occur before or simultaneously with the first observer's "cause." As Bohr himself remarked, the "notion of complementarity" therefore "exhibits a certain resemblance [to] the principle of relativity."[77] In each case, the object of observation is inescapably bound up with the subject of observation, such that any accurate description of the phenomenon in question must specify the particular vantage point (for special relativity) or experimental arrangement (for complementarity) that produces the phenomenon as such. Given, then, that Einstein himself had produced the insight that "objectivity only exists 'within the framework of [a] theory,'"[78] it is surprising that he reacted as viscerally as he did against the principle of complementarity.

Considering Einstein's commitment to a particular kind of Spinozism, however, his discomfort becomes more understandable. Filtered as it is through the Newtonian physics that Einstein retains even as he overthrows it,[79] "Spinoza" loses in Einstein's hands nearly all his monstrosity. Far from mixing up opposites that ought to remain separate, Einstein's Spinoza is *primarily* a determinist, and as such maintains the very distinctions that a thoroughgoing pantheology would dismantle and concatenate—in particular, the distinctions between subject and object and cause and effect. Einstein bristled at the notion that a quantum particle, commonly encoded as "object," might have no determinate properties independently of its intra-actions with agencies of observation, or "subjects." (Still troubled by this possibility in 1950, Einstein reportedly stopped his colleague and eventual biographer Abraham Pais on a walk home from work to ask whether he believed the moon itself only existed when someone was looking at it.)[80] Conversely, Einstein found it "quite intolerable" that such an object might, in fact, behave as a subject—"that an electron exposed to radiation," for example, "should choose *of its own free will*, not only its moment to jump off, but also its direction."[81] As we will recall, Einstein's "Spinozism" had led him to deny free will even to God and human beings, so he found the notion that subatomic particles might be free from causal determinism to be intellectually inadmissible and, frankly, emotionally unbearable. "In that case," he confessed to Max and Hedwig Born, "I would rather be a cobbler or even an employee in a gaming house, than a physicist."[82] For as he insisted throughout his life, Einstein's being a physicist relied on "the truly religious conviction that this universe of ours is something perfect and susceptible to the rational striving for knowledge."[83] And in this light, quantum theory was in equal parts unscientific and irreligious, proclaiming as it did the irrationality and unknowability of even the most basic components of a (therefore imperfect) universe. One might as well work in a gaming house.

Far from serving as simple escape fantasy, however, Einstein's casino simultaneously encapsulated and ridiculed the indeterminate universe of quantum mechanics. If physics could no more predict an effect from a cause than a gambler could foresee a roll of the dice, then what good was it? After all, if a physicist could calculate all the forces at work in a single roll (mass, velocity, torque, air resistance, distance to table, friction of surface, etc.), then she could, in fact, predict the outcome each time. There must, then, be some way to subject the quantum dice to a similar calculation—to do better than probability by getting at the determinate, determined reality of things. Einstein admitted that his conviction in this regard was more intuitive than it was demonstrable: "I must *confess* that my scientific instinct reacts against forgoing the demand for strict causality," he wrote in a 1928 article in the *St. Louis Post-Dispatch*.[84] And again, as his choice of verbs insinuates, this scientific instinct was identical to his theological instinct. Thus, Einstein wrote in a constantly cited letter to Born that "Quantum mechanics is certainly imposing. But an inner voice tells me that it is not yet the real thing. The theory tells us a lot, but does not really bring us any closer to the secret of the 'old one.' I, at any rate, am convinced that *He* is not playing at dice."[85] The quantum might look dicey to us here and now, but probability could not possibly be the final answer *sub specie aeternitatis*. There simply had to be a more fundamental truth beneath quantum indeterminacy, and Einstein spent the rest of his life in pursuit of it: "When I am judging a theory," Einstein wrote, "I ask myself whether, if I were God, I would have arranged the world in such a way."[86] And perhaps needless to say, if Einstein were God, *he* would most certainly not play dice.

The Great Debate

Convinced of the fundamental (if not currently practicable) separability of probability from actuality, subject from object, and cause from effect, Einstein devised a series of "thought experiments" (*Gedankenexperimenten*) that might demonstrate the penultimacy of complementarity—that is, its failure to describe "a reality of objects with definite spacetime coordinates and of causally determined events."[87] As we will recall, Bohr proclaimed that no such "reality" existed, and so responded to each of Einstein's experiments by demonstrating the *ultimacy* of complementarity—in one case, by appealing to Einstein's own theory of general relativity.[88] These exchanges culminated in 1935 with Einstein's joint publication of what would come to be known as the EPR paper (after its three authors: Einstein, Boris Podolsky, and Nathan Rosen), along with Bohr's speedy rejoinder. This exchange not only provided the terms for decades of quantum debate and experimentation, but also prompted the arguable demise of Einstein's deterministic monism.

Most briefly stated, the EPR paper seeks to demonstrate that "quantum mechanics is not complete."[89] What the authors mean is that it fails to describe the "physical reality" of systems independently of their environment. As EPR insist, "any serious consideration of a physical theory must take into account the distinction between the objective reality, which is independent of any theory, and the physical concepts with which the theory operates."[90] Bohr, as we have seen, denies this distinction, arguing alongside Einstein's own theory of relativity that "objective" reality has no meaning outside of the physical-theoretical framework that coproduces it. By contrast, EPR seeks to demonstrate alongside Einstein's metaphysics (but arguably against his physics) that there is, in fact, a distinction between objects and subjects, systems and measurement, or reality and theory. Particles *have* properties independently of our measurements, but quantum mechanics cannot detect them "without disturbing the system"; therefore, they argue, quantum mechanics is "incomplete."[91]

EPR's thought experiment proceeds as follows: allow "two systems, I and II," to interact such that they become correlated with one another.[92] Without breaking the correlation, send the systems (or particles) off with equal force in opposite directions. Now measure, say, the position of system I and you will be able to derive the position of system II; that is, if system I can be found five meters due south of the point of origin, then system II will be located five meters due north of it. One could follow the same procedure for momentum. Either way, the experimenter will have determined the value of system II "without in any way disturbing" it, thereby demonstrating that the system *possesses* said value independently of any measurement of it.[93] But insofar as quantum mechanics cannot determine the theory-independent values whose existence they have just demonstrated, EPR conclude that the quantum "does not provide a complete description of . . . physical reality."[94]

The only way out of this bind, EPR suggest, would be to assert that the act of measuring system I somehow influences system II. Considering that the systems would be physically separate, however—and considering that according to special relativity, nothing can travel faster than light—the authors assert that such instantaneous influence of system I over system II would be absurd; in their words, "no reasonable definition of reality could be expected to permit this."[95] With this brief aside, the authors unintentionally laid the foundation of their undoing decades later in the hands of John Bell and Alain Aspect.[96] At the time, however, the authors believed they were making a *reductio ad absurdam* argument: since separate systems clearly cannot interact simultaneously, the measurement of system I cannot in any way influence the state of system II. As such, system II must possess measurement-independent values— values to which quantum mechanics therefore has no access, and which expose its systemic flaws.

In a brief, final paragraph, the authors admit that it is unclear whether the complete description of reality they are seeking actually "exists" (as if it might be "out there" somewhere, lying in wait to be discovered so that it might supplant the incomplete quantum). But appropriately, they end their provocation with a collective profession of faith: "we believe," they affirm, "that such a theory is possible."[97]

Unimaginatively sharing the title of the paper to which it responds, Bohr's rejoinder turns on his rejection of the authors' definition of "physical reality."[98] Rather than permitting us to retain such Newtonian concepts, he argues, quantum mechanics requires both "a final renunciation of the classical ideal of causality" and "a radical renunciation of our attitude towards the problem of physical reality."[99] Unlike the classical universe, Bohr explains, the world of quantum mechanics does not admit any a priori distinction between the theoretical-experimental apparatus on the one hand and "reality" on the other; rather, "reality" means nothing other than "the observations obtained under specified circumstances."[100] In this particular regard, Bohr again reminds his colleagues that quantum mechanics is no different from "the general theory of relativity," which likewise called into question "the absolute character of physical phenomena" and demanded the specification of physical-theoretical points of reference for any stated measurement.[101] The problem, then, with EPR's *Gedankenexperiment* is that it forgets the nature of quantum (or indeed relativistic) reality, asserting a system's independence from the overarching experimental arrangement that produces it. What the authors overlook, according to Bohr, is that it is not possible to "determine," say, the position (q) of system II without *determining* it; that is, it is not possible simply to infer q_2 by measuring q_1. Rather, given the persistent correlation of the systems, the measurement of q_1 changes "*the very conditions which define*" the possible outcomes for q_2.[102] In other words, systems I and II cannot be regarded as separate from the experimental apparatus, or from one another.

Faced with Bohr's defense, Einstein had no response other than another characteristic confession of faith. It was possible, he conceded, that "reality" might be nothing more than the relations between interconstituted subjects and objects, the measuring and the measured, and theories and physical phenomena. It was possible, in other words, that quantum mechanics does, in fact, provide a "complete" description of "reality." But "to believe" as much, he wrote, "is so very contrary to my scientific conception that I cannot forgo the search for a more complete conception."[103]

Reality and Difference

Indeed, Einstein never did forgo this search. Until the day he died, he was convinced that there was something deeply wrong with quantum ontology.

And to return to the main thread of our inquiry, this conviction can be said to be the product of Einstein's theology, which asserted at once the mystery of the divine cosmos and its comprehensibility—a theology that, despite its "humility," nevertheless claimed to know the ways of the unknowable. This tension mirrors the tension between Einstein's relativistic physics and his absolutist metaphysics—a conflict that seems to have baffled Bohr in particular. As Carl Sagan narrates one of their famous encounters,

> Einstein said, "God does not play dice with the cosmos." And on another occasion he asserted, "God is subtle but he is not malicious." In fact Einstein was so fond of such aphorisms that the Danish physicist Niels Bohr turned to him on one occasion and with some exasperation said, "Stop telling God what to do."[104]

According to Stent, Bohr's irritation with Einstein's unshakeable faith in a causally deterministic cosmos reveals that the "actual subject" of the mythic Einstein-Bohr debates was "not physical theory, but God."[105] At stake, Stent suggests, was the existence of a superrational power anchoring the dicey universe, with Einstein holding onto "the traditional monotheistic viewpoint of modern science" and Bohr breaking through to a genuine, postmodern "atheism."[106] In this light, "the Great Debate" can be seen as enacting the final growing pains of an increasingly secular Western science, struggling to do away once and for all with its theological past.

It is striking, however, that Bohr's riposte does not contest the existence of God so much as Einstein's claim to know (and even dictate) how God must behave. Bohr was baffled by Einstein's appeal to a single, immutable order of things beyond, behind, or beneath the world as it variously takes shape under differing theoretical and experimental conditions. Thanks to his refusal to make proclamations about such a single, immutable order, Bohr is often encoded as an "anti-realist," denying the existence of a reality beneath appearances. Bohr's strongest statement in this regard insists that "there is no quantum world. There is only an abstract quantum physical description. It is wrong to think that the task of physics is to figure out how nature *is*. Physics concerns what we can *say* about nature."[107] Bohr's meaning, however, is far from clear; in fact, this statement and similar "anti-realist" assertions[108] can be interpreted in strikingly divergent ways.

First, there is Einstein's reading, which ascribes to Bohr an irresponsible disregard for the real world. As David Kaiser reports, "Bohr's insistence on observation and interaction appeared to Einstein as nothing but [what he called] an 'epistemology-soaked orgy.'"[109] Amusingly, Einstein also likened

Bohr's orgy to the painstaking rereadings of traditional Jewish scholarly practice, referring to his post-Christian opponent as "the Talmudic philosopher" whose obsession with interpretive plurality meant that he couldn't "give a straw for 'reality.'"[110] Against Einstein, the quantum pioneer Wolfgang Pauli spins Bohr's disregard for "reality" into a pragmatic virtue. Bohr's point, he explains, is that it makes no sense to waste time asking about measurement-independent values when such values are inescapably the product of our measurements. Reversing Einstein's charge of theological hairsplitting (and ironically likening him to traditional *Christian* philosophers), Pauli insists that "one should no more rack one's brain about the problem of whether something one cannot know anything about exists all the same, than about the ancient question of how many angels are able to sit on the point of a needle. But it seems to me," he muses, "that Einstein's questions are always of this kind."[111] Pauli's pragmatic valence becomes lost (or simply meaningless) in the eyes of the physicist-theologian Stanley Jaki who, in a revival of the old charge of acosmism, accuses Bohr of having "abolished the ontological reality of the universe itself" with his insistence that "there is no quantum world."[112] Offering perhaps the strongest reading of "anti-realism" among Bohr's numerous interpreters, Jaki suggests that Bohr's refusal to speculate about the universe apart from our interaction with it is tantamount to his denying its existence altogether. In this acosmic light, it is perhaps not surprising that Bohr himself has been charged or credited—depending on the hermeneut—with having imported "traditional Far Eastern philosophy" into the otherwise Abrahamic milieu of modern science.[113]

Finally, in the opposite interpretive direction, Karen Barad develops Bohr's pragmatism into a full-scale ontological principle, arguing that Bohr's relational, experimentally specific measurements *are* his reality. According to Bohr, she explains, "the primary ontological unit is not independent entities with inherent boundaries but rather *phenomena*," a term that Bohr calls upon to refer, in his words, to "the observations obtained under specified circumstances, including an account of the whole experimental arrangement."[114] There is, then, no such thing as a particle-in-itself, carrying around properties of position, momentum, energy, and spin. Rather, there is, say, a particle-entangled-with-another-and-measured-by-a-human-designed-and-human-monitored-spin-detector-along-the-mathematically-determined-x-axis. Or there is a photon-as-it-is-humanly-recorded-in-a-wave-pattern-on-a-photographic-screen-after-having-interfered-with-other-photons-passing-through-a-metal-plate-with-two-slits-cut-out-of-it-by-a-laser-manufactured-in-Minnesota-out-of-materials-mined-in-South-Africa-and-indigenous-Australia. Or there is a Danish-observer-who-set-up-a-which-path-detector-after-breakfast-and-lost-the-interference-pattern-he'd-been-expecting-before-breakfast. What "there is," in short, is a bottomless entanglement of subjects and objects, observers and observed, circumstances and experiments: queer mixtures that amount to Bohrian "phenomena." As Barad encapsulates such multiplicities, "*phenomena are the ontological inseparability . . . of intra-acting agencies. . . .* phenomena are ontologically primitive relations without preexisting relata."[115]

Again, it is this inseparability of relationally produced subjects and objects, causes and effects, and agents and patients that provoked and sustained Einstein's unending discomfort with the quantum. And indeed, a similar discomfort motivates the effort among those theorists who seek to avoid these subjective entanglements by means of the "many worlds interpretation" (MWI) that preserves classical causality by locating every possible outcome in its own universe; as physicist Colin Bruce proclaims, "only in a quantum [that is, MWI] world does it become possible to measure something without affecting it at all."[116] In both Einstein's and MWI's critiques, Bohr and his "Copenhagen Interpretation" take on the role of modern European animists, "unable" to distinguish between humans and nonhumans, self and other, internality and externality. What kind of a scientist can't get himself out of the way in order to see things objectively?

As we have seen in variously animist worldviews, however, the refusal of a priori binarism does not amount to a denial of difference—much less does it add up to a proclamation that "all is one." To the contrary, animist differences are constantly, relationally, and locally produced, so that a stick in the hands of an adept healer during ritual practice is alive, whereas the same stick in the hands of a U.S. curator is not. The things the Ashanika call maggots are grilled fish to a vulture, who moreover sees herself as human and the "human" as prey. What animist ontologies deny is that these beings carry around properties independently of the shifting intra-actions that bestow those properties upon them. And we detect a similar operation in Barad's reading of Bohr: there is no inherent quantum distinction between subject and object or observer and observed. Rather, there are experimentally specific distinctions that take shape differently depending on the apparatus, which "*enacts a cut delineating the object from the agencies of observation.*"[117] This "cut" amounts to Barad's Bohrian principle of distinction: it produces subjects and causes as different from objects and effects, but only within the framework of a specific, multiagential apparatus. Viewed in this light, Bohr's ontology amounts not to an "anti-realism," but to an "agential realism," by means of which real subjects and objects take shape as (and only as) the products of particular material-discursive frameworks.

As Barad explains, "it is through specific agential intra-actions that the bound-aries and properties of the components become determinate."[118] To be clear, *this does not mean there is no reality*. It means that realities are constantly, dif-ferentially, relationally, and perspectivally generated.

With all of this in mind, then, we can read Bohr's critique of Einstein's theology not as a call to atheism, but rather as an invitation to a more consis-tent pantheism—one whose *theos* genuinely abandons the lingering anthro-pocentrism of "reason" in order to take on the complex perspectivism of its *cosmos*. Indeed, we have repeatedly seen Einstein run away from the meta-physical implications not only of quantum physics, but also of his own theory of relativity, insisting as he repeatedly does on unifying, objectifying, and determining the cosmos with his non-gambling God. When Bohr rejects this theo-cosmic vision, we can see by means of Barad that he is not rejecting "reality," but rather recoding it as relationally and multiply situated—insights Bohr attributes equally to quantum mechanics and general relativity. What, then, would this recoding of reality mean for Einstein's theology? How would his "cosmic religious sense" hit if it sensed cosmic multiplicity? What would "Spinoza's God" look like if it amounted not to an anchor beneath or beyond the shifting perspectives of relativity and the quantum, but to these world-making perspectives themselves?

PANTHEOLOGIES

Dei sive omnēs

Ever since we uncovered a constitutive multiplicity at work in Spinoza's "single substance," we have sought to rethink his *Deus sive natura* from the perspec-tive of multiplicity, which is to say from the perspective of perspective itself. In Spinoza, we found a *pan* composed of infinite attributes, each of which expresses God-or-nature holographically in and as each distinct thing. It is this necessary expression that leads Spinoza to conclude that the universe itself is necessary, which is to say determined: nothing can be other than the way it is. At the same time, in order to avoid the seeming absurdity of declaring par-ticular things divine, Spinoza splits the modes off from substance, calling them contingent rather than necessary, and thereby introducing an indeterminism into his own clockwork cosmos. Much like his eventual descendent Einstein, however, Spinoza can be interpreted here as fleeing the implications of his own thinking, assured as he was that "Nature is always the same, and its force and power of acting is everywhere the same."[119] Convinced of the unchanging nature of nature, Spinoza preserves the traditionally monotheistic attributes of eternity and a certain kind of "reason" even as he vehemently denies the anthropomorphic Creator of popular religion and orthodox theology.

Reading Spinoza both with and against himself, the study at hand has sought to reconceive the "nature" that Spinoza's God "is." By means of an unruly con-catenation of old and new theories of immanence, it has uncovered a sympoi-etic, creative-destructive spiritual materiality that can neither be reduced to a single force nor gathered into a single world. Rather, these ceaseless copro-ductivities take shape as micro- and macrocosmic cosmoi that overlap, collide with, ignore, magnify, destroy, and inhabit one another. Divinity thus conceived would therefore be immanent, self-exceeding, relational, changing, and multi-ply perspectival, to such an extent that the "pantheism" in question would col-lide with a certain kind of polytheism. "All the gods that men ever discovered are still God," writes D. H. Lawrence in a more generous spirit than the one ani-mating his excoriation of Whitman: "and they contradict one another and fly down one another's throats, marvelously. Yet they are *all* God: the incalculable Pan."[120] To affirm the divinity of such manifold, contradictory, and incalculable unfoldings would be to affirm endless, particular loci of divinity—particular-ities akin, perhaps, to the "topick" gods of the English seventeenth century; or the Roman *genii loci* they modernize; or the ancient Greek *penates*, "local goddesses of the *oikos*"; or the Yoruban *orisha;* or the "radical polytheism" of Native American cosmology; or indeed the endless divinities into which not only the purportedly monistic Hindu worldview, but also the purported mono-theisms inexorably tumble.[121]

Such thinking would therefore affirm a kind of pancarnation: divinity's inability not to express itself in and as the endless, stubbornly un-totalized run of all things. This is not, of course, to say that everything is divine to every perceiving agent. Far less is it to say that everything is the same. Rather, it is to acknowledge that what looks like an inert rock from one perspective is a sacred ancestor from another; that the catfish one person serves for dinner could be kin to her partner and a great creative being to both of them; and that what looks in one light like the image of God is in another a peccary, and in another still the billion-year product of bacterial collaboration. Like Viveiros de Cas-tro's account of Amerindian cosmology, such perspectival pancarnation would be different from relativism: if the latter asserts that there are many ways to interpret the same world, the former would assert that worlds—and therefore divinities—take shape differently depending on the points of view that intra-agentially construct them.[122]

Ethics and Perspective

It is doubtful, however, that this distinction between perspectivism and relativism will suffice to allay the theist's concern over the so-called problem of evil. The concern, as we might recall, reliably stems from a monistic, even mereological understanding of pantheism as stating that "all things" add up to a divine totality. With this understanding in mind, the pantheistic insult is twofold: first, it seems to attribute to divinity "all the infirmities of the world," making God not only agent of every disease, disaster, and act of violence, but also its patient.[123] Second, pantheism thus conceived seems to endorse all things as they are, giving us no reason to try to change them. As Nancy Frankenberry summarizes this critique, "How are we to establish any priorities in the ordering of values and commitments if nature as a whole is considered divine and known to contain evil as well as good, destruction as much as creation?"[124] Frankenberry's answer to this question is that the ordering of values is no more a challenge for pantheism than it is for panentheism or even theism: in any of these frameworks, we are faced with the seeming indifference of the order of things to our ethical conduct, and with the need nevertheless to create ethical standards. "The rain falls on the just and the unjust alike," she reminds us, "whichever model of God one holds."[125]

Indeed, one could be less generous than Frankenberry and argue that classical theism is far more of an impediment to ethics than either pantheism or panentheism is, insisting as theism does on God's omnipotence, unchanging goodness, and preference for humanity over the rest of creation. As Einstein worries in his 1940 lecture, such a God becomes directly responsible for all the ills that befall us, relieving humans of any real accountability for having created the conditions that perpetuate such ills, or for acting otherwise.[126] After all, a God who is both willing and able to intervene in human affairs will do so when "he" deems it necessary to do so. And insofar as God does *not* intervene—even in the face of unprecedented levels of global suffering and cruelty—we can only be led to conclude that God must condone or even will, say, the escalating refugee crisis, phallo-nuclear brinkmanship, the normalization of sexual violence, the extinction of thousands of species for the sake of capitalist comfort, the unbridled resurgence of anti-black racism, and industrial agriculture's obliteration of untold scores of nonhuman animals.

Just a few years after Einstein wrote the "Science and Religion" lecture undermining the personal God, Dietrich Bonhoeffer issued a similar critique of what he called God as a "working hypothesis."[127] From his Gestapo prison cell in 1944,

Bonhoeffer explained that there had been no significant "religious" response to Hitler's deportation and extermination of European Jews (or of Roma, sexual deviants, the disabled, and the elderly) because Christians in particular had made God into a *deus ex machina*—a superman whom they believed would fly in from the rafters just in time to save people from cognitive or physical disaster.[128] Armed with such a salvific promise, Bonhoeffer lamented, most Christians felt relieved of any real responsibility for the catastrophe that would come to be called the *Shoah*, convinced as they were that God would eventually swoop in to fix it.

Three decades later, philosopher William R. Jones likewise accused traditional theism of condoning anti-blackness. If God is indeed omnipotent and invested in human affairs, he reasoned, then we can only conclude from the radically unequal distribution of suffering in the world that God must be a white racist.[129] After all, if such a God wanted to step in to put an end to black oppression—or even to mitigate it—then clearly, "he" would have done so. Jones went on to implore black liberationists to give up the God of white racism, which is to say the all-powerful God who relieves humanity of its responsibility for creating or changing racist conditions, assuring us that the world is running according to some mysterious divine plan.[130] Considering "God's" incompatibility with modern science, philosophy, and ethics—as well as his magnificent failure to end or even alleviate racism, suffering, and violence—the late twentieth and early twenty-first centuries have produced a slew of post-theistic reimaginings of divinity, from process theologies to existential theologies to liberation theologies to feminist theologies to womanist theologies to radical theologies to a/theologies to weak theologies to minimal theologies to eco-theologies to postcolonial theologies to theological naturalism to theologies of multiplicity and relation.[131] Each of these strategies positions itself squarely against the white-male-theistic God of power and might, and yet the allegedly modern West clings to him as if he had never died. In the immediate aftermath of Donald Trump's 2017 withdrawal from the Paris Climate Accord, for example, Republican Representative Tim Walberg of Michigan gave voice to an unreconstructed, even infantile theology by assuring his constituents that, "As a Christian I believe that there is a Creator in God who is much bigger than us. And I'm convinced that, if there is a real problem, he can take care of it."[132]

Influenced to a great extent by the post- and anti-theisms that have preceded it, the study at hand seeks to determine the theoretical and ethical force of the position even they tend uniformly to ridicule. Considering its constitutive attunement to interconstitution, pantheism in its pluralistic and even monistic forms combats the willful ignorance and ethical quietism of our astonishingly undead political theisms. To be sure, monistic pantheisms, especially in their deterministic forms, tend to replace such passivity with resignation to—or even deliberate affirmation of—the world as it is (as it must necessarily be). This is why we have opted for a pluralistic pantheology that teaches no such necessity, undermining the determinism of Spinoza and Einstein alike by means of their own physical philosophies. By attending to the contingency of intra-agential worldings, the pantheological effort at hand aligns itself with Haraway's cosmogonic "chthonic ones," affirming multispecies creative-destructive assemblages that endeavor to love and imagine and make worlds otherwise.

There is, then, no pantheological resignation to "the way things are," far less an endorsement of all things as "good." Rather, what pantheologies affirm when they say "all things are divine" is that all things participate—to greater or lesser intensity and to all manner of competing, collaborative, and disjunctive ends— in multiple, ongoing processes of cosmic makings and unravelings. Again, such pancarnation does not bless all things, events, or (un)becomings as "good," maintaining no a priori commitment to the human-measured benevolence of divinity. For this reason, one can justifiably respond to the perennial critic that *there is no "problem of evil"* when it comes to pantheologies. This is not at all to say that suffering, extinction, oppression, and violence are not pantheological concerns; to the contrary, the abandonment of an extra-cosmic problem-solver is motivated in part by the need to take responsibility for the messes we make. It is simply to say there is no *speculative* problem of evil—no logical incompatibility between pantheologies' visions of divinity and their experiences of the world. Indeed, such a "problem" is limited to those theisms that insist upon an anthropomorphic creator and an anthropocentric creation.

Classically stated, the problem of evil seeks to reconcile the existence of an omnipotent and benevolent God with the presence of suffering in the world. As Hume's Philo summarizes the dilemma, "is [God] willing to prevent evil, but not able? Then is he impotent. Is he able, but not willing? Then is he malevolent. Is he both able and willing? Whence then is evil?"[133] Committed as he is to affirming the untrammeled power and goodness of God, the theist then needs to perform cognitive backflips to explain God's inaction in the face of war, oppression, hurricanes, famine, plagues, and corporate capitalism. These backflips, or "theodicies" (justifications of the power and goodness of God in the face of a flawed creation), turn the problem upside-down in order to proclaim suffering a blessing in disguise, to lay the blame for evil on humanity rather than God, to override our plain experience of the world with a more fundamental and mysterious goodness, or to accomplish all of these at once.[134]

But such efforts become unnecessary in the absence of a single, anthropo-morphic creator. Indeed, there is no "problem of evil" for those non-monothe-istic cosmogonies that affirm a proliferation of shape-shifters, tricksters, and demiurges; their answer to the question of the origin of evil is simply that there have been competing interests among limited beings from the very beginning—and that the beginning has always been in the middle of things.[135] For self-identified animists, Graham Harvey explains, "the world and its various powers are neither good nor bad . . . but open, efficacious, and above all, relational."[136] "Evil" in such frameworks is therefore not a mystery to be explained but rather a concrete reality to negotiate and try to overcome.

In *Native Pragmatism*, philosopher Scott Pratt has assembled Narragansett, Iroquois, Algonquin, Penobscot, Haudenosaunee, and Ojibwa stories of "man-eaters" to demonstrate the ethical foundations of pragmatist philosophy within Native American communities. Rather than seeking to explain how the Great Spirit could allow cannibalism into an otherwise perfect creation, and rather than seeking the origin of this quintessentially antisocial behavior in either per-sonal or collective sin, Pratt explains that these stories are strictly concerned with restoring the specific social relations the cannibal threatens. Overwhelm-ingly, he finds, such stories recommend that the community show kindness and hospitality toward the fearsome other—even going so far as to welcome him as "grandfather"—in order to "diminish the danger and disruption of the cannibal and restore peace within a community or between nations."[137] Of course, offer-ing such radical hospitality is not possible in every situation. Sometimes the cannibal needs to be exiled or even killed to protect the life of the community. Kindness, then, is not "an absolute response mandated in every possible cir-cumstance," but rather a situational ethic, "chosen based on the circumstances at hand."[138]

Such a practical, contextual ethic tends not to emerge, however, when the operative cosmology presumes an anthropomorphic lawgiver who rules the universe. Demonstrating this distinction, Native American theologian and activist Vine Deloria recalls "going to an Indian home shortly after the death of a child."[139] The family's grief-stricken mother has been visited by a local Roman Catholic priest, who assures her that her child, having been baptized, is assuredly "with Jesus," and that therefore she should not grieve. Insofar as Jesus has overcome the death that Adam brought upon us, the priest concluded, "the mother could see the hand of God in the child's death and needn't worry about its cause," nor need she worry that perhaps she had done something to deserve the suffering that God had visited upon her. But as Deloria explains, "the mother had not wondered about the reason for the child's death. Her child had fallen from a second story window and suffered internal injuries. [The child] had lingered several days with a number of ruptured organs and had eventually and mercifully died."[140]

Because the Christian tradition cannot abide death, it explains death as the consequence of sin rather than the result of nonnegotiable physical processes. "In Indian religions," by contrast, "death is a natural occurrence and not a special punishment from an arbitrary God." Death in this context is a sadness to be mourned, but not "an occasion for probing the rationale of whatever reality exists beyond ourselves." It calls for a lived response, not a "series of logical syllogisms."[141] Pantheologically speaking, then, if we begin with multiple, finite, and immanent forces rather than a single anthropomorphic deity, we can stop wasting time on abstract justifications and set about trying to change the conditions that produce suffering in the first place (Pratt), and to create rituals of mourning wherever change is not possible (Deloria). As James summarizes the matter, "in any pluralistic metaphysic, the problems that evil presents are practical, not speculative."[142]

To be sure, such pluralistic metaphysics would need to determine what "evil" means, and whose suffering counts, in any given situation. In the absence of an extra-cosmic governor, there can be no extra-cosmic ethic—no static or a priori delineation of the boundaries of "good" and "evil." Rather, as Spinoza explains in consonance with Pratt, such terms describe relations rather than essences; the things composing God-or-nature possess no moral valences (or any other qualities, for that matter) on their own but only in relation to other things.[143] Under the reign of an anthropomorphic creator who made the whole universe for the sake of humanity, ethics forgets this relationality. Such theism pretends that good and evil are somehow inherent to things, but in fact designates them as one or the other "to the extent that they please or offend human senses, serve or oppose human interests."[144] Summarizing the position against which he stakes his entire metaphysics, Spinoza writes,

> When men became convinced that everything that is created is created on their behalf, they were bound to consider as the most important quality in every individual thing that which was most useful to them and to regard as of the highest excellence all those things by which they were most benefitted. Hence they came to form these abstract notions to explain the natures of things: Good, Bad, Order, Confusion, Hot, Cold, Beauty, Ugliness.[145]

In the absence of such an anthropomorphic creator and his anthropocentric creation, however, there is no assurance that human interests are any more

significant than bovine, mineral, or bacterial interests. Rather than being absolute terms, good and evil become as perspectival as anything else: the maggots
that are disgusting to most humans are delicious to fish and vultures; they
are destructive to certain crops but crucial to the recycling of organic waste
upon which the crop cycle relies; and they infest wounds under certain conditions but debride them under others. Again, this is not to say that all things
are equivalent or that, pantheologically speaking, there can be no values. It is
simply to say that such values are always situated, so that it would be the task
of any multiplicitous immanentism to own up to its situation. To account, for
example, for its preference for low-wage jobs and low-cost energy over moun-
taintops (or vice versa); its preference for animal welfare over stylish shoes
(or vice versa); or its conviction that anti-racist, labor-related, feminist, and
ecological efforts are resonant and interdependent endeavors, such that the
logic of preference undermines all of them.[146]

All or Nothing

The remaining question is whether there is any appreciable difference between
immanentism, thus conceived, and atheism. As we will recall, critics across
the centuries and from all corners of the philosophical universe have accused
pantheism of being indistinguishable from atheism: Bayle leveled this charge
against Spinoza; Jacobi and Schopenhauer revived it from opposite perspectives against Spinoza's Romantic enthusiasts; American preachers took it up
against the transcendentalists; and Richard Dawkins still hurls it at anyone who
tries to add a valence of sacredness to an otherwise selfish and mechanistic set
of natural processes. In the first half of this chapter, we saw Einstein accused of
"authentic atheism . . . camouflaged as cosmic pantheism"—a charge that persisted despite Einstein's insistence that he was by no means an atheist. Even his
admirers tended to assume that Einstein's "cosmic religious feeling" amounted
to a denial of God; as the president of England's National Secular Society
announced, Einstein's retention of the word "God" was ultimately a joke. After
all, if God does not have any particular preference for humanity and cannot
intervene in worldly affairs, then "he" might as well not exist.[147] At stake here
seems to be the question of impersonalism: if God is nothing more than the
order of the universe—deterministic or not—then what use is God?

Attempting to navigate between Einstein's critics and his defenders in the
wake of the scandal of 1940, Paul Tillich accused Einstein of having staked
his argument against an impoverished understanding of divine personality.

The God whom Einstein rejects, Tillich insists, is a God in whom no decent theologian believes—that is, an extra-cosmic superman who might put an end to the war, win the Super Bowl, or make the bus arrive on time. But God is no such character (or caricature); rather, God is the "ground of being" that is also an "abyss"—at once manifest in all that is and "hidden in its unexhaustible depth."[148] As we have seen, Einstein had a profound sense of this simultaneous revelation and concealment of divinity, but tended to override the latter with the former, convinced as he was that the mysterious nature of God must be fully rational and determinate. Tillich pushes Einstein's thinking back toward the apophatic, reminding him that if divinity is essentially mysterious, then anything we say about it falls short of encapsulating it; in Tillich's language, all religious speech is "symbolic." And—here is where Einstein has misunderstood theology—"one of these symbols is 'Personal God.'"[149]

Tillich concedes that, in popular usage, practitioners often forget this strictly symbolic valence. But when theologians speak of a "personal God," he explains, they are both asserting and negating the predication at the same time. What they mean is that God is both "ground and abyss" of all human personality, and as such God must be manifest in human personality even as "He" exceeds it.[150] According to Tillich, Einstein seems partially to understand this excessive manifestation when he calls God "supra-personal." But for Einstein, the supra-personal tumbles into the impersonal, whereas for Tillich, the supra-personal must mean *super*personal—above the personal—so personal as to defy worldly analogy. And at this point, Tillich solidifies his theological correction by means of that Great Undead Chain of Being, explaining that although all symbols ultimately fail, the supra-personal God is *best* analogized by the human personality "He" both encapsulates and exceeds. The problem with calling God "impersonal," he explains, is that it attempts to symbolize God by the less-than-personal, attributing to God the sort of being (presumably) possessed by rocks and plants and nonhuman animals. In other words, Einstein's impersonal God moves in the wrong direction. As Tillich puts it, "the depth of being cannot be symbolized by objects taken from a realm which is lower than the personal, from the realm of things or sub-personal living beings."[151]

To be sure, this is a perplexing assertion. What Tillich *means* is that in our ongoing effort to speak about the God who surpasses creation, we must at the very least attribute to God the highest of creaturely attributes. The highest of creaturely attributes is human personality. So, Tillich concludes, we must at the very least say that God is personal in order to say that God also exceeds the personal, and that he does so in a straightforwardly vertical, specifically upward, direction. With this logic, however, Tillich replicates the very certainty about uncertainty that has perplexed us in Einstein: on the one hand, Tillich is asserting the inaccessible mystery of God, and on the other hand, he is saying he knows where this mystery is and what its minimal contours must be. Start with the human, he tells us, retain those characteristics as you ascend, and eventually you'll hit something like God. Something closer, at least, than Einstein has got with his "allegedly supra-personal" but actually "sub-personal" God: the God of "monism and pantheism" that lies beneath, rather than above, personality.[152]

What is most confusing about Tillich's conviction, however, is that his own language employs the very downward metaphorics he denies can apply to God. It is as if two different people wrote the phrase, "the depth of being cannot be symbolized by objects taken from a realm which is lower than the personal," one of whom moves downward to analogize the divine and the other of whom moves up. How can Tillich possibly say that the *depth* of being cannot be symbolized by that which is low? And what, for that matter, are we to make of his calling God "ground," much less "abyss"? How is it that Tillich can assert that only lofty symbols can apply to God when he regularly appeals to such a lowly, fundamental symbolic?

To be sure, the study at hand is not attempting to produce a coherent Tillichian apophatics. Nor is it seeking to proclaim it incoherent. Rather, the point of this brief sojourn with Tillich-on-Einstein has been to demonstrate once again the theological insufficiency of the tired old vertical axis that runs from rocks to God. Indeed, Tillich simply reverses the analogical dive-bomb of which he accuses Einstein, elevating his otherwise "sub-personal" God into a "supra-personal" God and thereby solidifying the anthropomorphic theology he insists he rejects. And in both cases, I would suggest that the problem is the categorical confinement of personhood to humanity.

Much like Spinoza's, Einstein's primary theological concern is to unsettle the anthropomorphic God who reigns over an anthropocentric creation. His solution is an "impersonal" God—the God of mathematics and celestial harmony. But this God's eternal imperturbability and refusal of all relation takes "him" promptly out of the world with which Einstein is allegedly identifying God. Hence the charges of atheism and irrelevance; one might as well pray to the Pythagorean theorem. Conversely, Tillich seeks to secure God's transcendence of all human categories, but in the process establishes humanity as the symbolic ground upon which the "supra-personal" God is based; one might as well pray to one's father.

But what if, instructed by the new animisms, we refuse to confine the category of personhood to humanity? What if anything we can call agential—which is to say anything in active relation with other things, anything that participates in the ongoing creation, destruction, and re-worlding of worlds—can *from some perspective* also be called a person? In that case, there would be an alternative to the equally unpalatable theologemes of anthropocentrism on the one hand and impersonalism on the other. In that case, to call all things divine would be to call divinity *omni*personal, taking shape as every kind of person, depending on the circumstance. Such a reconfiguration of personhood would unsettle the theistic notion that humanity is the pinnacle of creation, along with the attendant assumption that divinity looks more like a human being than a dingo, an ocean, or the electromagnetic force. At the same time, it would avoid the non-relational force of the "impersonal," affirming that humans exist in interpersonal assemblages with nonhuman animals, plants, minerals, and bacteria. To call these agents "persons" is to say they can be petitioned, violated, tolerated, adored, apologized to, and collaborated with—and to call them divine is to ascribe to them the creative-destructive capacity of cosmogenesis.

Put otherwise, if divinity loses its association with humanity and takes on more pantheological proportions—so that everything in the cosmos is *in some sense* and from some perspective an expression of divinity—then the scope of personhood widens considerably. Pantheologically, we are not only surrounded but also constituted by nonhuman persons who can feel, hurt, rejoice, and who for those reasons deserve our respect and care—or at the very least our thoughtful deliberation whenever we decide to override the intentions of some assemblages (say, those of termites, their nests, mounds, shelter tubes, and gut bacteria) with others (say, those of a concrete foundation for a wood-frame house; its feline, canine, and human inhabitants; and *their* gut bacteria). And again, if all these persons are in some sense divine, then divinity becomes not impersonal but rather omni-personal—as operative in and irreducible to a bed of reeds as it is in and to a mustard seed, a coyote, your insufferable neighbor, Hegel's snuffbox, or Poliinio's dressing gown.

Otherwise Worlds

"Every day is a god," writes the poet Annie Dillard in one of her particularly pantheological moods; "each day is a god and holiness holds forth in time."[153] And so she greets the morning-god of Puget Sound; the bird-god her cat drags in, scorched and half-alive; the girl-god who follows her at sunset; those boyish, Pan-ish gods, "pagan and fernfoot"; her eggs, the coffee, a spider, a moth—all of it god-soaked, creating, created.[154] Surrounded by gods, however, Dillard also comes to realize she is abandoned by God—by the God of power and might who might stop a plane from falling from the sky, save a child from third-degree burns, or "stick a nickel's worth of sense into our days."[155] To affirm that each day is a god is therefore to admit that the gods of days are all we have—created creators, some of them on our side and some of them most certainly not. "No gods have the power to save," Dillard confesses. "There are only days. The one great God abandoned us to days, to time's tumult of occasions, abandoned us to the gods of days each brute and amok in his hugeness and idiocy."[156] To affirm days, worlds, or worldings as divine is therefore not to proclaim them good— certainly not only good—but rather to affirm them, for better or worse, as the source and end of all we are. And to try to make them otherwise.

Again, though, we might ask whether worlds and their immanent cosmogonists need to be encoded as divine in order to inspire such recognition, respect, and re-worldings. And clearly, the answer is no; theories and praxes of immanence tend to get along just fine without divinizing the mechanisms of their production. In the absence of such necessity, then, one starts to wonder whether the *theos* makes any difference at all to the *pan* or whether, as Schopenhauer charges, pantheism even in this carefully pluralized, indeterminate, multispecies form is simply looking for a way to add God back into an otherwise secular ontology.[157] Just in case it has not become clear that the position tends to be denigrated from every imaginable theo-political standpoint, we can focus this concern through Val Plumwood's ecofeminist critique. "In many forms of pantheism," Plumwood worries, "Nature is treated as fully sentient and as having, through its possession of spirit . . . human qualities;" in short, she charges, "the human is taken as the basic model."[158] According to Plumwood, such lingering anthropocentrism especially plagues goddess spiritualities, which siphon all agency into "a centralized source . . . a hidden presence throughout the whole, inhabiting the shell" of any given organism "and animating it."[159]

Convinced alongside Plumwood that "such a deity is theft," this study has sought to resist both anthropomorphism and centralization (or unification, totality, monism, etc.), recognizing that "the great plurality of particular beings in nature [are] capable of their *own* autonomy, agency and ecological or spiritual meaning"—so long as this "ownness" signifies an "interconnectedness"—or more precisely, *intra*-connectedness, which is to say sympoiesis.[160] In this manner, the pantheological convocation at hand may well elude this set of charges, ascribing destructive-creativity not to a humanlike force within all things, but to all things themselves. "But if we have such an account," Plumwood nevertheless fires back, "why should we need a deity?" Granted, one might quibble here with the lingering singular, explaining that pantheologies attend not to *a* deity, but rather to unending sites of divinity that reveal and conceal themselves from an infinite number of perspectives. But the spirit of the question remains: however single or multiple, why appeal to divinity at all?

There are numerous ways to respond to this question, any of which a hypothetical pantheologian might decide is more compelling or productive than the others. The first would be to claim an *affective* difference between ascribing agency to intra-connected world-making assemblages and ascribing divinity to them. To call all things divine, one might argue, is to profess a certain humility and awe in relation to them, and thereby to mark them as worthy of reverence. Einstein, for example, professed a "rapturous amazement" at the order of the universe, which revealed the "utterly insignificant" nature of human means and ends.[161] This humble astonishment, or "cosmic religious sense," marked for Einstein an admittedly narrow yet absolute distinction between the pantheism he professed and the atheism he seemed to court. As he explained to the theatre critic Alfred Kerr, who expressed disbelief at Einstein's purported "religiousness,"

> Try and penetrate with our limited means the secrets of nature and you will find that, behind all the discernible concatenations, there remains something subtle, intangible and inexplicable. Veneration for this force beyond anything that we can comprehend is my religion. To that extent I am, in point of fact, religious.[162]

A similarly awestruck veneration marks the theological naturalism of biologist and complexity theorist Stuart Kauffman, who "honorably steal[s]" the word "God" to refer to the "ceaseless creativity in the natural universe."[163] Kauffman is well aware that he will be accused of atheism by theists and atheists alike, convinced as both sides are that "God" can only mean an extra-cosmic superman. But as he explains it, the immanent self-organization of the universe is "so stunning, so overwhelming, so worthy of awe, gratitude, and respect, that it is God enough for many of us."[164]

With Kauffman, then, as with Einstein, Schleiermacher, and to some extent Spinoza, we find pantheism inspiring a gratified kind of amazement. At first, such amazement may seem a dramatic departure from the panic, horror, and fear that the identity of God and world has more regularly provoked. And yet I would suggest that these seemingly opposite emotions are just differing concrescences of the same basic mood or affect, which we might call wonder, awe, or astonishment. Although they have lost most of their duplicity in modern usage, these translations of the Greek *thaumazein*, the Hebrew *yir'ah*, or the German

Wunder have historically held together seemingly opposite valences.[165] Under the influence of an ambivalent wonder, the wonderer undergoes a complicated dance of attraction and revulsion, admiration and horror, love and fear—much like the *panic* coursing through both the lovers and enemies of Pan, (beginning with his terrified mother). From Bayle to Boyle to the Orientalists to the anti-transcendentalists to the anti-Gaians, we have seen such a multifarious affect arise again and again in response to the multifarious "monstrous." As Caroline Walker Bynum has reminded us, "A *mixture* is a monster (*monstrum*), a boundary or category violation, the addition of one species to another. . . . Mixtures are objects of *stupor* or *admiratio*, unusual occurrences at which we feel terror or wonder."[166] And again, insofar as it inexorably mixes up agent and patient, creator and created, matter and spirit, and all their co-constitutive categories, pantheism in its pluralist forms keeps the lover and the loather alike in a kind of horrified awe.

The decision either to abide or run from this discomfiting mood can be said to constitute a second, *ethical* difference between the "all-god" and the "no-God." Put succinctly, to recognize all things as divine—not by virtue of some "essence" they share, but in their material particularities—intensifies our sense of relatedness to all things, and this sense can open onto responsibility on the one hand or disavowal on the other. Thus, in Alice Walker's *The Color Purple*, Shug explains to Celie that the reason Celie imagines God to be a white man is that white men "wrote the Bible." But far from believing God to be a monarch, a slave owner, an overseer, or any sort of man at all, Shug tells Celie, "I believe God is everything. . . . Everything that is or ever was or ever will be."[167] Fueled by a love of Shug fierce enough to overcome her shame and self-doubt, Celie embarks on a journey—not of abandoning God, but of transvaluing "him"—of giving up "the old white man" for "everything." "My first step from the old white man was trees," Celie tells her readers; "then air. Then birds. Then other people. But one day when I was sitting quiet and feeling like a motherless child, which I was, it came to me: that feeling of being part of everything, not separate at all. I knew that if I cut a tree, my arm would bleed."[168] Celie's pantheological attunement thus heightens her compassion toward those nonhuman others that, she realizes, are both different from her and entangled with her. Like the allegedly undisturbed "system II" of EPR's thought experiment, Celie's allegedly separate arm bleeds with the lacerated tree.

We can find a similarly "entangled empathy" at work in Octavia Butler's Afrofuturist *Parable of the Sower* and *Parable of the Talents*.[169] The main and messianic character of this "Earthseed" duology is a woman named Lauren Oya Olamina, who suffers from a condition called "hyperempathy syndrome":

she shares the pain—and, albeit less often, the pleasure—of the people around her. As a child, Lauren writes in her journal, "I . . . bled through the skin when I saw someone else bleeding. I couldn't help doing it."[170] Although this particular symptom subsides when she hits puberty, Lauren continues to suffer alongside both human and nonhuman others, including even those birds, squirrels, and rats who eat the family's food and therefore "ha[ve] to be killed."[171] This extraordinary responsiveness to suffering, which Lauren often simply calls "sharing," provides the visceral basis of the theology around which she eventually gathers the "Earthseed" community she helps deliver northward from the ravaged Los Angeles suburbs: "God is change," she writes, which is to say God is that which makes, unmakes, and remakes all things.[172]

Like Walker's "everything," Butler's "change" is neither anthropomorphic nor "good" ("At least three years ago," she writes in her second journal entry, "my father's God stopped being my God").[173] Rather, as the ongoing processes of becoming and unbecoming, God-as-change just *is*. But insofar as this isness is inherently dynamic, recognizing God as change amounts to recognizing the malleability of God: "God is Pliable, / Trickster, / Teacher, / Chaos, / Clay. God exists to be shaped."[174] Instead of praying to this God, then, Lauren entreats her community to *make* the God who makes them; that is, "to shape God and to accept and work with the shapes that God imposes on us."[175] Along with womanist process theologian Monica Coleman, Lauren's God can be read as panentheistically different from the world to which it is inexorably bound.[176] Or this God can be read more pantheologically as the product of entirely immanent forces, some of which lie within human control but most of which lie beyond it. For the purposes at hand, the difference is immaterial; the point is simply that, like Walker, Butler connects the affirmation of a dynamic God-within-all-things to an increased receptivity and responsibility to each of those things. Reflecting on her adolescent brother's extended torture and eventual murder, Lauren finds herself hypothesizing that "if hyperempathy syndrome were a more common complaint, people couldn't do such things. They could kill if they had to, and bear the pain of it or be destroyed by it. But if everyone could feel everyone else's pain, who would torture? Who would cause anyone unnecessary pain?"[177]

It is no accident that the hyper-empathic Celie and Lauren are both African American characters, seeking to make lives for themselves and their communities in a constitutively anti-black world—to form what Ashon Crawley calls "otherwise worlds."[178] If, as Frank Wilderson has argued, the Western imaginary has encoded "a Black [as] the very antithesis of a Human subject,"[179] then these characters generate their cosmogonic theologies from a situation of categorical, political, and existential dehumanization. It is precisely this dehumanization that allows them to bleed with trees and suffer with squirrels. Conversely, their hyper-empathy leaves them vulnerable to further exploitation: Celie is passed from an abusive stepfather to an abusive husband, and Lauren learns that the four other "sharers" in her fledgling Earthseed community have been held in varying forms of economic and sexual slavery during the period of social, economic, and environmental unraveling known as "the Pox."[180] Insofar as hyper-empathy is bound up with conditions of oppression, it ought not to be romanticized. Rather, it should be acknowledged as the particularly painful ethical attunement of those who are not afforded the anesthesia of human (which is almost always to say white and male) exceptionalism. And because such exceptionalism has traditionally been secured by "the old white man" God, the hyper-empathy that lies beyond it (and Him) is able, in turn, to open divinity out to all things.

The third difference one might hold between a pluralist pantheism and atheism is *symbolic*. This, we might recall, is Grace Jantzen's position: feminist analysis must not abandon but recode "God," she insists, lest "he" retain his conceptual power.[181] Such power is the product of concrete historical conditions of violent exploitation; as Hortense Spillers reminds us, the "dominant symbolic activity, the ruling episteme that releases the dynamic of naming and valuation, remains grounded in the originating metaphors of captivity and mutilation."[182] Far from being "merely" symbolic, then, the symbolic works to encode, reaffirm, and endorse violence against dark, feminized others in particular: "sticks and bricks might break our bones," Spillers warns, "but words will most definitely kill us."[183] Words, then, must change. And if it is indeed the case that the word "God" is the product and guarantor of the whole structure of Western metaphysics—if the hierarchical distinction between God and world reflects and holds in place the hierarchical distinctions between light and darkness, male and female, spirit and matter, reason and passion, and humanity and environment—then one might argue that this particular word requires the most change of all, even to the point of God's being recoded *as* change: as the ongoing, intraspecies processes that world and unworld worlds.

With all these possibilities exhausted, the last way to respond to the purported equivocity between pantheologies thus conceived and atheism would be simply to defer to the critic ("Every time someone puts an objection to me," Deleuze once explained in an interview, "I want to say: 'OK, OK, let's go on to something else'").[184] The aim of the exploration at hand has been to sketch the historical and conceptual contours of the identification of God and world, of *theos* and *pan*, and if the reader finds such a position uncompelling, she is of course free to reject it—or even better, to reconceive it altogether. The author here finds herself channeling the sixth-century apophatic Pseudo-Dionysius, who (un)concludes his treatise on the omni-onomastic God,

> These, then, are the divine names. . . . I have explained them as well as I can. But of course I have fallen short of what they actually mean. . . . If so I ask you to be charitable, to correct my unwished-for ignorance, to offer an argument to one needing to be taught, to help my faltering strength and to heal my unwanted frailty.[185]

For if God can be found in and named by all things, then anything short of everything will certainly miss its infinite marks.

PANDEMONIUM

"Pan again!" said Dr. Bull, irritably. "You seem to think Pan is everything."
"So he is," said the Professor, "in Greek. He means everything."
"Don't forget," said the Secretary, looking down, "that he also means Panic."
—G. K. Chesterton, "The Man Who Was Thursday"

Of all the pagan gods whom Christianity excised, "no presence has been more haunting than Pan's," writes Robin Lane Fox.[1] This ought not to be surprising; after all, Pan has never been a great respecter of boundaries. If any deity were to cross a maze of onto-spatiotemporal divides to trouble our sleep, it would likely be this polyamorous polymorph. To be sure, he has spent millennia alluring the poets—who have arguably been more possessed by this god than by any other[2]—from the Elizabethans through the Romantics and Victorians straight to Ralph Waldo Emerson, who exclaimed, "the great God Pan is not dead, as was rumored. No God ever dies. Perhaps of all the gods of New England and of ancient Greece, I am most constant at his shrine."[3] Listening closely, we can hear Pan haunting even those humans less likely than the poets to be attuned to him—especially when their exceptionalism seems threatened. Indeed, whether or not the parties involved have acknowledged his presence, Pan has shown up in debates over zoological nomenclature,[4] in eco-activist struggles,[5] and, as I have suggested, in panicked dismissals of pantheism—among Christians above all, whose dangerous proximity to the heresy demands that they continue to ward it off at all costs.

At this late hour, I should make it clear: I am not calling for a post-monotheistic retrieval of the cult of Pan. Aside from believing such a return to be impossible, I find it undesirable: however proto-cyborgian and species-queer, an ithyphallic goat-man is not a god into whom I'd suggest we pile our theo-erotic energies. Neither am I advocating a (re-)turn to any number of other pan-theisms; rather I have simply hoped to figure out what such a thing would mean in the first place and why it has traditionally been so difficult to consider it as a coherent position. In particular, I have tried to uncover some of the sources of the aggressive and automatic dismissals of the position, sources that reliably amount to crossed boundaries, mixed-up categories, and monstrous combinations that usually have something to do with race, sex, and gender. For this reason, it seems to me that the pantheism that truly threatens the Western symbolic would not proclaim that "all is one"; after all, the "one" is just the "two" being honest with itself: there is one Real, the logic goes, and everything in the world exists as a more or less perfect instantiation of it. And such perfection, as we have seen, is invariably measured according to race, gender, and species.

The most threatening, and therefore most promising, pantheism would therefore not be the "all is one" variety, but rather the mixed-up, chimeric kind, whose *theos* is neither self-identical nor absolute, but a mobile and multiply-located concatenation of pan-species intra-carnation. And one particularly salient, but evanescent, node of such symbiotic pancarnation happens to be Pan himself, who crosses divisions of topography, species, function, ontology, time, space, culture, and decency not in order to make them "all one," but rather to present us with strange new sites of divinity. In such a provisionally named pantheology, divinity would be not static but evolving. As Emerson ventures,

> Onward and on, the eternal Pan
> Who layeth the world's incessant plan
> Halteth never in one shape,
> But forever doth escape
> Like wave or flame, into new forms
> Of gem, and air, of plants and worms.[6]

Pantheologically, those events we call gods would be discovered, sustained, killed off, resurrected, shared, transmogrified, and multiplied between and among temporary clusters of relation. As it has in those queerly intraspecies assemblages of Arcadia, Nazareth, Uluru, the Amazon, Turtle Island, Gaia, and untold multitudes of symbiotic ecosystems, divinity thus construed would show up in unforeseen crossings and alliances. It would frighten and delight us, save and ruin us with visions of the worlds and gods we've made, and glimpses of those that might yet emerge from our multispecies midst.

NOTES

Introduction: The Matter with Pantheism

1. Richard H. Popkin, "Introduction," in ibid., ix and viii; Thomas M. Lennon and Michael Hickson, "Pierre Bayle," in *The Stanford Encyclopedia of Philosophy*, ed. Edward N. Zalta, http://plato.stanford.edu/archives/fall2014/entries/bayle.

2. Bayle, *Dictionary*, 288. Where applicable, references to the French edition will follow English page numbers by a slash (/). See Bayle, *Dictionnaire Historique Et Critique*, 4 vols. (Amsterdam: 1740).

3. Ibid., 298/4:261, "si sensibles que jamais un esprit droit ne fera capable de les méconnoître."

4. Ibid., 311/4:261nN.IV, "c'est ce qui surpasse tous les monstres, et tous les déréglements chimériques des plus folles têtes qu'on ait jamais enfermés dans les petites maisons."

5. Ibid., 300/4:259, "He supposes [*il suppose*, as though it were a premise rather than a conclusion] that there is only one substance in nature, and that this unique substance is endowed [*douée*] with an infinity of attributes—thought and extension among others."

6. See, for example, Rene Descartes, "Principles of Philosophy," in *The Philosophical Writings of Descartes* (Cambridge: Cambridge University Press, 1985), 211, 215.

7. See, for example, Part IV, Proposition 4, in which Spinoza writes that "the power whereby each single thing . . . preserves its own being is the very power of God, or Nature ("*Potentia qua res singulars et consequenter homo suum esse conservat, est ipsa Dei sive Naturae potentia*"), Baruch Spinoza, "Ethics," in *Ethics, Treatise on the Emendation of the Intellect, and Selected Letters*, ed. Seymour Feldman (Indianapolis: Hackett, 1992), 145; Spinoza, *Ethica* (CreateSpace Independent Publishing Platform, 2014), 160. For a discussion of Spinoza's treatment of Descartes, see pp. 2, 44–45, above.

8. Spinoza, *Theological-Political Treatise*, trans. Samuel Shirley (Indianapolis: Hackett, 1998), 74.

9. Michel Foucault, *Abnormal: Lectures at the Collège De France, 1974–1975*, ed. Valerio Marchetti and Antonella Salomoni, trans. Graham Burchell (London: Picador, 2004), 63.

10. Aristotle, *The Metaphysics*, trans. Hugh Lawson-Tancred (New York: Penguin, 1998), 986a.

11. Bayle, *Dictionary*, 307nN/4:260nN.II.

12. Ibid., 296–7/4:259, "la plus monstrueuse Hypothese qui se puisse imaginer, la plus absurd, et la plus diamétralement oppose aux notions les plus évidentes de notre esprit."

13. Ibid., 301, 307, 311, 306nN, 293.

14. Cited in Roger Scruton, *Spinoza: A Very Short Introduction* (New York: Oxford University Press, 2002), 14.

15. The term "pantheist" first appears in a treatise by the Irish philosopher John Toland, who professes to be among their number without quite elucidating their doctrine: John Toland, *Socinianism Truly Stated; Being an Example of Fair Dealing in All Theological Controvrsys. To Which Is Prefixt, Indifference in Disputes: Recommended by a Pantheist to an Orthodox Friend* (London, 1705), 7. The term "pantheism," however, is initially attributable not to Toland, but to the man who ridiculed him, equating Toland's position, which "believes in no God aside from nature, or the workings of the world," with atheism (*nullum alium Deum habeat, praeter naturam, aut mundi machinam*): "This is Atheism or Pantheism (*hoc est Atheïsmum aut Pantheïsmum*)," de la Faye writes, thereby coining the latter (Jacques de la Faye, *Defensio Religionis, Nec Non Mosis Et Gentis Judaicae, Contra Duas Dissertationes Joh. Tolandi, Quarum Una Inscribitur Adeisidaemon, Altera Vera Antiquitates Judaicae*, [Ultrajecti: Apud Guilielmum Broedelet, 1709], 19, 23; with gratitude to Andrew Szegedy-Maszak for the translation). The work to which de la Faye is responding directly is John Toland, *Adeisidaemon, Sive Titus Livius. A Superstitione Vindicatus* (Hagae-Comitis: Apud Thomam Johnson, 1709). A populist, even practical version of Toland's highly monistic form of pantheism can be found in John Toland, *Pantheisticon: Or, the Form of Celebrating the Socratic-Society* (Charleston, SC: Nabu Press, 2010 [1720]).

16. Benjamin Lazier, *God Interrupted: Heresy and the European Imagination Between the World Wars* (Princeton, NJ: Princeton University Press, 2012), 73.

17. John Milton, "On the Morning of Christ's Nativity," in *The Complete Poetry and Essential Prose of John Milton*, ed. William Kerrigan, John Rumrich, and M. Fallon (New York: Modern Library, 2007 [1629]); Ben Jonson, "Pan's Anniversary; or, the Shepherd's Holiday," in *The Works of Ben Jonson*, ed. William Gifford (New York: Appelton, 1879); Edmund Spenser, "The Shepheardes Calendar," in *The Yale Edition of the Shorter Poems of Edmund Spenser*, ed. William Oram, et. al. (New Haven, CT: Yale University Press, 1989); Johann Wolfgang von Goethe, "Ganymed," in *Goethe: The Collected Works*, ed. Christopher Middleton (Princeton, NJ: Princeton University Press, 1994 [1774]); William Wordsworth, "Lines: Composed a Few Miles above Tintern Abbey," in *The Collected Poems of William Wordsworth (Wordsworth Poetry Library)* (Ware, UK: Wordsworth Editions, 1998); Percy Bysshe Shelley, "Song of Pan," in *The Major Works, Including Poetry, Prose, and Drama*, ed. Zachary Leader and Michael O'Neill, Oxford World's Classics (Oxford: Oxford University Press, 2009); Alfred Lord Tennyson, "The Higher Pantheism," in *The Major Works*, ed. Adam Roberts, Oxford World's Classics (Oxford: Oxford University Press, 2009); Elizabeth Barrett Browning, "The Dead Pan," in *Aurora Leigh and Other Poems*, ed. John Robert Glorney Bolton and Julia Bolton Holloway (New York: Penguin, 1996). For an exhaustive roundup of references to Pan in Western literature, see Patricia Merivale, *Pan the Goat-God: His Myth in Modern Times* (Cambridge, MA: Harvard University Press, 1969).

18. Even contemporary Spinozists will often insist that his position is not *really* pantheistic. For a roundup of these sources, see Seymour Feldman, "Introduction," in *Ethics, Treatise on the Emendation of the Intellect, and Selected Letters*, ed. Seymour Feldman (Indianapolis: Hackett, 1992), 11; Horst Lange, "Goethe and Spinoza: A Reconsideration," *Goethe Yearbook* 18 (2011): 15.

19. Ninian Smart, "God's Body," *Union Seminary Quarterly Review* 37, no. 1 and 2 (1891–1982): 51.

20. Douglas Hedley maintains there is nothing one might call a Western "pantheist tradition" because "'pantheism' has largely been a term of condemnation" (Douglas Hedley, "Pantheism, Trinitarian Theism and the Idea of Unity: Reflections on the Christian Concept of God," *Religious Studies* 32, no. 1 [March, 1996]: 64, 63). Michael Levine claims it is difficult even to know "what pantheism means," since it is often just "a term of 'theological abuse'" (Michael Levine, *Pantheism: A Non-Theistic Concept of Deity* [New York: Routledge, 1994], 25, 17n2). And Philip Clayton insists that "no philosophically adequate form of pantheism has been developed in Western philosophy" (Philip Clayton, *The Problem of God in Modern Thought* [Grand Rapids: Eerdmans, 2000], 389).

21. Gilles Deleuze, *Expressionism in Philosophy: Spinoza*, trans. Martin Joughin (New York: Zone Books, 1992), 177.

22. James Cone, *A Black Theology of Liberation* (New York: Lippincott, 1970), 40; Sallie McFague, *The Body of God: An Ecological Theology* (Minneapolis: Fortress Press, 1993), 134; Ivone Gebara, *Longing for Running Water: Ecofeminism and Liberation* (Minneapolis: Fortress Press, 1999), 123.

23. Philip Clayton, "Emerging God," *The Christian Century* 13 (2004): https://www
.christiancentury.org/article/2004-01/emerging-god. For a variety of process panen-
theisms, see John B. Cobb and David Ray Griffin, *Process Theology: An Introductory
Exposition* (Philadelphia: Westminster John Knox, 1996); Catherine Keller, *Face of the
Deep: A Theology of Becoming* (New York: Routledge, 2003); Catherine Keller, *Cloud
of the Impossible: Negative Theology and Planetary Entanglement* (New York: Columbia
University Press, 2014); Monica Coleman, *Making a Way out of No Way: A Womanist
Theology*, Innovations: African American Religious Thought (Minneapolis: Fortress
Press, 2008); Loriliai Biernacki and Philip Clayton, *Panentheism across the World's
Traditions* (Oxford: Oxford University Press, 2014).

24. Grace Jantzen, *Becoming Divine: Towards a Feminist Philosophy of Religion*
(Bloomington: Indiana University Press, 1999), 267.

25. Cited in Rebecca Goldstein, *Betraying Spinoza: The Renegade Jew Who Gave Us
Modernity* (New York: Schocken, 2006), 17; emphasis added; Scruton, *Spinoza: A Very
Short Introduction*, 9.

26. Cited in Scruton, *Spinoza: A Very Short Introduction*, 9–10.

27. Cited in ibid., 10. For a longer-form text of the condemnation, see Goldstein,
Betraying Spinoza, 17ff.

28. Excommunication was not an uncommon tool of theo-political discipline in
seventeenth-century Sephardic Amsterdam (Yirmiyahu Yovel, *Spinoza and Other
Heretics: The Marrano of Reason*, 2 vols., vol. 1 [Princeton, NJ: Princeton University
Press, 1989], 9). In most cases, however, the accused could repent and be readmitted
to the community. Spinoza was presented with no such option; as Rebecca Goldstein
has noted, "the terms of his excommunication were the harshest imposed by his community, uncharacteristically including no possibility of reconciliation or redemption."
Goldstein goes on to express perplexity at the "unusual vehemence and finality of the
denunciation. . . . Why was Spinoza alone deemed irredeemable?" (Goldstein, *Betraying Spinoza*, 13).

29. In 1225, Pope Honorius III condemned Eriugena's proto-pantheism as "pullu-
lating with worms of heretical perversity," and dismissed the whole position as "Irish
porridge" (Alasdair MacIntyre, "Pantheism," in *Encyclopedia of Philosophy, 2nd ed.*,
ed. Donald M. Borchert [Detroit: MacMillian Reference USA, 2006], 95). In these
short words alone, we can detect a mess of fears of crossed boundaries concerning
sex (perversity), species (worms, who are of course the "lowest" of animals), race (the
Irishman ridiculed by the noble Roman), and food, whose preparation is traditionally
the purview of women. On Almaric, see Paul Harrison, *Elements of Pantheism: Religious Reverence of Nature and the Universe* (Coral Springs, FL: Llumina, 2004), 26.
On Bruno, see Ingrid D. Rowland, *Giordano Bruno: Philosopher/Heretic* (New York:
Farrar, Straus and Giroux, 2008). On Porete, see M. G. Sargent, "The Annihilation of
Marguerite Porete," *Viator* 28 (1997). On Edwards, see William Mander, "Pantheism," in
The Stanford Encyclopedia of Philosophy, ed. Edward N. Zalta, http://plato.stanford.edu
/archives/win2012/entries/pantheism. On Eckhart, see Edmund Colledge and Bernard

McGinn, eds., *Meister Eckhart: The Essential Sermons, Commentaries, Treatises, and Defense*, Classics of Western Spirituality (Mahwah, NJ: Paulist Press, 1981), 5–61.

30. Richard Hardack, *Not Altogether Human: Pantheism and the Dark Nature of the American Renaissance* (Amherst: University of Massachussetts Press, 2012), 6.

31. Nathaniel Smith Richardson, "The Pantheistic Movement," *The Church Review, and Ecclesiastical Register* 1, no. 4 (1849): 563.

32. Ibid., 556.

33. Ibid.

34. Rev. Morgan Dix, *Lectures on the Pantheistic Idea of an Impersonal Deity, as Contrasted with the Christian Faith Concerning Almighty God* (New York: Hurd and Houghton, 1864), 34; Alexis de Tocqueville, *Democracy in America*, trans. Gerald Bevan (New York: Penguin, 2003), 521; Herman Melville, *Moby-Dick*, Norton Critical Editions (New York: Norton, 2002), 367. On the seductions of pantheism for the white, male, American subject, see "The Seductive God," in Hardack, *Not Altogether Human*, 15–59.

35. Melville cited in Hardack, *Not Altogether Human*, 56.

36. Melville cited in ibid., 56; emphasis added. Elsewhere in the same letter to Hawthorne, Melville writes, "*Spread and expand yourself,* and bring yourself to the *tinglings of life that are felt in the flowers and the woods,* that are felt in the planets. . . . What nonsense! . . . This 'all' feeling, though, there is some truth in it. You must have often felt it, lying on the grass on a warm summer's day. Your legs seem to send out shoots into the earth. Your hair feels like leaves upon your head. This is the *all* feeling" (Melville cited in ibid., 87).

37. Luce Irigaray, "Plato's *Hystera,*" in *Speculum of the Other Woman* (Ithaca, NY: Cornell University Press, 1985).

38. Edward Said, *Orientalism* (New York: Vintage, 1979), 138, 206, 234; Victor Li, *The Neo-Primitivist Turn: Critical Reflections on Alterity, Culture, and Modernity* (Toronto: University of Toronto Press, 2006), 67–86.

39. Hardack, *Not Altogether Human*, 23–24, 78, 62.

40. See, most powerfully, Outka's analysis of Emerson's infamous "eyeball" passage as "at least an unconscious recoiling" from a scene in Crèvocoeur's *Letters from An American Farmer*, in which the author stumbles upon a slave being slowly tortured to death in a cage in the wilderness (Paul Outka, *Race and Nature from Transcendentalism to the Harlem Renaissance* (New York: Palgrave Macmillan 2013), 37–43.

41. Ibid., 23.

42. D. H. Lawrence catches this connection in the mid-twentieth century, ridiculing American Renaissance authors for filtering a cheap version of the European Pan through romantic portrayals of black and Native Americans, whom Lawrence renders in consistently insulting caricature. See D. H. Lawrence, *Studies in Classic American Literature*, ed. James T. Boulton, The Cambridge Edition of the Letters and Works of D. H. Lawrence (Cambridge: Cambridge University Press, 2003); D. H. Lawrence, "Democracy," in *Phoenix*, ed. Edward McDonald (New York: Viking, 1936); D. H. Lawrence, "Pan in America," *Southwest Review* (January, 1926).

43. On the transcendentalist fascination with Indian philosophy, see Dale Riepe, *The Philosophy of India and Its Impact on American Thought* (Springfield, IL: Thomas, 1970); J. P. Rao Rayapati, *Early American Interest in Vedanta: Pre-Emersonian Interest in Vedic Literature and Vedantic Philosophy* (Delhi: Asia Publishing, 1973).

44. Richardson, "The Pantheistic Movement," 548. Cf. Dix, who explains that pantheism "is first encountered by the student when he investigates the Brahminism of India; and it formed the basis of the Egyptian and Chaldean religions, and of the philosophy of Greece" (Dix, *Pantheistic Idea*, 32).

45. Richardson, "The Pantheistic Movement," 548, 556.

46. Ibid., 548.

47. Ibid., 563.

48. Ibid., 565.

49. Ibid., 556, 548.

50. Ibid., 548.

51. Ibid., 564.

52. Ibid., 563.

53. C. E. Plumptre, *General Sketch of the History of Pantheism: From the Earliest Times to the Age of Spinoza*, 2 vols., vol. 1, Cambridge Library Series—Religion (Cambridge, UK: Cambridge University Press, 2011 [1878]), 133.

54. Ibid., 31, 29.

55. Ibid., 133.

56. Ibid., 264.

57. Ibid., 234.

58. Ibid., 128.

59. See Richard King, *Orientalism and Religion: Postcolonial Theory, India and 'the Mystic East'* (New York: Routledge, 1999), 104.

60. Plumptre, *History of Pantheism, Vol. 1*, 1, 264.

61. On Gandhi's having reappropriated orientalist representations of passivity and femininity as an anti-colonialist strategy, see King, *Orientalism and Religion*, 134.

62. Bayle, *Dictionary*, 288. My thanks to Stephen Angle for helping me navigate Bayle's strange rendition of Chinese Buddhism.

63. Ibid., 291nB, 290nB.

64. Ibid., 291nB. Similarly, Rudolf Otto attempts to clear Meister Eckhart of centuries-old charges of heresy by foisting quietism, amoralism, and pantheism onto the Vedas (see King, *Orientalism and Religion*, 125–127).

65. Bayle, *Dictionary*, 291nB; emphasis added.

66. Ibid., 301.

67. Jantzen, *Becoming Divine*, 267.

68. As Rosemary Radford Ruether has argued, "the way [Classical Western cultural traditions] have construed the idea of the male monotheistic God, and the relation of this God to the cosmos as its Creator, have reinforced symbolically the relations of domination of men over women, masters over slaves, and (male ruling-class) humans

over animals and over the earth" (Rosemary Radford Ruether, *Gaia and God: An Eco-feminist Theology of Earth Healing* ([San Francisco: Harper, 1992], 3).

69. Jantzen, *Becoming Divine*, 267.

70. Just a few examples of such feminist theologians include Gebara, *Longing for Running Water*; Mary Daly, *Gyn/Ecology: The Metaethics of Radical Feminism* (New York: Beacon, 1990); Ruether, *Gaia and God: An Ecofeminist Theology of Earth Healing*.

71. For the distinction between the tree and the rhizome, see Gilles Deleuze and Félix Guattari, *A Thousand Plateaus*, trans. Brian Massumi (Minneapolis: University of Minnesota Press, 1987), 3–25.

72. Jantzen, *Becoming Divine*, 10; emphasis original.

73. Ibid., 269.

74. It is remarkably difficult to demonstrate the presence of an absence, but I am struck in particular by the single, unelaborated reference to "feminist pantheism" in Pamela Anderson's review of the book (Pamela Sue Anderson, "Jantzen, Grace, Becoming Divine: Towards a Feminist Philosophy of Religion," *Theology and Sexuality* 13 [September 1, 2000]). Cf. the absence of any reference to pantheism in Anderson's epistolary response to the same text (Pamela Sue Anderson and Grace Jantzen, "Correspondence with Grace Jantzen," *Feminist Theology* 9, no. 25 [2000]). See also the absence of any reference to pantheism in an academic obituary for Jantzen that focuses mainly on *Becoming Divine* ("Grace Jantzen [1948–2006]," ibid.15, no. 1 [2006]). Even Laurel Schneider's excellent review of the book, which reads Jantzen's constructive project quite closely and critically, does not mention pantheism: Laurel Schneider, "Becoming Divine: Towards a Feminist Philosophy of Religion," *Journal of the American Academy of Religion* 70, no. 3 (2002). Morny Joy does cite Jantzen's post-Christian turn to pantheism, but only in order to say that Jantzen did not have the opportunity to develop the position fully: see Morny Joy, "Rethinking the 'Problem of Evil' with Hannah Arendt and Grace Jantzen," in *New Topics in Feminist Philosophy of Religion: Contestations and Transcendence Incarnate*, ed. Pamela Sue Anderson (New York: Springer, 2010), 30–31.

75. Novalis (Freiherr Friedrich von Hardenberg), *Gesammelte Werke*, vol. 4 (Bühler: Herrliberg-Zürich, 1946), 259.

76. Goethe, letter to Jacobi (9 June 1785) cited in Detley Pätzold, "Deus Sive Natura. J. G. Herder's Romanticized Reading of Spinoza's Physico-Theology," in *The Book of Nature in Early Modern and Modern History*, ed. Klaas van Berkel and Arjo Vanderjagt (Leuven: Peeters, 2006), 161.

77. See note 16, above.

78. Dix, *Pantheistic Idea*, 56.

79. "Against pantheism I have mainly the objection that it states nothing. To call the world God is not to explain it, but only to enrich the language with a superfluous synonym for the word world. It comes to the same thing whether we say 'the world is God' or 'the world is the world'" (Arthur Schopenhauer, *Parerga and Paralipomena*, trans. E. F. J. Payne, 2 vols., vol. 2 [Oxford: Clarendon Press, 2000], 99).

80. Ibid., 1: 114.

81. See Nancy Frankenberry, "Classical Theism, Panentheism, and Pantheism: On the Relation between God Construction and Gender Construction," *Zygon* 28, no. 1 (March, 1993): 44.

82. G. W. F. Hegel, *Lectures on the Philosophy of Religion*, trans. R. F. Brown, P. C. Hodgson, and J. M. Stewart (Berkeley: University of California Press, 1988 [1827]), 180.

83. "*Es ist also nichts in endlicher Wirklichkeit . . . nach Spinosa ist, was 'ist', allein 'Gott'. Das Gegenteil also von allem de mist wahr, was die behaupten, die Spinosa Atheismus Schuld geben: bei ihm ist 'zu viel Gott'.*" G. W. F. Hegel, *Lectures on the History of Philosophy: Medieval and Modern Philosophy*, trans. E. S. Haldane and Frances H. Simson, 3 vols., vol. 3 (Lincoln: University of Nebraska Press, 1995), 281–82; G. W. F. Hegel, *Vorlesungen Über Die Geschichte Der Philosophie* (Leiden: Adriani, 1908), 891. Where relevant, the translated page number will be followed by the original page number, separated with a slash (/).

84. According to Hegel, pantheism was a primarily "oriental" intuition: "For example," he writes, "the Orientals state that Krishna, Vishnu, and Brahma say regarding themselves: 'I am the luster or the brilliance in metals, the Ganges among rivers, the life in the living, the understanding in those who have understanding.'" (Hegel, *Philosophy of Religion*, 124.) This teaching is, for Hegel, equivalent to Spinozism; as Parkinson explains, "In [Spinoza's] philosophy, all content sinks into emptiness, into a purely formal unity, much as in Indian thought Siva is the great whole, not distinguished from Brahma" (G. H. R. Parkinson, "Hegel, Pantheism, and Spinoza," *Journal of the History of Ideas* 38, no. 3 [1977]: 459).

85. Richardson, "The Pantheistic Movement," 548; cf. Arthur O. Lovejoy, "The Dialectic of Bruno and Spinoza," in *The Summum Bonum*, ed. Evander Bradley McGilvary (Berkeley, CA: The University Press, 1904), 174.

86. William Ellery Channing, *The Works of William E. Channing, D. D.*, 11th complete ed., 6 vols., vol. 1 (Boston: Channing, 1849 [1841]), xii.

87. Goethe, letter to Jacobi (9 June 1785), cited in Pätzold, "Deus Sive Natura," 161.

88. See Lazier, *God Interrupted*, 106.

89. Richardson, "The Pantheistic Movement," 551, 553, 562.

90. Lazier, *God Interrupted*, 79.

91. Spinoza sets forth the impossibility of God's violating the order of nature (events commonly known as "miracles") in Spinoza, *Theological-Political Treatise*, 73–74.

92. Mersenne in Miguel A. Granada, "Mersenne's Critique of Giordano Bruno's Conception of the Relation between God and the Universe: A Reappraisal," *Perspectives on Science* 18, no. 1 (Spring, 2010): 37. Divine constraint was one of the major charges that led to Giordano Bruno's execution at the hands of the Inquisition. For an elaboration of Bruno's positions and their consequences, see Mary-Jane Rubenstein, *Worlds Without End: The Many Lives of the Multiverse* (New York: Columbia University Press, 2014), 88–105.

93. Schopenhauer concludes, "It would be more correct to identify the world with the devil" (Schopenhauer, *Parerga and Paralipomena*, 2, 101).

94. Bayle, *Dictionary*, 312nN.

95. C. S. Lewis, *Mere Christianity* (San Francisco: HarperCollins, 2001), 37.

96. See, for example, Jonathan David Hill, *Made-from-Bone: Trickster Myths, Music, and History from the Amazon*, Interpretations of Culture in the New Millennium (Urbana: University of Illinois Press, 2009); Babacar M'Baye, *The Trickster Comes West: Pan-African Influence in Early Black Diasporan Narratives* (Jackson: University Press of Mississippi, 2009); Eduardo Viveiros de Castro, "Exchanging Perspectives: The Transformation of Objects into Subjects in Amerindian Ontologies," *Common Knowledge* 10, no. 3 (2004): 477; Graham Harvey, *Animism: Respecting the Living World* (New York: Columbia University Press, 2006), 128–29; Deborah Bird Rose, "Death and Grief in a World of Kin: Dwelling in Larger-Than-Human Communities," in *The Handbook of Contemporary Animism*, ed. Graham Harvey (New York: Routledge, 2015).

97. Sylvia Marcos, "The Sacred Earth of the Nahuas," in *Taken from the Lips: Gender and Eros in Mesoamerican Religions, Religion in the Americas* (Boston: Brill, 2006), 39.

98. Friedrich Nietzsche, *On the Genealogy of Morals*, trans. Walter Kaufmann (New York: Vintage Books, 1989), 17.

99. Lazier, *God Interrupted*, 87.

100. Dix, *Pantheistic Idea*, 55.

101. Gunton in Jantzen, *Becoming Divine*, 273.

102. Lawrence, *Studies in Classic American Literature*, 174.

103. Judith Butler, "Imitation and Gender Insubordination," in *The Lesbian and Gay Studies Reader*, ed. Henry Abelove, Michele Aina Barale, and David M. Halperin (New York: Routledge, 1993); Homi Bhabha, *The Location of Culture*, Routledge Classics (New York: Routledge, 2004), 122.

104. Laurel Schneider has made a similar argument in passing: "The mistake that most theologians make at this point is to assume that without a categorical, substantive distinction between God and world then nothing is 'left' for God but the world, and we face the tired straw man of pantheism, as if a word that literally means 'everything-god' makes meaningful distinction between things and between events theologically impossible. But that is the case only within the confines of the logic of the One" (Laurel Schneider, *Beyond Monotheism: A Theology of Multiplicity* [New York: Routledge, 2008], 162).

105. Janzten makes this point in Jantzen, *Becoming Divine*, 273.

106. Grace Jantzen, "Feminism and Pantheism," *Monist* 80, no. 2 (April, 1997): 272.

107. G. W. F. Hegel, *Phenomenology of Spirit*, trans. A. V. Miller (New York: Oxford University Press, 1977), 9. Hegel is speaking specifically about Schelling's Absolute, which can be seen as a romantic appropriation of Spinoza. See F. C. Copleston, "Pantheism in Spinoza and the German Idealists," *Philosophy* 21, no. 78 (April, 1946): 50. Indeed, one finds Hegel leveling a similar charge against Spinoza himself, "to the effect that everything goes into the unity of Spinoza's substance as into the eternal night" (cited in Parkinson, "Hegel, Pantheism, and Spinoza," 458–59).

108. Jantzen, "Feminism and Pantheism," 281.

109. Dix, *Pantheistic Idea*, 20; emphasis added.

110. On the feminized and racialized nature of the biblical *tehom*, see Keller, *Face of the Deep*, 150ff.

111. William Lane Craig, "Pantheists in Spite of Themselves," in *For Faith and Clarity: Philosophical Contributions to Christian Theology*, ed. James K. Beilby (Ada, MI: Baker Academic, 2006), 142–43.

112. Ibid., 144.

113. Walt Whitman, "Song of Myself," in *The Complete Poems*, ed. Francis Murphy (New York: Penguin Classics, 2005), 94.

114. Lawrence, *Studies in Classic American Literature*, 150.

115. Ibid.

116. Ibid., 151.

117. Ibid., 156.

118. "all living creatures helplessly hurtling together into one great snowball" (ibid., 159). For a double-reading of Whitman as offering on the one hand a "static One" and on the other "possibles in the plural, genuine possibles," see William James, "Pragmatism and Religion," in *Pragmatism and Other Writings*, ed. Giles Gunn (New York: Penguin, 2000).

119. "A lot of the most exciting recent work around 'queer' spins the term outward along dimensions that can't be subsumed under gender and sexuality at all: the ways that race, ethnicity, postcolonial nationality criss-cross with these and *other* identity-constituting, identity-fracturing discourses, for example" (Eve Kosofsky Sedgwick, *Tendencies* [Durham, NC: Duke University Press, 1993], 8–9).

120. Stephen Webb, *American Providence: A Nation with a Mission* (New York: Continuum, 2006), 129–30.

121. On the Christian transformation of the earth from source of life to standing-reserve, see Lynn White Jr., "The Historical Roots of Our Ecological Crisis," *Science* 155, no. 3767 (1967).

122. Richard Dawkins, *The God Delusion* (New York: Mariner Books, 2008), 40.

123. MacIntyre, "Pantheism," 98.

124. Keith E. Yandell, "Pantheism," in *Routledge Encyclopedia of Philosophy*, ed. Edward Craig (New York: Routledge, 1998), 202.

125. William James, *A Pluralistic Universe* (Lincoln, NE: University of Nebraska Press, 1996 [1908]), 31. Subsequent references will be cited internally.

126. Of Christian doctrine, James writes, "it has not sweep and infinity enough to meet the requirements of even the illiterate natives of India. . . . The theological machinery that spoke so livingly to our ancestors . . . sounds as odd to most of us as if it were some outlandish savage religion" (ibid., 29).

127. "This world *may*, in the last resort, be a block-universe; but on the other hand it *may* be a universe only strung-along, not rounded in and closed. . . . you decide; it *shall be* as if true, for *you*. And your acting thus may in certain special cases be a means of making it securely true in the end" (James, *A Pluralistic Universe*, 328–29).

128. See ibid., 117, 33.

129. "*As* absolute," James explains, "or *sub specie eternitatis*, or *quatenus infinitus est*, the world repels our sympathy because it has no history" (ibid., 47; emphasis original).

130. Ernst Haeckel, *The History of Creation, or the Development of the Earth and Its Inhabitants by the Actions of Natural Causes: A Popular Exposition of the Doctrine of Evolution in General, and of That of Darwin, Goethe, and Lamarck in Particular*, trans. E. Ray Lankester, 2 vols. (New York: Appleton, 1914), 2:497–98.

131. On Haeckel's place in the history of scientific racism, see Robert J. Richards, *The Tragic Sense of Life: Ernst Haeckel and the Struggle over Evolutionary Thought* (Chicago: University of Chicago Press, 2008), 269–78.

132. Ernst Haeckel, *Monism as Connecting Religion and Science: The Confession of Faith of a Man of Science*, trans. J. Gilchrist (London: Black, 1895), 9, 5–6.

133. Ibid.

134. For a treatment of the evolution of this term in James's work, see Rubenstein, *Worlds Without End*, 3–5, 85, 189–90.

135. This God looks, not like the God of theism, but rather like the biblical God; in fact, James likens him to "the God, say, of David or of Isaiah. *That* God is an essentially finite being *in* the cosmos, not with the cosmos in him, and indeed he has a very local habitation there, and very one-sided local and personal attachments." Later in this lecture, James's theology verges on affirming a monistic God, with a bit of imperfection tagged on: "The finite God . . . may conceivably have *almost* nothing outside of himself; he may already have . . . absorbed all but the minutest fraction of the universe; but that fraction, however small, reduces him to the status of a relative being" (James, *A Pluralistic Universe*, 111, 125).

136. Lawrence, *Studies in Classic American Literature*, 151.

137. Clayton, *The Problem of God in Modern Thought*, 389.

138. James, *A Pluralistic Universe*, 38.

149. Jane Bennett, *Vibrant Matter: A Political Ecology of Things* (Durham, NC: Duke University Press, 2010), 23.

140. "Discursive practices are ongoing agential intra-actions of the world" (Karen Barad, *Meeting the Universe Halfway: Quantum Physics and the Entanglement of Matter and Meaning* [Durham, NC: Duke University Press, 2007], 173).

141. Hegel, *History of Philosophy*, 3, 281/891.

142. Bayle, *Dictionary*, 307nN/4:260nN.II.

143. While he would not support the sense in which his logic is deployed here, the quotation is taken from Thomas Aquinas, *Summa Theologiae*, trans. Fathers of the English Dominican Province, 5 vols. (Allen, TX: Christian Classics, 1981), 1.2.3.

144. Déborah Danowski and Eduardo Viveiros de Castro, *The Ends of the World*, trans. Rodrigo Nunes (Malden, MA: Polity Press, 2017), 22. Although Danowski, Viveiros de Castro, Latour, and Haraway have all taken up the language, it is Isabelle Stengers who first construes Gaia as an "intrusion." See Isabelle Stengers, "Penser À Partir Du Ravage Écologique," in *De L'univers Clos Au Monde Infini*, ed. Émilie Hache (Paris: Éditions Dehors, 2014).

145. Bayle, *Dictionary*, 291; Faye, *Defensio Religionis*, 23. See introduction, note 16.

PANIC

1. "Pan," in *Oxford Classical Dictionary, Third Edition*, ed. Simon Hornblower and Antony Spawforth (Oxford: Oxford University Press, 2006).

2. See Wilfred H. Schoff, "Tammuz, Pan and Christ," *The Open Court* 26, no. 9 (September 1912).

3. "Hymn to Pan," in *The Homeric Hymns: A Translation, with Introduction and Notes*, ed. Diane J. Rayor (Berkeley: University of California Press, 2004), line 2; Patricia Merivale, *Pan the Goat-God: His Myth in Modern Times* (Cambridge, MA: Harvard University Press, 1969), 4.

4. Robin Lane Fox, *Pagans and Christians* (New York: Knopf, 1987), 131.

5. "Pan," in *Oxford English Dictionary Online*.

6. Cornutus (d. 65 ce), cited in Merivale, *Goat-God*, 9–10.

7. Isidore of Seville, cited in ibid., 10.

8. Sharon Lynn Coggan, "Pandaemonia: A Study of Eusebius' Recasting of Plutarch's Story of the 'Death of Great Pan'" (Dissertation: Syracuse University, 1992), 87.

9. "Pan," in *Harper's Dictionary of Classical Literature and Antiquities*, ed. Harry Thurston Peck (New York: Cooper Square, 1963).

10. "Pan," in *Oxford Classical Dictionary*. See also Coggan, "Pandaemonia," 86.

11. Coggan, "Pandaemonia," 95, 86–87.

12. Donna Haraway, *When Species Meet* (Minneapolis: University of Minnesota Press, 2007), 4.

13. G. K. Chesterton, "The Man Who Was Thursday," in *The Man Who Was Thursday: And Related Pieces*, ed. Stephen Medcalf (Oxford: Oxford University Press, 1996), 150.

1. PAN

1. William James, *A Pluralistic Universe* (Lincoln: University of Nebraska Press, 1996 [1908]), 36; William James, "The One and the Many," in *Pragmatism and Other Writings*, ed. Giles Gunn (New York: Penguin, 2000), 62.

2. James, *A Pluralistic Universe*, 30.

3. Alexander Pope, "An Essay on Man," in *The Major Works*, ed. Pat Rogers, Oxford World's Classics (Oxford: Oxford University Press, 2009), 279.

4. Ernst Haeckel, *Monism as Connecting Religion and Science: The Confession of Faith of a Man of Science*, trans. J. Gilchrist (London: Black, 1895), 3.

5. Frederick C. Beiser, *The Fate of Reason: German Philosophy from Kant to Fichte* (Cambridge, MA: Harvard University Press, 1987), 48.

6. For an account of this controversy and the consequent retrieval of Spinoza, see ibid., 44–108; Tracie Matysik, "Spinozist Monism: Perspectives from Within and

Without the Monist Movement," in *Monism: Science, Philosophy, Religion, and the History of a Worldview*, ed. Todd Weir (New York: Palgrave Macmillan, 2012).

7. As Friedrich Schelling lampoons the affair, "the terrible truth was uttered in this way: All philosophy, absolutely all, which is based on pure reason alone, is, or will become, Spinozism. All men were now warned of the abyss; it was clearly laid bare before all eyes. The only remedy which still seemed possible was seized; only that bold utterance could bring on the crisis; it alone could frighten Germans away from this ruinous philosophy and lead them back to the Heart, to inwardness of feeling and to faith" (F. W. J. Schelling, *Philosophical Investigations into the Essence of Human Freedom* (Albany: State University of New York Press, 2007 [1809]), 21.

8. Beiser, *The Fate of Reason*, 44–45.

9. Horst Lange, "Goethe and Spinoza: A Reconsideration," *Goethe Yearbook* 18 (2011): 14, 18, 22–23.

10. F. W. J. Schelling, *The Ages of the World* (Albany: State University of New York Press, 2000), 103. Concerning Spinoza's neglecting the human, Schelling wrote, "instead of descending into the depths of his self-consciousness and descrying the emergence thence of the two worlds in us—the ideal and the real—he passed himself by; instead of explaining from our nature how finite and infinite, originally united in us, proceed reciprocally from each other, he lost himself forwith in the idea of an infinite outside us" (Schelling, *Ideas for a Philosophy of Nature, as Introduction to the Study of This Science*, trans. Errol E. Harris and Peter Heath [Cambridge: Cambridge University Press, 1988], 27).

11. See F. C. Copleston, "Pantheism in Spinoza and the German Idealists," *Philosophy* 21, no. 78 (April, 1946): 51.

12. Todd H. Weir, "The Riddles of Monism: An Introductory Essay," in *Monism: Science, Philosophy, Religion, and the History of a Worldview*, ed. Todd Weir (New York: Palgrave Macmillan, 2012), 16.

13. "The reason that [Spinoza's] God is not spirit," Hegel explains, "is that He is not the Three in One" (*er nicht 'der dreieinige' ist*)." G. W. F Hegel, *Lectures on the History of Philosophy: Medieval and Modern Philosophy*, trans. E. S. Haldane and Frances H. Simson, vol. 3 (Lincoln: University of Nebraska Press, 1995), 288; Hegel, *Vorlesungen Über Die Geschichte Der Philosophie* (Leiden: Adriani, 1908), 895. Where relevant, page numbers for the German text will follow the translated page numbers by a slash (/). Similarly, Schelling echoes centuries of Christian critiques of Judaism as unyielding, legalistic, and lacking in spirit and love when he writes that "Spinozism in its rigidity could be regarded like Pygmalion's statue, needing to be given a soul through the warm breath of love" (Schelling, *Freedom*, 23).

14. Hegel, *Lectures on the Philosophy of Religion*, trans. R. F. Brown, P. C. Hodgson, and J. M. Stewart (Berkeley: University of California Press, 1988 [1827]), 180.

15. Ibid., 123.

16. Ibid., 180.

17. Hegel, *History of Philosophy*, 3, 281.

18. Hegel, *Philosophy of Religion*, 180.

19. Ibid.

20. Hegel, *History of Philosophy*, 3, 288/895.

21. Hegel, *Philosophy of Religion*, 124.

22. Hegel, *History of Philosophy*, 3, 252.

23. See pp. 6–8, above. See also Dale Riepe, *The Philosophy of India and Its Impact on American Thought* (Springfield, IL: Thomas, 1970), 25–69; J. P. Rao Rayapati, *Early American Interest in Vedanta: Pre-Emersonian Interest in Vedic Literature and Vedantic Philosophy* (Delhi: Asia Publishing House, 1973), 1–23.

24. "The Oriental theory of absolute identity was brought by Spinoza . . . directly into line . . . with the European and Cartesian philosophy, in which it soon found a place" (Hegel, *History of Philosophy*, 3, 252.) "If it is objected," explains G. H. R. Parkinson, "that there is no evidence that Spinoza knew anything of Indian thought, Hegel would reply that he understands 'oriental thought' to include Jewish thought" (G. H. R. Parkinson, "Hegel, Pantheism, and Spinoza," *Journal of the History of Ideas* 38, no. 3 [1977]: 459).

25. Hegel, *Philosophy of Religion*, 123; emphasis added.

26. Ibid., 124.

27. Hegel, *History of Philosophy*, 3, 288/895.

28. Ibid., 288.

29. "*das Denken sich auf den Standpunkt des Spinosismus gestellt haben muss; Spinosist zu sein, ist der wesentliche . . . 'Anfang' alles Philosophierens*" (ibid., 257/873). Cf. his statement later in the essay that "you are either a Spinozist or not a philosopher at all" (ibid., 283).

30. The *Philosophy of Religion* is structured according to this tripartite movement; see Hegel, *Philosophy of Religion*, v–vii.

31. Hegel, *History of Philosophy*, 3, 472.

32. See, for example, Hegel, *Introduction to the Philosophy of History*, trans. Leo Rauch (Indianapolis: Hackett, 1988), 24–25.

33. Schelling, *Ages*, 105.

34. On Hegel, see Copleston, "Pantheism," 53. As for Schelling, he insisted that, properly conceived, pantheism maintains a "complete differentiation" of God and creation, thereby defending his "pantheism" against charges of indifference by rejecting its constitutive identification of God and world (Schelling, *Freedom*, 11).

35. Schelling, *Freedom*, 13, 32. Perhaps surprisingly, Martin Heidegger articulates this difference-in-identity more clearly than Schelling does himself: "Identity," he explains, "is the belonging together of what is different in one; still more generally expressed, the unity of a unity and an opposition." Considering this, "a sentence such as 'God is everything' must from the beginning not be understood to mean a mere, boundless identicalness of God and all things in the sense of a lawless primeval hodgepodge. . . . the one is precisely not the same as the other, but different. But in this difference as a relation it belongs together with the other" (Martin Heidegger, *Schelling's Treatise on*

the Essence of Human Freedom, trans. Joan Stambaugh [Athens: Ohio University Press, 1985], 77–79).

36. "With Fichte," Schelling explains, "the fundamental thought of the I, that is, of a living unity of that which has being and Being, aroused the hope of an elevated Spinozism that led to what is vital" (Schelling, *Ages*, 106).

37. Schelling, *Freedom*, 92; emphasis added.

38. Ibid., 38.

39. Schelling does not reject the name, as long as his position is understood to involve the fundamental difference of God and creation, as well as the centrality of the human (ibid., 91).

40. Yirmiyahu Yovel, *Spinoza and Other Heretics: The Adventures of Immanence*, 2 vols., vol. 2 (Princeton, NJ: Princeton University Press, 1989), 46.

41. Hegel, *The Encyclopaedia Logic: Part I of the Encyclopaedia of Philosophical Sciences with the Zusätze*, trans. T. F. Geraets, W. A. Suchting, and H. S. Harris (Indianapolis: Hackett, 1991), 85.

42. Heidegger, *Schelling's Treatise*, 86–87.

43. "God . . . is only the nature of man regarded objectively" (Ludwig Feuerbach, *The Essence of Christianity*, trans. George Eliot [Amherst, NY: Prometheus Books, 1989], 270).

44. Wilhelm Halbfass, *India and Europe: An Essay in Understanding* (Albany: State University of New York Press, 1988), 70. Offering his own rendition of the Vedantic Moha Mudgara, Herder writes, "Vishnu is in you, in me, in all beings; / It is foolish to ever feel offense. / See all souls in your own, / and banish the delusion of being different" (cited in ibid., 70–71).

45. Ibid., 74.

46. Ibid., 76. The resulting text is Friedrich von Schlegel, *Über Die Sprache Und Weisheit Der Indier* (Heidelberg: Mohr und Zimmer, 1808).

47. Halbfass, *India and Europe*, 76.

48. See, for example, Donald Lopez's account of Henry Steel Olcott's voyage to Sri Lanka: Donald S. Lopez, "Belief," in *Critical Terms for Religious Studies*, ed. Mark C. Taylor (Chicago: University of Chicago Press, 1998), 30.

49. Schlegel cited in Halbfass, *India and Europe*, 77; emphasis added.

50. Schlegel cited in ibid.

51. Ibid., 77.

52. Hegel, *Philosophy of Religion*, 289, 291. Hegel acknowledged, of course, the vast proliferation of deities "among the Hindus," but judged this "fanciful polytheism" to be the result of a failure to think finite spirit itself. Steeped in the "abstraction" of the one substance, "Hindus" ascribe equal importance to natural and spiritual beings: "they do not yet know that their own content or specification is nobler than the content of a spring or a tree" (289).

53. See Yovel, *Adventures of Immanence*, 2, 29.

54. Richard King, *Indian Philosophy: An Introduction to Hindu and Buddhist Thought* (Washington, D.C.: Georgetown University Press, 1999), 54.

55. See ibid., 56–57; Andrew J. Nicholson, *Unifying Hinduism: Philosophy and Identity in Indian Intellectual History* (New York: Columbia University Press, 2010), 24–38. According to Nicholson, "Medieval Vedāntins distinguished two basic positions. One theory, Pariṇāmavāda, states that the world is a real transformation (*pariṇāma*) of Brahman. Just as clay is transformed into the multiple forms of pots, saucers, cups, and so forth, Brahman is the material cause, transforming itself into the many real entities visible in the world. The alternative to this model is Vivartavāda, the theory that the world is merely an unreal manifestation (*vivarta*) of Brahman. . . . The most visible advocates of Vivartavāda are the Advaitins, the followers of Śankara who went on to establish a powerful network of monastic schools across India. In the Pariṇāmavāda camp we find the majority of other schools of Vedānta, who see the phenomenal world as real" (ibid., 27).

56. Christopher Isherwood, Introduction, in *Vedanta for the Western World*, ed. Christopher Isherwood (Hollywood: Marcel Rodd, 1945), 1.

57. Richard King, *Orientalism and Religion: Postcolonial Theory, India and 'the Mystic East'* (New York: Routledge, 1999), 103. For a longer, more philosophical, and less political history of this development, see Nicholson, *Unifying Hinduism*.

58. King, *Orientalism and Religion*, 133.

59. Cited in ibid., 93.

60. James, "The One and the Many," 68.

61. Focusing on the dualistic and empirical schools of Vedāntic philosophy, Andrew Nicholson insists that "it is . . . not fair to say that the early Upanisads were themselves propounding a pure monistic or idealistic philosophy." Even within Sankara's writings, Nicholson insists, it is not clear that the world is simply "an unreal manifestation of Brahman;" his earlier works tend to afford a greater ontological status to the material universe, which some commentators insist he never abandoned (Nicholson, *Unifying Hinduism*, 25, 31).

62. Hegel, *Philosophy of Religion*, 123.

63. Ibid., 123, 180.

64. Jonathan Israel, Introduction, in *Spinoza: Theological-Political Treatise*, ed. Jonathan Israel, Cambridge Texts in the History of Philosophy (Cambridge: Cambridge University Press, 2007), xxxi.

65. Baruch Spinoza, *Theological-Political Treatise*, trans. Samuel Shirley (Indianapolis: Hackett, 1998), 2, 5, 8, 55, 56, 163.

66. Ibid., 73.

67. Spinoza, "Ethics," in *Ethics, Treatise on the Emendation of the Intellect, and Selected Letters*, ed. Seymour Feldman (Indianapolis: Hackett, 1992), 58.

68. Spinoza, *Theological-Political Treatise*, 72.

69. Ibid.

70. Ibid.

71. Ibid.

72. On the escalating political interests of monotheistic theology, see Laurel Schneider, *Beyond Monotheism: A Theology of Multiplicity* (New York: Routledge, 2008).

73. Spinoza, *Theological-Political Treatise*, 163.

74. Ibid., 73.

75. Ibid., 74; emphasis added.

76. Ibid., 74.

77. See, for example, ibid., 76–77.

78. Ibid., 74. See pp 1–7, above.

79. Ibid.

80. See, for example, Part IV, Proposition 4, in which Spinoza writes that "the power whereby each single thing . . . preserves its own being is the very power of God, or Nature (*Potentia qua res singulars et consequenter homo suum esse conservat, est ipsa Dei sive Naturae potentia*)" (Spinoza, "Ethics," 145; Baruch Spinoza, *Ethica* [CreateSpace Independent Publishing Platform, 2014], 160). Where relevant, page numbers for the Latin edition will follow English page numbers, separated by a slash (/).

81. Spinoza, "Ethics," 65, 57. "In seeking to show that Nature does nothing in vain," Spinoza writes, "that is, nothing that is not to man's advantage—they seem to have shown only this, that Nature and the gods are as crazy as mankind" (ibid., 58).

82. Rene Descartes, "Principles of Philosophy," in *The Philosophical Writings of Descartes* (Cambridge: Cambridge University Press, 1985), 210.

83. "Substance is thought to belong most obviously to bodies; and so we say that both animals and plants and their parts are substances, and so are natural bodies such as fire and water and earth and everything of the sort, and all things that are parts of these or composed of these . . . e.g. the heaven and its parts, stars and moon and sun" (Aristotle, "Metaphysics," in *The Complete Works of Aristotle: The Revised Oxford Translation*, ed. Jonathan Barnes [Princeton: Princeton University Press, 1971], 7.2.1028b9–13).

84. Descartes, "Principles of Philosophy," 210.

85. Ibid.

86. "By mode . . . we understand exactly the same as what is elsewhere meant by *attribute* or *quality*. But we employ the term *mode* when we are thinking of a substance as being affected or modified; when the modification enables the substance to be designated as a substance of such and such a kind, we use the term *quality*; and finally, when we are simply thinking in a more general way of what is in a substance, we use the term *attribute*" (ibid., 211).

87. Spinoza, "Ethics," 34.

88. "Every substance is necessarily infinite" (ibid.).

89. "*Per Deum intelligo ens absolute infinitum hoc est substantiam constantem infinitis attributis quorum unumquodque aeternam et infinitam essentiam exprimit*" (ibid., 31; emphasis added/7).

90. Spinoza, "Short Treatise on God, Man, and His Well-Being," in *Complete Works*, ed. Michael L. Morgan (Indianapolis: Hackett, 2002), 42.

91. Spinoza, "Ethics," 67.

92. On the principle of complementarity, see Karen Barad, *Meeting the Universe Halfway: Quantum Physics and the Entanglement of Matter and Meaning* (Durham, NC: Duke University Press, 2007), 303–4.

93. Hegel, *History of Philosophy*, 3, 260.

94. Ibid., 263.

95. Spinoza, "Ethics," 46/24.

96. Ibid., 67; emphasis added.

97. Jonathan Bennett, "Spinoza's Metaphysics," in *The Cambridge Companion to Spinoza*, ed. Don Garrett (Cambridge: Cambridge University Press, 1996), 65.

98. Spinoza, "Short Treatise," 40; emphasis added.

99. Gilles Deleuze, *Expressionism in Philosophy: Spinoza*, trans. Martin Joughin (New York: Zone Books, 1992), 13; emphasis added; emphasis deleted from "expresses"; Gilles Deleuze, *Spinoza Et Le Problème De L'expression* (Paris: Éditions de Minuit, 1968), 9.

100. Deleuze, *Expressionism*, 59.

101. Spinoza, "Ethics," 80, 71. In sum, mind and body for Spinoza "are one and the same individual thing, conceived now under the attribute of Thought and now under the attribute of Extension" (ibid., 81; cf. 104–6).

102. As Spinoza cryptically and far too quickly explains to a contemporary who asked about the human incapacity to perceive more than two attributes, "the infinite ideas in which [each thing] is expressed cannot constitute one and the same mind of a particular thing, but an infinity of minds" (Spinoza, "Letter 66"). Presumably, he is referring to types of minds other than human minds. See also the explanation in Alan Donagan, "Spinoza's Theology," in *The Cambridge Companion to Spinoza*, ed. Don Garrett (Cambridge: Cambridge University Press, 1996), 354.

103. Spinoza, "Ethics," 72.

104. Bennett, "Spinoza's Metaphysics," 87. See Harry Austryn Wolfson, *The Philosophy of Spinoza*, 2 vols. (Cambridge, MA: Harvard University Press, 1934). Commentators who position themselves to varying degrees against Wolfson include Paul Eisenberg, "On the Attributes and Their Alleged Independence of One Another: A Commentary on Spinoza's *Ethics* Ip10," in *Spinoza: Issues and Directions*, ed. Edwin Curley and Pierre-François Moreau (Leiden: E. J. Brill, 1990); F. S. Haserot, "Spinoza's Definition of Attribute," in *Studies in Spinoza*, ed. S. P. Kashap (Berkeley: University of California Press, 1972); Martial Gueroult, *Spinoza: Dieu, vol. 1* (Paris: Aubier Montaigne, 1968); Valtteri Viljanen, "Spinoza's Ontology," in *The Cambridge Companion to Spinoza's Ethics*, ed. Olli Koistinen (Cambridge: Cambridge University Press, 2009).

105. Hegel, *Philosophy of History*, 260.

106. "*Per attributam intelligo id quod intellectus de substantia percipit tanquam ejusdem essentiam constituens*" (Spinoza, "Ethics," 31/7).

107. Ibid., 31; emphasis added/7.

108. Viljanen, "Spinoza's Ontology," 65. Parkinson makes a different but equally convincing case when he reminds us that if the intellect perceives that the attributes

constitute substance, it must be correct, insofar as "knowledge of the second and third kinds is necessarily true" (Parkinson, "Hegel, Pantheism, and Spinoza," 454).

109. Spinoza, "Ethics," 36; emphasis added.

110. Hegel, *History of Philosophy*, 3, 281/891.

111. Spinoza, "Ethics," 40, 65.

112. Ibid., 45.

113. See discussion of Tschirnhaus, below. Hegel raises a similar and less sympathetic objection, as we have seen above. See also Arthur O. Lovejoy, "The Dialectic of Bruno and Spinoza," in *The Summum Bonum*, ed. Evander Bradley McGilvary (Berkeley, CA: The University Press, 1904).

114. "*Res particulares nihil sunt nisi Dei attributorum affections sive modi quibus Dei attributa certo et determinate modo exprimuntur*" (Spinoza, "Ethics," 48; emphasis added/28.)

115. Ehrenfried Walther von Tschirnhaus, "Letter 82: To the Acute and Learned Philosopher B.D.S., from Ehrenfried Walter Von Tschirnhaus," in *Spinoza: Complete Works*, ed. Michael L. Morgan (Indianapolis: Hackett, 2002), 956–57. I am indebted to Brian Fay for having made me aware of this letter, and for pointing me in this regard toward Nadler's account of the relationship between the attributes and modes.

116. Spinoza, "Letter 83: To the Most Noble and Learned Ehrenfried Walther Von Tschirnhaus, from B.D.S.," 958.

117. Steven Nadler, *Spinoza's 'Ethics': An Introduction*, Cambridge Introductions to Key Philosophical Texts (Cambridge: Cambridge University Press, 2006), 91–104.

118. Spinoza, "Ethics," 47.

119. Spinoza, "Letter 64: To the Learned and Experienced G. H. Schuller, from B.D.S."

120. Nadler, *Spinoza's "Ethics,"* 91–92; emphasis added.

121. Ibid., 93.

122. "*Quicquid est, in Deo est et nihil sine Deo esse neque concipi potest.*" (Spinoza, "Ethics," 40/17).

123. Deleuze, *Expressionism*, 16.

124. Yirmiyahu Yovel, *Spinoza and Other Heretics: The Marrano of Reason*, 2 vols., vol. 1 (Princeton, NJ: Princeton University Press, 1989), 162.

125. Spinoza, "Ethics," 50.

126. Yovel, *Marrano of Reason*, 1, 162.

127. Nadler, *Spinoza's "Ethics,"* 99.

128. Spinoza, "Ethics," 49.

129. Ibid., 64.

130. Ibid., 51.

131. Leibniz infamously accused Spinoza of having become the posthumous leader of "a new sect of Stoics" (cited in Jon Miller, "Spinoza and the Stoics on Substance Monism," in *The Cambridge Companion to Spinoza's Ethics*, ed. Olli Koistinen [Cambridge: Cambridge University Press, 2009], 99). On the differences between Spinoza and the Stoics, see Miller. See also Dirk Baltzly, "Stoic Pantheism," *Sophia* 42, no. 2 (October 2003).

On ancient Greek Stoic cosmology, see Mary-Jane Rubenstein, *Worlds Without End: The Many Lives of the Multiverse* (New York: Columbia University Press, 2014), 53–60.

132. Spinoza, "Short Treatise," 49.

133. Schelling, *Freedom*, 11, 18.

134. Ibid., 14.

135. Upon reading Spinoza, Nietzsche found his notorious loneliness shattered. He sent a postcard to Franz Overbeck saying, "I am utterly amazed, utterly enchanted. I have a *precursor* . . . he denies the freedom of the will, teleology, the moral world order, the unegoistic, and evil. . . . *In summa*, my solitude, which as on very high mountains, often made it hard for me to breathe and made my blood rush out, is at least a dualitude" (Nietzsche cited in Yovel, *Adventures of Immanence*, 2, 105).

136. Friedrich Nietzsche, *The Will to Power*, trans. Walter Kaufmann and R. J. Hollingdale (New York: Vintage, 1968), 268.

137. Ibid., 270.

138. Friedrich Nietzsche, *On the Genealogy of Morals*, trans. Walter Kaufmann (New York: Vintage Books, 1989), 45.

139. Nietzsche, *Will to Power*, 270.

140. Spinoza, "Ethics," 43.

141. Personal correspondence; emphasis original.

142. Personal correspondence.

143. Nietzsche, *Will to Power*, 270.

144. Spinoza, *Theological-Political Treatise*, 74.

145. Spinoza, "Ethics," 57.

146. Ibid., 54.

147. See proposition 32: "Will cannot be called a free cause, but only a necessary cause." Of finite will, Spinoza explains that "Will, like intellect, is only a definite mode of thinking, and so no single volition can exist or be determined to act unless it is determined by another cause, and this cause again by another, and so *ad infinitum*." Of the divine will, Spinoza insists that, far from stemming from "freedom," "it bears the same relationship to God's nature as does . . . everything else that we have shown to follow from the necessity of the divine nature" (ibid., 53, 54).

148. Ibid., 37.

149. "God, or substance consisting of infinite attributes, each of which expresses eternal and infinite essence, necessarily exists. If you deny this, conceive, if you can, that God does not exist. Therefore his essence does not involve existence. But this is absurd [insofar as, according to Proposition 7, "existence belongs to the nature of substance"]. Therefore God necessarily exists" (ibid.).

150. Bennett, "Spinoza's Metaphysics," 64.

151. Spinoza, "Ethics," 102.

152. Spinoza, *Theological-Political Treatise*, 77. As Deleuze points out, Spinoza calls upon St. Paul to affirm the immanence of God in all things (and, perhaps unintentionally,

the extent to which our vision of God is constructed by virtue of our vision of the material universe). As Deleuze cites Spinoza paraphrasing Romans 1:20, "the invisible things of God from the creation of the world are clearly seen, being understood by the things that are made" (Deleuze, *Expressionism*, 59). See Spinoza, *Theological-Political Treatise*, 58–59.

153. Spinoza, "Ethics," 65; Spinoza, "Treatise on the Emendation of the Intellect," 246, 259, 233, 250.

154. Spinoza, "Ethics," 60.

155. Copleston, "Pantheism," 45.

156. Deleuze, *Expressionism*, 100.

157. "Pragmatism," he argues, "must equally abjure absolute monism and absolute pluralism. . . . The world is one in so far as its parts hang together by any definite connexion. It is many just so far as any definite connexion fails to obtain. . . . This leaves us with the common-sense world, in which we find things partly joined and partly disjoined" (James, "The One and the Many," 70, 72).

158. For a spirited elucidation of this "problem," see Lovejoy, "The Dialectic of Bruno and Spinoza."

159. Deleuze, *Expressionism*, 81.

160. Schelling, *Ages*, 105; Schelling, *Freedom*, 22–23.

161. Hegel, *Philosophy of History*, 19–56; Schelling, *Freedom*, 9, 92.

162. Schelling, *Freedom*, 92; Schelling, *Philosophische Untersuchungen Über Das Wesen Der Menschlichen Freiheit Und Die Damit Zusammenhängended Gegenstände* (Reutlingen: J. N. Ensslin, 1834), 121; emphasis added.

163. Haeckel, *Monism*, 79.

Panterruption

1. W. R. Irwin, "The Survival of Pan," *Publications of the Modern Language Association of America* 76, no. 3 (1961): 161.

2. Sharon Lynn Coggan, "Pandaemonia: A Study of Eusebius' Recasting of Plutarch's Story of the 'Death of Great Pan'" (Dissertation: Syracuse University, 1992), 88.

3. Ibid.

4. Ibid., 88, 85.

5. "Pan," in *Harper's Dictionary of Classical Literature and Antiquities*, ed. Harry Thurston Peck (New York: Cooper Square, 1963).

6. Robin Lane Fox, *Pagans and Christians* (New York: Knopf, 1987), 130.

7. "Pan," in *Oxford English Dictionary Online*.

8. "Pan," in *Oxford Classical Dictionary, Third Edition*, ed. Simon Hornblower and Antony Spawforth (Oxford: Oxford University Press, 2006).

9. Patricia Merivale, *Pan the Goat-God: His Myth in Modern Times* (Cambridge, MA: Harvard University Press, 1969), 1.

10. "It is reasonable . . . that Pan is the double-natured son of Hermes [since] . . . speech makes all things [*pân*] known and always makes them circulate and move about and is twofold, true and false. . . . The true part is smooth and divine and dwells aloft among the gods, but falsehood dwells below among common men, is rough like the tragic goat. . . . The Pan, who declares and always moves all is rightly called goat-herd, being the double-natured son of Hermes, smooth in his upper parts, rough and goat-like in his lower parts. And Pan, if he is the son of Hermes, is either speech or the brother of speech" (Plato, "Cratylus," in *Complete Works*, ed. John M. Cooper and D. S. Hutchinson [Indianapolis: Hackett, 1997], 408b-d).

11. Benjamin Hederich, "Pan," in *Gründliches Mythologisches Lexikon* (http://woerterbuchnetz.de/cgi-bin/WBNetz/wbgui_py?sigle=Hederich&mode=Vernetzung&lemid=HP00050#XHP00050).

12. The most common reference to Penelope as the mother of Pan can be found in Plutarch, "The Obsolescence of Oracles," in *Moralia* (Cambridge, MA: Harvard University Press, 1936), 419e.

13. "Hymn to Pan" in *The Homeric Hymns: A Translation, with Introduction and Notes*, ed. Diane J. Rayor (Berkeley: University of California Press, 2004), lines 36–37.

2. HYLE

1. Baruch Spinoza, "Ethics," in *Ethics, Treatise on the Emendation of the Intellect, and Selected Letters*, ed. Seymour Feldman (Indianapolis: Hackett, 1992), 54.

2. Ibid., 102; Baruch Spinoza, "Short Treatise on God, Man, and His Well-Being," in *Complete Works*, ed. Michael L. Morgan (Indianapolis: Hackett, 2002), 53.

3. Plato, "Timaeus," in *Timaeus and Critias*, ed. Thomas Kjeller Johansen (New York: Penguin, 1977), 30a.

4. Ibid., 50c-d, 49a.

5. Genesis 1:1–3.

6. Catherine Keller, *Face of the Deep: A Theology of Becoming* (New York: Routledge, 2003), 43–64.

7. Ibid., 239n4. See "The Epic of Creation (*Enuma Elish*)," in *Myths from Mesopotamia: Creation, the Flood, Gilgamesh, and Others*, ed. Stephanie Dalley (New York: Oxford, 2008).

8. Rosemary Radford Ruether, *Gaia and God: An Ecofeminist Theology of Earth Healing* (San Francisco: Harper, 1992), 22.

9. Aristotle, "Physics," in *The Complete Works of Aristotle*, ed. Jonathan Barnes (Princeton: Princeton University Press, 1984), 1.9.192a16–17.

10. The essence, or "nature," of any particular thing, he insists, is "the form . . . rather than the matter, for a thing is more properly said to be what it is when it exists in actuality than when it exists potentially" (ibid., 2.1.193b7–8).

11. Ibid., 1.9.192a26; Aristotle, "Metaphysics," in *The Complete Works of Aristotle: The Revised Oxford Translation*, ed. Jonathan Barnes (Princeton, NJ: Princeton University Press, 1971), 7.3.1029a24–26.

12. Aristotle, "Physics," 1.9.192a23–24.

13. Aristotle, "Metaphysics," 6.1.1026a6. Cf. *De Anima*, which observes that "there seems to be no case in which the soul can act or be acted upon without involving the body; e.g. anger, courage, appetite, and sensation generally. Thinking seems to be the most probable exception; but if this too proves to be a form of imagination or to be impossible without imagination, it too requires a body as a condition of its existence" (Aristotle, "On the Soul [De Anima]," in *The Complete Works of Aristotle: The Revised Oxford Translation*, ed. Jonathan Barnes [Princeton, NJ: Princeton University Press, 1971], 1.1.403a6–10).

14. "Form Vs. Matter," in *Stanford Encyclopedia of Philosophy*, https://plato .stanford.edu/entries/form-matter; quotation marks added. See Aristotle, "Metaphysics," 6.1.1025a30–32.

15. Aristotle, "Metaphysics," 7.3.1029a24.

16. Enzo Maccagnolo, "David of Dinant and the Beginnings of Aristotelianism in Paris," in *A History of Twelfth-Century Western Philosophy*, ed. Peter Dronke (New York: Cambridge University Press, 1992), 435.

17. David's fragment is published in Tristan Dagron, "David of Dinant—Sur Le Fragment <Hyle, Mens, Deus> Des Quaternuli," *Revue de Métaphysique et de Morale* 40 (2003): 424–25; translation mine.

18. William Turner, "David of Dinant," in *The Catholic Encyclopedia* (New York: Appleton, 2017 [1908]).

19. Albert charges David with equating the divine *nous* and prime matter, arguing that insofar as the divine substance is the efficient cause of the universe, it is wholly active, and therefore cannot possibly be confused with the passivity of matter (Albertus Magnus, "Summa Theologiae Sive Scientia De Mirabili Scientia Dei," ed. E. Borgnet [Paris: Vives, 1894], 2.12.72.1, 2.12.72.4.2). For his part, Thomas refers to three errors with respect to divine simplicity: that of Augustine, who calls God the world-soul; that of the Almaricians, who call God "the formal principle of all things; and that "of David of Dinant, who most absurdly taught that God was primary matter." Following Albert, Thomas explains that God is the efficient cause of creation, and as such cannot be material, since "primary matter . . . is merely potential, while the [efficient cause] is actual," and since— perplexingly—"potentiality is absolutely posterior to actuality" Thomas Aquinas, *Summa Theologiae*, trans. Fathers of the English Dominican Province, 5 vols. (Allen, TX: Christian Classics, 1981), 1.3.8.P. His demonstration of the priority of actuality over possibility comes a few articles earlier, when Thomas argues that "although in any single thing that passes from potentiality to actuality, the potentiality is prior in time to the actuality; nevertheless, absolutely speaking, actuality is prior to potentiality; for whatever is in potentiality can be reduced into actuality only by some being in actuality" (ibid., 1.3.1).

20. Giordano Bruno says that "Averroes" came close to asserting the primacy of matter, and that the *divinity* of matter was taught by "an Arab named Avicebron" or "the Moor Avicebron" in Giordano Bruno, "Cause, Principle and Unity," in *Cause, Principle and Unity and Essays on Magic*, ed. Richard J. Blackwell and Robert de Lucca, Cambridge Texts in the History of Philosophy (Cambridge: Cambridge University Press, 1998), 80, 55, 61.

21. The controversy with respect to Ibn Rushd turns on the question of whether calling matter eternal renders it equal (and therefore identical) to God. Believing that it did, Bishop Etienne Tempier condemned 219 "Averroist" theses in 1277. For a defense of the ontological difference in the face of the eternity of matter, see Oliver Leaman, *Averroes and His Philosophy* (Richmond, UK: Curzon, 1998), 63–71. Ibn Gabirol goes farther than Averroes, not only identifying matter with form but occasionally privileging the former over the latter. Passages that seem to assert and deny the ultimacy of matter respectively can be found in Ibn Gabirol, *The Font of Life (Fons Vitae)*, Mediaeval Philosophical Texts in Translation (Milwaukee, WI: Marquette University Press, 2014), 5.42.334, 3.9.99.

22. On the numerically shifting plurality of the movers, see Aristotle, "Metaphysics," 7.8.1073a–1074b; Mary-Jane Rubenstein, *Worlds Without End: The Many Lives of the Multiverse* (New York: Columbia University Press, 2014), 35.

23. Jane Bennett, *Vibrant Matter: A Political Ecology of Things* (Durham, NC: Duke University Press, 2010), vii. In the second *Critique*, for example, Immanuel Kant calls the term "living matter" a contradiction in terms, "since the essential character of matter is lifelessness, *inertia*" (Immanuel Kant, *Critique of Judgment*, cited in ibid.).

24. The most straightforwardly mechanistic account of such a clock as a "great automaton" can be found in Robert Boyle, *A Free Enquiry into the Vulgarly Received Notion of Nature* (Cambridge: Cambridge University Press, 1996 [1686]), 39, 60, 160. See also pp. 110–13, above. Ironically, as Jessica Riskin has demonstrated, the "classical" or "brute" mechanism of Cartesians, Newtonians, and the followers of Robert Boyle drained all agency out of the material world only to require a supernatural creator to get it going and keep it in motion (Jessica Riskin, *The Restless Clock: A History of the Centuries-Long Argument over What Makes Living Things Tick* [Chicago: University of Chicago Press, 2016], 4). Riskin contrasts this vision with the ultimately subjugated "active mechanism" of Leibniz, Lamarck, and Haeckel, according to whom machines were "self-constituting and self-transforming." "Modern scientific accounts of life," she explains, "have been shaped by a struggle between these two competing mechanisms, two scientific principles." As far as Riskin is concerned, Descartes, Kant, and Darwin are all poised between these two forms of mechanism (ibid., 7).

25. John Cottingham, "'A Brute to the Brutes?': Descartes' Treatment of Animals," *Philosophy* 53, no. 206 (October 1978): 552. This argument finds its most explicit articulation in Descartes' letter to Henry More: "it is more probable that worms, flies, caterpillars, and other animals move like machines than they have immortal souls. [. . . S]ince art copies nature, and people make various automatons which move without thought, it

seems reasonable that nature should produce its own automatons, which are even more splendid than artificial ones—namely the animals" ("To More, 5 February 1649," in Rene Descartes, *The Philosophical Writings of Descartes, Volume 3: The Correspondence*, ed. John Cottingham, et al. [Cambridge: Cambridge University Press, 1991], 366). On the reduction of animals to matter and matter to inertness, see James Stanescu, "Matter," in *Critical Terms for Animal Studies*, ed. Lori Gruen (Chicago: University of Chicago Press, forthcoming). Although Riskin acknowledges that Descartes occasioned such a reduction—among thinkers like Nicholas Malebranche and Thomas Hobbes in particular—she cautions against the misreading that denies activity, life, or perception to Cartesian animals. As Descartes clarifies in the same letter to More, "I spoke of thought, not of life or sense: for no one denies the life of animals" (Descartes cited in Riskin, *Restless Clock*, 69). According to Riskin, Descartes' philosophy therefore occupies a fulcrum between the Scholastic and New Scientific worlds: "in the unstable moment of transition that he inhabited," she argues, "it seemed briefly possible to see living creatures as machines in the modern sense *and* as alive in the ancient sense" (ibid., 71).

26. Mary Midgley, "Introduction—the Not-So-Simple Earth," in *Earthly Realism: The Meaning of Gaia*, ed. Mary Midgley (Charlottesville, VA: Societas, 2007), 5.

27. With the advent of capital and bourgeois society, Marx writes, "for the first time nature becomes purely an object for humankind, purely as a matter of utility; ceases to be recognized as a power for itself; and the theoretical discovery of its autonomous laws appears merely as a ruse so as to subjugate it to human needs, whether as an object of consumption or as a means of production." Any attribution of agency to the nonhuman world is then ridiculed as *"nature-idolatry"* (Karl Marx, *Grundrisse: Foundations of the Critique of Political Economy*, trans. Martin Nicolaus [New York: Penguin, 1993], 410).

28. Bennett, *Vibrant Matter*, ix.

29. Ibid., vii; Jane Bennett, "Thing-Power," in *Political Matter: Technoscience, Democracy, and Public Life*, ed. Bruce Braun and Sarah J. Whatmore (Minneapolis: University of Minnesota Press, 2010), 43.

30. Bennett, *Vibrant Matter*, 25.

31. Mel Chen, *Animacies: Biopolitics, Racial Mattering, and Queer Affect* (Durham, NC: Duke University Press, 2012), 11.

32. On the racialization of lead—in particular, the positioning of white American children between black American children and Chinese workers—and the fear of "phallic licking" of toys, see ibid., 159–88.

33. For (sympathetic) critiques of the "newness" of such materialisms, see Sara Ahmed, "Imaginary Prohibitions: Some Preliminary Remarks on the Founding Gestures of the 'New Materialism,'" *European Journal of Women's Studies* 15, no. 23 (2008); Margret Grebowicz and Helen Merrick, *Beyond the Cyborg: Adventures with Donna Haraway* (New York: Columbia University Press, 2013), 24–25.

34. Val Plumwood, *Feminism and the Mastery of Nature* (New York: Routledge, 1993), 121; emphasis added.

35. This story is retold in Alice Lee Marriott, *American Indian Mythology* (New York: Apollo, 1968), 22–26.

36. Paula Gunn Allen, *The Sacred Hoop: Recovering the Feminine in American Indian Traditions* (Boston: Beacon, 1992), 60.

37. Deborah Bird Rose, "Death and Grief in a World of Kin: Dwelling in Larger-Than-Human Communities," in *The Handbook of Contemporary Animism*, ed. Graham Harvey (New York: Routledge, 2015), 138–39.

38. Ibid., 145; Deborah Bird Rose, "Val Plumwood's Philosophical Animism: Attentive Interactions in the Sentient World," *Environmental Humanities* 3 (2013): 95; Val Plumwood, "Nature in the Active Voice," *Ecological Humanities* 46 (2009): 6/11.

39. Tim Ingold, "Rethinking the Animate, Re-Animating Thought," *Ethnos: Journal of Anthropology* 71, no. 1 (2011): 14.

40. David J. Furley, *The Greek Cosmologists: The Formation of the Atomic Theory and Its Earliest Critics* (Cambridge: Cambridge University Press, 1987), 18.

41. Diogenes Laertius, *Lives of the Eminent Philosophers*, trans. R. D. Hicks, 2 vols., Loeb Classical Library (Cambridge, MA: Harvard University Press, 1942), 1:1.1.27, 1:2.2.3, 2:9.9.57, 2:9.1.7, 2:8.2.76.

42. "For all things come from earth, and all things end by becoming earth. For we are all sprung from earth and water. All things that come into being and grow are earth and water" (Arthur Fairbanks, "Xenophanes: Fragments and Commentary," in *The First Philosophers of Greece*, ed. Arthur Fairbanks [London: Paul, Trench, Trubner, 1898], fragments 8–10). On the perplexing (and gendered) absence of earth as an original principle among most of the early Greek philosophers, see David Macauley, *Elemental Philosophy: Earth, Air, Fire, and Water as Environmental Ideas* (Albany, NY: State University of New York Press, 2011), 20–21.

43. C. E. Plumptre, *General Sketch of the History of Pantheism: From the Earliest Times to the Age of Spinoza*, 2 vols., vol. 1, Cambridge Library Series—Religion (Cambridge, UK: Cambridge University Press, 2011 [1878]), 188.

44. Fairbanks, "Xenophanes: Fragments and Commentary," fragment 6.

45. Diogenes Laertius explains, "The substance of God is spherical, in no way resembling man. He is all eye and all ear, but does not breathe; he is the totality of mind and thought" (Diogenes Laertius, *Lives*, 1:9.2.19).

46. Ibid., 2:7.1.139.

47. J. M. Ross, Introduction, in *Cicero: The Nature of the Gods* (New York: Penguin, 1972), 42.

48. Michael Lapidge, "Stoic Cosmology," in *The Stoics*, ed. J. M. Rist (Berkeley, CA: University of California Press, 1978), 164.

49. The relevant fragments can be found in Hans Frederich August von Anim, ed. *Zeno Et Zenonis Discipuli. Exemplar Anastatice Iteratum*, 4 vols., vol. 1, Stoicorum Veterum Fragmenta (Leipzig: Teubneri, 1921), 1.125–29.

50. *Chryssipi Fragmenta Logica Et Physica*, 4 vols., vol. 2, Stoicorum Veterum Fragmenta, ed. Hans Frederich August von Anim (Leipzig: Teubneri, 1903), 2.6.22, 2.1071.

51. David E. Hahm, *The Origins of Stoic Cosmology* (Columbus, OH: Ohio State University Press, 1977), 31–33.

52. Diogenes Laertius, *Lives*, 2:7.1.139.

53. Elizabeth Asmis, "Lucretius' Venus and Stoic Zeus," *Hermes* 110 (1982): 459.

54. Diogenes Laertius, *Lives*, 2:7.1.137.

55. See J. Mansfield, "Providence and the Destruction of the Universe in Early Stoic Thought: With Some Remarks on the 'Mysteries of Philosophy,'" in *Studies in Hellenistic Religion*, ed. M. J. Vermaseren (Leiden: Brill, 1979).

56. See Rubenstein, *Worlds Without End*, 55–56.

57. See Everett Ferguson, *Backgrounds of Early Christianity* (Grand Rapids, MI: Eerdmans, 2003), 354–70; Tuomas Rasimus, Troels Engberg-Pedersen, and Ismo Dunderberg, eds., *Stoicism in Early Christianity* (Grand Rapids, MI: Baker Academic, 2010).

58. Edward Adams, "Graeco-Roman and Ancient Jewish Cosmology," in *Cosmology and New Testament Theology*, ed. Jonathan T. Pennington and Sean M. McDonald (New York: Clark, 2008), 16.

59. On Leucippus, see Diogenes Laertius, *Lives*, 2:9.6.30–33. On Democritus, see ibid., 2:9.7.34–49. On Epicurus, see ibid., 2:10.1–154. On the two different atomist models of chaos, which he calls "the stochastic cloud" and "the laminar flow," see Michel Serres, *The Birth of Physics*, trans. Jack Hawkes (Manchester, UK: Clinamen Press, 2000), 136.

60. Lucretius, *The Nature of Things*, trans. A. E. Stallings (New York: Penguin, 2007), 1.83, 1.148. All Latin references have been taken from the Loeb edition: Lucretius, *De Rerum Natura*, trans. W. H. D. Rouse; revised by Martin Ferguson Smith, Loeb Classical Library (Cambridge, MA: Harvard University Press, 1975).

61. Lucretius's chief example in this regard is of the murder of Iphigenia, whose father Agamemnon believes he has to sacrifice her to ensure safe sailing conditions for his fleet (Lucretius, *The Nature of Things*, 1.80–101). On the uselessness of rituals, he writes, "O foolish race of mortals. . . . It is not piety to cover up your head for show, / To bow and scrape before a stone, or stop by as you go / At every altar, flinging yourself upon the ground face down, / Lifting your palms at the gods' shrines, nor piety to drown / Altars in the blood of brutes" (ibid., 5.1194–1201). Subsequent references to this text will be cited internally.

62. Mary Midgley makes the latter argument in Mary Midgley, *Science and Poetry* (New York: Routledge, 2001), 23–27. As far as I am aware, no one has held the former position apart from Giordano Bruno, who states without further elaboration that Epicurean matter is "the divine nature" (Bruno, "Cause, Principle and Unity," 55).

63. For a classic and charming description of such gods as "too remote and too happy, like good secluded Epicureans, to meddle with earthly things," see George Santayana, *Three Philosophical Poets, Lucretius, Dante, and Goethe* (New York: CreateSpace, 2013 [1910]), 16.

64. "For godhead by its nature must enjoy eternal life / In utmost peace, removed from us and far from mortal strife, / Apart from any suffering, apart from any danger, / Powerful of itself, not needing us, and both a stranger / To our attempts to win it over and untouched by anger" (Lucretius, *The Nature of Things*, 44–49).

65. The call for peace can be found at ibid., 1.29–39. The theological summary can be found at ibid., 1.44–49. On the puzzling location of the theological statement, see Paul Friedländer, "The Epicurean Theology in Lucretius' First Prooemium (Lucr. I. 44–49)," *Transactions and Proceedings of the American Philological Association* 70 (1939).

66. See Asmis, "Lucretius' Venus and Stoic Zeus," 458; Kirk Summers, "Lucretius and the Epicurean Tradition of Piety," *Classical Philology* 90, no. 1 (1995); Monica Gale, *Myth and Poetry in Lucretius* (Cambridge: Cambridge University Press, 1996), 47–48.

67. Lucretius, *The Nature of Things*, 1.937–54.

68. Asmis, "Lucretius' Venus and Stoic Zeus," 458.

69. I am thinking here of the specific vegetality of Deleuzian rhizomes: "In contrast to centered (even polycentric) systems with hierarchical modes of communication and established paths," he writes with Guattari, "the rhizome is an acentered, nonhierarchical, nonsignifying system without a General and without an organizing memory or central automaton, defined solely by a circulation of states" (Gilles Deleuze and Félix Guattari, *A Thousand Plateaus*, trans. Brian Massumi [Minneapolis: University of Minnesota Press, 1987], 21).

70. Asmis, "Lucretius' Venus and Stoic Zeus," 469.

71. Ibid.

72. On the thirteenth- and fourteenth-century readers of Lucretius, see Guido Billanovich, "'Veterum Vestigia Vatum' Nei Carmi Dei Preumanisti Padovani," *Italia Medievale e Umanistica* 1 (1958). For a lively account of Bracciolini's discovery, see Stephen Greenblatt, *The Swerve: How the World Became Modern* (New York: Norton, 2011), 14–50.

73. See Hans Blumenberg, *The Legitimacy of the Modern Age*, trans. Robert M. Wallace (Cambridge, MA: MIT Press, 1983), 549–96.

74. Giordano Bruno, "On the Infinite Universe and Worlds," in *Giordano Bruno: His Life and Thought with Annotated Translation of His Work on the Infinite Universe and Worlds*, ed. Dorothea Singer (New York: Schuman, 1950), 270.

75. The phrase comes from Dorothea Singer, ed., *Giordano Bruno: His Life and Thought with Annotated Translation of His Work on the Infinite Universe and Worlds* (New York: Schuman, 1950), 51.

76. Bruno, "Cause, Principle and Unity," 101, 55.

77. Ibid., 55. Cf. 64: "The Epicureans have said some good things, although they have not risen beyond the material quality." Subsequent references to this text will be cited internally.

78. Giordano Bruno, *The Ash Wednesday Supper*, trans. Edward A. Gosselin and Lawrence S. Lerner, Renaissance Society of America Reprint Texts (Toronto: University of Toronto Press, 1995), 95.

79. See David Hume, *Dialogues Concerning Natural Religion* (Indianapolis: Hackett, 1998), part 2, esp. 16–22.

80. "*la quale é principio di vita vegetatione et senso in tutte le cose, che vivono, vegetano, et senteno*" (Giordano Bruno, *De La Causa, Principio, Et Uno* [Venice 1584],

"Epistola Dedicatoria," unpaginated p. 6). Where applicable, Italian page numbers will follow English page numbers, separated by a slash (/).

81. On the distinction between principle and cause, see Bruno, "Cause, Principle and Unity," 36–37.

82. Here, Bruno is equating matter with Plato's *khôra*, which is merely "space" in the *Timaeus*. This is the first of many steps the dialogue will take to elevate the traditionally feminized principles of creation.

83. This is no exaggeration; in his commentary on the *De Anima*, Averroes wrote, "I believe that [Aristotle] was a model in nature and the exemplar which nature found for showing final human perfection" (cited in Richard C. Taylor, "Averroes," in *The Cambridge Companion to Arabic Philosophy*, ed. Peter Adamson and Richard C. Taylor [Cambridge: Cambridge University Press, 2005], 189).

84. In the framing dialogue, Elitropio summarizes "the precepts of [Filoteo's] philosopy" as the insight "that contraries coincide both in principle and in reality" (Bruno, "Cause, Principle and Unity," 23). Nicholas marked the coincidence of all opposites in God, who "is above all affirmation and all negation" and as such, must be, for example, both the absolutely maximum and the absolutely minimum (insofar as minimum-ness means maximum smallness). See Nicholas of Cusa, *On Learned Ignorance*, trans. H. Lawrence Bond, Nicholas of Cusa: Selected Writings (New York: Paulist Press, 1997), 91–92. It is striking for the purposes of this pantheological exploration to note that Bruno is deploying this mechanism in relation to the universe rather than to God, implying their ultimate identity.

85. See p. 52, above.

86. "The universe has a first principle taken as a unity, and no longer considered doubled into material principle and formal principle" (Bruno, "Cause, Principle and Unity," 69).

87. On the irreducible manyness of oneness in Bruno, see Antonio Calcagno, *Giordano Bruno and the Logic of Coincidence: Unity and Multiplicity in the Philosophical Thought of Giordano Bruno*, ed. Eckhard Bernstein, Renaissance and Baroque Studies and Texts (New York: Peter Lang, 1998).

88. Nicholas of Cusa, *On Learned Ignorance*, 2.4.113.

89. There is no incontrovertible evidence that Spinoza read Bruno, but commentators often deduce that he either may or must have done so. For these positions, respectively, see Steven Nadler, *Spinoza: A Life* (Cambridge: Cambridge University Press, 2001), 111; J. Lewis McIntyre, *Giordano Bruno* (London: Macmillan, 1903), 337–43.

For an analysis of the dialectical similarities between the two thinkers and their shared roots in Neoplatonic philosophy, see Arthur O. Lovejoy, "The Dialectic of Bruno and Spinoza," in *The Summum Bonum*, ed. Evander Bradley McGilvary (Berkeley, CA: The University Press, 1904).

90. Discono to Teofilo: "You reveal a plausible way of supporting Anaxagoras's opinion that all things are in all things, for since the spirit, or soul, or the universal form is in all things, everything can be produced from everything." Teofilo responds:

"That is not only plausible but true, for that spirit is found in all things which, even if they are not living creatures, are animate" (Bruno, "Cause, Principle and Unity," 44). Anaxagoras taught that the milk a child ingests, for example, can only become bone and blood "if there is already bone and blood in the milk" (Patricia Curd, "Anaxagoras," *Stanford Encyclopedia of Philosophy*, https://plato.stanford.edu/entries/anaxagoras. This universally mixed state of affairs can be traced for Anaxagoras back to the pre-cosmic state, an inhomogeneous interpenetration of every substance that would come to be with every other substance. (See Patricia Curd, "Anaxagoras and the Theory of Everything," in *The Oxford Handbook of Presocratic Philosophy*, ed. Patricia Curd and Daniel W. Graham [Oxford: Oxford University Press, 2008]).

91. See Mary-Jane Rubenstein, "End Without End: Cosmology and Infinity in Nicholas of Cusa," in *Desire, Faith, and the Darkness of God: Essays in Honor of Denys Turner*, ed. Eric Bugyis and David Newheiser (Notre Dame, IN: University of Notre Dame Press, 2016), 21–22, 27–28.

92. Nicholas of Cusa, *On Learned Ignorance*, 2.2.101.

93. Ibid., 2.5.117. For a contemporary cosmo-theological exposition of this principle, see Catherine Keller, *Cloud of the Impossible: Negative Theology and Planetary Entanglement* (New York: Columbia University Press, 2014), 114–15.

94. Singer, *Giordano Bruno*, 177.

95. "The Bruno myth can be summarized as follows: An itinerant renegade friar, Bruno defied contemporary ecclesiastical authority and doctrines. . . . He thus became the first martyr of modern science at the hands of the Church and thereby a precursor of Galileo. The moral of this nineteenth-century story is that Science, the bearer of knowledge, struggles to an inevitable victory over the Church, the champion of ignorance and superstition" (Edward A Gosselin and Lawrence S. Lerner, Introduction, in Bruno, *The Ash Wednesday Supper*, 12).

96. C. E. Plumptre, "Giordano Bruno: His Life and Philosophy," *Westminster Review* 132, no. 2 (1889): 117–18.

97. Ibid., 117.

98. "Giordano Bruno and Galileo Galilei," *The Popular Science Monthly Supplement* 13–18 (1878): 112.

99. Ann Druyan and Steven Soter, "Episode 1: Standing up in the Milky Way," in *Cosmos: A Spacetime Odyssey* (Cosmos Studios, Fuzzy Door Productions, Santa Fe Studios, 2014), 26:29–33.

100. On the death and eventual resurrection of this idea, see Rubenstein, *Worlds Without End*, 106–76.

101. Bruno, "On Magic."

102. Saumarez cited in Riskin, *Restless Clock*, 205.

103. As Lee Smolin explains the Newtonian worldview, "this framework views nature as consisting of nothing but particles with timeless properties, whose motions and interactions are determined by timeless laws. . . . Within this view of nature, nothing happens except the rearrangement of particles according to timeless laws, so according

to these laws the future is already completely determined by the present, as the present was by the past" (Lee Smolin, *Time Reborn: From the Crisis in Physics to the Future of the Universe* [New York: Houghton Mifflin Harcourt, 2013], xxiii). Or, in Elizabeth Grosz's words, "the [Newtonian] material world is that which is capable of unrolling or unfolding what has been already rolled or folded, that is, caused: it is the inevitable unwinding or unfolding, the relaxation, of what has been cocked and set, dilated, in a pregiven trajectory" (Elizabeth Grosz, *Becoming Undone: Darwinian Reflections on Life, Politics, and Art* [Durham, NC: Duke University Press, 2011], 29). For a defense of Newton *himself* against the charge of passivity and strict determinism, see Peter Dear, *The Intelligiblity of Nature: How Science Makes Sense of the World* (Chicago: University of Chicago Press, 2006), 31–38.

104. William Pietz, "Fetishism and Materialism: The Limits of Theory in Marx," in *Fetishism as Cultural Discourse*, ed. Emily Apter and William Pietz (Ithaca, NY: Cornell University Press, 1993), 139.

105. Plumptre, "Giordano Bruno," 117.

106. David Hume, "The Natural History of Religion," in *Dialogues and the Natural History of Religion*, ed. J. C. A. Gaskin (Oxford: Oxford University Press, 1998); Friedrich Max Müller, *Natural Religion: The Gifford Lectures Delivered before the University of Glasgow in 1888* (New York: AMS Press, 1975 [1889]); Emile Durkheim, *The Elementary Forms of Religious Life*, trans. Karen E. Fields (New York: Free Press, 1995 [1912]); James George Frazer, *The Illustrated Golden Bough: A Study in Magic and Religion; Abridged by Robert K. G. Temple* (New York: Simon & Schuster, 1996); Mircea Eliade, *Patterns in Comparative Religion*, trans. Rosemary Sheed (New York: World, 1963).

107. Edward Burnett Tylor, "The Philosophy of Religion Among the Lower Races of Mankind," *The Journal of the Ethnological Society of London* 2, no. 4 (1870): 370; Edward Burnett Tylor, *Religion in Primitive Culture* (New York: Harper and Row, 1958 [1871]), 10.

108. Tylor, *Religion in Primitive Culture*, 9. Subsequent references to this text will be cited internally.

109. On the proliferation of such racialized hierarchies of religion among eighteenth- and nineteenth-century comparativists, see Jonathan Z. Smith, "Religion, Religions, Religious," in *Critical Terms for Religious Studies*, ed. Mark C. Taylor (Chicago: University of Chicago Press, 1998), 276–79. Indeed, Val Plumwood has argued that the whole category of animism was the product of a largely nineteenth-century European effort to solidify a racial hierarchy among the humans they had encountered in conquered lands; see Rose, "Plumwood's Philosophical Animism," 96.

110. On the soul of animals (nonhuman and human), see Aristotle, "On the Soul (De Anima)," 3.9.432a15–433a10. On the vegetal, or "nutritive" soul, see ibid., 3.12.434a23–434b10.

111. Tylor, "Philosophy of Religion," 372.

112. Paul Christopher Johnson, "An Atlantic Genealogy of 'Spirit Possession,'" *Comparative Studies in Society and History* 53, no. 2 (2011): 412.

113. See Introduction, note 30. On the condemnation of Eriugena, see Alasdair MacIntyre, "Pantheism," in *Encyclopedia of Philosophy, 2nd ed.*, ed. Donald M. Borchert (Detroit: MacMillian, 2006), 95. On Eriugena's immanentism and pantheism, see Eugene Thacker, *After Life* (Chicago: University of Chicago Press, 2010), 57–58, 70–72, 173–75.

114. See chapter 1, note 21.

115. Tylor, "Philosophy of Religion," 374.

116. Ernst Haeckel, *Monism as Connecting Religion and Science: The Confession of Faith of a Man of Science*, trans. J. Gilchrist (London: Black, 1895), 3–4; emphasis added.

117. On this lineage, see Rose, "Plumwood's Philosophical Animism," 96–98.

118. As Hallowell explains it, "the study of social organization, defined as human relations of a certain kind, is perfectly intelligible as an objective approach to the study of this subject in any culture. But if, in the world view of a people, 'persons' as a class include entities other than human beings, then our objective approach is not adequate. . . . A different perspective is required for this purpose" (Hallowell, "Ojibwa Ontology," 359).

119. Ibid., 366.

120. Ibid., 363, 365, 369, 374, 369.

121. Ibid., 361; emphasis added.

122. Ibid., 377.

123. Ibid., 362.

124. As Matthew Hall explains, among "new" animists, "Tylor's notion of residing spirits or souls in plants (and animals and rocks) is increasingly rejected in favour of the idea that in indigenous cultures plants are actually understood (and related to) as other-than-human persons" (Matthew Hall, "Talk Among the Trees: Animist Plant Ontologies and Ethics," in *The Handbook of Contemporary Animism*, ed. Graham Harvey [New York: Routledge, 2015], 387–88).

125. Ingold, "Rethinking the Animate," 10.

126. Rose, "Plumwood's Philosophical Animism," 98.

127. Graham Harvey, *Animism: Respecting the Living World* (New York: Columbia University Press, 2006), xi.

128. This example is Justine Quijada's (personal communication).

129. On the inherently "intra-active" nature of quantum particles, see Karen Barad, *Meeting the Universe Halfway: Quantum Physics and the Entanglement of Matter and Meaning* (Durham, NC: Duke University Press, 2007), 97–131.

130. Déborah Danowski and Eduardo Viveiros de Castro, *The Ends of the World*, trans. Rodrigo Nunes (Malden, MA: Polity Press, 2017), 68–69.

131. Deborah Bird Rose, *Dingo Makes Us Human: Life and Land in an Australian Aboriginal Culture* (Cambridge: Cambridge University Press, 2000).

132. Rose, "Death and Grief," 139–40.

133. Ibid., 142.

134. Ibid., 141.

135. Such ethnographies form the basis of Sigmund Freud, *Totem and Taboo*, trans. James Strachey, Complete Psychological Works of Sigmund Freud (New York: Norton, 1990 [1913]).

136. These concepts, he insisted, are all "exact equivalents" (Durkheim, *Elementary Forms*, 196).

137. Ibid., 191.

138. Ibid.

139. Harvey, *Animism*, 130. Radin's rejection of this notion can be found in Paul Radin, "Religion of the North American Indians," *Journal of American Folklore* 27 (1914). Hallowell's can be found in Hallowell, "Ojibwa Ontology," 382.

140. Ingold, "Rethinking the Animate," 11.

141. Ibid; cf. Tim Ingold, "The Art of Translation in a Continuous World," in *Beyond Boundaries: Understanding, Translation, and Anthropological Discourse*, ed. Gisli Pálsson (Oxford: Berg, 1993), 218–19.

142. Ingold, "Rethinking the Animate," 10.

143. Rose, "Death and Grief," 137.

144. "American pragmatism begins along the border between Native and European America as an attitude of resistance against the dominant attitudes of European colonialism" (Scott L. Pratt, *Native Pragmatism: Rethinking the Roots of American Philosophy* [Bloomington: Indiana University Press, 2002], xiv).

145. Hall, "Talk Among the Trees," 393.

146. Ibid., 394.

147. My thanks to Justine Quijada for having pointed out this ironic reinscription of "Western" dualisms.

148. Hall, "Talk Among the Trees," 391–92.

149. The phrase comes from Margulis, who was understandably resistant to being so dismissed. "They say it's a kind of science only a woman could do," she said, "that 'Earth Mother' crap—and that's a back door way of putting it down, of saying it's not really top quality science" (Margulis cited in James Strick, "Exobiology at Nasa: Incubator for the Gaia and Serial Endosymbiosis Theories," in *Earth, Life, and System: Evolution and Ecology on a Gaian Planet*, ed. Bruce Clarke [New York: Fordham University Press, 2015], 100). Margulis was reacting in particular to the ridicule she had suffered by virtue of her endorsement of James Lovelock's Gaia hypothesis. On this endorsement and the backlash against Margulis, see Charles Mann, "Lynn Margulis: Science's Unruly Earth Mother," *Science* 252 (April 19, 1991).

150. Dorion Sagan, "Life on a Margulisian Planet: A Son's Philosophical Reflections," in *Earth, Life, and System: Evolution and Ecology on a Gaian Planet*, ed. Bruce Clarke (New York: Fordham University Press, 2015), 33. Maturana's and Varela's articulation of autopoiesis can be found in Francisco Varela, Humberto Maturana, and Ricardo B. Uribe, "Autopoiesis: The Organization of Living Systems, Its Characterization and a Model," *BioSystems* 5 (1974). A more popular expansion can be found in Humberto Maturana and Francisco Varela, *Autopoiesis and Cognition: The Realization of the Living* (Dordrecht: Reidel, 1980), 78–79.

151. Lynn Margulis and Dorion Sagan, *What Is Life?* (New York: Simon and Schuster, 1995), 23.

152. Sagan, "Life on a Margulisian Planet," 33–34.

153. The idea (and term) was originally proposed by Konstantin Meresckowski; see Konstantin Mereschkowsky, "Theorie Der Zwei Plasmaarten Als Grundlage Der Symbiogenesis, Einer Neuer Lehre Von Der Ent-Stehung Der Organismen," *Biologisches Centralblatt* 30 (1910).

154. This study was first published under a previous surname as Lynn Sagan, "On the Origin of Mitosing Eukaryotic Cells," *Journal of Theoretical Biology* 14 (March 1967); and later developed into a monograph: Lynn Margulis, *The Origin of Eukaryotic Cells: Evidence and Research Implications for a Theory of the Origin and Evolution of Microbial, Plant, and Animal Cells on the Precambrian Earth* (New Haven, CT: Yale University Press, 1970). Endosymbiosis accounts for the development of prokaryotic cells, which lack nuclei and divide by mitosis, into eukaryotic cells, which possess nuclei along with other complex structures—including, most perplexingly, mitochondria—and which divide by mitosis (on this riddle, see Jan Sapp, "On Symbiosis, Microbes, Kingdoms, and Domains," in *Earth, Life, and System: Evolution and Ecology on a Gaian Planet*, ed. Bruce Clarke [New York: Fordham University Press, 2015], 111). What Margulis realized was that "mitochondria so closely resembled certain free-living aerobic bacteria . . . that the most likely explanation was that these . . . originated as free-living bacteria engulfed serially over time, but not digested, by a mycoplasma-like ancestral cell" (James Strick, "Exobiology at Nasa: Incubator for the Gaia and Serial Endosymbiosis Theories," ibid., 93–94). According to Margulis's theory, then, eukaryotes were the product of prokaryotes' encapsulation of bacteria and the resulting symbiotic development between them.

155. For Margulis's sustained critique of, and departure from, neo-Darwinism (which she accuses of being a religious institution, complete with unquestionable dogmas and sacred texts), see Lynn Margulis, "Big Trouble in Biology: Physiological Autopoiesis Versus Mechanistic Neo-Darwinism," in *Slanted Truths: Essays on Gaia, Symbiosis, and Evolution*, ed. Lynn Margulis and Dorion Sagan (New York: Copernicus, 1997).

156. Margulis cited in Mann, "Margulis," 379.

157. Bruno Latour, "How to Make Sure Gaia Is Not a God? With Special Attention to Toby Tyrrell's Book *On Gaia*," *Os Mil Nomes de Gaia: do Antropocentro à Idade da Terra*, https://osmilnomesdegaia.files.wordpress.com/2014/11/bruno-latour.pdf.

158. Myra J. Hird, *The Origins of Sociable Life: Evolution after Science Studies* (New York: Palgrave Macmillan, 2009), 86.

159. "of all the organisms on earth today," write Margulis and Sagan, "only prokaryotes (bacteria) are individuals. All other live beings ('organisms'—such as animals, plants, and fungi) are metabolically complex communities of a multitude of tightly organized beings" (Margulis, "Big Trouble," 273). From a molecular and even quantum perspective, of course, one might argue that even prokaryotes are composed of a vast

series of interactions—or as Karen Barad would have it, "intra-actions"—which make even the smallest particle a relational product of material-discursive practices (Barad, *Meeting*, 33).

160. Margulis cited in Mann, "Margulis," 378; Sagan, "Life on a Margulisian Planet," 16.

161. Margulis and Sagan, *What Is Life?*, 26.

162. Scott F. Gilbert, Jan Sapp, and Alfred I. Tauber, "A Symbiotic View of Life: We Have Never Been Individuals," *The Quarterly Review of Biology* 87, no. 4 (2012): 327. The authors appeal to Margulis's favorite example, *Mastotermes darwiniensis*, as a "'poster organism' for the chimeric individual. . . . How can a worker termite be considered an individual," they ask, "when it is the hive that is the reproductive unit of the species, and the worker cannot even digest cellulose without its gut symbiont, *Mixotricha paradoxa*, which is itself a genetic composite of at least five other species?" (ibid.)

163. Dorion Sagan, "The Human Is More Than Human: Interspecies Communities and the New 'Facts of Life,'" *Cultural Anthropology* (April 24, 2011).

164. Donna Haraway, "Sowing Worlds: A Seed Bag for Terraforming with Earth Others," in *Beyond the Cyborg: Adventures with Donna Haraway*, ed. Margret Grebowicz and Helen Merrick (New York: Columbia University Press, 2013), 145.

165. Nicholas Gane and Donna Haraway, "When We Have Never Been Human, What Is to Be Done? Interview with Donna Haraway," *Theory, Culture & Society* 23, no. 7–8 (2006): 141.

166. Evolutionary biologist Ernst Mayr called the discovery "the single most important event in the history of the organic world" before going on to reject the possibility that the earth itself might be an autopoietic symbiont: "it's startling," he confesses, "to find a reputable scientist arguing such fantasies" (Mayr cited in Mann, "Margulis," 378).

167. Against the popular monism associated with the Gaia hypothesis, Margulis insists that "the Gaia hypothesis is not, as many claim, that 'the Earth is a single organism.' Yet the Earth, in the biological sense, has a body sustained by complex physiological processes" (Lynn Margulis, *Symbiotic Planet: A New Look at Evolution* [New York: Basic Books, 1998], 115).

168. Lynn Margulis and James Lovelock, "Biological Modulations of the Earth's Atmosphere," *Icarus* 21 (1974): 473.

169. Ibid., 471. Cf. Margulis, *Symbiotic Planet*, 116–18, 123–25.

170. From the Margulis archive, cited in Michael Ruse, *The Gaia Hypothesis: Science on a Pagan Planet* (Chicago: University of Chicago Press, 2013), 176.

171. From the Margulis archive, cited in ibid., 177.

172. Strick, "Exobiology," 88.

173. Mann, "Margulis," 380.

174. Strick, "Exobiology," 89; Hird, *Origins*, 116; Lovelock cited in Ruse, *The Gaia Hypothesis*; Margulis cited in Strick, "Exobiology," 100; Dorion Sagan, "Life on a Margulisian Planet: A Son's Philosophical Reflections," ibid., 19.

Panfusion

1. Patricia Merivale, *Pan the Goat-God: His Myth in Modern Times* (Cambridge, MA: Harvard University Press, 1969), 9.

2. "Pan," in *Harper's Dictionary of Classical Literature and Antiquities*, ed. Harry Thurston Peck (New York: Cooper Square, 1963).

3. "To Pan," in *Orphic Hymns, Classical Texts Library*, http://www.theoi.com/Text /OrphicHymns1.html#10.

4. "Pan," in *Oxford English Dictionary Online* (Oxford: Oxford University Press, 2014); "Pan," in *Oxford Classical Dictionary, Third Edition*, ed. Simon Hornblower and Antony Spawforth (Oxford: Oxford University Press, 2006); Wilfred H. Schoff, "Tammuz, Pan and Christ," *The Open Court* 26, no. 9 (September, 1912): 517.

5. See Porphyry, *On Images*, trans. Edwin Hamilton Gifford http://classics.mit.edu /Porphyry/images.html, fragment 9.

6. See Mary-Jane Rubenstein, *Worlds Without End: The Many Lives of the Multiverse* (New York: Columbia University Press, 2014), chapter 1.

7. See Merivale, *Goat-God*, 76.

8. Plutarch, *On the Obsolescence of the Oracles*, in Sharon Lynn Coggan, "Pandaemonia: A Study of Eusebius' Recasting of Plutarch's Story of the 'Death of Great Pan'" (Dissertation: Syracuse University, 1992), ii.

9. Plutarch, *Obsolescence*, in ibid., 1.

10. In a nutshell: the Romans on the ship misheard the Greeks on the island. The latter were celebrating the annual death of their agricultural deity, Tammuz, and cried out ritualistically, "Tammuz, Tammuz, Tammuz, the very great is dead (πανμεγας τεθνηκε)." Mistaking the god's name for his own, the captain Thamus and his passengers believed the news was just, "παμμεγας τεθνηκε," which their nonnative Greek parleyed into Παν ο μεγας τεθνκε ("Pan the great is dead"). See Schoff, "Tammuz, Pan and Christ," 521.

11. Eusebius in Coggan, "Pandaemonia," 1. As Coggan demonstrates, it was Eusebius who shifted the meaning of the Greek *daimon* from "divine being" to "evil spirit" (See Coggan, "Pandaemonia," 2–3).

12. Ibid., ii. According to Robin Lane Fox, this "Pan pun was premature, for his was the one reported death of Tiberius's reign which nobody believed. Cults of Pan continued in the very heart and identity of cities, the 'Pan hill' in the middle of Alexandria or the grottoes and springs of Caesarea Panias, where the god's presence persisted on the city's third-century coinage" (Robin Lane Fox, *Pagans and Christians* [New York: Knopf, 1987], 130).

13. Jeffrey Burton Russell, *The Prince of Darkness: Radical Evil and the Power of Good in History* (Ithaca, NY: Cornell University Press, 1992), 17. See also Schoff, "Tammuz, Pan and Christ," 517; Merivale, *Goat-God*, 28–31; James Hillman and W. H. Roscher, *Pan and the Nightmare* (Irving, TX: Spring Publications, 1979), 64, 160.

14. Richard Hardack, *Not Altogether Human: Pantheism and the Dark Nature of the American Renaissance* (Amherst: University of Massachussetts Press, 2012), 68.

15. Ibid.

16. Hawthorne, cited in ibid., 69.

17. D. H. Lawrence, "Pan in America," *Southwest Review* (January, 1926): 114.

18. Ibid., 115.

19. Ibid.

20. Ibid., 104.

3. Cosmos

1. See p. 21, above.

2. Philip Clayton, *The Problem of God in Modern Thought* (Grand Rapids: Eerdmans, 2000), 401.

3. Ibid.

4. Homer used the term in the former sense; Herodotus in the latter; see Edward Adams, "Graeco-Roman and Ancient Jewish Cosmology," in *Cosmology and New Testament Theology*, ed. Jonathan T. Pennington and Sean M. McDonald (New York: Clark, 2008), 6.

5. "Yes, Callicles, wise men claim that partnership and friendship, orderliness, self-control, and justice hold together heaven and earth, and gods and men, and that is why they call this universe a *world order* [*kósmos*], my friend, and not an undisciplined world-disorder [*akosmosían*]" (Plato, "Gorgias," in *Complete Works*, ed. John M. Cooper and D. S. Hutchinson [Indianapolis: Hackett, 1997], 507e-508a).

6. For an elaboration of Platonic, Aristotelian, Epicurean, and Stoic cosmologies, see Mary-Jane Rubenstein, *Worlds Without End: The Many Lives of the Multiverse* (New York: Columbia University Press, 2014), 21–69.

7. "World," *Oxford English Dictionary Online*.

8. See Steven J. Dick, *Plurality of Worlds: The Origins of the Extraterrestrial Life Debate from Democritus to Kant* (Cambridge: Cambridge University Press, 1982), 44–60.

9. See Rubenstein, *Worlds Without End*, 159–93.

10. Elizabeth A. Povinelli, *Geontologies: A Requiem to Late Liberalism* (Durham, NC: Duke University Press, 2016), 122; cf. Deborah Bird Rose, "Death and Grief in a World of Kin: Dwelling in Larger-Than-Human Communities," in *The Handbook of Contemporary Animism*, ed. Graham Harvey (New York: Routledge, 2015), 139; Matthew Hall, "Talk Among the Trees: Animist Plant Ontologies and Ethics," ibid., 389.

11. Déborah Danowski and Eduardo Viveiros de Castro, *The Ends of the World*, trans. Rodrigo Nunes (Malden, MA: Polity Press, 2017), 64.

12. Thomas M. Norton-Smith, *The Dance of Person and Place: One Interpretation of American Indian Philosophy*, Suny Series in Living Indigenous Philosophies (Albany: State University of New York Press, 2010), 47.

13. Robin Wall Kimmerer, *Braiding Sweetgrass: Indigenous Wisdom, Scientific Knowledge, and the Teaching of Plants* (Minneapolis: Milkweed, 2013), 4.

14. Plato, "Timaeus," in *Timaeus and Critias*, ed. Thomas Kjeller Johansen (New York: Penguin, 1977), 30d-31a.

15. Ibid., 40b-c.

16. Homer, "Hymn to Gaia," in *Homeric Hymns*, ed. Nicholas Richardson, Penguin Classics (New York: Penguin, 2003), 140.

17. Hesiod's Gaia is "the eternal ground" of the "starry Sky" (Ouranos), the hills, the sea, and all the Olympian deities—along with the Cyclops, Titans, Furies, Giants, Nymphs, and three hundred-limbed "haughty sons with monstrous forms" (Hesiod, in *Theogony and Works and Days*, ed. Theogony [Ann Arbor: University of Michigan Press, 2006], 26.117–27.118, 125, 129, 131; 29.185–7). When her son-husband Ouranos hides these monstrous ones away, Gaia devises a plan to free them and create even more monstrosities by castrating him, an action her son Kronos boldly undertakes (ibid., 28.178–80). Bruno Latour reads this and subsequent plots as the actions of a scheming monster (Bruno Latour, *Facing Gaia: Eight Lectures on the New Climatic Regime*, trans. Catherine Porter [Medford, MA: Polity, 2017], 83). Somehow, Latour misses Hesiod's focus throughout the *Theogony* on Gaia's effulgent production of all things, as well as the fierce maternal protectiveness that leads her time and again to concoct such "schemes" in the face of paternal aggression.

18. Jessica Riskin, *The Restless Clock: A History of the Centuries-Long Argument over What Makes Living Things Tick* (Chicago: University of Chicago Press, 2016), 3.

19. Ibid., 4.

20. Seneca cited in Robert Boyle, *A Free Enquiry into the Vulgarly Received Notion of Nature* (Cambridge: Cambridge University Press, 1996 [1686]), 51.

21. Ibid., 47, cf. 158; subsequent references will be cited internally. The editors of Boyle's volume confess to being perplexed by the object of Boyle's criticism here (xvi-xvii), but when Boyle introduces these contemporary idolators as the intellectual progeny of numerous "Jews and Christians," he might well be referring to Spinoza, with whom he corresponded between 1661 and 1663, with Henry Oldenburg serving as intermediary (see Simon Duffy, "The Difference Between Science and Philosophy: The Spinoza-Boyle Controversy Revisited," *Paragraph* 29, no. 2 [July, 2006]; Filip Buyse, "Boyle, Spinoza and the Hartlib Circle: The Correspondence That Never Took Place," *Societate si Politica* 7, no. 2 [2013]). Moreover, considering the publication date, it seems possible that the Christian "sect" in question refers to the small but vocal set of European political radicals who appealed to a Spinozan sort of Protestantism to contest the increasing dogmatism and hierarchy of the reformed churches. Marshaling Spinoza against Luther's authority of Scripture and in favor of his unmediated relationship to God, these "freethinkers" demanded "tolerance, freedom of speech and conscience, democracy, a universal religion, and the separation of church and state" (Frederick C. Beiser, *The Fate of Reason: German Philosophy from Kant to Fichte* [Cambridge, MA: Harvard University Press, 1987], 50).

22. Lawrence Principe includes *Atalanta Fugiens* as one of the "common and well known" texts of Boyle's age, and as one to which he was most likely responding in his *Sceptical Chymist* (1661) (Lawrence M. Principe, *The Aspiring Adept: Robert Boyle and His Alchemical Quest* [Princeton, NJ: Princeton University Press, 2000], 48–49).

23. H. M. E. De Jong, ed. *Michael Maier's Atalanta Fugiens* (Lake Worth, FL: Nicolas-Hays, 2014).

24. It is not clear whether or not Boyle was familiar with the works of the Ash Wednesday heretic, but Bruno would beg to differ with him on the matter of matter's agency in Genesis. Citing "Moses" as an advocate of the notion that "nature produces everything out of its own matter," Bruno paraphrases Genesis 1:20 and 24: "'Let the earth bring forth its animals, let the waters bring forth living creatures.' It is as if he had said: Let matter bring them forth. . . . that is, he gave the waters a procreative power" (Giordano Bruno, "Cause, Principle and Unity," in *Cause, Principle and Unity and Essays on Magic*, ed. Richard J. Blackwell and Robert de Lucca, Cambridge Texts in the History of Philosophy [Cambridge: Cambridge University Press, 1998], 83).

25. Boyle, *Free Enquiry*, 13.

26. Isaac Newton, *The Principia*, trans. Andrew Motte, Great Minds Series (Amherst, NY: Prometheus books, 1995 [1687]), 13.

27. See ibid., 442–43.

28. These mysterious functions included the initial creation of matter, its division into the "shining" and "opaque" subtypes that respectively constitute stars and planets, and the repulsive force that counteracts gravity sufficiently to keep the universe from collapsing into itself. On the initial creation of matter, see Isaac Newton, *Opticks* (CreateSpace Independent Publishing Platform, 2013 [1704]), 206–7. On the other functions, see Isaac Newton, *Four Letters from Sir Isaac Newton to Doctor Bentley, Containing Some Arguments in Proof of a Deity* (London: Dodsley, 1756 [1692–1693]), 2–4, 20.

29. Newton, *Letters to Bentley*, 15. Leibniz ridicules this idea in his correspondence with Newton's defender, Samuel Clarke: "according to this doctrine," wrote Leibniz, "God Almighty needs to wind his watch from time to time, otherwise it would cease to move. He did not, it seems, have sufficient foresight to make it a perpetual motion" (Leibniz, First Letter, in G. W. Leibniz and Samuel Clarke, *Correspondence* [Indianapolis: Hackett, 2000], 40).

30. Newton, *Letters to Bentley*, 1.

31. Richard Bentley, *Matter and Motion Cannot Think, or, a Confutation of Atheism from the Faculties of the Soul* (London: Parkhurst and Mortluck, 1692), 14; capitalization regularized throughout this source.

32. Ibid., 33.

33. Pierre-Simon Laplace, *A Philosophical Essay on Probabilities*, trans. Frederick Wilson Truscott and Frederick Lincoln Emory (New York: Wiley, 1902 [1814]), 4.

34. Ibid.

35. The tale can be found throughout popular literature on the history of science; for just one example, see Richard Dawkins, *The God Delusion* (New York: Mariner, 2008), 68.

36. See, for example, Ernest Pasquier, "Les Hypothèses Cosmogoniques," *Revue néo-scolastique* 5, no. 18 (1898): 125n1; Stephen Hawking, "Does God Play Dice?" http://www .hawking.org.uk/does-god-play-dice.html.

37. Laplace, *Exposition Du Système Du Monde* (Brussels: De Vroom, 1827), 522–23; translation mine.

38. Lee Smolin, *Time Reborn: From the Crisis in Physics to the Future of the Universe* (New York: Houghton Mifflin Harcourt, 2013), xxii.

39. Lynn White, Jr., "The Historical Roots of Our Ecological Crisis," *Science* 155, no. 3767 (1967): 1205.

40. On this progression, see Catherine Keller, "'Nothingsomething' on My Mind: *Creatio Ex Nihilo* or *Ex Profundis*?" in *Theologies of Creation: Creatio Ex Nihilo and Its New Rivals*, ed. Thomas Jay Oord (New York: Routledge, 2015); Mary-Jane Rubenstein, "Myth and Modern Physics: On the Power of Nothing," ibid.

41. White, Jr., "The Historical Roots of Our Ecological Crisis," 1205.

42. Starhawk cited in Isabelle Stengers, "Reclaiming Animism," *E-flux* 36 (July 2012).

43. Dorion Sagan and Lynn Margulis, "Gaia and Philosophy," in *Slanted Truths: Essays on Gaia, Symbiosis, and Evolution*, ed. Lynn Margulis and Dorion Sagan (New York: Copernicus, 1997), 152.

44. James Strick, "Exobiology at Nasa: Incubator for the Gaia and Serial Endosymbiosis Theories," in *Earth, Life, and System: Evolution and Ecology on a Gaian Planet*, ed. Bruce Clarke (New York: Fordham University Press, 2015), 82.

45. Margulis and James Lovelock, "Biological Modulations of the Earth's Atmosphere," *Icarus* 21(1974): 471.

46. Ibid.

47. James Lovelock and Sidney Epton, "The Quest for Gaia," *New Scientist* (February 6, 1975): 304.

48. Lovelock, *Homage to Gaia: The Life of an Independent Scientist* (Oxford: Oxford University Press, 2000), 253.

49. Sagan and Margulis, "Gaia and Philosophy," 145.

50. Lovelock, *Gaia: A New Look at Life on Earth* (New York: Oxford University Press, 1979), 11.

51. Ibid.

52. Interview with Lovelock, cited in Michael Ruse, *The Gaia Hypothesis: Science on a Pagan Planet* (Chicago: University of Chicago Press, 2013), 32.

53. Richard Dawkins, *The Extended Phenotype: The Long Reach of the Gene* (Oxford: Oxford University Press, 2016 [1982]), 359.

54. See a summary of this position in Strick, "Exobiology," 89.

55. W. Ford Doolittle, "Is Nature Really Motherly?" *The CoEvolution Quarterly* (Spring 1981): 61.

56. Dawkins has called Gaia the "BBC Theorem," insofar as it makes nature appear beautiful and awe-inspiring rather than selfish and warlike. Even Stephen Jay Gould was worried about the social metaphors of cooperation and harmony Gaia had adopted (see Ruse, *The Gaia Hypothesis*, 30, 32). In this matter, it seems Gould has strategically forgotten Darwin's own adoption of Malthusian economics into his principle of natural selection, rendering existence a perpetual struggle for scarce resources (see Priscilla Stuckey, "The Animal Versus the Social: Rethinking Individual and Community in Western Cosmology," in *The Handbook of Contemporary Animism*, ed. Graham Harvey [New York: Routledge, 2015], 196–98). As Bruno Latour insists, no discourse can speak unmetaphorically, but somehow "scientists are . . . convinced that they, and they alone, speak literally" (Bruno Latour, "How to Make Sure Gaia Is Not a God? With Special Attention to Toby Tyrrell's Book *on Gaia*," *Os Mil Nomes de Gaia: do Antropocentro à Idade da Terra*, https://osmilnomesdegaia.files.wordpress.com/2014/11/bruno-latour.pdf [2014]: 10).

57. As Latour points out, the widespread distaste for this metaphor is both telling and absurd, considering the omnipresence of the prefix "geo-" in the earth sciences. "Geo- and Gaia share exactly the same etymology," he reminds us; "both come from the same entity Gè, actually a chthonic divinity much older than the Olympian gods and goddesses, the primitive power." The reason "that the invocation of Gaia is sure to trigger confusion, to agitate, to provoke" is that it "make[s] people think anew about this innocent prefix 'geo' which had become dead and stale. . . . What the prefix 'geo' no longer provokes, 'Gaia' does" (Latour, "How to Make Sure," 2).

58. John Maynard and Robert May, cited in Ruse, *The Gaia Hypothesis*, 32–33.

59. John Postgate, "Gaia Gets Too Big for Her Boots," *New Scientist* (April 7, 1988): 60.

60. Ibid.

61. Ibid.

62. See Evelyn Fox Keller, "One Woman and Her Theory," ibid. (July 3, 1986).

63. Dorion Sagan, "Life on a Margulisian Planet: A Son's Philosophical Reflections," in *Earth, Life, and System: Evolution and Ecology on a Gaian Planet*, ed. Bruce Clarke (New York: Fordham University Press, 2015), 19.

64. Doolittle, "Motherly," 61.

65. Lovelock and Epton, "The Quest for Gaia," 304. In an interview, Lovelock characteristically says and unsays this analogy, describing "the Earth as an organism, or if not an organism, as a self-regulating system" (Lovelock cited in Ruse, *The Gaia Hypothesis*, 5).

66. Margulis, *Symbiotic Planet: A New Look at Evolution* (New York: Basic Books, 1998), 115, cf. 106, 120.

67. Margulis and Oona West, "Gaia and the Colonization of Mars," in *Slanted Truths: Essays on Gaia, Symbiosis, and Evolution*, ed. Margulis and Sagan (New York: Copernicus, 1997), 225.

68. Charles Darwin, *The Variation of Animals and Plants under Domestication*, 2 vols. (London: Murray, 1868), 2:404. Cf. Deleuze and Guattari: "It is already going too

far to postulate an order descending from the animal to the vegetable, then to molecules, to particles. Each multiplicity is symbiotic; its becoming ties together animals, plants, microorganisms, mad particles, a whole galaxy" (Gilles Deleuze and Félix Guattari, *A Thousand Plateaus*, trans. Brian Massumi [Minneapolis: University of Minnesota Press, 1987], 250).

69. Myra J. Hird, *The Origins of Sociable Life: Evolution After Science Studies* (New York: Palgrave Macmillan, 2009), 26.

70. Margulis and Lovelock, "The Atmosphere as Circulatory System of the Biosphere—the Gaia Hypothesis," in *Slanted Truths: Essays on Gaia, Symbiosis, and Evolution*, ed. Margulis and Sagan (New York: Copernicus, 1997), 131.

71. Margulis and Lovelock, "Modulations," 474.

72. Ibid., 475.

73. "The earth . . . is sympoietic, not autopoietic. Mortal worlds . . . do not make themselves, no matter how complex and multileveled the systems" (Donna Haraway, *Staying with the Trouble: Making Kin in the Chthulucene* [Durham, NC: Duke University Press, 2016], 33).

74. Lovelock, *Homage*, 253–54.

75. Vine Deloria Jr., "If You Think About It, You Will See That It Is True," in *Spirit & Reason: The Vine Deloria, Jr., Reader*, ed. Barbara Deloria, Kristen Foehner, and Sam Scinta (Golden, CO: Fulcrum, 1999), 49.

76. Lovelock, *Healing Gaia: Practical Medicine for the Planet* (New York: Harmony, 1991), 31; emphasis added.

77. Margulis, "Big Trouble in Biology: Physiological Autopoiesis Versus Mechanistic Neo-Darwinism," in *Slanted Truths: Essays on Gaia, Symbiosis, and Evolution*, ed. Margulis and Sagan (New York: Copernicus, 1997), 277.

78. Ibid., 277–78.

79. Luciano Onori and Guido Visconti, "The Gaia Theory: From Lovelock to Margulis. From a Homeostatic to a Cognitive Autopoietic Worldview," *Rendiconti lincei / Scienze fisiche e naturali* 23 (2012): 375.

80. Sagan, Margulis, and Guerrero, "Descartes, Dualism, and Beyond," in *Slanted Truths: Essays on Gaia, Symbiosis, and Evolution*, ed. Margulis and Sagan (New York: Copernicus, 1997), 178.

81. Ibid., 179.

82. Valerie Brown, "Bacteria 'R' Us," *Pacific Standard*, https://psmag.com/bacteria-r-us-61e66d1b6792#.xxy87z7si (December 2, 2010); Sagan, "The Human Is More Than Human: Interspecies Communities and the New 'Facts of Life,'" *Cultural Anthropology* (April 24, 2011); Hird, *Origins*, 25; Hird, "Naturally Queer," *Feminist Theory* 5 (2004): 86.

83. Sagan, Margulis, and Guerrero, "Descartes."

84. See chapter 2, note 28.

85. Margulis, "The Conscious Cell," *Annals of the New York Academy of Sciences* 929, no. 1 (April 2001): 57. Eduardo Kohn similarly attributes thought to

all life in Eduardo Kohn, *How Forests Think: Toward an Anthropology Beyond the Human* (Oakland: University of California Press, 2013). Against this line of thinking-about-thinking, Daniel Dennett insists on distinguishing between bacterial "pseudominds or protominds, or semiminds, or hemi-semi-demi-minds from the real thing," which is to say human intentionality enabled by neurons (Daniel C. Dennett, *Kinds of Minds: Toward an Understanding of Consciousness* [New York: Basic Books, 1997], 18).

86. Margulis, *Symbiotic Planet*, 10. Earlier in the same work, Margulis writes that "humans are the work not of God but of thousands of millions of years of interactions among highly responsive microbes" (ibid., 4).

87. Margulis and West, "Gaia and the Colonization of Mars," 222–23.

88. Margulis, *Symbiotic Planet*, 123; emphasis added.

89. Lovelock interview from the David Suzuki documentary, *The Sacred Balance*, cited in Ruse, *The Gaia Hypothesis*, 181; emphasis added.

90. Lovelock interview cited in ibid., 186.

91. Sagan and Margulis, "Gaia and Philosophy," 186.

92. Lovelock interview from Suzuki, cited in Ruse, *The Gaia Hypothesis*, 182.

93. Sagan and Margulis, "A Good Four-Letter Word," 206.

94. Toby Tyrrell, *On Gaia: A Critical Investigation of the Relationship between Life and Earth* (Princeton, NJ: Princeton University Press, 2013), 1–2, 4.

95. It is this faith that Tyrrell is seeking most energetically to undermine: "I believe that a 'Gaia mindset' unconsciously predisposes [us] toward undue optimism," he writes. "As far as planetary stewardship is concerned there could be serious adverse consequences of adopting an incorrect and overly optimistic paradigm view of how the earth operates as a system" (ibid., 211). The same argument was made decades ago in Doolittle, "Motherly," 62–63.

96. Tyrrell, *On Gaia*, 198.

97. Latour, "How to Make Sure," 9.

98. Ibid., 14.

99. Ibid., 4.

100. Ibid., 15.

101. Lovelock cited in ibid., 12.

102. Ibid.

103. Ibid., 3, 7, 9, 2, 5, 22.

104. Ibid., 5.

105. Jacques Derrida, "How to Avoid Speaking: Denials," in *Derrida and Negative Theology*, ed. Harold Coward and Toby Foshay (Albany, NY: State University of New York Press, 1992).

106. Latour, "How to Make Sure," 23.

107. Meister Eckhart, "Sermon 52: Beati Paupers Spiritu, Quoniam Ipsorum Est Regnum Caelorum," in *The Essential Sermons, Commentaries, Treatise, and Defense*, ed. Edmund Colledge and Bernard McGinn (New York: Paulist, 1981), 202.

108. Ibid., 200–201.

109. These include his affirming the identity of the soul with God, the righteous person and Christ, and Christ with the world (Propositions 10, 11–12, 20–21, 3), as well as the eternity of the cosmos (Proposition 2). See John XXII, "*In Agro Dominico*," https://www.scribd.com/doc/9651895/Bull-In-Agro-Dominico-by-John-XXII (March 27, 1329).

110. To the original sentence, "But let's try nonetheless for the remainder of this lecture to see what could protect Gaia from being a God of natural religion," Latour now adds, "which does not mean that we wish religion out of the picture, on the contrary, but simply that we don't want religious views of the providential God of Totality to be dragged into an apparent discussion about 'material objects'. And the danger is very real because of the obligatory shift to holism." (Bruno Latour, "How to Make Sure Gaia Is Not a God of Totality? With Special Attention to Toby Tyrrell's Book on Gaia," http://bruno-latour.fr/sites/default/files/138-THOUSAND-NAMES_0.pdf (September 2014).

111. See the conference's position paper at https://thethousandnamesofgaia.files.wordpress.com/2014/07/position-paper-ingl-para-site.pdf.

112. The term was first proposed in Paul J. Crutzen and Eugene F. Stoermer, "The Anthropocene," *IGBP [International Geosphere-Biosphere Programme] Newsletter* 41(2000). It was adopted at the 35th Annual Geological Congress, which named the Anthropocene an "epoch," which falls categorically between an age or stage and a period or era. They also voted to date the epoch beginning from the year 1950. See http://www2.le.ac.uk/offices/press/press-releases/2016/august/media-note-anthropocene-working-group-awg.

113. On the difficulties of dating the Anthropocene, see Povinelli, *Geontologies*, 9–11; William Connolly, *Facing the Planetary: Entangled Humanism and the Politics of Swarming* (Durham, NC: Duke University Press, 2017), 31.

114. Crutzen, cited in Dipesh Chakrabarty, "The Climate of History: Four Theses," *Critical Inquiry* 35, no. 2 (Winter 2009): 209.

115. Timothy Morton, *Hyperobjects: Philosophy and Ecology after the End of the World* (Minneapolis: University of Minnesota Press, 2013), 6, 129.

116. Haraway, *Trouble*, 56; Connolly, *Planetary*, 9.

117. Danowski and Viveiros de Castro, *The Ends of the World*, 111. See also Eileen Crist, "On the Poverty of Our Nomenclature," in *Anthropocene or Capitalocene? Nature, History, and the Crisis of Capitalism*, ed. Jason W. Moore (Oakland, CA: PM Books, 2016).

118. For a critical appraisal of such proposals, see Elmar Alvater, "The Capitalocene, or, Geoengineering Against Capitalism's Planetary Boundaries," ibid.

119. Haraway, *Trouble*, 3.

120. James Cone, "Whose Earth Is It Anyway?" *Cross Currents* (2000): 43.

121. Danowski and Viveiros de Castro, *The Ends of the World*, 83.

122. "Gaia est celle qui fait intrusion dans une histoire que les descendants de la revolution industrielle avaient ractontée comme celle de l'emanciaption humaine se libérant des contraintes de 'la nature'" (Isabelle Stengers, "Penser À Partir Du Ravage Écologique," in *De L'univers Clos Au Monde Infini*, ed. Émilie Hache [Paris: Éditions Dehors, 2014], 148).

123. Stengers, *In Catastrophic Times: Resisting the Coming Barbarism*, ed. Tom Cohen and Claire Colebrook, trans. Andrew Goffey, Critical Climate Change (London: Open Humanities Press, 2015), 43. In a recent essay, Stengers clarifies that "Elle [Gaia] met en question l'avenir de tous les inhabitants de la terre, sauf, sans doute, celui des populations innombrables de micro-organismes qui, depuis des milliards d'années, sont les co-auteurs de son existence continue" (Stengers, "Penser," 149). And although Stengers does preserve the gendering of Gaia, she makes it clear that Gaia is not here to sing us lullabies: "Ce pourrait être la figure d'une mère, mais non pas d'une mère bonne et aimante, plutôt d'une mère redoutable, qu'il ne faut pas offenser, aussi d'une mère assez indifférente, sans intérêt particulier pour le destin de sa progéniture" (ibid., 148).

124. Stengers, *Catastrophic Times*, 48.

125. Latour, *Facing Gaia*, 75–79.

126. Danowski and Viveiros de Castro, *The Ends of the World*, 39. On "negentropy" as the function of entropy in open systems that produces local order and complexity, see Erwin Schrödinger, *What Is Life?* (New York: Macmillan, 1945); Eric D. Schneider and Dorion Sagan, *Into the Cool: Energy Flow, Thermodynamics, and Life* (Chicago: University of Chicago Press, 2005); Clayton Crockett, "Earth: What Can a Planet Do?" in *An Insurrectionist Manifesto: Four New Gospels for a Radical Politics, with an Afterward by Catherine Keller*, ed. Ward Blanton, et al. (New York: Columbia University Press, 2016).

127. Danowski and Viveiros de Castro, *The Ends of the World*, 39.

128. Stengers, *Catastrophic Times*, 45.

129. Lovelock, *The Vanishing Face of Gaia: A Final Warning* (New York: Basic Books, 2009), 5.

130. Stengers, *Catastrophic Times*, 8; Jason W. Moore, "Introduction," in *Anthropocene or Capitalocene? Nature, History, and the Crisis of Capitalism*, ed. Jason W. Moore (Oakland, CA: PM Press, 2016).

131. Margulis, *Symbiotic Planet*, 119.

132. Ibid., 20.

133. Danowski and Viveiros de Castro, *The Ends of the World*, 9.

134. Latour, *Facing Gaia*, 117.

135. William James, "The One and the Many," in *Pragmatism and Other Writings*, ed. Giles Gunn (New York: Penguin, 2000), 60.

136. Ibid., 62.

137. This reference can be found in the transcript of Latour's original lectures: Bruno Latour, "Facing Gaia: Six Lectures on the Political Theology of Nature," (2013): 19–20. Cf. Catherine Keller's deployment of the Joycean "chaosmos" in Catherine Keller, *Face of the Deep: A Theology of Becoming* (New York: Routledge, 2003), 12–13, 170–71.

138. Danowski and Viveiros de Castro, *The Ends of the World*, 4.

139. Ibid., 29–30.

140. Ibid., 104.

141. Ibid.

142. Ibid.

143. Ibid., 107–8, 112.

144. Latour, *Facing Gaia*, 245.

145. Ibid., 152.

146. Stengers, *Catastrophic Times*, 53. Similarly, Haraway writes that we may need to "revisio[n] the world as coding trickster with whom we must learn to converse" (Haraway, "The Promises of Monsters: A Regenerative Politics for Inappropriate/D Others," in *The Haraway Reader* [New York: Taylor and Francis, 2004], 68).

147. Stengers cited in Danowski and Viveiros de Castro, *The Ends of the World*, 111; emphasis added.

148. Connolly, *Planetary*, 34.

149. Connolly, *A World of Becoming* (Durham, NC: Duke University Press, 2011), 91; Connolly, *Planetary*, 12.

150. Haraway, *Companion Species Manifesto: Dogs, People, and Significant Otherness* (Chicago: Prickly Paradigm, 2003), 3.

151. Haraway, "Monsters," 77; Haraway, "Introduction: A Kinship of Feminist Figurations," in *The Haraway Reader* (New York: Routledge, 2004), 3.

152. Haraway, "Kinship," 3; Haraway, *Modest_Witness@Second_Millennium. Femaleman_Meets_Oncomouse* (New York: Routledge, 1997), 75; Haraway, "Sowing Worlds: A Seed Bag for Terraforming with Earth Others," in *Beyond the Cyborg: Adventures with Donna Haraway*, ed. Margret Grebowicz and Helen Merrick (New York: Columbia University Press, 2013), 137; Haraway, *When Species Meet*, Posthumanities (Minneapolis: University of Minnesota Press, 2007), 3; Haraway, "Monsters," 69; Haraway, *Modest Witness*, 79, 43.

153. Haraway, *Trouble*, 53.

154. Ibid.

155. Ibid., 57.

156. Ibid., 52, 101.

157. Ibid., 2; emphasis added. Cf. Exodus 3:14.

158. With this term, Povinelli is seeking to eliminate the distinction between life (onto-) and nonlife (geo-), which has led to the poisoning and destruction of the Aboriginal landscape, and which is unsupportable even within the regime of Western biology. Tjipel, for example, is a dreamtime teenage girl who was transformed into a creek in northern Australia, and whom late liberalism has converted into a desertified ecosystem. Both mythologically and ecologically speaking, Tjipel is "an assemblage . . . of living and nonliving substances" that animates and constitutes the "landscape" (Povinelli, *Geontologies*, 100).

159. Danowski and Viveiros de Castro, *The Ends of the World*, 112.

160. Ibid., 108.

161. Ibid., 69.

162. For an ethnographic roundup of such Amerindian perspectivism, see Eduardo Viveiros de Castro, "Cosmological Deixis and Amerindian Perspectivism," *Royal Anthropological Institute of Great Britain and Ireland* 4, no. 3 (September 1998): 471.

163. Ibid., 477.

164. Danowski and Viveiros de Castro, *The Ends of the World*, 70.

165. Eduardo Viveiros de Castro, "Exchanging Perspectives: The Transformation of Objects into Subjects in Amerindian Ontologies," *Common Knowledge* 10, no. 3 (2004): 471, 472, 475.

166. Ibid., 472.

167. Tania Stolze Lima, "The Two and Its Many: Reflections on Perspectivism in a Tupi Cosmology," *Ethnos: Journal of Anthropology* 64, no. 1 (1999): 116.

168. Ibid., 117.

169. Viveiros de Castro, "Exchanging Perspectives," 472; emphasis added to "things," deleted from "that."

170. Danowski and Viveiros de Castro, *The Ends of the World*, 72.

171. Nicholas of Cusa, *On Learned Ignorance*, trans. H. Lawrence Bond, Nicholas of Cusa: Selected Writings (New York: Paulist Press, 1997), 2.12.162. For a fuller treatment of Cusa's theo-cosmology, see Catherine Keller, *Cloud of the Impossible: Negative Theology and Planetary Entanglement* (New York: Columbia University Press, 2014), 87–126; Mary-Jane Rubenstein, "End Without End: Cosmology and Infinity in Nicholas of Cusa," in *Desire, Faith, and the Darkness of God: Essays in Honor of Denys Turner*, ed. Eric Bugyis and David Newheiser (Notre Dame, IN: University of Notre Dame Press, 2016).

172. Nicholas of Cusa, *On Learned Ignorance*, 2.12.172.

173. On Bruno's relationship to Copernicus, see Giordano Bruno, *The Ash Wednesday Supper*, trans. Stanley L. Jaki (Paris: Mouton, 1975), 86, 89, 90. On worlds as solar systems, see Giordano Bruno, "On the Infinite Universe and Worlds," in *Giordano Bruno: His Life and Thought with Annotated Translation of His Work on the Infinite Universe and Worlds*, ed. Dorothea Singer (New York: Schuman, 1950), 304; Miguel A. Granada, "Kepler and Bruno on the Infinity of the Universe and of Solar Systems," *Journal for the History of Astronomy* 39 (2008).

174. Saul Perlmutter, Adam Reiss, and Brian Schmidt were awarded the 2011 Nobel Prize in physics for their discovery. See the "advanced information" section at https://www.nobelprize.org/nobel_prizes/physics/laureates/2011/advanced-physicsprize2011.pdf.

175. On the vexed history of the cosmological constant, which Einstein posited and then revoked, see Robert P. Kirshner, *The Extravagant Universe: Exploding Stars, Dark Energy, and the Accelerating Cosmos* (Princeton, NJ: Princeton University Press, 2002), xi, 215–21. Einstein's original paper can be found in Albert Einstein, "Cosmological Considerations on the General Theory of Relativity (1917)," in *Cosmological Constants: Papers in Modern Cosmology*, ed. Jeremy Bernstein and Gerald Feinberg (New York: Columbia University Press, 1986). The term "dark energy" was coined by Michael Turner at the University of Chicago, who meant with the adjective "dark" to signal this pressure's undetectability and incomprehensibility; in short, physicists cannot see it and do not know what it is, or why its value is so outlandishly out of sync with the

calculations of quantum field theory (see Joshua A. Frieman, Michael S. Turner, and Dragan Huterer, "Dark Energy and the Accelerating Universe," *arXiv* 0803.0982 [March 7, 2008]).

176. Sean M. Carroll, *From Eternity to Here: The Quest for the Ultimate Theory of Time* (New York: Dutton, 2010), 62.

177. "*This is the way the world ends/ This is the way the world ends/ This is the way the world ends/ Not with a bang but a whimper*" (T. S. Eliot, *Collected Poems: 1909–1962* [New York: Harcourt Brace, 1991], 82; emphasis original).

178. Marcelo Gleiser, *A Tear at the Edge of Creation: A Radical New Vision for Life in an Imperfect Universe* (New York: Free Press, 2010), 128; Brian Greene, *The Fabric of the Cosmos: Space, Time, and the Texture of Reality* (New York: Vintage, 2005), 301.

179. Kirshner, *Extravagant Universe*, 258; Schmidt interviewed in NOVA, *Runaway Universe*, (PBS, November 11, 2000).

180. Seth Shostak, "The Lugubrious Universe," *Huffington Post*, November 26, 2010, emphasis original.

181. For detailed explanations and comparative analyses of these scenarios, see Rubenstein, *Worlds Without End*, 159–93.

182. Alex Vilenkin, *Many Worlds in One: The Search for Other Universes* (New York: Hill and Wang, 2006), 93; cf. Andrei Linde, "The Self-Reproducing Inflationary Universe," *Scientific American* 271, no. 5 (November, 1994). The connection between the discovery of dark energy and the sudden turn to the multiverse can also be found in Alex Vilenkin and Jaume Garriga, "Many Worlds in One," *Physical Review* D64, no. 043511 (2001): 1–5; John Gribbin, *In Search of the Multiverse* (London: Allen Lane, 2009), 135; Laura Mersini-Houghton, "Thoughts on Defining the Multiverse," *arXiv* 0804.4280 (April 27, 2008); Brian Greene, *The Hidden Reality: Parallel Universes and the Deep Laws of the Cosmos* (New York: Knopf, 2011), 7.

183. For an accessible introduction to this "problem," see Alan P. Lightman, "The Accidental Universe: Science's Crisis of Faith," *Harper's Magazine*, December 22, 2011.

184. On the multiverse as the most respectable solution to the fine-tuning problem, see Steven Weinberg, "The Cosmological Constant Problem," *arXiv* astro-ph, no. 0005265v1 (May 12, 2000); Steven Weinberg, "Living in the Multiverse," in *Universe or Multiverse*, ed. Bernard Carr (Cambridge: Cambridge University Press, 2007).

185. See Max Tegmark, *Our Mathematical Universe: My Quest for the Ultimate Nature of Reality* (New York: Vintage, 2015).

186. Latour, *Facing Gaia*, 163.

187. Laura Mersini-Houghton, "Birth of the Universe from the Multiverse," *arXiv* 0809.3623 (September 22, 2008).

188. Anthony Aguirre and Matthew C. Johnson, "A Status Report on the Observability of Cosmic Bubble Collisions," https://arxiv.org/pdf/0908.4105v2.pdf (September 21, 2009).

189. Paul J. Steinhardt and Neil Turok, "The Cyclic Model Simplified," *New Astronomy Reviews* 49, no. 206 (May 2005).

190. John D. Barrow, "Living in a Simulated Universe," in *Universe or Multiverse?*, ed. Bernard Carr (Cambridge: Cambridge University Press, 2007).

191. Rubenstein, *Worlds Without End*, 235.

192. Danowski and Viveiros de Castro, *The Ends of the World*, 72.

PANCARNATION

1. Jeffrey Burton Russell, *The Prince of Darkness: Radical Evil and the Power of Good in History* (Ithaca, NY: Cornell University Press, 1992), 17. Milton associates Pan explicitly with the devil in his *Paradise Regained*.

2. John Milton, "On the Morning of Christ's Nativity," in *The Complete Poetry and Essential Prose of John Milton*, ed. William Kerrigan, John Rumrich, and M. Fallon (New York: Modern Library, 2007 [1629]), 8.85. Cf. Milton's reference to "universal Pan" in John Milton, "Paradise Lost," in *The Complete Poetry and Essential Prose of John Milton*, ed. William Kerrigan, John Rumrich, and M. Fallon (New York: Modern Library, 2007 [1667]), 4.266.

3. Wilfred H. Schoff, "Tammuz, Pan and Christ," *The Open Court* 26, no. 9 (September 1912): 526. Rabelais did not come up with this connection himself; it can be traced back at least to Paulus Marsus, who in 1482 sets the death of Pan "in the nineteenth year of Tiberius' reign: at which time indeed Christ died.... Now what does Pan mean," he reasons, "if not all. Thus the lord of all and of universal nature had died.... not the lord of the woods, but the ruler of the material substance of the universe" (cited in Patricia Merivale, *Pan the Goat-God: His Myth in Modern Times* [Cambridge, MA: Harvard University Press, 1969], 13).

4. François Rabelais, *Gargantua and Pantagruel*, trans. M. A. Screech (New York: Penguin, 2006 [1535–64]), 24.

5. Ibid., 749.

6. Ibid.

7. Ibid., 750.

8. Schoff, "Tammuz, Pan and Christ," 527.

9. Edmund Spenser, "The Shepheardes Calendar," in *The Yale Edition of the Shorter Poems of Edmund Spenser*, ed. William Oram, et. al. (New Haven, CT: Yale University Press, 1989), 99–100.

10. Ben Jonson, "Pan's Anniversary; or, the Shepherd's Holiday," in *The Works of Ben Jonson*, ed. William Gifford (New York: Appelton, 1879), Hymn II, 763.

11. Elizabeth Barrett Browning, "The Dead Pan," in *Aurora Leigh and Other Poems*, ed. John Robert Glorney Bolton and Julia Bolton Holloway (New York: Penguin, 1996), 117.

12. Søren Kierkegaard (Anti-Climacus), *The Sickness Unto Death: A Christian Psychological Exposition for Upbuilding and Awakening*, trans. Edna H. Hong and Howard V. Hong (Princeton, NJ: Princeton University Press, 1983 [1849]), 117.

13. Ibid.

14. Rev. Morgan Dix, *Lectures on the Pantheistic Idea of an Impersonal Deity, as Contrasted with the Christian Faith Concerning Almighty God* (New York: Hurd and Houghton, 1864), 565.

15. Ralph Waldo Emerson, "An Address," in *The Essential Writings of Ralph Waldo Emerson*, ed. Brooks Atkinson (New York: Modern Library, 2000 [1838]), 68.

16. Laurel Schneider, "Promiscuous Incarnation," in *The Embrace of Eros: Bodies, Desires, and Sexuality in Christianity*, ed. Margaret Kamitsuka (Minneapolis: Fortress Press, 2010), 232.

17. Ibid., 242.

18. Ibid.

19. Donna Haraway, "Ecce Homo, Ain't (Ar'n't) I a Woman, and Inappropriate/D Others: The Human in a Posthuman Landscape," in *The Haraway Reader* (New York: Taylor and Francis, 2004), 151.

20. Ibid.

21. Ibid., 151–52.

22. Catherine Keller, *The Cloud of the Impossible: Negative Theology and Planetary Entanglement* (New York: Columbia University Press, 2014), 118.

23. Ibid.

4. THEOS

1. Although I will invoke the categories of God and gods when historically appropriate or rhetorically useful, I share William Robert's preference for the category of "divinity" insofar as it "names a sensible transcendence. . . . Divinity is not god. 'God' remains vertically transcendent, transcendentally transcendental, inaccessibly *beyond*. Divinity happens, arrives, through a sensible transcendental threshold" (William Robert, *Revivals: Of Antigone* [Albany: State University of New York Press, 2015], 45).

2. By appealing to created creators, I am following the heretical lead of John Scotus Eriugena (810–877), whose works were condemned throughout the late medieval period for having conflated God with nature. In his *Periphyseon*, Eriugena proposes that "the whole" is composed of four "species": "that which creates and is not created . . . *that which is created and also creates* . . . that which is created and does not create . . . [and that which] neither creates nor is created" (*Periphyseon* 1.441b, cited in Eugene Thacker, *After Life* [Chicago: University of Chicago Press, 2010], 173; emphasis added). Over the course of this text, Eriugena proceeds dialectically to identify these categories, proclaiming God to be nothing else than "all things." On Eriugena's "dark pantheism," see ibid., 170–84. On the "shared incomprehensibility" of humanity, God, and cosmos, see Thomas A. Carlson, *The Indiscrete Image: Infinitude and Creation of the Human* (Chicago: University of Chicago Press, 2008), 85–94.

3. "Thousands Attend Einstein Jubilee Celebration in New York City," *Jewish Daily Bulletin*, April 18, 1929.

4. "The attack was led by the Nobel laureate physicist Philipp Lenard, who denounced what he called the 'mathematically botched-up theories of Einstein,'" and who exhorted his countrymen, "We must recognize that it is unworthy of a German to be the intellectual follower of a Jew. Natural science, properly so-called, is of completely Aryan origin. . . . *Heil Hitler!*" (Carl Sagan, "The Other World That Beckons: A Profile of Albert Einstein," *New Republic*, https://newrepublic.com/article/117028/world-beckons [September 16, 1978]). To revisit the connections between Spinozism and "Oriental" philosophy, see pp. 33–41, above.

5. "Death of a Cardinal," *Time*, May 1, 1944.

6. "Einstein Believes in 'Spinoza's God,'" *The New York Times*, April 25, 1929.

7. J. D. B. Mail, "Cardinal O'Connell's Full Statement Against Professor Einstein's Theories," *Jewish Daily Bulletin*, April 18, 1929.

8. "Is there any standard that has not been challenged in our post-war world? Is there any absolute system of ethics, of economics or of law, whose stability and permanence is not assailed somewhere?" (George Sylvester Viereck, *Glimpses of the Great* [New York: Macauley, 1930], 356). On the connection between this creeping moral relativism, the theory of relativity, and a generalized waning belief in God as the moral lawgiver, see "Dr. Ward Attacks Einstein Theories," *The New York Times*, November 10, 1930.

9. Cited in Max Jammer, *Einstein and Religion: Physics and Theology* (Princeton, NJ: Princeton University Press, 1999), 49.

10. "*Ich glaube an Spinozas Gott der sich in gesetzlicher Harmonie des Seienden offenbart, nicht an Gott der Sich mit Schicksalen und Handlungen der Menschen abgibt.*" Cited in "Einstein Believes," translation altered slightly.

11. Viereck, *Glimpses of the Great*, 372, 375.

12. "Einstein Believes."

13. "Einstein points to a unity . . . a scientific formula for monotheism. He does away with all thought of dualism or pluralism. There can be no room for any aspect of polytheism. This latter thought perhaps may have caused the Cardinal to speak out. Let us call a spade a spade" (Rabbi Goldstein cite in ibid.).

14. "Vatican Finds Professor Einstein Is an Atheist," *Jewish Daily Bulletin*, May 26, 1929.

15. Albert Einstein, "Religion and Science," *The New York Times Magazine*, November 9, 1930.

16. See the poem Einstein wrote about Spinoza, which begins, "How I love this noble man / More than I can say with words (*Wie lieb ich diesen edlen Mann/Mehr als ich mit Worten sagen kann*)" (Albert Einstein, "Zu Spinozas Ethik," http://www.autodidactproject.org/other/einstein9-spinoza8.html).

17. Einstein, "Religion and Science."

18. See "Dr. Ward Attacks Einstein Theories; "Dr. Coffin Praises Child's Simplicity," *The New York Times*, November 10, 1930; "'Intellectual' View of God Is Assailed," *The New York Times*, November 10, 1930; "Urges Faith in Leaders: Dean Gates Deplores Followers Who Are Critical," *The New York Times*, November 10, 1930.

19. "Einstein's Faith Defended," *The New York Times*, November 10, 1930.

20. "Science and Religion," *Time*, September 23, 1940, 52.

21. Ibid.

22. Albert Einstein, "Science and Religion," in *Ideas and Opinions*, ed. Cal Seelig and Sonja Bargmann (New York: Three Rivers, 1982 [1940]), 45. Subsequent references will be cited internally.

23. "No event can occur to contravene Nature, which preserves an eternal and immutable order" (Baruch Spinoza, *Theological-Political Treatise*, trans. Samuel Shirley [Indianapolis: Hackett, 1998], 73).

24. Dietrich Bonhoeffer, *Letters and Papers from Prison*, ed. Eberhard Bethge et al., trans. Isabel Best et al., Dietrich Bonhoeffer Works, vol. 8 (Minneapolis, MN: Augsburg Fortress, 2010), 366–67.

25. "Give up Idea of Personal God, Einstein Urges," *Chicago Daily Tribune*, September 11, 1940; "Religion of Good Urged by Einstein," *The New York Times*, September 11, 1940; "Einstein Urges Abandonment of Personal God Doctrine," *The Washington Post*, September 11, 1940; Einstein, "Science and Religion." For a summary of the local news pieces, see Jammer, *Einstein and Religion*, 98–103.

26. Cited in Jammer, *Einstein and Religion*, 98.

27. Rev. Morgan Dix, *Lectures on the Pantheistic Idea of an Impersonal Deity, as Contrasted with the Christian Faith Concerning Almighty God* (New York: Hurd and Houghton, 1864), 56.

28. "Religion of Good," 27.

29. See Jammer, *Einstein and Religion*, 103–7.

30. Ibid., 98–101; David Rowe and Robert Schulmann, *Einstein on Politics* (Princeton, NJ: Princeton University Press, 2007), 235.

31. In Jammer, *Einstein and Religion*, 99.

32. Dr. Jacob Singer, "Einstein's Religion: A Sermon Preached before Temple Isaiah-Israel, Chicago," January 4, 1931: 5–7; Jammer, *Einstein and Religion*, 99.

33. Cited in Jammer, *Einstein and Religion*, 102.

34. In ibid., 104–5.

35. In ibid., 106.

36. See Yirmiyahu Yovel, *Spinoza and Other Heretics: The Marrano of Reason*, 2 vols., vol. 1 (Princeton, NJ: Princeton University Press, 1989), 16–26.

37. "There are yet people who say there is no God. But what really makes me angry is that they quote me for support of such views" (Einstein cited in Jammer, *Einstein and Religion*, 97).

38. In his nearest avowal of pantheism, Einstein explains, "this firm belief . . . in a superior mind that reveals itself in the world of experience, represents my conception

of God. In common parlance, this may be described as 'pantheistic' (Spinoza)" (Albert Einstein, "On Scientific Truth," in *Ideas and Opinions*, ed. Cal Seelig and Sonja Bargmann [New York: Three Rivers Press, 1984 [1929]], 262). In his nearest disavowal of pantheism, Einstein writes, "I am not an Atheist. I do not know if I can describe myself as a Pantheist" (Viereck, *Glimpses of the Great*, 372–73). Either way, he did not seem particularly attached to or repelled by the label; it simply was not his focus. As he explained to Viereck, "I am fascinated by Spinoza's Pantheism. I admire even more his . . . deal[ing] with the soul and body as one, and not two separate things" (ibid., 373). Insofar as Spinoza's unification of mind and body are predicated upon his unification of God and Nature, however, an acceptance of the former would logically require an acceptance of the latter. If it is the case that Spinoza can be called a pantheist (and if he cannot, it is not clear who can), then it is also the case that Einstein can be called a pantheist.

39. Einstein cited in Abraham Pais, *Subtle Is the Lord: The Science and the Life of Albert Einstein* (Oxford: Oxford University Press, 2005 [1982]), vi.

40. Einstein, "On Scientific Truth," 262.

41. Albert Einstein, "On Science," in *Cosmic Religion with Other Opinions and Aphorisms, with an Appreciation by George Bernard Shaw* (New York: Covici-Friede, 1931), 98.

42. Albert Einstein, "The Religious Spirit of Science," in *Ideas and Opinons*, ed. Cal Seelig and Sonja Bargmann (New York: Three Rivers, 1984 [1934]), 40.

43. Einstein, "Religion and Science," 1.

44. Einstein, "Science and Religion," 46.

45. He then goes on to say, "I know that philosophically a murderer is not responsible for his crime, nevertheless I must protect myself from unpleasant contacts. I may consider him guiltless. But I prefer not to take tea with him" (Einstein cited in Viereck, *Glimpses of the Great*, 368).

46. Albert Einstein, "What I Believe," *Forum and Century* 45, no. 3 (March, 1936 [October, 1930]): 174.

47. Einstein cited in Jammer, *Einstein and Religion*, 92.

48. "In Mme. [Marie] Curie I can see no more than a brilliant exception. Even if there were more woman scientists of like caliber they would serve as no argument against the fundamental weakness of the feminine organization" (Einstein, "Miscellaneous," 105).

49. Einstein, "Science and Religion," 44–45. On Einstein's own effort to "free [him] self from the chains of the merely personal," a quest which, despite his atheist upbringing, began in childhood as a religious pursuit and then made a scientific turn in early adolescence, see Arthur Fine, *The Shaky Game: Einstein, Realism, and the Quantum Theory* (Chicago: University of Chicago Press, 1986), 110; Gerald Holton, "Einstein's Third Paradise," *Daedalus* 132, no. 4 (Fall 2003); Lorraine Daston, "A Short History of Einstein's Paradise Beyond the Personal," in *Einstein for the 21st Century: His Legacy in Science, Art, and Modern Culture*, ed. Peter L. Galison, Gerald Holton, and Silvan Schweber (Princeton, NJ: Princeton University Press, 2008).

50. Einstein, "Religious Spirit," 40.

51. This longing to intuit the universe constitutes the essence of all genuine religion for Schleiermacher, who begins his *Speeches on Religion* with an encomium to "the holy rejected Spinoza." "The high world spirit permeated him," Schleiermacher effuses, "the infinite was his beginning and end, the universe his only and eternal love" (Friedrich Schleiermacher, *On Religion: Speeches to Its Cultured Despisers* [Cambridge: Cambridge University Press, 1998], 24). Although Einstein does not explicitly invoke Schleiermacher, Max Jammer says it is "very likely" he had read him, and either way, they shared an intellectual ancestor in Spinoza (Jammer, *Einstein and Religion*, 129–30). Einstein does explicitly invoke Spinoza's *amor dei intellectualis* in Albert Einstein, "Religion and Science: Irreconcilable?" in *Ideas and Opinions*, ed. Cal Seelig and Sonja Bargmann (New York: Three Rivers, 1984 [1948]), 52.

52. Einstein cited in Yehuda Elkana, "Einstein and God," in *Einstein for the 21st Century: His Legacy in Science, Art, and Modern Culture*, ed. Peter L. Galison, Gerald Holton, and Silvan Schweber (Princeton, NJ: Princeton University Press, 2008), 36.

53. On the individual scientist's progress, Einstein explains that "it is enough if one tries to comprehend only a little of this mystery every day" (Einstein cited in ibid.). On his own advancement of physics with respect to his predecessors, he writes, "Newton, forgive me; you found just about the only way possible in your age for a man of highest reasoning and creative power. The concepts that you created are even today still guiding our thinking in physics, although we now know that they will have to be replaced by others . . . if we aim at a profounder understanding of relationships" (Albert Einstein, *Autobiographical Notes*, trans. Paul Arthur Schilpp (1999 [1949]), 31).

54. The cosmologist Marcelo Gleiser has thus described the scientific pursuit as an expanding "island of knowledge," whose borders onto the unknown expand along with its known territory: "with every discovery, the Island [grows] broader, but so [do] the unknowns, the new questions that scientists [are] able to ask" (Marcelo Gleiser, *The Island of Knowledge: The Limits of Science and the Search for Meaning* [New York: Basic Books, 2014], 55–56).

55. Dean R. Fowler, "Einstein's Cosmic Religion," *Zygon* 14, no. 3 (September 1979): 269.

56. See pp. 108–18, above.

57. Albert Einstein, "On the Electrodynamics of Moving Bodies (1905)," in *The Collected Papers of Albert Einstein, Volume 2: The Swiss Years: Writings, 1900–1909* (Princeton, NJ: Princeton University Press, 1989); Albert Einstein, "The Field Equations of Gravitation (1915)," in *The Collected Papers of Albert Einstein, Volume 6: The Berlin Years: Writings, 1914–1917* (Princeton, NJ: Princeton University Press, 1997).

58. "I stand at the window of a railway carriage which is travelling uniformly, and drop a stone on the embankment, without throwing it. . . . I see the stone descend in a straight line. A pedestrian who observes the misdeed from the footpath notices that the stone falls to earth in a parabolic curve. . . . The stone traverses a straight line relative to a system of co-ordinates rigidly attached to the carriage, but relative to a system of co-ordinates rigidly attached to the ground (embankment) it descries

a parabola" (Albert Einstein, *Relativity: The Special and the General Theory*, trans. Robert W. Lawson [New York: Three Rivers, 1961], 10–11).

59. Einstein's most famous example in this regard concerns a train struck by lightning in two places, A (toward the back of the train) and B (toward the front). From the perspective of the embankment, the two bolts strike simultaneously, whereas from the perspective of the train, bolt B hits before bolt A. Neither of these is more correct than the other; rather, the measure of correctness depends upon the specification of the vantage point. In short, "events which are simultaneous with reference to the embankment are not simultaneous with respect to the train and *vice versa*. . . . Every reference body . . . has its own particular time" (ibid., 30–31).

60. Ibid., vii.

61. Niels Bohr, "Physical Science and the Study of Religion," in *Studia Orientalia Ioanni Pedersen Septuagenario A. D. Vii Id. Nov. Anno Mcmliii a Collegis Discipulis Amicis Dicata* (Copenhagen: Munksgaard, 1953), 387.

62. We should note that such full-fledged perspectivism did not emerge until Einstein developed the theory of general relativity, and even at that point, Einstein himself was notoriously allergic to declarations like: "everything in life is relative and we have the right to turn the whole world mischievously topsy-turvy" (Einstein cited in Viereck, *Glimpses of the Great*, 356–57). In fact, he had initially wanted to call his special theory of relativity "invariance theory" by virtue of the inalterable, indeed absolute nature, neither of space nor of time, but of their totality. For although "constantly moving observers will disagree about the difference in time (Δt) or the difference in space (Δx) separately," they must agree about the difference in spacetime itself. Technically speaking, then, "the 'spacetime distance squared' $[(\Delta x)^2 - (\Delta y)^2]$ does *not* depend on the inertial reference frame" (Lorraine Daston and Peter L. Galison, *Objectivity* [New York: Zone Books, 2007], 303). As Einstein came to realize, however, this referential independence only holds for bodies in "*uniform rectilinear and non-rotary motion*"; in other words, it leaves out gravity (Einstein, *Relativity*, 69). Once the consideration of gravity pushes Einstein from special to general relativity, spacetime loses its invariance because "space and time become players in the evolving cosmos. They come alive. Matter here causes space to warp there, which causes matter over there to move, which causes space way over there to warp even more, and so on. General relativity provides the choreography for an entwined cosmic dance of space, time, matter, and energy" (Brian Greene, *The Fabric of the Cosmos: Space, Time, and the Texture of Reality* [New York: Vintage, 2005], 73).

63. Stephen Snobelen, "'The True Frame of Nature': Isaac Newton, Heresy, and the Reformation of Natural Philosophy," in *Heterodoxy in Early Modern Science and Religion*, ed. John Hedley Brooke and Ian Maclean (Oxford: Oxford University Press, 2005), 254.

64. Erwin Schrödinger, "Mind and Matter: The Tarner Lectures, Delivered at Trinity College, Cambridge," in *What Is Life?: The Physical Aspect of the Living Cell. With Mind and Matter and Autobiographical Sketches* (Cambridge: Cambridge University Press, 2016 [1956]), 149.

65. Ibid.

66. Erwin Schrödinger, "Autobiographical Sketches," in *What Is Life?: The Physical Aspect of the Living Cell. With Mind and Matter and Autobiographical Sketches* (Cambridge: Cambridge University Press, 2016), 167.

67. Protestant theologian Dean Fowler makes a similar argument, asserting that "Einstein's cosmic religion develops in a direction opposite [to] that of the implications of his thought" (Fowler, "Einstein's Cosmic Religion," 277). In the context of the rest of Fowler's work, however, it seems that he sets forth this argument in order to lay the groundwork for a specifically Christian process theology, rather than to push Einstein's theory of relativity into the pantheism his espousal of Spinoza seems to promise. See Dean R. Fowler, "A Process Theology of Interdependence," *Theological Studies* 40, no. 1 (March 1, 1979).

68. Albert Einstein, "Cosmological Considerations on the General Theory of Relativity (1917)," in *Cosmological Constants: Papers in Modern Cosmology*, ed. Jeremy Bernstein and Gerald Feinberg (New York: Columbia University Press, 1986).

69. On the resolution of nebulae into galaxies, see "Finds Spiral Nebulae Are Stellar Systems," *The New York Times*, November 23, 1924. For an explanation of Hubble's Law, which accounts for the relative velocity of receding galaxies, see Alan H. Guth, "The Inflationary Universe," in *Cosmology: Historical, Literary, Philosophical, Religious, and Scientific Perspectives*, ed. Norris S. Hetherington (New York: Garland, 1993), 413.

70. Even though the big bang hypothesis emerged from a set of solutions to his own field equations, Einstein was notoriously uncomfortable with this idea, as well—reportedly because it was too redolent of the "let there be light" of Genesis 1. According to Georges Lemaître's account of the conversation in which he first introduced the idea, Einstein responded, "Non, pas cela, cela suggère trop la creation" (Georges Lemaître, "Rencontre Avec A. Einstein," *Revue des Questions Scientifiques* 129 [1958]: 130).

71. On the likelihood of Einstein's having uttered this phrase or something much like it, see Galina Weinstein, "George Gamow and Albert Einstein: Did Einstein Say the Cosmological Constant Was the 'Biggest Blunder' He Ever Made in His Life?" https://arxiv.org/pdf/1310.1033.pdf (October 3, 2013). On the longer story of the effort to determine the nature and value of a counter-gravitational force, see John D. Norton, "The Cosmological Woes of Newtonian Gravitation Theory," in *The Expanding Worlds of General Relativity*, ed. H. Goenner, et al. (Boston: The Center for Einstein Studies, 1999). In the wake of the 1998 discovery of dark energy, it has become commonplace to claim that Einstein was right, after all: there is a counter-gravitational force (Λ). But insofar as dark energy is *accelerating* the expansion of the universe, it only intensifies the metaphysical insult of Hubble's discovery and the resulting big bang hypothesis: space-time is in no way static, eternal, unchanging, or for that matter rationally constructed and maintained. The point of Einstein's having inserted lambda into his equations was not to name a repulsive force *per se*, but rather to hold spacetime in eternal equilibrium. And in this sense, he was excruciatingly far from having anticipated anything like dark energy.

72. Einstein, "On the Development of Our Views Concerning the Nature and Constitution of Radiation (1909)."

73. For a diagrammed explanation of these experiments, see Karen Barad, *Meeting the Universe Halfway: Quantum Physics and the Entanglement of Matter and Meaning* (Durham, NC: Duke University Press, 2007), 97–106.

74. See pp. 108–18, above.

75. Barad, *Meeting*, 115.

76. Gunther S. Stent, "Does God Play Dice?" *The Sciences* (March 1979): 18.

77. Bohr, "Physical Science," 388.

78. Daston and Galison, *Objectivity*, 304.

79. In a 1927 eulogy marking the 200th anniversary of Newton's death, Einstein expressed in particular his lasting commitment, relativistic innovations notwithstanding, to the Newtonian principle of "strict causality," writing, "May the spirit of Newton's method give us the power to restore unison between physical reality and the profoundest characteristic of Newton's teaching—strict causality" (Einstein cited in Fine, *Shaky Game*, 100).

80. Pais, *Subtle Is the Lord*, 5.

81. Albert Einstein, letter to Max and Hedwig Born, 29 April 1924, in Albert Einstein, Max Born, and Hedwig Born, *The Born-Einstein Letters: Correspondence between Albert Einstein and Max and Hedwig Born from 1916 to 1955*, trans. Irene Born (New York: Walker, 1971), 82.

82. Ibid.

83. Einstein, "Irreconcilable," 52.

84. Einstein, "Fundamental Concepts of Physics and Their Most Recent Changes," *St. Louis Post-Dispatch* supplement (December 9, 1928): 4; emphasis added.

85. Einstein, letter to Max Born, 4 December 1926, in Einstein, Born, and Born, *Born-Einstein Letters*, 91.

86. Einstein cited in Elkana, "Einstein and God," 38.

87. Stent, "Dice," 19. See this article for a remarkably concise account of Einstein's *Gedankenexperimenten* and Bohr's refutations thereof.

88. In an effort to disprove time-energy complementarity, the experiment in question had involved a number of photons in a box with a clock and a shutter to let some particles escape so that the energy of the system might be measured accurately at equally accurate times. By suspending the hypothetical box from a spring balance, Bohr reminded Einstein that "a clock moving in a gravitational field is subject to time-dilation effects"; in other words, "the very act of weighing a clock effectively changes the way it keeps time" (Jim Baggott, *Beyond Measure: Modern Physics, Philosophy and the Meaning of Quantum Theory* [Oxford: Oxford University Press, 2004], 128). According to Stent, "After this fiasco with his photon-in-the-box experiment Einstein stopped trying to find logical flaws in the instrumental aspect of Bohr's complementarity notion. He conceded the universal validity of Heisenberg's uncertainty principle and thereafter concentrated on the metaphysical aspect of complementarity" (Stent, "Dice," 20).

89. Einstein, B. Podolsky, and N. Rosen, "Can Quantum-Mechanical Descriptions of Reality Be Considered Complete?" *Physical Review* 47 (1935): 777.

90. Ibid.

91. Ibid.

92. Ibid., 779.

93. Ibid., 780.

94. Ibid.

95. Ibid.

96. To adjudicate between EPR and Bohr, John Bell follows EPR's own *Gedanken-experiment*, devising an apparatus that would determine the spins of particles along three complementary axes to discover whether or not they possess measurement-independent values. What Bell concluded theoretically has been confirmed experimentally by Alain Aspect and his colleagues: the measurement of system I does, in fact, affect system II. This conclusion does not, however, violate special relativity, for it is not the case that any signal travels between the two systems. Rather, the two systems compose one physical entity; in Bohr's language, they amount, along with the experimental apparatus that determines them, to one *phenomenon*. As Jammer summarizes this principle of "nonlocality," "there exist instantaneous noncausal correlations between spatially-separated physical systems" (Jammer, *Einstein and Religion*, 236). Or as Brian Greene more colloquially puts it, "something we do over here . . . *can* be subtly entwined with something that happens over there . . . *without* anything being sent from here to there. . . . Intervening space . . . does not ensure that two objects are separate" (Greene, *Fabric*, 80). For a popular introduction to this phenomenon, which Schrödinger named "entanglement," see ibid., 77–123.

97. Einstein, Podolsky, and Rosen, "Complete," 780.

98. Niels Bohr, "Can Quantum-Mechanical Description of Physical Reality Be Considered Complete?" ibid. 38: 697.

99. Ibid.

100. Bohr cited in Barad, *Meeting*, 119.

101. Bohr, "Complete," 702.

102. Ibid., 700.

103. Einstein cited in Stent, "Dice," 20–21.

104. Sagan, "Other World."

105. Stent, "Dice," 21–22.

106. Ibid., 22.

107. Bohr cited in Baggott, *Beyond Measure*, 109; emphasis added.

108. These include his saying, "our task is not to penetrate into the essence of things, the meaning of which we don't know anyway, but rather to develop concepts which allow us to talk in a productive way about phenomena in nature" (Bohr cited in David I. Kaiser, "Bringing the Human Actors Back on Stage: The Personal Context of the Einstein-Bohr Debate," *British Journal for the History of Science* 27 [1994]: 140).

109. Ibid., 139.

110. Einstein cited in Baggott, *Beyond Measure*, 135.

111. Dipankar Home and Andrew Whitaker, *Einstein's Struggles with Quantum Theory: A Reappraisal* (New York: Springer, 2007), 151.

112. Stanley L. Jaki, *God and the Cosmologists* (Washington, DC: Real View, 1989), 138–39.

113. Stent, "Dice," 23.

114. Barad, *Meeting*, 139; Bohr cited in ibid., 119.

115. Ibid., 139.

116. Colin Bruce, *Schrödinger's Rabbits: The Many-Worlds of Quantum* (Washington, DC: Joseph Henry, 2004), 154. On MWI's longing for the classical universe, which is to say its "cognitive repression" of the relational constitution of particles and physicists, see Evelyn Fox Keller, "Cognitive Repression in Contemporary Physics," in *Reflections on Gender and Science* (New Haven: Yale University Press, 1985).

117. Barad, *Meeting*, 114.

118. Ibid., 139.

119. Baruch Spinoza, "Ethics," in *Ethics, Treatise on the Emendation of the Intellect, and Selected Letters*, ed. Seymour Feldman (Indianapolis: Hackett, 1992), 102.

120. D. H. Lawrence, "The Novel," in *Selected Critical Writings*, ed. Michael Herbert, Oxford World Classics (Oxford: Oxford University Press, 1998 [1925]).

121. Donna Haraway, "The Promises of Monsters: A Regenerative Politics for Inappropriate/D Others," in *The Haraway Reader* (New York: Taylor and Francis, 2004), 65; Greg Woolf, "Divinity and Power in Ancient Rome," in *Religion and Power: Divine Kingship in the Ancient World and Beyond*, ed. Nicole Maria Brisch, *University of Chicago Oriental Institute Seminars* (Chicago: Oriental Institute of the University of Chicago, 2008); Monica Coleman, *Making a Way out of No Way: A Womanist Theology*, Innovations: African American Religious Thought (Minneapolis: Fortress Press, 2008), 109–10; Eduardo Viveiros de Castro, "Exchanging Perspectives: The Transformation of Objects into Subjects in Amerindian Ontologies," *Common Knowledge* 10, no. 3 (2004): 482; Page Dubois, *A Million and One Gods: The Persistence of Polytheism* (Cambridge, MA: Harvard University Press, 2014), 86–128; Laurel Schneider, *Beyond Monotheism: A Theology of Multiplicity* (New York: Routledge, 2008), 27–38, 153–63.

122. Viveiros de Castro, "Exchanging Perspectives," 471.

123. "The most infamous things the pagan poets have dared to sing against Venus and Jupiter do not approach the horrible idea that Spinoza gives us of God, for at least the poets did not attribute to the gods all the crimes that are committed and all the infirmities of the world. But according to God there is no other agent and no other recipient than God . . ." (Pierre Bayle, *Historical and Critical Dictionary: Selections*, trans. Richard H. Popkin [Indianapolis: Hackett, 1991], 301–2nN).

124. Nancy Frankenberry, "Classical Theism, Panentheism, and Pantheism: On the Relation between God Construction and Gender Construction," *Zygon* 28, no. 1 (March, 1993): 39.

125. Ibid., 40.

126. Einstein, "Science and Religion," 46.

127. Bonhoeffer, *Letters and Papers from Prison*, 325.

128. "Religious people speak of God when human knowledge . . . has come to an end, or when human resources fail—in fact, it is always the *deus ex machina* they bring on the scene, either for the apparent solution of insoluble problems, or as strength in human failure" (Bonhoeffer, LPP, 281–82).

129. William R. Jones, *Is God a White Racist?: A Preamble to Black Theology* (Boston: Beacon, 1998 [1973]), 4–6.

130. Jones calls his alternative "humanocentric theism," whose preference for humanity I would not retain, but which does the work of unsettling divine racism by making God more of a panentheistic persuader than a theistic dictator. See ibid., 185–202. A more recent appeal to the particularity of humanity that insists on humans' constitutive relation to other creatures and the earth can be found in Carol Wayne White, *Black Lives and Sacred Humanity: Toward an African American Religious Naturalism* (New York: Fordham University Press, 2016).

131. See, among countless others, Alfred North Whitehead, *Process and Reality:* (New York: Free Press, 1979); John B. Cobb and David Ray Griffin, *Process Theology: An Introductory Exposition* (Philadelphia: Westminster John Knox, 1996); Coleman, *Making a Way*; Catherine Keller, *Face of the Deep: A Theology of Becoming* (New York: Routledge, 2003); Catherine Keller, *God and Power: Counter-Apocalyptic Journeys* (Minneapolis: Fortress Press, 2005); Paul Tillich, *The Courage to Be* (New Haven: Yale University Press, 2014); Mark C. Taylor, *Erring: A Postmodern a/Theology* (Chicago: University of Chicago Press, 1984); John Caputo, *The Weakness of God: A Theology of the Event* (Indianapolis: Indiana University Press, 2006); Hent de Vries, *Minimal Theologies: Critiques of Secular Reason in Adorno and Levinas* (Baltimore: Johns Hopkins University Press, 2005); James Cone, *A Black Theology of Liberation* (New York: Lippincott, 1970); Rita Nakashima Brock and Rebecca Ann Parker, *Proverbs of Ashes: Violence, Redemptive Suffering, and the Search for What Saves Us* (New York: Beacon, 2002); Mary Daly, *Gyn/Ecology: The Metaethics of Radical Feminism* (New York: Beacon, 1990); Delores Williams, *Sisters in the Wilderness: The Challenge of Womanist God-Talk* (Maryknoll, NY: Orbis, 2013); Whitney Bauman, *Religion and Ecology: Developing a Planetary Ethic* (New York: Columbia University Press, 2014); Rosemary Radford Ruether, *Gaia and God: An Ecofeminist Theology of Earth Healing* (San Francisco: HarperSanFrancisco, 1992); White, *Black Lives and Sacred Humanity: Toward an African American Religious Naturalism*; Catherine Keller and Laurel Schneider, eds., *Polydoxy: Theology of Multiplicity and Relation* (New York: Routledge, 2011); Schneider, *Beyond Monotheism*.

132. Walberg cited in Jacob J. Erickson, "'I Worship Jesus, Not Mother Earth': Exceptionalism and the Paris Withdrawal," *Religion Dispatches* (June 2, 2017).

133. David Hume, *Dialogues Concerning Natural Religion* (Indianapolis: Hackett, 1998), 63.

134. For a historical and contemporary roundup of such efforts and an ethically motivated rejection of all of them, see Kenneth Surin, *Theology and the Problem of Evil* (Eugene, OR: Wipf and Stock, 1986), 70–141. More recently, Timothy Knepper has pointed out that, even in analytic circles, there are two times as many philosophers of religion criticizing the endeavor as engaging in it (Timothy David Knepper, *The Ends of Philosophy of Religion: Terminus and Telos* (New York: Palgrave Macmillan, 2013), 4.

135. According to Vine Deloria, "the beginning and end of time are of no apparent concern for many tribal religions." Rather than explaining how the world came to be at the absolute origin of things, creation stories are practical tools for coming to terms with disorder. Thus, Deloria suggests, "what we have previously been pleased to call creation stories might not be such at all. They might be simply the collective memories of a great and catastrophic event through which people came to understand themselves and the universe they inhabited. Creation stories may simply be the survivors' memories of reasonably large and destructive events" (Vine Deloria Jr., *God Is Red* [New York: Grosset & Dunlap, 1973], 91–92, 154). On multiagential cosmogonies, see Viveiros de Castro, "Exchanging Perspectives," 477; Graham Harvey, *Animism: Respecting the Living World* (New York: Columbia University Press, 2006), 128–29; Sylvia Marcos, "The Sacred Earth of the Nahuas," in *Taken from the Lips: Gender and Eros in Mesoamerican Religions, Religion in the Americas* (Boston: Brill, 2006), 39.

136. Harvey, *Animism*, 129.

137. Scott L. Pratt, *Native Pragmatism: Rethinking the Roots of American Philosophy* (Bloomington and Indianapolis: Indiana University Press, 2002), 93.

138. Ibid., 95–96.

139. Vine Deloria Jr., *Custer Died for Your Sins: An Indian Manifesto* (New York: Macmillan, 1969), 119.

140. Ibid., 119–20.

141. Ibid., 120.

142. William James, *A Pluralistic Universe* (Lincoln, NE: University of Nebraska Press, 1996 [1908]), 124.

143. "Good and evil are only relations"; not things or actions. "Therefore good and evil do not exist in Nature" (Baruch Spinoza, "Short Treatise on God, Man, and His Well-Being," in *Complete Works*, ed. Michael L. Morgan [Indianapolis: Hackett, 2002], 59).

144. Spinoza, "Ethics," 62.

145. Ibid., 60.

146. On this latter set of entanglements, see James Cone, "Whose Earth Is It Anyway?" *Cross Currents* (2000); Carol J. Adams and Lori Gruen, eds., *Ecofeminism: Feminist Intersections with Other Animals and the Earth* (New York: Bloomsbury, 2014).

147. In his polemical *God and the Universe*, Chapman Cohen writes that Einstein's "religion" amounts to a "practical atheism." After all, he asks, "What significance have all the churches, synagogues, mosques, and other gathering places of the religiously afflicted if they are worshipping a God who takes no interest in their fates or their actions[?]" (cited in Jammer, *Einstein and Religion*, 50).

148. Paul Tillich, "The Idea of a Personal God," *The Union Review* 2 (November, 1940): 9–10.

149. Ibid., 10.

150. Ibid.

151. Ibid.

152. Ibid.

153. Annie Dillard, *Holy the Firm* (New York: Harper Perennial, 1998 [1977]), 11.

154. Ibid., 11, 27, 28, 30, 61, 13, 15–17.

155. Ibid., 61.

156. Ibid., 43.

157. "Pantheism presupposes theism as having preceded it; for only in so far as we start from a God and thus have him already in advance and are intimate with him, can we ultimately bring ourselves to identify him with the world really in order to dispose of him in a seemly manner" (Arthur Schopenhauer, *Parerga and Paralipomena*, trans. E. F. J. Payne, 2 vols., vol. 2 (Oxford: Clarendon, 2000), 100.

158. Val Plumwood, *Feminism and the Mastery of Nature* (New York: Routledge, 1993), 127.

159. Ibid. Plumwood is thinking primarily of the neopagan activist and ecofeminist Starhawk, whose theological multiplicity does tend to be gathered into a single divine-worldly reality. "The Goddess has infinite aspects and thousands of names," Starhawk explains; "She is the reality behind many metaphors. She *is* reality, the manifest deity, omnipresent in all of life, in each of us. The Goddess is not separate from the world—She *is* the world, and all things in it: moon, sun, earth, star, stone, seed, flowing river, wind, wave, leaf and branch, bud and blossom, fang and claw, woman and man. In Witchcraft, flesh and spirit are one" (Starhawk, *The Spiral Dance: A Rebirth of the Ancient Religion of the Great Goddess* (San Francisco: HarperCollins, 1999 [1979]), 32).

160. Plumwood, *Feminism and the Mastery of Nature*, 128.

161. Einstein, "Religious Spirit," 40.

162. Einstein cited in Jammer, *Einstein and Religion*, 39–40.

163. Stuart A. Kauffman, *Reinventing the Sacred: A New View of Science, Reason, and Religion* (New York: Basic Books, 2010), 44–45, xi.

164. Ibid., 6.

165. On the double-valence of wonder, see Mary-Jane Rubenstein, *Strange Wonder: The Closure of Metaphysics and the Opening of Awe*, Insurrections: Critical Studies in Religion, Politics, and Culture (New York: Columbia University Press, 2009), 9–12, 33–39, 185–96.

166. Caroline Walker Bynum, *Metamorphosis and Identity* (New York: Zone Books, 2001), 117.

167. Walker, *The Color Purple*, 178.

168. Ibid.

169. This term has been coined by philosopher Lori Gruen, who uses it to refer in particular to humans' differential and constitutive relationship to the more-than-human world (see Gruen, *Entangled Empathy: An Alternative Ethic for Our Relationships with Animals* [New York: Lantern Books, 2014], 65–68).

170. Octavia E. Butler, *Parable of the Sower* (New York: Grand Central, 2000 [1993]), 11.

171. Ibid., 37–38.

172. Ibid., 3.

173. Ibid., 7.

174. Ibid., 25.

175. Ibid.

176. Coleman, *Making a Way*, 140–41.

177. Butler, *Sower*, 115.

178. Ashon T. Crawley, *Blackpentecostal Breath: The Aesthetics of Possibility* (New York: Fordham University Press, 2016), 27.

179. Frank B. Wilderson, *Red, White, and Black: Cinema and the Structure of U.S. Antagonisms* (Durham, NC: Duke University Press, 2010), 9.

180. Octavia E. Butler, *Parable of the Talents* (New York: Grand Central, 2000 [1998]), 8.

181. See pp. 11–12, above.

182. Hortense J. Spillers, *Black, White, and in Color: Essays on American Literature and Culture* (Chicago: University of Chicago Press, 2003), 208.

183. Ibid., 209.

184. Gilles Deleuze and Claire Parnet, "A Conversation: What Is It? What Is It For?" in *Dialogues II* (New York: Columbia University Press, 2007), 1.

185. Pseudo-Dionysius, "The Divine Names," in *The Complete Works*, ed. Colm Luibheid, *Classics of Western Spirituality* (New York: Paulist Press, 1987), 981c–d.

PANDEMONIUM

1. Robin Lane Fox, *Pagans and Christians* (New York: Knopf, 1987), 130.

2. On the astonishing proliferation of poetic renditions of Pan in English literature, see Patricia Merivale, *Pan the Goat-God: His Myth in Modern Times* (Cambridge, MA: Harvard University Press, 1969).

3. Henry David Thoreau, "A Week on the Concord and Merrimack Rivers," in *A Week on the Concord and Merrimack Rivers, Walden, the Maine Woods, Cape Cod* (New York: Library of America, 1985 [1849]), 53.

4. Because of their proximity to humans, chimpanzees were first placed in the genus *Homo*. Threatened by this categorical confusion of humanity and "ape," later taxonomists rechristened chimps with the genus name *Pan*, which "refers to the mythical Greek god of forests, flocks, and shepherds, represented with the head, chest, and arms of a man and the legs and sometimes horns and ears of a goat" (Clyde Jones et al., "Pan Troglodytes," *Mammalian Species* 529 [May 17, 1966]). This explanation is perplexing, insofar as chimps have very little to do with goats. But they have quite a lot to do with "men," so it seems taxonomists named them after Pan because of his *half*-humanity (I have no idea what they made of Pan's divinity with respect to chimps!). The species name is *troglodytes* (cave dwellers), which is a strange name for animals who do not live in caves, but which both connects chimps to the fabled "cavemen" that "we" used to be and intensifies the connection to Pan. As late as 1985, the International Committee on Zoological Nomenclature was considering sneaking *homo* back into the *type* name, but the deciding vote was contingent upon the rejection of including *homo* anywhere in the official nomenclature of chimps ("International Commission on Zoological Nomenclature," "Opinion 1368: The Generic Names *Pan* and *Panthera* [Mammalia, Carnivora]: Available as from Oken, 1916," *Bulletin of Zoological Nomenclature* 42, no. 4 [December, 1985]). Here, then, we see Pan invoked to shoulder the burden of liminality—to keep humanity safely separate from its too-close kin. I am indebted to Lori Gruen for having uncovered these sources, and for talking me through this particular thicket of theo-humanimality.

5. The three reasons most commonly invoked for Christian opposition to the transnational Earth Charter are its purported pantheism, its reference to the earth as "mother," and its support for women's reproductive rights. See Thomas Sieger Derr, "The Earth Charter and the United Nations," *Religion & Liberty* 11, no. 2; Bron Taylor, *Dark Green Religion: Nature, Spirituality, and the Planetary Future* (Berkeley: University of California Press, 2010).

6. Ralph Waldo Emerson, "Wood Notes Ii," in *The Early Poems of Ralph Waldo Emerson*, ed. Nathan Haskell Dole (New York: Crowell, 1899), 87.

BIBLIOGRAPHY

Adams, Carol J., and Lori Gruen, eds. *Ecofeminism: Feminist Intersections with Other Animals and the Earth*. New York: Bloomsbury Academic, 2014.

Adams, Edward. "Graeco-Roman and Ancient Jewish Cosmology." In *Cosmology and New Testament Theology*, edited by Jonathan T. Pennington and Sean M. McDonald, 5–27. New York: T & T Clark, 2008.

Aguirre, Anthony, and Matthew C. Johnson. "A Status Report on the Observability of Cosmic Bubble Collisions." https://arxiv.org/pdf/0908.4105v2.pdf (September 21, 2009).

Ahmed, Sara. "Imaginary Prohibitions: Some Preliminary Remarks on the Founding Gestures of the 'New Materialism." *European Journal of Women's Studies* 15, no. 23 (2008): 23–39.

Allen, Paula Gunn. *The Sacred Hoop: Recovering the Feminine in American Indian Traditions*. Boston: Beacon Press, 1992.

Alvater, Elmar. "The Capitalocene, or, Geoengineering Against Capitalism's Planetary Boundaries." In *Anthropocene or Capitalocene? Nature, History, and the Crisis of Capitalism*, edited by Jason W. Moore, 138–53. Oakland, CA: PM Press, 2016.

Anderson, Pamela Sue. "Jantzen, Grace, Becoming Divine: Towards a Feminist Philosophy of Religion." *Theology and Sexuality* 13 (September 1, 2000): 121–25.

Anderson, Pamela Sue, and Grace Jantzen. "Correspondence with Grace Jantzen." *Feminist Theology* 9, no. 25 (2000): 112–19.

Anim, Hans Frederich August von, ed. *Chryssipi Fragmenta Logica Et Physica.* 4 vols. Vol. 2, Stoicorum Veterum Fragmenta. Leipzig: B. G. Teubneri, 1903.

——, ed. *Zeno Et Zenonis Discipuli. Exemplar Anastatice Iteratum.* 4 vols. Vol. 1, Stoicorum Veterum Fragmenta. Leipzig: B. G. Teubneri, 1921.

Aquinas, Thomas. *Summa Theologiae.* Translated by Fathers of the English Dominican Province. 5 vols. Allen, TX: Christian Classics, 1981.

Ariel, David. *Kabbalah: The Mystic Quest in Judaism.* New York: Rowman & Littlefield, 2006.

Aristotle. "Metaphysics." Translated by W. D. Ross. In *The Complete Works of Aristotle: The Revised Oxford Translation,* edited by Jonathan Barnes. Princeton, NJ: Princeton University Press, 1971.

——. *The Metaphysics.* Translated by Hugh Lawson-Tancred. New York: Penguin, 1998.

——. "On the Soul (De Anima)." Translated by J. A. Smith. In *The Complete Works of Aristotle: The Revised Oxford Translation,* edited by Jonathan Barnes, 641–92. Princeton, NJ: Princeton University Press, 1971.

——. "Physics." Translated by R. P. Hardie and R. K. Gaye. In *The Complete Works of Aristotle,* edited by Jonathan Barnes. Princeton, NJ: Princeton University Press, 1984.

Asmis, Elizabeth. "Lucretius' Venus and Stoic Zeus." *Hermes* 110 (1982): 458–70.

Baggott, Jim. *Beyond Measure: Modern Physics, Philosophy and the Meaning of Quantum Theory.* Oxford: Oxford University Press, 2004.

Baltzly, Dirk. "Stoic Pantheism." *Sophia* 42, no. 2 (October, 2003): 3–33.

Barad, Karen. *Meeting the Universe Halfway: Quantum Physics and the Entanglement of Matter and Meaning.* Durham, NC: Duke University Press, 2007.

Barrow, John D. "Living in a Simulated Universe." In *Universe or Multiverse?,* edited by Bernard Carr, 481–86. Cambridge: Cambridge University Press, 2007.

Bauman, Whitney. *Religion and Ecology: Developing a Planetary Ethic.* New York: Columbia University Press, 2014.

Bayle, Pierre. *Dictionnaire Historique Et Critique.* 4 vols. Amsterdam: 1740.

——. *Historical and Critical Dictionary: Selections.* Translated by Richard H. Popkin. Indianapolis: Hackett, 1991.

Beiser, Frederick C. *The Fate of Reason: German Philosophy from Kant to Fichte.* Cambridge, MA: Harvard University Press, 1987.

Bennett, Jane. "Thing-Power." In *Political Matter: Technoscience, Democracy, and Public Life,* edited by Bruce Braun and Sarah J. Whatmore, 35–62. Minneapolis: University of Minnesota Press, 2010.

——. *Vibrant Matter: A Political Ecology of Things.* Durham, NC: Duke University Press, 2010.

Bennett, Jonathan. "Spinoza's Metaphysics." In *The Cambridge Companion to Spinoza,* edited by Don Garrett, 61–88. Cambridge: Cambridge University Press, 1996.

Bentley, Richard. *Matter and Motion Cannot Think, or, a Confutation of Atheism from the Faculties of the Soul.* London: Thomas Parkhurst and Henry Mortluck, 1692.

Bhabha, Homi. *The Location of Culture*. Routledge Classics. New York: Routledge, 2004.

Biernacki, Loriliai, and Philip Clayton. *Panentheism Across the World's Traditions*. Oxford: Oxford University Press, 2014.

Billanovich, Guido. "'Veterum Vestigia Vatum' Nei Carmi Dei Preumanisti Padovani." *Italia Medievale e Umanistica* 1 (1958): 155–243.

Blumenberg, Hans. *The Legitimacy of the Modern Age*. Translated by Robert M. Wallace. Cambridge, MA: MIT Press, 1983.

Bohr, Niels. "Can Quantum-Mechanical Description of Physical Reality Be Considered Complete?". *Physical Review* 38 (1935): 696–702.

——. "Physical Science and the Study of Religion." In *Studia Orientalia Ioanni Pedersen Septuagenario A. D. Vii Id. Nov. Anno Mcmliii a Collegis Discipulis Amicis Dicata*, 385–90. Copenhagen: Munksgaard, 1953.

Bonhoeffer, Dietrich. *Letters and Papers from Prison*, edited by Eberhard Bethge et al., translated by Isabel Best et al. Dietrich Bonhoeffer Works, vol. 8. Minneapolis, MN: Augsburg Fortress, 2010.

Boyle, Robert. *A Free Enquiry into the Vulgarly Received Notion of Nature*. Cambridge: Cambridge University Press, 1996 [1686].

Brock, Rita Nakashima, and Rebecca Ann Parker. *Proverbs of Ashes: Violence, Redemptive Suffering, and the Search for What Saves Us*. New York: Beacon Press, 2002.

Brown, Valerie. "Bacteria 'R' Us." *Pacific Standard*. https://psmag.com/bacteria-r-us-61e66d1b6792#.xxy87z7si (December 2, 2010).

Browning, Elizabeth Barrett. *Aurora Leigh*. Oxford World's Classics. Oxford: Oxford University Press, 2008.

——. "The Dead Pan." In *Aurora Leigh and Other Poems*, edited by John Robert Glorney Bolton and Julia Bolton Holloway, 351–59. New York: Penguin, 1996.

Bruce, Colin. *Schrödinger's Rabbits: The Many-Worlds of Quantum*. Washington, DC: Joseph Henry, 2004.

Bruno, Giordano. *The Ash Wednesday Supper*. Translated by Edward A. Gosselin and Lawrence S. Lerner. Renaissance Society of America Reprint Texts. Toronto: University of Toronto Press, 1995.

——. *The Ash Wednesday Supper*. Translated by Stanley L. Jaki. Paris: Mouton & Co., 1975.

——. "Cause, Principle and Unity." Translated by Richard J. Blackwell. In *Cause, Principle and Unity and Essays on Magic*, edited by Richard J. Blackwell and Robert de Lucca. Cambridge Texts in the History of Philosophy, 1–102. Cambridge: Cambridge University Press, 1998.

——. *De La Causa, Principio, Et Uno*. Venice: 1584.

——. "On Magic." Translated by Richard J. Blackwell. In *Cause, Principle and Unity and Essays on Magic*, edited by Richard J. Blackwell and Robert de Lucca. Cambridge Texts in the History of Philosophy, 103–42. Cambridge: Cambridge University Press, 1998.

———. "On the Infinite Universe and Worlds." In *Giordano Bruno: His Life and Thought with Annotated Translation of His Work on the Infinite Universe and Worlds*, edited by Dorothea Singer. New York: Schuman, 1950.

Butler, Judith. "Imitation and Gender Insubordination." In *The Lesbian and Gay Studies Reader*, edited by Henry Abelove, Michele Aina Barale, and David M. Halperin, 307–20. New York: Routledge, 1993.

Butler, Octavia E. *Parable of the Sower*. New York: Grand Central Publishing, 2000 [1993].

———. *Parable of the Talents*. New York: Grand Central Publishing, 2000 [1998].

Buyse, Filip. "Boyle, Spinoza and the Hartlib Circle: The Correspondence That Never Took Place." *Societate si Politica* 7, no. 2 (2013).

Bynum, Caroline Walker. *Metamorphosis and Identity*. New York: Zone Books, 2001.

Calcagno, Antonio. *Giordano Bruno and the Logic of Coincidence: Unity and Multiplicity in the Philosophical Thought of Giordano Bruno*. Renaissance and Baroque Studies and Texts, edited by Eckhard Bernstein. New York: Peter Lang, 1998.

Caputo, John. *The Weakness of God: A Theology of the Event*. Bloomington: Indiana University Press, 2006.

Carlson, Thomas A. *The Indiscrete Image: Infinitude and Creation of the Human*. Chicago: University of Chicago Press, 2008.

Carroll, Sean M. *From Eternity to Here: The Quest for the Ultimate Theory of Time*. New York: Dutton, 2010.

Chakrabarty, Dipesh. "The Climate of History: Four Theses." *Critical Inquiry* 35, no. 2 (Winter 2009): 197–222.

Channing, William Ellery. *The Works of William E. Channing, D.D.* 11th complete ed., 6 vols. Vol. 1, Boston: G. G. Channing, 1849 [1841].

Chen, Mel. *Animacies: Biopolitics, Racial Mattering, and Queer Affect*. Durham, NC: Duke University Press, 2012.

Chesterton, G. K. "The Man Who Was Thursday." In *The Man Who Was Thursday: And Related Pieces*, edited by Stephen Medcalf, 1–166. Oxford: Oxford University Press, 1996.

Clayton, Philip. "Emerging God." *The Christian Century* 13 (2004): https://www .religion-online.org/article/emerging-god.

———. *The Problem of God in Modern Thought*. Grand Rapids: Eerdmans, 2000.

Cobb, John B., and David Ray Griffin. *Process Theology: An Introductory Exposition*. Philadelphia: Westminster John Knox Press, 1996.

Coggan, Sharon Lynn. "Pandaemonia: A Study of Eusebius' Recasting of Plutarch's Story of the 'Death of Great Pan.'" Dissertation: Syracuse University, 1992.

Coleman, Monica. *Making a Way out of No Way: A Womanist Theology*. Innovations: African American Religious Thought. Minneapolis, MN: Fortress Press, 2008.

Colledge, Edmund, and Bernard McGinn, eds. *Meister Eckhart: The Essential Sermons, Commentaries, Treatises, and Defense*, Classics of Western Spirituality. Mahwah, NJ: Paulist Press, 1981.

Cone, James. *A Black Theology of Liberation.* New York: Lippincott, 1970.

——. "Whose Earth Is It Anyway?". *Cross Currents* (2000): 36–46.

Connolly, William. *Facing the Planetary: Entangled Humanism and the Politics of Swarming.* Durham, NC: Duke University Press, 2017.

——. *A World of Becoming.* Durham, NC: Duke University Press, 2011.

Copleston, F. C. "Pantheism in Spinoza and the German Idealists." *Philosophy* 21, no. 78 (April, 1946): 42–56.

Cottingham, John. "'A Brute to the Brutes?': Descartes' Treatment of Animals." *Philosophy* 53, no. 206 (October 1978): 551–59.

Craig, William Lane. "Pantheists in Spite of Themselves." In *For Faith and Clarity: Philosophical Contributions to Christian Theology*, edited by James K. Beilby, 135–56. Ada, MI: Baker Academic, 2006.

Crawley, Ashon T. *Blackpentecostal Breath: The Aesthetics of Possibility.* New York: Fordham University Press, 2016.

Crist, Eileen. "On the Poverty of Our Nomenclature." In *Anthropocene or Capitalocene? Nature, History, and the Crisis of Capitalism*, edited by Jason W. Moore, 14–33. Oakland, CA: PM Books, 2016.

Crockett, Clayton. "Earth: What Can a Planet Do?". In *An Insurrectionist Manifesto: Four New Gospels for a Radical Politics, with an Afterward by Catherine Keller*, edited by Ward Blanton, Clayton Crockett, Jeffrey Robbins, and Noëlle Vahanian, 21–59. New York: Columbia University Press, 2016.

Crutzen, Paul J., and Eugene F. Stoermer. "The Anthropocene." *IGBP [International Geosphere-Biosphere Programme] Newsletter* 41 (2000): 17–18.

Curd, Patricia. "Anaxagoras." *Stanford Encyclopedia of Philosophy* https://plato.stanford. edu/entries/anaxagoras/ (October 1, 2015): 2.2.

——. "Anaxagoras and the Theory of Everything." In *The Oxford Handbook of Presocratic Philosophy*, edited by Patricia Curd and Daniel W. Graham, 230–49. Oxford: Oxford University Press, 2008.

Dagron, Tristan. "David of Dinant—Sur Le Fragment <Hyle, Mens, Deus> Des Quaternuli." *Revue de Métaphysique et de Morale* 40 (2003): 419–36.

Daly, Mary. *Gyn/Ecology: The Metaethics of Radical Feminism.* New York: Beacon, 1990.

Danowski, Déborah, and Eduardo Viveiros de Castro. *The Ends of the World.* Translated by Rodrigo Nunes. Malden, MA: Polity Press, 2017.

Darwin, Charles. *The Variation of Animals and Plants under Domestication.* 2 vols. London: John Murray, 1868.

Daston, Lorraine. "A Short History of Einstein's Paradise Beyond the Personal." In *Einstein for the 21st Century: His Legacy in Science, Art, and Modern Culture*, edited by Peter L. Galison, Gerald Holton, and Silvan Schweber, 15–26. Princeton, NJ: Princeton University Press, 2008.

Daston, Lorraine, and Peter L. Galison. *Objectivity.* New York: Zone Books, 2007.

Dawkins, Richard. *The Extended Phenotype: The Long Reach of the Gene*. Oxford: Oxford University Press, 2016 [1982].

——. *The God Delusion*. New York: Mariner Books, 2008.

Dear, Peter. *The Intelligiblity of Nature: How Science Makes Sense of the World*. Chicago: University of Chicago Press, 2006.

"Death of a Cardinal." *Time*, May 1, 1944, 54.

De Jong, H. M. E., ed. *Michael Maier's Atalanta Fugiens*. Lake Worth, FL: Nicolas-Hays, Inc., 2014.

Deleuze, Gilles. *Expressionism in Philosophy: Spinoza*. Translated by Martin Joughin. New York: Zone Books, 1992.

——. *Spinoza Et Le Problème De L'expression*. Paris: Éditions de Minuit, 1968.

Deleuze, Gilles, and Félix Guattari. *A Thousand Plateaus*. Translated by Brian Massumi. Minneapolis: University of Minnesota Press, 1987.

Deleuze, Gilles, and Claire Parnet. "A Conversation: What Is It? What Is It For?" Translated by Hugh Tomlinson and Barbara Habberjam. In *Dialogues Ii*, 1–35. New York: Columbia University Press, 2007.

Deloria, Vine, Jr. *Custer Died for Your Sins: An Indian Manifesto*. New York: Macmillan, 1969.

——. *God Is Red*. New York: Grosset & Dunlap, 1973.

——. "If You Think About It, You Will See That It Is True." In *Spirit and Reason: The Vine Deloria, Jr., Reader*, edited by Barbara Deloria, Kristen Foehner and Sam Scinta. Golden, CO: Fulcrum, 1999.

Dennett, Daniel C. *Kinds of Minds: Toward an Understanding of Consciousness*. New York: Basic Books, 1997.

Derr, Thomas Sieger. "The Earth Charter and the United Nations." *Religion and Liberty* 11, no. 2 http://www.acton.org/pub/religion-liberty/volume-11-number-2/earth-charter -and-united-nations.

Derrida, Jacques. "How to Avoid Speaking: Denials." In *Derrida and Negative Theology*, edited by Harold Coward and Toby Foshay. Albany: State University of New York Press, 1992.

Descartes, Rene. *The Philosophical Writings of Descartes, Volume 3: The Correspondence*. Edited by John Cottingham, Dugald Murdoch, Robert Stoothoff, and Anthony Kenny. Cambridge: Cambridge University Press, 1991.

——. "Principles of Philosophy." Translated by John Cottingham. In *The Philosophical Writings of Descartes*, 177–292. Cambridge: Cambridge University Press, 1985.

de Vries, Hent. *Minimal Theologies: Critiques of Secular Reason in Adorno and Levinas*. Baltimore: Johns Hopkins University Press, 2005.

Dick, Steven J. *Plurality of Worlds: The Origins of the Extraterrestrial Life Debate from Democritus to Kant*. Cambridge: Cambridge University Press, 1982.

Dillard, Annie. *Holy the Firm*. New York: Harper Perennial, 1998 [1977].

Diogenes Laertius. *Lives of the Eminent Philosophers*. Translated by R. D. Hicks. Loeb Classical Library. 2 vols. Cambridge, MA: Harvard University Press, 1942.

Dix, Rev. Morgan. *Lectures on the Pantheistic Idea of an Impersonal Deity, as Contrasted with the Christian Faith Concerning Almighty God*. New York: Hurd and Houghton, 1864.

Donagan, Alan. "Spinoza's Theology." In *The Cambridge Companion to Spinoza*, edited by Don Garrett, 343–82. Cambridge: Cambridge University Press, 1996.

Doolittle, W. Ford. "Is Nature Really Motherly?". *The CoEvolution Quarterly* (Spring 1981): 58–63.

"Dr. Coffin Praises Child's Simplicity." *The New York Times*, November 10, 1930, 22.

Druyan, Ann, and Steven Soter. "Episode 1: Standing up in the Milky Way." In *Cosmos: A Spacetime Odyssey*: Cosmos Studios, Fuzzy Door Productions, Santa Fe Studios, 2014.

"Dr. Ward Attacks Einstein Theories." *The New York Times*, November 10, 1930, 22.

Dubois, Page. *A Million and One Gods: The Persistence of Polytheism*. Cambridge, MA: Harvard University Press, 2014.

Duffy, Simon. "The Difference between Science and Philosophy: The Spinoza-Boyle Controversy Revisited." *Paragraph* 29, no. 2 (July, 2006): 115–38.

Durkheim, Emile. *The Elementary Forms of Religious Life*. Translated by Karen E. Fields. New York: Free Press, 1995 [1912].

Eckhart, Meister. "Sermon 52: Beati Paupers Spiritu, Quoniam Ipsorum Est Regnum Caelorum." In *The Essential Sermons, Commentaries, Treatise, and Defense*, edited by Edmund Colledge and Bernard McGinn. New York: Paulist Press, 1981.

Einstein, Albert. *Autobiographical Notes*. Translated by Paul Arthur Schilpp. 1999 [1949].

——. "Cosmological Considerations on the General Theory of Relativity (1917)." In *Cosmological Constants: Papers in Modern Cosmology*, edited by Jeremy Bernstein and Gerald Feinberg, 16–26. New York: Columbia University Press, 1986.

——. "The Field Equations of Gravitation (1915)." Translated by Alfred Engel. In *The Collected Papers of Albert Einstein, Volume 6: The Berlin Years: Writings, 1914–1917*, 117–20. Princeton, NJ: Princeton University Press, 1997.

——. "Fundamental Concepts of Physics and Their Most Recent Changes." *St. Louis Post-Dispatch* Supplement (December 9, 1928): 7.

——. "Miscellaneous." In *Cosmic Religion with Other Opinions and Aphorisms, with an Appreciation by George Bernard Shaw*, 104–9. New York: Covici-Friede, 1931.

——. "On Science." In *Cosmic Religion with Other Opinions and Aphorisms, with an Appreciation by George Bernard Shaw*, 97–103. New York: Covici-Friede, 1931.

——. "On Scientific Truth." In *Ideas and Opinions*, edited by Cal Seelig and Sonja Bargmann, 261–62. New York: Three Rivers Press, 1984 [1929].

——. "On the Development of Our Views Concerning the Nature and Constitution of Radiation [1909]." In *The Collected Papers of Albert Einstein, Volume 2: The Swiss Years: Writings, 1900–1909*, 379–94. Princeton, NJ: Princeton University Press, 1989.

——. "On the Electrodynamics of Moving Bodies (1905)." Translated by Anna Beck. In *The Collected Papers of Albert Einstein, Volume 2: The Swiss Years: Writings, 1900–1909*, 140–71. Princeton, NJ: Princeton University Press, 1989.

——. *Relativity: The Special and the General Theory*. Translated by Robert W. Lawson. New York: Three Rivers Press, 1961.

——. "Religion and Science." *The New York Times Magazine*, November 9, 1930, 1.

——. "Religion and Science: Irreconcilable?". In *Ideas and Opinions*, edited by Cal Seelig and Sonja Bargmann, 49–52. New York: Three Rivers Press, 1984 [1948].

——. "The Religious Spirit of Science." In *Ideas and Opinons*, edited by Cal Seelig and Sonja Bargmann, 40. New York: Three Rivers Press, 1984 [1934].

——. "Science and Religion." In *Ideas and Opinions*, edited by Cal Seelig and Sonja Bargmann, 41–49. New York: Three Rivers Press, 1982 [1940].

——. "What I Believe." *Forum and Century* 45, no. 3 (March, 1936 [October, 1930]): 174–76.

——. "Zu Spinozas Ethik." http://www.autodidactproject.org/other/einstein9-spinoza8.html.

Einstein, Albert, Max Born, and Hedwig Born. *The Born-Einstein Letters: Correspondence Between Albert Einstein and Max and Hedwig Born from 1916 to 1955*. Translated by Irene Born. New York: Walker & Co., 1971.

Einstein, Albert, B. Podolsky, and N. Rosen. "Can Quantum-Mechanical Descriptions of Reality Be Considered Complete?". *Physical Review* 47 (1935): 777–80.

"Einstein Believes in 'Spinoza's God.'" *The New York Times*, April 25, 1929, 60.

"Einstein's Faith Defended." *The New York Times*, November 10, 1930, 22.

"Einstein Urges Abandonment of Personal God Doctrine." *The Washington Post*, September 11, 1940, 1–2.

Eisenberg, Paul. "On the Attributes and Their Alleged Independence of One Another: A Commentary on Spinoza's *Ethics* Ip10." In *Spinoza: Issues and Directions*, edited by Edwin Curley and Pierre-François Moreau. Leiden: E. J. Brill, 1990.

Eliade, Mircea. *Patterns in Comparative Religion*. Translated by Rosemary Sheed. New York: World, 1963.

Eliot, T. S. *Collected Poems: 1909–1962*. New York: Harcourt Brace, 1991.

Elkana, Yehuda. "Einstein and God." In *Einstein for the 21st Century: His Legacy in Science, Art, and Modern Culture*, edited by Peter L. Galison, Gerald Holton and Silvan Schweber, 35–47. Princeton, NJ: Princeton University Press, 2008.

Emerson, Ralph Waldo. "An Address." In *The Essential Writings of Ralph Waldo Emerson*, edited by Brooks Atkinson, 61–78. New York: The Modern Library, 2000 [1838].

——. "Wood Notes II." In *The Early Poems of Ralph Waldo Emerson*, edited by Nathan Haskell Dole, 66–82. New York: Thomas Y. Crowell & Co., 1899.

"The Epic of Creation (*Enuma Elish*)." Translated by Stephanie Dalley. In *Myths from Mesopotamia: Creation, the Flood, Gilgamesh, and Others*, edited by Stephanie Dalley. Oxford World's Classics, 233–77. New York: Oxford, 2008.

Erickson, Jacob J. "'I Worship Jesus, Not Mother Earth': Exceptionalism and the Paris Withdrawal." *Religion Dispatches* (June 2, 2017): http://religiondispatches.org/i-worship-jesus-not-mother-earth-american-christian-exceptionalism-and-the-paris-withdrawal/?utm_source=Religion+Dispatches+Newsletter&utm_campaign=ceoa251ec4-RD_Daily_Newsletter&utm_medium=email&utm_term=0_742d86f519-ceoa251ec4-42408801.

Fairbanks, Arthur. "Xenophanes: Fragments and Commentary." Translated by Arthur Fairbanks. In *The First Philosophers of Greece*, edited by Arthur Fairbanks, 65–85. London: K. Paul, Trench, Trubner, 1898.

Faye, Jacques de la. *Defensio Religionis, Nec Non Mosis Et Gentis Judaicae, Contra Duas Dissertationes Joh. Tolandi, Quarum Una Inscribitur Adeisidaemon, Altera Vera Antiquitates Judaicae*. Ultrajecti: Apud Guilielmum Broedelet, 1709.

Feldman, Seymour. "Introduction." In *Ethics, Treatise on the Emendation of the Intellect, and Selected Letters*, edited by Seymour Feldman, 1–20. Indianapolis: Hackett, 1992.

Ferguson, Everett. *Backgrounds of Early Christianity*. Grand Rapids, MI: Eerdmans, 2003.

Feuerbach, Ludwig. *The Essence of Christianity*. Translated by George Eliot. Amherst, NY: Prometheus Books, 1989.

"Finds Spiral Nebulae Are Stellar Systems." *The New York Times*, November 23, 1924, 6.

Fine, Arthur. *The Shaky Game: Einstein, Realism, and the Quantum Theory*. Chicago: University of Chicago Press, 1986.

"Form vs. Matter." In *Stanford Encyclopedia of Philosophy*. https://plato.stanford.edu/entries/form-matter/, February 8, 2016.

Foucault, Michel. *Abnormal: Lectures at the Collège De France, 1974–1975*. Edited by Valerio Marchetti and Antonella Salomoni, translated by Graham Burchell. London: Picador, 2004.

Fowler, Dean R. "Einstein's Cosmic Religion." *Zygon* 14, no. 3 (September 1979): 267–78.

——. "A Process Theology of Interdependence." *Theological Studies* 40, no. 1 (March 1, 1979): 44–58.

Fox, Robin Lane. *Pagans and Christians*. New York: Knopf, 1987.

Frankenberry, Nancy. "Classical Theism, Panentheism, and Pantheism: On the Relation Between God Construction and Gender Construction." *Zygon* 28, no. 1 (March, 1993): 29–46.

Frazer, James George. *The Illustrated Golden Bough: A Study in Magic and Religion; Abridged by Robert K. G. Temple*. New York: Simon & Schuster, 1996.

Freud, Sigmund. *Totem and Taboo*. Translated by James Strachey. Complete Psychological Works of Sigmund Freud. New York: Norton, 1990 [1913].

Friedländer, Paul. "The Epicurean Theology in Lucretius' First Prooemium (Lucr. I. 44–49)." *Transactions and Proceedings of the American Philological Association* 70 (1939): 368–79.

Frieman, Joshua A., Michael S. Turner, and Dragan Huterer. "Dark Energy and the Accelerating Universe." *arXiv* 0803.0982 (March 7, 2008).

Furley, David J. *The Greek Cosmologists: The Formation of the Atomic Theory and Its Earliest Critics*. Cambridge: Cambridge University Press, 1987.

Gabirol, Ibn. *The Font of Life (Fons Vitae)*. Mediaeval Philosophical Texts in Translation. Milwaukee, WI: Marquette University Press, 2014.

Gale, Monica. *Myth and Poetry in Lucretius*. Cambridge: Cambridge University Press, 1996.

Gane, Nicholas, and Donna Haraway. "When We Have Never Been Human, What Is to Be Done? Interview with Donna Haraway." *Theory, Culture, and Society* 23, no. 7–8 (2006): 135–58.

Gebara, Ivone. *Longing for Running Water: Ecofeminism and Liberation.* Minneapolis, MN: Fortress Press, 1999.

Gilbert, Scott F., Jan Sapp, and Alfred I. Tauber. "A Symbiotic View of Life: We Have Never Been Individuals." *The Quarterly Review of Biology* 87, no. 4 (2012): 325–41.

"Giordano Bruno and Galileo Galilei." *The Popular Science Monthly Supplement* 13–18 (1878): 111–28.

"Give up Idea of Personal God, Einstein Urges." *Chicago Daily Tribune*, September 11, 1940, 23.

Gleiser, Marcelo. *The Island of Knowledge: The Limits of Science and the Search for Meaning.* New York: Basic Books, 2014.

——. *A Tear at the Edge of Creation: A Radical New Vision for Life in an Imperfect Universe.* New York: Free Press, 2010.

Goethe, Johann Wolfgang von. "Ganymed." In *Goethe: The Collected Works*, edited by Christopher Middleton, 30–33. Princeton, NJ: Princeton University Press, 1994 [1774].

Goldstein, Rebecca. *Betraying Spinoza: The Renegade Jew Who Gave Us Modernity.* New York: Schocken, 2006.

"Grace Jantzen (1948–2006)." *Feminist Theology* 15, no. 1 (2006): 121–23.

Granada, Miguel A. "Kepler and Bruno on the Infinity of the Universe and of Solar Systems." *Journal for the History of Astronomy* 39 (2008): 469–95.

——. "Mersenne's Critique of Giordano Bruno's Conception of the Relation Between God and the Universe: A Reappraisal." *Perspectives on Science* 18, no. 1 (Spring 2010): 26–49.

Grebowicz, Margret, and Helen Merrick. *Beyond the Cyborg: Adventures with Donna Haraway.* New York: Columbia University Press, 2013.

Greenblatt, Stephen. *The Swerve: How the World Became Modern.* New York: Norton, 2011.

Greene, Brian. *The Fabric of the Cosmos: Space, Time, and the Texture of Reality.* New York: Vintage, 2005.

——. *The Hidden Reality: Parallel Universes and the Deep Laws of the Cosmos.* New York: Knopf, 2011.

Gribbin, John. *In Search of the Multiverse.* London: Allen Lane, 2009.

Grosz, Elizabeth. *Becoming Undone: Darwinian Reflections on Life, Politics, and Art.* Durham, NC: Duke University Press, 2011.

Gruen, Lori. *Entangled Empathy: An Alternative Ethic for Our Relationships with Animals.* New York: Lantern Books, 2014.

Gueroult, Martial. *Spinoza: Dieu (Vol. 1).* Paris: Aubier Montaigne, 1968.

Guth, Alan H. "The Inflationary Universe." In *Cosmology: Historical, Literary, Philosophical, Religious, and Scientific Perspectives*, edited by Norris S. Hetherington, 411–45. New York: Garland, 1993.

Haeckel, Ernst. *The History of Creation, or the Development of the Earth and Its Inhabitants by the Actions of Natural Causes: A Popular Exposition of the Doctrine of Evolution in General, and of That of Darwin, Goethe, and Lamarck in Particular.* Translated by E. Ray Lankester. 2 vols. New York: Appleton, 1914.

——. *Monism as Connecting Religion and Science: The Confession of Faith of a Man of Science.* Translated by J. Gilchrist. London: Adam and Charles Black, 1895.

Hahm, David E. *The Origins of Stoic Cosmology.* Columbus: Ohio State University Press, 1977.

Halbfass, Wilhelm. *India and Europe: An Essay in Understanding.* Albany: State University of New York Press, 1988.

Hall, Matthew. "Talk Among the Trees: Animist Plant Ontologies and Ethics." In *The Handbook of Contemporary Animism,* edited by Graham Harvey, 385–94. New York: Routledge, 2015.

Hallowell, A. Irving. "Ojibwa Ontology, Behavior, and World View." In *Contributions to Anthropology: Selected Papers of A. Irving Hallowell,* 357–90. Chicago: University of Chicago Press, 1976.

Haraway, Donna. *Companion Species Manifesto: Dogs, People, and Significant Otherness.* Chicago: Prickly Paradigm Press, 2003.

——. "Ecce Homo, Ain't (Ar'n't) I a Woman, and Inappropriate/D Others: The Human in a Posthuman Landscape." In *The Haraway Reader,* 47–61. New York: Taylor and Francis, 2004.

——. "Introduction: A Kinship of Feminist Figurations." In *The Haraway Reader,* 1–6. New York: Routledge, 2004.

——. *Modest Witness@Second_Millennium: Femaleman_Meets_Oncomouse.* New York: Routledge, 1997.

——. "The Promises of Monsters: A Regenerative Politics for Inappropriate/D Others." In *The Haraway Reader,* 63–124. New York: Taylor and Francis, 2004.

——. "Sowing Worlds: A Seed Bag for Terraforming with Earth Others." In *Beyond the Cyborg: Adventures with Donna Haraway,* edited by Margret Grebowicz and Helen Merrick. New York: Columbia University Press, 2013.

——. *Staying with the Trouble: Making Kin in the Chthulucene.* Durham, NC: Duke University Press, 2016.

——. *When Species Meet.* Minneapolis: University of Minnesota Press, 2007.

Hardack, Richard. *Not Altogether Human: Pantheism and the Dark Nature of the American Renaissance.* Amherst: University of Massachussetts Press, 2012.

Harrison, Paul. *Elements of Pantheism: Religious Reverence of Nature and the Universe.* Coral Springs, FL: Llumina Press, 2004.

Harvey, Graham. *Animism: Respecting the Living World.* New York: Columbia University Press, 2006.

Haserot, F. S. "Spinoza's Definition of Attribute." In *Studies in Spinoza,* edited by S. P. Kashap, 28. Berkeley: University of California Press, 1972.

Hawking, Stephen. "Does God Play Dice?" http://www.hawking.org.uk/does-god-play -dice.html.

Hederich, Benjamin. *Gründliches Mythologisches Lexikon.* http://woerterbuchnetz.de /cgi-bin/WBNetz/wbgui_py?sigle=Hederich&mode=Vernetzung&lemid=HP0005 0#XHP00050.

Hedley, Douglas. "Pantheism, Trinitarian Theism and the Idea of Unity: Reflections on the Christian Concept of God." *Religious Studies* 32, no. 1 (March, 1996): 61–77.

Hegel, G. W. F. *The Encyclopaedia Logic: Part I of the Encyclopaedia of Philosophical Sciences with the Zusätze.* Translated by T. F. Geraets, W. A. Suchting, and H. S. Harris. Indianapolis: Hackett, 1991.

——. *Introduction to the Philosophy of History.* Translated by Leo Rauch. Indianapolis: Hackett, 1988.

——. *Lectures on the History of Philosophy: Medieval and Modern Philosophy.* Translated by E. S. Haldane and Frances H. Simson. 3 vols. Vol. 3, Lincoln: University of Nebraska Press, 1995.

——. *Lectures on the Philosophy of Religion.* Translated by R. F. Brown, P. C. Hodgson, and J. M. Stewart. Berkeley: University of California Press, 1988 [1827].

——. *Phenomenology of Spirit.* Translated by A. V. Miller. New York: Oxford University Press, 1977.

——. *Vorlesungen Über Die Geschichte Der Philosophie.* Leiden: A. H. Adriani, 1908.

Heidegger, Martin. *Schelling's Treatise on the Essence of Human Freedom.* Translated by Joan Stambaugh. Athens: Ohio University Press, 1985.

Hesiod. Translated by Catherine M. Schlegel and Henry Weinfield. In *Theogony and Works and Days,* edited by Theogony. Ann Arbor: University of Michigan Press, 2006.

Hill, Jonathan David. *Made-from-Bone: Trickster Myths, Music, and History from the Amazon.* Interpretations of Culture in the New Millennium. Urbana: University of Illinois Press, 2009.

Hillman, James, and W. H. Roscher. *Pan and the Nightmare.* Irving, TX: Spring Publications, 1979.

Hird, Myra J. "Naturally Queer." *Feminist Theory* 5 (2004): 85–89.

——. *The Origins of Sociable Life: Evolution after Science Studies.* New York: Palgrave Macmillan, 2009.

Holton, Gerald. "Einstein's Third Paradise." *Daedalus* 132, no. 4 (Fall 2003): 26–34.

Home, Dipankar, and Andrew Whitaker. *Einstein's Struggles with Quantum Theory: A Reappraisal.* New York: Springer, 2007.

Hornblower, Simon, and Antony Spawforth, eds. *Oxford Classical Dictionary, Third Edition.* Oxford: Oxford University Press, 2006.

Hume, David. *Dialogues Concerning Natural Religion.* Indianapolis: Hackett, 1998.

——. "The Natural History of Religion." In *Dialogues and the Natural History of Religion,* edited by J. C. A. Gaskin. Oxford: Oxford University Press, 1998.

Ingold, Tim. "The Art of Translation in a Continuous World." In *Beyond Boundaries: Understanding, Translation, and Anthropological Discourse*, edited by Gisli Pálsson. Oxford: Berg, 1993.

——. "Rethinking the Animate, Re-Animating Thought." *Ethnos: Journal of Anthropology* 71, no. 1 (2011): 9–20.

"'Intellectual' View of God Is Assailed." *The New York Times*, November 10, 1930.

Irigaray, Luce. "Plato's *Hystera*." Translated by Gillian C. Gill. In *Speculum of the Other Woman*, 243ff. Ithaca, NY: Cornell University Press, 1985.

Irwin, W. R. "The Survival of Pan." *Publications of the Modern Language Association of America* 76, no. 3 (1961): 159–67.

Isherwood, Christopher, ed. *Vedanta for the Western World*. Hollywood, CA: Marcel Rodd, 1945.

Israel, Jonathan. "Introduction." Translated by Jonathan Israel and Michael Silverthorne. In *Spinoza: Theological-Political Treatise*, edited by Jonathan Israel. Cambridge Texts in the History of Philosophy, viii–xxxiv. Cambridge: Cambridge University Press, 2007.

Jaki, Stanley L. *God and the Cosmologists*. Washington, DC: Real View, 1989.

James, William. "The One and the Many." In *Pragmatism and Other Writings*, edited by Giles Gunn, 58–73. New York: Penguin, 2000.

——. *A Pluralistic Universe*. Lincoln: University of Nebraska Press, 1996 [1908].

——. "Pragmatism and Religion." In *Pragmatism and Other Writings*, edited by Giles Gunn, 119–32. New York: Penguin, 2000.

Jammer, Max. *Einstein and Religion: Physics and Theology*. Princeton, NJ: Princeton University Press, 1999.

Jantzen, Grace. *Becoming Divine: Towards a Feminist Philosophy of Religion*. Bloomington: Indiana University Press, 1999.

——. "Feminism and Pantheism." *Monist* 80, no. 2 (April 1997): 266–85.

Johnson, Paul Christopher. "An Atlantic Genealogy of 'Spirit Possession.'" *Comparative Studies in Society and History* 53, no. 2 (2011): 393–425.

John XXII. "*In Agro Dominico*." https://www.scribd.com/doc/9651895/Bull-In-Agro -Dominico-by-John-XXII (March 27, 1329).

Jones, Clyde, Cheri A. Jones, J. Knox Jones Jr., and Don E. Wilson. "Pan Troglodytes." *Mammalian Species* 529 (May 17, 1966): 1–9.

Jones, William R. *Is God a White Racist? A Preamble to Black Theology*. Boston: Beacon Press, 1998 [1973].

Jonson, Ben. "Pan's Anniversary; or, the Shepherd's Holiday." In *The Works of Ben Jonson*, edited by William Gifford. New York: D. Appelton and Co., 1879.

Joy, Morny. "Rethinking the 'Problem of Evil' with Hannah Arendt and Grace Jantzen." In *New Topics in Feminist Philosophy of Religion: Contestations and Transcendence Incarnate*, edited by Pamela Sue Anderson, 17–32. New York: Springer, 2010.

Kaiser, David I. "Bringing the Human Actors Back on Stage: The Personal Context of the Einstein-Bohr Debate." *British Journal for the History of Science* 27 (1994): 129–52.

Kauffman, Stuart A. *Reinventing the Sacred: A New View of Science, Reason, and Religion.* New York: Basic Books, 2010.

Keller, Catherine. *Cloud of the Impossible: Negative Theology and Planetary Entanglement.* New York: Columbia University Press, 2014.

——. *Face of the Deep: A Theology of Becoming.* New York: Routledge, 2003.

——. *God and Power: Counter-Apocalyptic Journeys.* Minneapolis, MN: Fortress Press, 2005.

——. "'Nothingsomething' on My Mind: *Creatio Ex Nihilo* or *Ex Profundis*?". In *Theologies of Creation: Creatio Ex Nihilo and Its New Rivals*, edited by Thomas Jay Oord, 31–40. New York: Routledge, 2015.

Keller, Catherine, and Laurel Schneider, eds. *Polydoxy: Theology of Multiplicity and Relation.* New York: Routledge, 2011.

Keller, Evelyn Fox. "Cognitive Repression in Contemporary Physics." In *Reflections on Gender and Science*, 139–49. New Haven, CT: Yale University Press, 1985.

——. "One Woman and Her Theory." *New Scientist* (July 3, 1986): 46–52.

Kierkegaard, Søren. *The Sickness unto Death: A Christian Psychological Exposition for Upbuilding and Awakening.* Translated by Edna H. Hong and Howard V. Hong. Princeton, NJ: Princeton University Press, 1983 [1849].

Kimmerer, Robin Wall. *Braiding Sweetgrass: Indigenous Wisdom, Scientific Knowledge, and the Teaching of Plants.* Minneapolis, MN: Milkweed, 2013.

King, Richard. *Indian Philosophy: An Introduction to Hindu and Buddhist Thought.* Washington, DC: Georgetown University Press, 1999.

——. *Orientalism and Religion: Postcolonial Theory, India and 'the Mystic East'.* New York: Routledge, 1999.

Kirshner, Robert P. *The Extravagant Universe: Exploding Stars, Dark Energy, and the Accelerating Cosmos.* Princeton, NJ: Princeton University Press, 2002.

Knepper, Timothy David. *The Ends of Philosophy of Religion: Terminus and Telos.* New York: Palgrave Macmillan, 2013.

Kohn, Eduardo. *How Forests Think: Toward an Anthropology Beyond the Human.* Berkeley: University of California Press, 2013.

Lange, Horst. "Goethe and Spinoza: A Reconsideration." *Goethe Yearbook* 18 (2011): 11–33.

Lapidge, Michael. "Stoic Cosmology." In *The Stoics*, edited by J. M. Rist, 160–85. Berkeley: University of California Press, 1978.

Laplace, Pierre-Simon, marquis de. *Exposition Du Système Du Monde.* Brussels: De Vroom, 1827.

——. *A Philosophical Essay on Probabilities.* Translated by Frederick Wilson Truscott and Frederick Lincoln Emory. New York: J. Wiley, 1902 [1814].

Latour, Bruno. *Facing Gaia: Eight Lectures on the New Climatic Regime.* Translated by Catherine Porter. Medford, MA: Polity, 2017.

——. "Facing Gaia: Six Lectures on the Political Theology of Nature." (2013).

——. "How to Make Sure Gaia Is Not a God? With Special Attention to Toby Tyrrell's Book *on Gaia*." *Os Mil Nomes de Gaia: do Antropocentro à Idade da Terra* https://osmilnomesdegaia.files.wordpress.com/2014/11/bruno-latour.pdf (2014).

——. "How to Make Sure Gaia Is Not a God of Totality? With Special Attention to Toby Tyrrell's Book *on Gaia*." http://bruno-latour.fr/sites/default/files/138-THOUSAND -NAMES_0.pdf (September, 2014).

Lawrence, D. H. "Democracy." In *Phoenix*, edited by Edward McDonald, 699–718. New York: Viking, 1936.

——. "The Novel." In *Selected Critical Writings*, edited by Michael Herbert. Oxford World Classics, 179–90. Oxford: Oxford University Press, 1998 [1925].

——. "Pan in America." *Southwest Review* (January, 1926): 102–15.

——. *Studies in Classic American Literature: The Cambridge Edition of the Letters and Works of D. H. Lawrence*. Edited by James T. Boulton. Cambridge: Cambridge University Press, 2003.

Lazier, Benjamin. *God Interrupted: Heresy and the European Imagination Between the World Wars*. Princeton, NJ: Princeton University Press, 2012.

Leaman, Oliver. *Averroes and His Philosophy*. Richmond, UK: Curzon, 1998.

Leibniz, G. W., and Samuel Clarke. *Correspondence*. Indianapolis: Hackett, 2000.

Lemaître, Georges. "Rencontre Avec A. Einstein." *Revue des Questions Scientifiques* 129 (1958): 129–32.

Lennon, Thomas M., and Michael Hickson. "Pierre Bayle." In *The Stanford Encyclo- pedia of Philosophy*, edited by Edward N. Zalta. http://plato.stanford.edu/archives /fall2014/entries/bayle, Fall 2014.

Levine, Michael. *Pantheism: A Non-Theistic Concept of Deity*. New York: Routledge, 1994.

Lewis, C. S. *Mere Christianity*. San Francisco: HarperCollins, 2001.

Li, Victor. *The Neo-Primitivist Turn: Critical Reflections on Alterity, Culture, and Modernity*. Toronto: University of Toronto Press, 2006.

Lightman, Alan P. "The Accidental Universe: Science's Crisis of Faith." *Harper's Maga- zine*, December 22, 2011.

Lima, Tania Stolze. "The Two and Its Many: Reflections on Perspectivism in a Tupi Cosmology." *Ethnos: Journal of Anthropology* 64, no. 1 (1999): 107–31.

Linde, Andrei. "The Self-Reproducing Inflationary Universe." *Scientific American* 271, no. 5 (November, 1994): 48–55.

Lopez, Donald S. "Belief." In *Critical Terms for Religious Studies*, edited by Mark C. Taylor. Chicago: University of Chicago Press, 1998.

Lovejoy, Arthur O. "The Dialectic of Bruno and Spinoza." In *The Summum Bonum*, edited by Evander Bradley McGilvary, 141–74. Berkeley, CA: The University Press, 1904.

Lovelock, James. *Gaia: A New Look at Life on Earth*. New York: Oxford University Press, 1979.

——. *Healing Gaia: Practical Medicine for the Planet*. New York: Harmony, 1991.

——. *Homage to Gaia: The Life of an Independent Scientist*. Oxford: Oxford University Press, 2000.

——. *The Vanishing Face of Gaia: A Final Warning*. New York: Basic Books, 2009.

Lovelock, James, and Sidney Epton. "The Quest for Gaia." *New Scientist* (February 6, 1975): 304–6.

Lucretius. *De Rerum Natura*. Translated by W. H. D. Rouse; revised by Martin Ferguson Smith. Loeb Classical Library. Cambridge, MA: Harvard University Press, 1975.

——. *The Nature of Things*. Translated by A. E. Stallings. New York: Penguin, 2007.

Macauley, David. *Elemental Philosophy: Earth, Air, Fire, and Water as Environmental Ideas*. Albany: State University of New York Press, 2011.

Maccagnolo, Enzo. "David of Dinant and the Beginnings of Aristotelianism in Paris." In *A History of Twelfth-Century Western Philosophy*, edited by Peter Dronke, 429–42. New York: Cambridge University Press, 1992.

MacIntyre, Alasdair. "Pantheism." In *Encyclopedia of Philosophy, 2nd Ed.*, edited by Donald M. Borchert, 94–99. Detroit: MacMillian Reference USA, 2006.

Magnus, Albertus. "Summa Theologiae Sive Scientia De Mirabili Scientia Dei." edited by E. Borgnet, http://albertusmagnus.uwaterloo.ca/Downloading.html. Paris: Vives, 1894.

Mail, J. D. B. "Cardinal O'Connell's Full Statement Against Professor Einstein's Theories." *Jewish Daily Bulletin*, April 18, 1929, 7.

Mander, William. "Pantheism." In *The Stanford Encyclopedia of Philosophy*, edited by Edward N. Zalta: http://plato.stanford.edu/archives/win2012/entries/pantheism/, Winter 2012.

Mann, Charles. "Lynn Margulis: Science's Unruly Earth Mother." *Science* 252 (April 19, 1991): 378–81.

Mansfield, J. "Providence and the Destruction of the Universe in Early Stoic Thought: With Some Remarks on the 'Mysteries of Philosophy'." In *Studies in Hellenistic Religion*, edited by M. J. Vermaseren, 129–88. Leiden: Brill, 1979.

Marcos, Sylvia. "The Sacred Earth of the Nahuas." In *Taken from the Lips: Gender and Eros in Mesoamerican Religions*. Religion in the Americas, 31–39. Boston: Brill, 2006.

Margulis, Lynn. "Big Trouble in Biology: Physiological Autopoiesis Versus Mechanistic Neo-Darwinism." In *Slanted Truths: Essays on Gaia, Symbiosis, and Evolution*, edited by Lynn Margulis and Dorion Sagan, 265–82. New York: Copernicus, 1997.

——. "The Conscious Cell." *Annals of the New York Academy of Sciences* 929, no. 1 (April, 2001): 55–70.

——. *The Origin of Eukaryotic Cells: Evidence and Research Implications for a Theory of the Origin and Evolution of Microbial, Plant, and Animal Cells on the Precambrian Earth*. New Haven, CT: Yale University Press, 1970.

——. *Symbiotic Planet: A New Look at Evolution*. New York: Basic Books, 1998.

Margulis, Lynn, and James Lovelock. "The Atmosphere as Circulatory System of the Biosphere—the Gaia Hypothesis." In *Slanted Truths: Essays on Gaia, Symbiosis, and Evolution*, edited by Lynn Margulis and Dorion Sagan, 127–43. New York: Copernicus, 1997.

——. "Biological Modulations of the Earth's Atmosphere." *Icarus* 21 (1974): 471–89.

Margulis, Lynn, and Dorion Sagan. *What Is Life?* New York: Simon and Schuster, 1995.

Margulis, Lynn, and Oona West. "Gaia and the Colonization of Mars." In *Slanted Truths: Essays on Gaia, Symbiosis, and Evolution*, edited by Lynn Margulis and Dorion Sagan, 221–34. New York: Copernicus, 1997.

Marriott, Alice Lee. *American Indian Mythology*. New York: Apollo Editions, 1968.

Marx, Karl. *Grundrisse: Foundations of the Critique of Political Economy*. Translated by Martin Nicolaus. New York: Penguin, 1993.

Maturana, Humberto, and Francisco Varela. *Autopoiesis and Cognition: The Realization of the Living*. Dordrecht: Reidel, 1980.

Matysik, Tracie. "Spinozist Monism: Perspectives from Within and Without the Monist Movement." In *Monism: Science, Philosophy, Religion, and the History of a Worldview*, edited by Todd Weir, 107–34. New York: Palgrave Macmillan, 2012.

M'Baye, Babacar. *The Trickster Comes West: Pan-African Influence in Early Black Diasporan Narratives*. Jackson: University Press of Mississippi, 2009.

McFague, Sallie. *The Body of God: An Ecological Theology*. Minneapolis, MN: Fortress Press, 1993.

McIntyre, J. Lewis. *Giordano Bruno*. London: Macmillan, 1903.

Melville, Herman. *Moby-Dick*. Norton Critical Editions. New York: Norton, 2002.

Mereschkowsky, Konstantin. "Theorie Der Zwei Plasmaarten Als Grundlage Der Symbiogenesis, Einer Neuer Lehre Von Der Ent-Stehung Der Organismen." *Biologisches Centralblatt* 30 (1910): 353–67.

Merivale, Patricia. *Pan the Goat-God: His Myth in Modern Times*. Cambridge, MA: Harvard University Press, 1969.

Mersini-Houghton, Laura. "Birth of the Universe from the Multiverse." *arXiv* 0809.3623 (September 22, 2008).

——. "Thoughts on Defining the Multiverse." *arXiv* 0804.4280 (April 27, 2008).

Midgley, Mary. "Introduction—the Not-So-Simple Earth." In *Earthly Realism: The Meaning of Gaia*, edited by Mary Midgley, 1–8. Charlottesville, VA: Societas, 2007.

——. *Science and Poetry*. New York: Routledge, 2001.

Miller, Jon. "Spinoza and the Stoics on Substance Monism." In *The Cambridge Companion to Spinoza's Ethics*, edited by Olli Koistinen, 99–117. Cambridge: Cambridge University Press, 2009.

Milton, John. "On the Morning of Christ's Nativity." In *The Complete Poetry and Essential Prose of John Milton*, edited by William Kerrigan, John Rumrich, and M. Fallon, 18–29. New York: Modern Library, 2007 [1629].

——. "Paradise Lost." In *The Complete Poetry and Essential Prose of John Milton*, edited by William Kerrigan, John Rumrich, and M. Fallon. New York: Modern Library, 2007 [1667].

Moore, Jason W. "Introduction." In *Anthropocene or Capitalocene? Nature, History, and the Crisis of Capitalism*, edited by Jason W. Moore, 1–11. Oakland, CA: PM Press, 2016.

Morton, Timothy. *Hyperobjects: Philosophy and Ecology After the End of the World*. Minneapolis: University of Minnesota Press, 2013.

Müller, Friedrich Max. *Natural Religion: The Gifford Lectures Delivered before the University of Glasgow in 1888*. New York: AMS Press, 1975 [1889].

Nadler, Steven. *Spinoza: A Life*. Cambridge: Cambridge University Press, 2001.

——. *Spinoza's "Ethics": An Introduction*. Cambridge Introductions to Key Philosophical Texts. Cambridge: Cambridge University Press, 2006.

Newton, Isaac. *Four Letters from Sir Isaac Newton to Doctor Bentley, Containing Some Arguments in Proof of a Deity*. London: R. and J. Dodsley, 1756 [1692–3].

——. *Opticks*. CreateSpace Independent Publishing Platform, 2013 [1704].

——. *The Principia*. Translated by Andrew Motte. Great Minds Series. Amherst, NY: Prometheus Books, 1995 [1687].

Nicholas of Cusa. *On Learned Ignorance*. Translated by H. Lawrence Bond. Nicholas of Cusa: Selected Writings. New York: Paulist Press, 1997.

Nicholson, Andrew J. *Unifying Hinduism: Philosophy and Identity in Indian Intellectual History*. New York: Columbia University Press, 2010.

Nietzsche, Friedrich. *On the Genealogy of Morals*. Translated by Walter Kaufmann. New York: Vintage Books, 1989.

——. *The Will to Power*. Translated by Walter Kaufmann and R. J. Hollingdale. New York: Vintage, 1968.

Norton, John D. "The Cosmological Woes of Newtonian Gravitation Theory." In *The Expanding Worlds of General Relativity*, edited by H. Goenner, J. Renn, J. Ritter, and T. Sauer, 271–322. Boston: The Center for Einstein Studies, 1999.

Norton-Smith, Thomas M. *The Dance of Person and Place: One Interpretation of American Indian Philosophy*. Suny Series in Living Indigenous Philosophies. Albany: State University of New York Press, 2010.

NOVA. *Runaway Universe*. PBS, November 11, 2000.

Novalis [Hardenberg, Freiherr Friedrich von]. *Gesammelte Werke*. Vol. 4. Bühler: Herrliberg-Zürich, 1946.

Onori, Luciano, and Guido Visconti. "The Gaia Theory: From Lovelock to Margulis. From a Homeostatic to a Cognitive Autopoietic Worldview." *Rendiconti lincei / Scienze fisiche e naturali* 23 (2012): 375–86.

Outka, Paul. *Race and Nature from Transcendentalism to the Harlem Renaissance*. New York: Palgrave Macmillan, 2013.

Oxford English Dictionary Online. Oxford: Oxford University Press, 2014.

Pais, Abraham. *Subtle Is the Lord: The Science and the Life of Albert Einstein*. Oxford: Oxford University Press, 2005 [1982].

Parkinson, G. H. R. "Hegel, Pantheism, and Spinoza." *Journal of the History of Ideas* 38, no. 3 (1977): 449–59.

Pasquier, Ernest. "Les Hypothèses Cosmogoniques." *Revue néo-scolastique* 5, no. 18 (1898): 123–40.

Pätzold, Detley. "Deus Sive Natura. J. G. Herder's Romanticized Reading of Spinoza's Physico-Theology." In *The Book of Nature in Early Modern and Modern History*, edited by Klaas van Berkel and Arjo Vanderjagt, 155–66. Leuven: Peeters, 2006.

Peck, Harry Thurston, ed. *Harper's Dictionary of Classical Literature and Antiquities.* New York: Cooper Square, 1963.

Perry, Seamus, ed. *Coleridge's Notebooks: A Selection.* Oxford: Oxford University Press, 2002.

Pietz, William. "Fetishism and Materialism: The Limits of Theory in Marx." In *Fetishism as Cultural Discourse*, edited by Emily Apter and William Pietz. Ithaca, NY: Cornell University Press, 1993.

Plato. "Cratylus." In *Complete Works*, edited by John M. Cooper and D. S. Hutchinson. Indianapolis: Hackett, 1997.

——. "Gorgias." Translated by Donald J. Zeyl. In *Complete Works*, edited by John M. Cooper and D. S. Hutchinson, 791–869. Indianapolis: Hackett, 1997.

——. "Timaeus." Translated by Desmond Lee. In *Timaeus and Critias*, edited by Thomas Kjeller Johansen, 28–126. New York: Penguin Books, 1977.

Plumptre, C. E. *General Sketch of the History of Pantheism: From the Earliest Times to the Age of Spinoza.* Cambridge Library Series—Religion. 2 vols. Vol. 1, Cambridge: Cambridge University Press, 2011 [1878].

——. "Giordano Bruno: His Life and Philosophy." *Westminster Review* 132, no. 2 (1889): 117–238.

Plumwood, Val. *Feminism and the Mastery of Nature.* New York: Routledge, 1993.

——. "Nature in the Active Voice." *Australian Humanities Review* 46 (2009): 113–29.

Plutarch. "The Obsolescence of Oracles." In *Moralia.* Cambridge, MA: Harvard University Press, 1936.

Pope, Alexander. "An Essay on Man." In *The Major Works*, edited by Pat Rogers. Oxford World's Classics, 270–309. Oxford: Oxford University Press, 2009.

Porphyry. *On Images.* Translated by Edwin Hamilton Gifford. http://classics.mit.edu /Porphyry/images.html.

Postgate, John. "Gaia Gets Too Big for Her Boots." *New Scientist* (April 7, 1988): 60.

Povinelli, Elizabeth A. *Geontologies: A Requiem to Late Liberalism.* Durham, NC: Duke University Press, 2016.

Pratt, Scott L. *Native Pragmatism: Rethinking the Roots of American Philosophy.* Bloomington: Indiana University Press, 2002.

Principe, Lawrence M. *The Aspiring Adept: Robert Boyle and His Alchemical Quest.* Princeton, NJ: Princeton University Press, 2000.

Pseudo-Dionysius. "The Divine Names." In *The Complete Works*, edited by Colm Luibheid. Classics of Western Spirituality. New York: Paulist Press, 1987.

Rabelais, François. *Gargantua and Pantagruel.* Translated by M. A. Screech. New York: Penguin, 2006 [1535–64].

Radin, Paul. "Religion of the North American Indians." *Journal of American Folklore* 27 (1914): 335–73.

Rasimus, Tuomas, Troels Engberg-Pedersen, and Ismo Dunderberg, eds. *Stoicism in Early Christianity.* Grand Rapids, MI: Baker Academic, 2010.

Rayapati, J. P. Rao. *Early American Interest in Vedanta: Pre-Emersonian Interest in Vedic Literature and Vedantic Philosophy.* Delhi: Asia Publishing House, 1973.

Rayor, Diane J., ed. *The Homeric Hymns: A Translation, with Introduction and Notes.* Berkeley: University of California Press, 2004.

"Religion of Good Urged by Einstein." *The New York Times*, September 11, 1940, 27.

Richards, Robert J. *The Tragic Sense of Life: Ernst Haeckel and the Struggle over Evolutionary Thought.* Chicago: University of Chicago Press, 2008.

Richardson, Nathaniel Smith. "The Pantheistic Movement." *The Church Review, and Ecclesiastical Register* 1, no. 4 (1849): 548–65.

Richardson, Nicholas, ed. *Homeric Hymns*, Penguin Classics. New York: Penguin, 2003.

Riepe, Dale. *The Philosophy of India and Its Impact on American Thought.* Springfield, IL: Thomas, 1970.

Riskin, Jessica. *The Restless Clock: A History of the Centuries-Long Argument over What Makes Living Things Tick.* Chicago: University of Chicago Press, 2016.

Robert, William. *Revivals: Of Antigone.* Albany: State University of New York Press, 2015.

Rose, Deborah Bird. "Death and Grief in a World of Kin: Dwelling in Larger-Than-Human Communities." In *The Handbook of Contemporary Animism*, edited by Graham Harvey, 137–47. New York: Routledge, 2015.

——. *Dingo Makes Us Human: Life and Land in an Australian Aboriginal Culture.* Cambridge: Cambridge University Press, 2000.

——. "Val Plumwood's Philosophical Animism: Attentive Interactions in the Sentient World." *Environmental Humanities* 3 (2013): 93–109.

Ross, J. M. "Introduction." In *Cicero: The Nature of the Gods*, 7–63. New York: Penguin, 1972.

Rowe, David, and Robert Schulmann. *Einstein on Politics.* Princeton, NJ: Princeton University Press, 2007.

Rowland, Ingrid D. *Giordano Bruno: Philosopher/Heretic.* New York: Farrar, Straus and Giroux, 2008.

Rubenstein, Mary-Jane. "End Without End: Cosmology and Infinity in Nicholas of Cusa." In *Desire, Faith, and the Darkness of God: Essays in Honor of Denys Turner*, edited by Eric Bugyis and David Newheiser, 13–36. Notre Dame, IN: University of Notre Dame Press, 2016.

——. "Myth and Modern Physics: On the Power of Nothing." In *Theologies of Creation: Creatio Ex Nihilo and Its New Rivals*, edited by Thomas Jay Oord, 7–16. New York: Routledge, 2015.

——. *Strange Wonder: The Closure of Metaphysics and the Opening of Awe.* Insurrections: Critical Studies in Religion, Politics, and Culture. New York: Columbia University Press, 2009.

——. *Worlds Without End: The Many Lives of the Multiverse.* New York: Columbia University Press, 2014.

Ruether, Rosemary Radford. *Gaia and God: An Ecofeminist Theology of Earth Healing.* San Francisco, CA: HarperSanFrancisco, 1992.

Ruse, Michael. *The Gaia Hypothesis: Science on a Pagan Planet*. Chicago: University of Chicago Press, 2013.

Russell, Jeffrey Burton. *The Prince of Darkness: Radical Evil and the Power of Good in History*. Ithaca, NY: Cornell University Press, 1992.

Sagan, Carl. "The Other World That Beckons: A Profile of Albert Einstein." *New Republic* https://newrepublic.com/article/117028/world-beckons (September 16, 1978).

Sagan, Dorion. "The Human Is More Than Human: Interspecies Communities and the New 'Facts of Life.'" *Cultural Anthropology* (April 24, 2011): https://culanth.org/fieldsights/228-the-human-is-more-than-human-interspecies-communities-and-the-new-facts-of-life.

——. "Life on a Margulisian Planet: A Son's Philosophical Reflections." In *Earth, Life, and System: Evolution and Ecology on a Gaian Planet*, edited by Bruce Clarke, 13–38. New York: Fordham University Press, 2015.

Sagan, Dorion, and Lynn Margulis. "Gaia and Philosophy." In *Slanted Truths: Essays on Gaia, Symbiosis, and Evolution*, edited by Lynn Margulis and Dorion Sagan, 145–57. New York: Copernicus, 1997.

——. "A Good Four-Letter Word." In *Slanted Truths: Essays on Gaia, Symbiosis, and Evolution*, edited by Lynn Margulis and Dorion Sagan, 201–6. New York: Copernicus, 1997.

Sagan, Dorion, Lynn Margulis, and Ricardo Guerrero. "Descartes, Dualism, and Beyond." In *Slanted Truths: Essays on Gaia, Symbiosis, and Evolution*, edited by Lynn Margulis and Dorion Sagan. New York: Copernicus, 1997.

Sagan, Lynn. "On the Origin of Mitosing Eukaryotic Cells." *Journal of Theoretical Biology* 14 (March 1967): 225–74.

Said, Edward. *Orientalism*. New York: Vintage, 1979.

Santayana, George. *Three Philosophical Poets, Lucretius, Dante, and Goethe*. New York: CreateSpace, 2013 [1910].

Sapp, Jan. "On Symbiosis, Microbes, Kingdoms, and Domains." In *Earth, Life, and System: Evolution and Ecology on a Gaian Planet*, edited by Bruce Clarke, 105–26. New York: Fordham University Press, 2015.

Sargent, M. G. "The Annihilation of Marguerite Porete." *Viator* 28 (1997): 253–79.

Schelling, F. W. J. *The Ages of the World*. Albany: State University of New York Press, 2000.

——. *Ideas for a Philosophy of Nature, as Introduction to the Study of This Science*. Translated by Errol E. Harris and Peter Heath. Cambridge: Cambridge University Press, 1988.

——. *Philosophical Investigations into the Essence of Human Freedom*. Albany: State University of New York Press, 2007 [1809].

——. *Philosophische Untersuchungen Über Das Wesen Der Menschlichen Freiheit Und Die Damit Zusammenhängended Gegenstände*. Reutlingen: J. N. Ensslin, 1834.

Schlegel, Friedrich von. *Über Die Sprache Und Weisheit Der Indier*. Heidelberg: Mohr und Zimmer, 1808.

Schleiermacher, Friedrich. *On Religion: Speeches to Its Cultured Despisers*. Cambridge: Cambridge University Press, 1998.

Schneider, Eric D., and Dorion Sagan. *Into the Cool: Energy Flow, Thermodynamics, and Life*. Chicago: University of Chicago Press, 2005.

Schneider, Laurel. "Becoming Divine: Towards a Feminist Philosophy of Religion." *Journal of the American Academy of Religion* 70, no. 3 (2002): 644–47.

——. *Beyond Monotheism: A Theology of Multiplicity*. New York: Routledge, 2008.

——. "Promiscuous Incarnation." In *The Embrace of Eros: Bodies, Desires, and Sexuality in Christianity*, edited by Margaret Kamitsuka. Minneapolis, MN: Fortress Press, 2010.

Schoff, Wilfred H. "Tammuz, Pan and Christ." *The Open Court* 26, no. 9 (September, 1912): 513–32.

Schopenhauer, Arthur. *Parerga and Paralipomena*. Translated by E. F. J. Payne. 2 vols. Vol. 1, Oxford: Clarendon Press, 2000.

——. *Parerga and Paralipomena*. Translated by E. F. J. Payne. 2 vols. Vol. 2, Oxford: Clarendon Press, 2000.

Schrödinger, Erwin. "Autobiographical Sketches." Translated by Verena Schrödinger. In *What Is Life? The Physical Aspect of the Living Cell. With Mind and Matter and Autobiographical Sketches*, 167–84. Cambridge: Cambridge University Press, 2016.

——. "Mind and Matter: The Tarner Lectures, Delivered at Trinity College, Cambridge." In *What Is Life? The Physical Aspect of the Living Cell. With Mind and Matter and Autobiographical Sketches*, 93–164. Cambridge: Cambridge University Press, 2016 [1956].

——. *What Is Life?* New York: Macmillan, 1945.

"Science and Religion." *Time*, September 23, 1940, 52–53.

Scruton, Roger. *Spinoza: A Very Short Introduction*. New York: Oxford University Press, 2002.

Sedgwick, Eve Kosofsky. *Tendencies*. Durham, NC: Duke University Press, 1993.

Serres, Michel. *The Birth of Physics*. Translated by Jack Hawkes. Manchester, UK: Clinamen Press, 2000.

Shelley, Percy Bysshe. "Song of Pan." In *The Major Works, Including Poetry, Prose, and Drama*, edited by Zachary Leader and Michael O'Neill. Oxford World's Classics, 509. Oxford: Oxford University Press, 2009.

Shostak, Seth. "The Lugubrious Universe." *The Huffington Post*, November 26, 2010.

Singer, Dorothea, ed. *Giordano Bruno: His Life and Thought with Annotated Translation of His Work on the Infinite Universe and Worlds*. New York: Schuman, 1950.

Singer, Dr. Jacob. "Einstein's Religion: A Sermon Preached before Temple Isaiah-Israel, Chicago." January 4, 1931.

Smart, Ninian. "God's Body." *Union Seminary Quarterly Review* 37, no. 1 and 2 (1891–1982): 51–59.

Smith, Jonathan Z. "Religion, Religions, Religious." In *Critical Terms for Religious Studies*, edited by Mark C. Taylor, 269–84. Chicago: University of Chicago Press, 1998.

Smolin, Lee. *Time Reborn: From the Crisis in Physics to the Future of the Universe.* New York: Houghton Mifflin Harcourt, 2013.

Snobelen, Stephen. "'The True Frame of Nature': Isaac Newton, Heresy, and the Reformation of Natural Philosophy." In *Heterodoxy in Early Modern Science and Religion*, edited by John Hedley Brooke and Ian Maclean, 223–62. Oxford: Oxford University Press, 2005.

Spenser, Edmund. "The Shepheardes Calendar." In *The Yale Edition of the Shorter Poems of Edmund Spenser*, edited by William Oram, et. al. New Haven, CT: Yale University Press, 1989.

Spillers, Hortense J. *Black, White, and in Color: Essays on American Literature and Culture.* Chicago: University of Chicago Press, 2003.

Spinoza, Baruch. *Ethica.* CreateSpace Independent Publishing Platform, 2014.

——. "Ethics." Translated by Samuel Shirley. In *Ethics, Treatise on the Emendation of the Intellect, and Selected Letters*, edited by Seymour Feldman, 31–223. Indianapolis: Hackett, 1992.

——. "Letter 64: To the Learned and Experienced G. H. Schuller, from B.D.S." In *Complete Works*, edited by Michael L. Morgan, 918–19. Indianapolis: Hackett, 2002.

——. "Letter 66: To the Noble and Learned Ehrenfried Walther Von Tschirnhaus, from B.D.S." In *Complete Works*, edited by Michael L. Morgan, 921. Indianapolis: Hackett, 2002.

——. "Letter 83: To the Most Noble and Learned Ehrenfried Walther Von Tschirnhaus, from B.D.S." In *Complete Works*, edited by Michael L. Morgan, 958. Indianapolis: Hackett, 2002.

——. "Short Treatise on God, Man, and His Well-Being." Translated by Samuel Shirley. In *Complete Works*, edited by Michael L. Morgan, 31–107. Indianapolis, IN: Hackett, 2002.

——. *Theological-Political Treatise.* Translated by Samuel Shirley. Indianapolis: Hackett, 1998.

——. "Treatise on the Emendation of the Intellect." In *Ethics, Treatise on the Emendation of the Intellect, and Selected Letters*, edited by Seymour Feldman, 233–62. Indianapolis: Hackett, 1992.

Stanescu, James. "Matter." In *Critical Terms for Animal Studies*, edited by Lori Gruen. Chicago: University of Chicago Press, forthcoming.

Starhawk. *The Spiral Dance: A Rebirth of the Ancient Religion of the Great Goddess.* San Francisco: HarperCollins, 1999 [1979].

Steinhardt, Paul J., and Neil Turok. "The Cyclic Model Simplified." *New Astronomy Reviews* 49, no. 206 (May 2005): 43–57.

Stengers, Isabelle. *In Catastrophic Times: Resisting the Coming Barbarism.* Translated by Andrew Goffey. Critical Climate Change, edited by Tom Cohen and Claire Colebrook London: Open Humanities Press, 2015.

——. "Penser À Partir Du Ravage Écologique." In *De L'univers Clos Au Monde Infini*, edited by Émilie Hache, 147–90. Paris: Éditions Dehors, 2014.

——. "Reclaiming Animism." *E-flux* 36 (July 2012): 1–10.

Stent, Gunther S. "Does God Play Dice?". *The Sciences* (March 1979): 18–23.

Strick, James. "Exobiology at Nasa: Incubator for the Gaia and Serial Endosymbiosis Theories." In *Earth, Life, and System: Evolution and Ecology on a Gaian Planet*, edited by Bruce Clarke, 80–104. New York: Fordham University Press, 2015.

Stuckey, Priscilla. "The Animal Versus the Social: Rethinking Individual and Community in Western Cosmology." In *The Handbook of Contemporary Animism*, edited by Graham Harvey, 191–208. New York: Routledge, 2015.

Summers, Kirk. "Lucretius and the Epicurean Tradition of Piety." *Classical Philology* 90, no. 1 (1995): 32–57.

Surin, Kenneth. *Theology and the Problem of Evil*. Eugene, OR: Wipf and Stock, 1986.

Taylor, Bron. *Dark Green Religion: Nature, Spirituality, and the Planetary Future*. Berkeley: University of California Press, 2010.

Taylor, Mark C. *Erring: A Postmodern a/Theology*. Chicago: University of Chicago Press, 1984.

Taylor, Richard C. "Averroes." In *The Cambridge Companion to Arabic Philosophy*, edited by Peter Adamson and Richard C. Taylor, 180–200. Cambridge: Cambridge University Press, 2005.

Tegmark, Max. *Our Mathematical Universe: My Quest for the Ultimate Nature of Reality*. New York: Vintage, 2015.

Tennyson, Alfred Lord. "The Higher Pantheism." In *The Major Works*, edited by Adam Roberts. Oxford World's Classics, 379. Oxford: Oxford University Press, 2009.

Thacker, Eugene. *After Life*. Chicago: University of Chicago Press, 2010.

Thoreau, Henry David. "A Week on the Concord and Merrimack Rivers." In *A Week on the Concord and Merrimack Rivers, Walden, the Maine Woods, Cape Cod*, 1–320. New York: Library of America, 1985 [1849].

"Thousands Attend Einstein Jubilee Celebration in New York City." *Jewish Daily Bulletin*, April 18, 1929, 3–4, 8.

Tillich, Paul. *The Courage to Be*. New Haven, CT: Yale University Press, 2014.

——. "The Idea of a Personal God." *The Union Review* 2 (November, 1940): 8–10.

Tocqueville, Alexis de. *Democracy in America*. Translated by Gerald Bevan. New York: Penguin, 2003.

Toland, John. *Adeisidaemon, Sive Titus Livius. A Superstitione Vindicatus*. Hagae-Comitis: Apud Thomam Johnson, 1709.

——. *Pantheisticon: Or, the Form of Celebrating the Socratic-Society*. Charleston, SC: Nabu Press, 2010 [1720].

——. *Socinianism Truly Stated; Being an Example of Fair Dealing in All Theological Controvrsys. To Which Is Prefixt, Indifference in Disputes: Recommended by a Pantheist to an Orthodox Friend*. London, 1705.

"To Pan." Translated by Thomas Taylor. In *Orphic Hymns*. Classical Texts Library. http://www.theoi.com/Text/OrphicHymns1.html#10.

Tschirnhaus, Ehrenfried Walther von. "Letter 82: To the Acute and Learned Philoso-pher B.D.S., from Ehrenfried Walter Von Tschirnhaus." In *Spinoza: Complete Works*, edited by Michael L. Morgan, 956–57. Indianapolis: Hackett, 2002.

Turner, William. "David of Dinant." In *The Catholic Encyclopedia*, http://www.newadvent.org/cathen/04645a.htm. New York: Robert Appleton Co., 2017 [1908].

Tylor, Edward Burnett. "The Philosophy of Religion Among the Lower Races of Mankind." *The Journal of the Ethnological Society of London* 2, no. 4 (1870): 369–81.

——. *Religion in Primitive Culture*. New York: Harper and Row, 1958 [1871].

Tyrrell, Toby. *On Gaia: A Critical Investigation of the Relationship Between Life and Earth*. Princeton, NJ: Princeton University Press, 2013.

"Urges Faith in Leaders: Dean Gates Deplores Followers Who Are Critical." *The New York Times*, November 10, 1930, 22.

Varela, Francisco, Humberto Maturana, and Ricardo B. Uribe. "Autopoiesis: The Organization of Living Systems, Its Characterization and a Model." *BioSystems* 5 (1974): 187–96.

"Vatican Finds Professor Einstein Is an Atheist." *Jewish Daily Bulletin*, May 26, 1929, 3.

Viereck, George Sylvester. *Glimpses of the Great*. New York: Macauley, 1930.

Vilenkin, Alex. *Many Worlds in One: The Search for Other Universes*. New York: Hill and Wang, 2006.

Vilenkin, Alex, and Jaume Garriga. "Many Worlds in One." *Physical Review* D64, no. 043511 (2001): 1–5.

Viljanen, Valtteri. "Spinoza's Ontology." In *The Cambridge Companion to Spinoza's Ethics*, edited by Olli Koistinen, 56–78. Cambridge: Cambridge University Press, 2009.

Viveiros de Castro, Eduardo. "Cosmological Deixis and Amerindian Perspectivism." *Royal Anthropological Institute of Great Britain and Ireland* 4, no. 3 (September 1998): 469–88.

——. "Exchanging Perspectives: The Transformation of Objects into Subjects in Amer-indian Ontologies." *Common Knowledge* 10, no. 3 (2004): 463–84.

Walker, Alice. *The Color Purple*. New York: Harcourt Brace, 1988.

Webb, Stephen. *American Providence: A Nation with a Mission*. New York: Continuum, 2006.

Weinberg, Steven. "The Cosmological Constant Problem." *arXiv* astro-ph, no. 0005265v1 (May 12, 2000).

——. "Living in the Multiverse." In *Universe or Multiverse*, edited by Bernard Carr, 29–42. Cambridge: Cambridge University Press, 2007.

Weinstein, Galina. "George Gamow and Albert Einstein: Did Einstein Say the Cosmological Constant Was the 'Biggest Blunder' He Ever Made in His Life?". *https://arxiv.org/pdf/1310.1033.pdf* (October 3, 2013).

Weir, Todd H. "The Riddles of Monism: An Introductory Essay." In *Monism: Science, Philosophy, Religion, and the History of a Worldview*, edited by Todd Weir, 1–44. New York: Palgrave Macmillan, 2012.

White, Carol Wayne. *Black Lives and Sacred Humanity: Toward an African American Religious Naturalism*. New York: Fordham University Press, 2016.

White, Lynn, Jr. "The Historical Roots of Our Ecological Crisis." *Science* 155, no. 3767 (1967): 1203–7.

Whitehead, Alfred North. *Process and Reality*. New York: Free Press, 1979.

Whitman, Walt. "Song of Myself." In *The Complete Poems*, edited by Francis Murphy, 63–124. New York: Penguin Classics, 2005.

Wilderson, Frank B. *Red, White, and Black: Cinema and the Structure of U.S. Antagonisms*. Durham, NC: Duke University Press, 2010.

Williams, Delores. *Sisters in the Wilderness: The Challenge of Womanist God-Talk*. Maryknoll, NY: Orbis Books, 2013.

Wolfson, Harry Austryn. *The Philosophy of Spinoza*. 2 vols. Cambridge, MA: Harvard University Press, 1934.

Woolf, Greg. "Divinity and Power in Ancient Rome." In *Religion and Power: Divine Kingship in the Ancient World and Beyone*, edited by Nicole Maria Brisch. University of Chicago Oriental Institute Seminars, 235–55. Chicago: Oriental Institute of the University of Chicago, 2008.

Wordsworth, William. "Lines: Composed a Few Miles above Tintern Abbey." In *The Collected Poems of William Wordsworth (Wordsworth Poetry Library)*, 241–43. Ware, UK: Wordsworth Editions, 1998.

Yandell, Keith E. "Pantheism." In *Routledge Encyclopedia of Philosophy*, edited by Edward Craig, 202–5. New York: Routledge, 1998.

Yovel, Yirmiyahu. *Spinoza and Other Heretics: The Adventures of Immanence*. 2 vols. Vol. 2, Princeton, NJ: Princeton University Press, 1989.

——. *Spinoza and Other Heretics: The Marrano of Reason*. 2 vols. Vol. 1, Princeton, NJ: Princeton University Press, 1989.

INDEX